Lecture Notes in Computer Science   15551

Founding Editors

Gerhard Goos
Juris Hartmanis

The series Lecture Notes in Computer Science (LNCS), including its subseries Lecture Notes in Artificial Intelligence (LNAI) and Lecture Notes in Bioinformatics (LNBI), has established itself as a medium for the publication of new developments in computer science and information technology research, teaching, and education.

LNCS enjoys close cooperation with the computer science R & D community, the series counts many renowned academics among its volume editors and paper authors, and collaborates with prestigious societies. Its mission is to serve this international community by providing an invaluable service, mainly focused on the publication of conference and workshop proceedings and postproceedings. LNCS commenced publication in 1973.

José Proença · Raul Fervari · Manuel A. Martins ·
Reinhard Kahle · Graham Pluck

Editors

Software Engineering and Formal Methods

SEFM 2024 Collocated Workshops

ReacTS 2024 and CIFMA 2024
Aveiro, Portugal, November 4–5, 2024
Revised Selected Papers

 Springer

Editors
José Proença (iD)
CISTER & Faculty of Sciences
University of Porto
Porto, Portugal

Manuel A. Martins (iD)
Department of Mathematics
Universidade de Aveiro
Aveiro, Portugal

Graham Pluck (iD)
Faculty of Psychology
Chulalongkorn University
Bangkok, Thailand

Raul Fervari (iD)
CONICET
Buenos Aires, Argentina

Reinhard Kahle (iD)
Universität Tübingen
Tübingen, Germany

ISSN 0302-9743   ISSN 1611-3349 (electronic)
Lecture Notes in Computer Science
ISBN 978-3-031-94747-6   ISBN 978-3-031-94748-3 (eBook)
https://doi.org/10.1007/978-3-031-94748-3

Preface

The 22nd International Conference on Software Engineering and Formal Methods (SEFM 2024) was organized in Aveiro on November 4–8, 2024, by the University of Aveiro, Portugal. This volume collects the proceedings of two collocated SEFM workshops:

- **ReacTS 2024:** International Workshop on Reconfigurable Transition Systems: Semantics, Logics and Applications.
- **CIFMA 2024:** 6th International Workshop on Cognition: Interdisciplinary Foundations, Models and Applications.

A single-blind, 3.03 reviews per submission ensured the quality of the nineteen papers (ten in ReacTS and nine in CIFMA) selected for this volume, from a total of thirty-two submissions. This process was guided by the workshop organizers and managed by the Program Committees members in a rigorous way, by respecting conflict of interest situations, and with the aim of providing useful reviews to all the authors. The workshops were held on November 4 and 5, and the discussions, always vibrant and characterized by interdisciplinary exchanges, benefited also from four keynote speeches. We would like to thank the members of the program committees, the keynote speakers, and the authors for their effort in contributing to a rich and interesting program. We also thank the SEFM chairs for taking care of the logistics and registration process of the collocated workshops.

February 2025

José Proença
Raul Fervari
Manuel A. Martins
Reinhard Kahle
Graham Pluck

Contents

CIFMA 2024

ReacTS 2024

ReacTS 2024 Organizers' Message

These are the post-proceedings of the first International Workshop on Reconfigurable Transition Systems: Semantics, Logics and Applications, ReacTS 2024, a workshop devoted to the different aspects involving Reconfigurable Transition Systems (RTS). RTS are dynamic relational structures (graphs) that evolve along their execution, in the sense that their accessibility relation, their set of nodes or their labelling change when their edges are crossed. These structures have proven to be suitable to compactly represent complex reactive and reconfigurable behaviours. Namely, the ability to react or adapt under the influence of certain events is a very distinctive feature of many diverse situations and objects. An autonomous vehicle that changes its route due to a new strike occurring, the behaviour of a software component after a memory disposal, or a DNA mutation as the result of a viral infection are different examples that witness the importance of modelling changes in a determined situation. Practical user cases have aroused the interest of the logic community in the study of variants of RTS, by developing formal methods to properly reason about such situations.

This workshop aims to bring together the whole community of researchers working on different ways to model reconfigurable and reactive systems from a formal perspective. This includes theoretical approaches (like hybrid logics, reactive frames, and model-update logics), or formalisms designed for specific purposes (like separation logic in software verification, dynamic epistemic logic in AI planning, and others). Also, the goal of the workshop is to devise novel approaches and potential applications, and share a common perspective on the discipline.

This first edition of ReacTS was affiliated with SEFM, and took place on November 4 and 5, in Aveiro, Portugal. Around 30 members of the scientific community participated in person along the three sessions during the two days, while another 10 participated online. The workshop included three outstanding invited talks by active members of the research community working in topics related to Reconfigurable Systems and their formal treatment. A short commentary on them is included below (in alphabetical order).

Carlos Areces, Axiomatizing Dynamic Logics without Substitution. Carlos Areces presented a recently developed approach to deal with axiomatizations of dynamic logics relying on Hybrid Logic.

Johan van Benthem, Graph Games and Dynamic Logics. Johan van Benthem discussed the state of the art on the design of dynamic logics to characterize and reason about graph games. In this regard, three options were presented to target different levels of detail in viewing dynamic scenarios: graph logics, game logics, and general logics of dynamical systems.

Sérgio Marcelino, Logics for path-dependent systems: from reactive to switch frames and beyond. Sérgio Marcelino's talk was focused on the use of graphs with higher-order arrows encoding path dependencies, to represent how a transition system evolves under certain circumstances. He also discussed some features and extensions to capture a wider range of applications.

The workshop received 20 submissions, comprising 12 long papers (12 pages each) and 8 short papers (5 pages each). Submissions followed a single-blind review process. Each paper received at least three reviews from members of the Program Committee (PC), with additional evaluations by external experts for some papers to assist the PC in making final decisions.

To ensure anonymity, papers submitted by PC members or the Chairs were reviewed and evaluated separately. Ultimately, 5 long papers and 5 short papers were selected for publication in the workshop proceedings, along with one invited paper by Johan van Benthem. The invited paper, evaluated by the Chairs, was accepted as a position paper in the area.

Additionally, 5 submissions considered relevant to the community but not selected for publication were invited for informal presentations at the workshop to promote their dissemination.

February 2025   Raul Fervari
                                                                           Manuel A. Martins

ReacTS 2024 Organization

Program Committee Chairs

Raul Fervari   Universidad Nacional de Córdoba and CONICET, Argentina

Manuel A. Martins   Universidade de Aveiro, Portugal

Program Committee

Carlos Areces	Universidad Nacional de Córdoba and CONICET, Argentina
Luís Soares Barbosa	Universidade do Minho, Portugal
Mario Benevides	Universidade Federal Fluminense, Brazil
Johan van Benthem	University of Amsterdam, The Netherlands & Stanford University, USA
Patrick Blackburn	University of Roskilde, Denmark
Valentin Cassano	Universidad Nacional de Río Cuarto and CONICET, Argentina
Madalena Chaves	Centre Inria d'Université Côte d'Azur, France
Gabriel Ciobanu	Romanian Academy, Romania
Diana Costa	Universidade de Lisboa, Portugal
Stéphane Demri	CNRS, Université Paris-Saclay, France
Hans van Ditmarsch	CNRS, University of Toulouse, France
Daniel Figueiredo	Universidade de Aveiro, Portugal
Sabine Frittella	Université d'Orleans, France
Dov Gabbay	King's College London, UK
Sujata Gosh	Indian Statistical Institute, Chennai, India
Andreas Herzig	CNRS, Université Paul Sabatier, France
Juha Kontinen	University of Helsinki, Finland
Alexandre Madeira	Universidade de Aveiro, Portugal
Sérgio Marcelino	University of Lisbon, Portugal
Regivan Santiago	Universidade Federal do Rio Grande do Norte, Brazil
François Schwarzentruber	ENS Rennes, France
Igor Sedlár	Czech Academy of Sciences, Czech Republic
Sonja Smets	University of Amsterdam, The Netherlands
Ionuţ Ţuţu	Romanian Academy, Romania
Fernando R. Velázquez-Quesada	University of Bergen, Norway
Fan Yang	Utrecht University, The Netherlands

Additional Reviewers

Benjamín Bedregal
Juliana Bueno
Pablo F. Castro
Suene Duarte
Renato Neves
Alexandre Rademaker
Raqueline A. M. Santos
Andrés R. Saravia
Renaud Vilmart
Chrysoula Vlachou

Behavioural Equivalences
over Reconfigurable Systems

Bogdan Aman[1,2(✉)] and Gabriel Ciobanu[1]

[1] Institute of Computer Science, Romanian Academy, Iasi Branch, Romania
{bogdan.aman,gabriel.ciobanu}@iit.academiaromana-is.ro
[2] Faculty of Computer Science, Alexandru Ioan Cuza University, Iasi, Romania

Abstract. We introduced and studied previously a process calculus that uses timeouts to describe the migration and communication taking place in distributed real-time systems. This calculus allows spatial reconfiguration regarding the mobility of agents, and reconfiguration of connectivity through communication of channel names. In this paper, we go further and study various behaviours of these distributed real-time systems, aiming to identify the most appropriate one (closer to a desired behaviour). For this, we describe an example consisting of a driver moving between locations, and define some behavioural equivalences involving multisets of actions, communicated resources and migration between locations.

1 Introduction

In multi-agent systems, the agents are numerous, mobile and required to collaborate by means of communication channels. Based on the communicated values and existing restrictions, these systems can reconfigure the communication connectivity and the spatial distribution of agents.

The π-calculus [19,21,22] was the first process calculus used to model the behaviour of agents in concurrent systems by reconfiguring the connectivity through communication of names on shared channel. Over the time, the π-calculus was used as a basis for defining process calculi that model reconfiguration of mobility and communication: e.g., mobile ambients [9], distributed π-calculus [18], AbC calculus [1]. The advantages of using a process calculus are: (i) the systems are described using only a small number of operators and primitives; (ii) communication between agents is by passing messages on shared channels; (iii) agents can be manipulated by using equational reasoning and behavioural equivalence. The ability of process calculi to create large systems by putting in parallel smaller ones using a parallel composition operator distinguish them from other models of computation [7,8,15,17,25].

By using timers, one can model systems that may change their behaviours also as a result of sustained inactivity: e.g., timed automata [2], timed distributed π-calculus [14], TiMo [12]. However, none of the existing formalisms is able to capture properties of timing, communication and mobility in distributed systems in a natural way. In [3,4], we considered an extension of TiMo called

J. Proença et al. (Eds.): SEFM 2024, LNCS 15551, pp. 7–21, 2026.
https://doi.org/10.1007/978-3-031-94748-3_1

rTiMo (real-Time Mobility) in which timers are used over migration and communication actions of agents in a explicit distributed system. The usefulness of rTiMo in describing real-time systems is given by: (i) the ability to model migration of agents between distributed locations; (ii) the execution of agents in parallel, while communication taken places only if the communicating agents reside at the same location; (iii) the possibility of using behavioural equivalence to detect equivalent systems that can replace existing parts of a system. Oversimplifying a little, rTiMo models spatial reconfiguration through communication of locations, and reconfiguration of connectivity through communication of channels.

Our current approach focuses on comparing the behaviours of the distributed real-time systems by taking into account the performed actions and their timers. Choosing an appropriate behavioural equivalence relation depends on the analyzed distributed system and on what properties need to be preserved. Since we consider systems modelled using the parallel composition operator, the defined equivalence relations should be compositional with respect to the other operators. To illustrate how our approach works, we consider the resource example from [15], we use rTiMo to model it, and define bisimulations to check that various constructed rTiMo models are equivalent or not. In this example, the system consist of four locations and a driver that has the possibility to move between these locations. However, the driver has to pay before moving to a new location, and it has the possibility to withdraw money from cash machines at each location in order to pay for the moving costs.

The structure of the paper is as follows. Section 2 contains the syntax and operational semantics of rTiMo, and the example of a resource system consisting of four locations and a driver moving between them. In Sect. 3, we define several bisimulations, study the connections among them and provide examples on how some systems are related. Conclusion and references end the paper.

2   Real-Time Mobility Calculus

In rTiMo calculus, the distributed real-time systems are defined as explicit parallel locations containing agents able to perform spatial reconfiguration through communication of locations and reconfiguration of connectivity through communication of channels. Agents use real-timed constraints over migration and communication actions such that sustained inactivity leads to a change in their behaviours. In rTiMo, the migration of agents between locations and the local communication between agents are performed in parallel, while a global clock is used to model the passage of time in the system when no migration or communication actions can be performed.

Each migration action has assigned a real-time timer that marks the time units needed to pass before an agent is able to move to the new location in order to continue its execution. The communication actions have also assigned real-time timers, such that agents have the possibility to communicate before the expiration of the timer. Two agents are able to communicate if they are at the same location, in the same time instance, they use the same channel to execute opposite actions (send/receive values), and their timers have not expired. The semantics of rTiMo is given by means of a labelled transition system in which the labels are multisets of actions performed in parallel in the same time instance.

A timeout of length $t \in \mathbb{R}_+$ assigned to migration and communication actions has the form $^{\Delta t}$. For instance, an agent $go^{\Delta 3}l$ then P should wait at the current location for 3 time units, before being able to migrate to location l where it can continue as P. An agent $a^{\Delta 5}!\langle z \rangle$ then P else Q waits to send z on channel a for at most 5 time units, while the agent $a^{\Delta 4}?(x)$ then P else Q waits for at most 4 time units to receive a value on channel a, value that will be used to instantiate the variable x appearing in P. If an agent that has P as possible continuation on the then branch and Q on the else branch on an input or output action succeeds in performing successfully the communication, it will continue by executing P at the current location; otherwise, in case of a timeout, it will continue by executing Q at the current location. An agent if $test$ then P else Q performs the $test$ in order to decide what is its continuation; it will continue as P is the $test$ returns $true$, and as Q is the $test$ returns $false$.

Table 1 contains the syntax of rTiMo , where the next assumptions are made:

- there exist the set $Loc = \{l, l', \ldots\}$ of locations, the set $Chan = \{a, a', \ldots\}$ of communication channels, and the set $Id = \{id, id', \ldots\}$ of agent identifiers;
- each agent identifier $id \in Id$ has an unique agent definition $id(u_1, \ldots, u_{m_{id}})$ $\overset{def}{=} P_{id}$ that uses m_{id} distinct parameters u_i that can be instantiated;
- $t, t', \ldots \in [0, \infty]$ are positive real-timeouts, $u, u', \ldots$ are variables and $v, v', \ldots$ are expressions that are recursively defined over variables, values and operations.

Table 1. rTiMo Syntax

Agents	P, Q	$::= a^{\Delta t}!\langle v \rangle$ then P else Q	(output)
		$\mid a^{\Delta t}?(u)$ then P else Q	(input)
		$\mid go^{\Delta t}l$ then P	(move)
		$\mid$ if $test$ then P else Q	(branch)
		$\mid \mathbf{0}$	(termination)
		$\mid id(v)$	(recursion)
		$\mid P \mid Q$	(parallel)
Located Agents	L	$::= l[[P]]$	
Systems	N	$::= L \mid L \mid N$	

Variables are bound only in agents of the form $a^{\Delta t}?(u)$ then P else Q, namely variable u is bound in the action $a^{\Delta t}?(u)$ and in the continuation P, while it is free in the continuation Q. $fv(N)$ and $fv(P)$ denote the sets of free variables appearing in a system N and in an agent P, respectively. An agent definition $id(u_1, \ldots, u_{m_{id}}) \stackrel{def}{=} P_{id}$ is correctly defined only if it holds that $fv(P_{id}) \subseteq \{u_1, \ldots, u_{m_{id}}\}$. An agent $\{v/u\}P$ is obtained from P by instantiating the free variable $u \in fv(P)$ with the value v; in order to avoid clashes of names we might need to perform some alpha-conversions (renaming of bound variables).

An agent $go^{\Delta t}l$ then P needs to wait at the current location for t time units, before being able to migrate to location l where it can continue its executing as P. We can use a flexible migration strategy in which a system is reconfigured by using location variables in go actions that will be instantiated with location names transmitted on communication channels. For example an agent $a^{\Delta 5}?(l)$ then $go^{\Delta t}l$ then P else Q can perform a migration to location l only if l is instantiated with a name received on channel a. In this way, it is possible to define agents that do not have a predefined migration route, but are able to reconfigure their migration routes by means of the communicated values between agents. Multisets of agents residing in each location are constructed using the parallel composition operator $|$, while an agent that finished its execution is denoted by $\mathbf{0}$. A system N is constructed from multisets of located agents of the form $l[[P]]$; a system is well-formed if it does not contain free variables.

Operational Semantics. In order to rearrange the agents of a system such that the operational semantic rules of Table 3 are applicable, we consider a structural equivalence relation $\equiv$ defined as the smallest congruence holding for the equalities in Table 2. By using the equalities from Table 2, we can transform any system N into an equivalent one $l_1[[P_1]] \mid \ldots \mid l_n[[P_n]]$, such that for each P_i (with $1 \leq i \leq n$) there does not exist Q_i and R_i such that $P_i \equiv Q_i \mid R_i$.

Table 2. rTiMo Structural Congruence

$N \mid l[[\mathbf{0}]] \equiv N$	(identity)
$N \mid N' \equiv N' \mid N$	(commutativity)
$(N \mid N') \mid N'' \equiv N \mid (N' \mid N'')$	(associativity)
$l[[P \mid Q]] \equiv l[[P]] \mid l[[Q]]$	((de)composition)

We give the operational semantics rules of rTiMo in Table 3 in which we use two types of labelled transition: $N \xrightarrow{\Lambda} N'$ and $N \xrightarrow{t} N'$. By means of a labelled transition $N \xrightarrow{\Lambda} N'$ we denote that after applying the multiset of actions λ in the system N, we obtain the system N'. If the multiset Λ consists only of an action λ, namely $\Lambda = \{\lambda\}$, instead of the labelled transition $N \xrightarrow{\{\lambda\}} N'$ we use the labelled transition $N \xrightarrow{\lambda} N'$. Also, by a labelled transition $N \xrightarrow{t} N'$ we denote that after allowing t time units to pass in the system N, we obtain the system N'.

In rule (MOVE0), we model an agent $go^{\Delta 0}l'$ then P at location l for which the timer of the migration action is 0 is able to migrate to location l' where it continues as P. In rule (COM), we model that two agents $a^{\Delta t}!\langle v \rangle$ then P else Q and

Table 3. rTiMo Operational Semantics

(DSTOP)	$l[[\mathbf{0}]] \overset{t}{\rightsquigarrow} l[[\mathbf{0}]]$
(DMOVE)	if $t \geq t'$ then $l[[go^{\Delta t}l'$ then $P]] \overset{t'}{\rightsquigarrow} l[[go^{\Delta t - t'}l'$ then $P]]$
(MOVE0)	$l[[go^{\Delta 0}l'$ then $P]] \xrightarrow{l \rhd l'} l'[[P]]$

$$(\text{COM}) \frac{t > 0 \text{ and } t' > 0}{l[[a^{\Delta t}!\langle v \rangle \text{ then } P \text{ else } Q \mid a^{\Delta t'}?(u) \text{ then } P' \text{ else } Q']] \xrightarrow{\{v/u\}@l} l[[P \mid \{v/u\}P']]}$$

$$(\text{DPUT}) \frac{t \geq t' > 0}{l[[a^{\Delta t}!\langle v \rangle \text{ then } P \text{ else } Q]] \overset{t'}{\rightsquigarrow} l[[a^{\Delta t - t'}!\langle v \rangle \text{ then } P \text{ else } Q]]}$$

(PUT0)	$l[[a^{\Delta 0}!\langle v \rangle \text{ then } P \text{ else } Q]] \xrightarrow{\Delta 0@l} l[[Q]]$

$$(\text{DGET}) \frac{t \geq t' > 0}{l[[a^{\Delta t}?(u) \text{ then } P \text{ else } Q]] \overset{t'}{\rightsquigarrow} l[[a^{\Delta t - t'}?(u) \text{ then } P \text{ else } Q]]}$$

(GET0)	$l[[a^{\Delta 0}?(u) \text{ then } P \text{ else } Q]] \xrightarrow{\Delta 0@l} l[[Q]]$

$$(\text{IFT}) \frac{test = true}{l[[\text{if } test \text{ then } P \text{ else } Q]] \xrightarrow{true@l} l[[P]]}$$

$$(\text{IFF}) \frac{test = false}{l[[\text{if } test \text{ then } P \text{ else } Q]] \xrightarrow{false@l} l[[Q]]}$$

$$(\text{DCALL}) \frac{l[[\{v/u\}P_{id}]] \overset{t}{\rightsquigarrow} l[[P'_{id}]] \text{ and } id(u) \overset{def}{=} P_{id}}{l[[id(v)]] \overset{t}{\rightsquigarrow} l[[P'_{id}]]}$$

$$(\text{CALL}) \frac{l[[\{v/u\}P_{id}]] \xrightarrow{call@l} l[[P'_{id}]] \text{ and } id(u) \overset{def}{=} P_{id}}{l[[id(v)]] \xrightarrow{call@l} l[[P'_{id}]]}$$

$$(\text{DPAR}) \frac{N_1 \overset{t}{\rightsquigarrow} N'_1 , N_2 \overset{t}{\rightsquigarrow} N'_2 \text{ and } N_1 \mid N_2 \not\xrightarrow{\lambda}}{N_1 \mid N_2 \overset{t}{\rightsquigarrow} N'_1 \mid N'_2}$$

$$(\text{PAR}) \frac{N_1 \xrightarrow{\Lambda_1} N'_1 \text{ and } N_2 \xrightarrow{\Lambda_2} N'_2}{N_1 \mid N_2 \xrightarrow{\Lambda_1 \cup \Lambda_2} N'_1 \mid N'_2}$$

$$(\text{DEQUIV}) \frac{N \equiv N', N' \overset{t}{\rightsquigarrow} N'' \text{ and } N'' \equiv N'''}{N \overset{t}{\rightsquigarrow} N'''}$$

$$(\text{EQUIV}) \frac{N \equiv N', N' \xrightarrow{\Lambda} N'' \text{ and } N'' \equiv N'''}{N \xrightarrow{\Lambda} N'''}$$

$a^{\Delta t}?(u)$ then P' else Q' at the same location l can communicate on channel a; the first agent sends the value v that will be used by the second agent to instantiate the variable u appearing in P'. If the communicated value v is a location, the system performs a spatial reconfiguration by changing the destination of an agent receiving v, while if it is a channel, it performs a connectivity reconfiguration by changing the channels used for communication by the agent receiving v. Note that the two agents do not change locations in the process of communication, and that they continue their execution as P and $\{v/u\}P'$, respectively. In rules (PUT0) and (GET0), we model an agent $a^{\Delta 0}!\langle v \rangle$ then P else Q (and

$a^{\Delta 0}?(u)$ then P else Q, respectively) at location l for which the timer of the communication action is 0, removing its communication action and continuing its execution as Q (without changing its location).

In rules (IFT) and (IFF), we model that an agent if *test* then P else Q needs to evaluate the *test* in order to decide if it continues its execution as P or Q without changing its location. In rule (CALL), we model that an agent $id(v)$ is replaced by the agent definition of id in which the variable u is instantiated by the value v. In rules (EQUIV) and (DEQUIV), we model the replacement of a system by an equivalent one with respect to the congruence relation $\equiv$. In rule (PAR), we model how to create large systems by putting in parallel smaller ones using a parallel composition operator.

In order to model the passage of time, we use the rules with names starting with D (Table 3). In rule (DPAR), we denote by $N_1 \mid N_2 \not\xrightarrow{\lambda}$ the fact that there does not exists an action λ nor a system $N_1' \mid N_2'$ such that $N_1 \mid N_2 \xrightarrow{\lambda} N_1' \mid N_2'$ by means of one of the rules (MOVE0), (COM), (PUT0), (GET0) or (CALL). Also, in rule (DPAR), the real-valued timeout t is used to denote that for this period of time none of the rules (MOVE0), (COM), (PUT0), (GET0) and (CALL) can be applied to $N_1 \mid N_2$. We use the negative premise $N_1 \mid N_2 \not\xrightarrow{\lambda}$ in rule (DPAR) in order to separate the application of actions and the passage of time, while keeping the set of rules consistent [16].

We define a complete computational step as executing a multiset of actions Λ followed by a time step of length t; formally, it is a derivation of the form:

$$N \xrightarrow{\Lambda} N_1 \overset{t}{\rightsquigarrow} N'.$$

If in a system N we perform a complete computational step leading to the system N, we say that N' is directly reachable from N. In case none of the rules (MOVE0), (COM), (PUT0), (GET0) and (CALL) can be applied in system N (namely, $\Lambda = \emptyset$), then we have only time passing, and thus we write $N \overset{t}{\rightsquigarrow} N'$ instead of $N \xrightarrow{\Lambda} N_1 \overset{t}{\rightsquigarrow} N'$.

In the next result we illustrate that if a system allows only passage of time to be performed, this does not lead to nondeterministic behaviours (the obtained system is unique after some time units), and the passage of time is continuous (we do not skip time instances to execute migration and communication actions).

Proposition 1. *For all systems N, N' and N'', the following hold:*

1. *If $N \overset{t}{\rightsquigarrow} N'$ and $N \overset{t}{\rightsquigarrow} N''$ then $N' \equiv N''$;*
2. *$N \overset{(t+t')}{\rightsquigarrow} N'$ iff $\exists N''$ such that $N \overset{t}{\rightsquigarrow} N''$ and $N'' \overset{t'}{\rightsquigarrow} N'$.*

Example 1. We consider the resource example from [15] depicted in Fig. 1. The system consists of four locations and directed arrows to indicate the roads one can drive along between locations. Driving along a road costs and this cost has to be payed by a driver before entering that road (e.g., to go from location a to

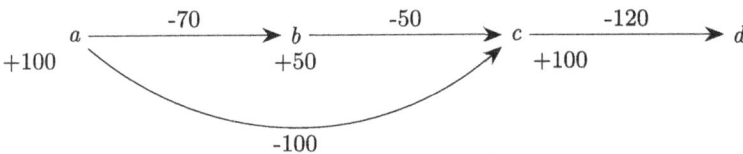

Fig. 1. A quantitative road system

location b costs \$70). However, the driver has the possibility to withdraw money
from cash machines at some locations (e.g., \$100 at location a, and \$50 at b).

When starting in location a with no initial money, a driver can withdraw
\$100 and is able to go next either to location b or to location c. If he decides
to go through location b, the driver is able to reach location d. However, if the
driver decides to go from location a directly to location c, he will not be able to
go further to location d (not enough money).

In what follows, we show that the system of Fig. 1 can be modelled in rTiMo.
To achieve this, we use some shorthand notations for agents unable to take the
else path:

$$a^{\Delta\infty}!\langle v \rangle \text{ then } P \text{ stands for } a^{\Delta\infty}!\langle v \rangle \text{ then } P \text{ else } Q;$$
$$a^{\Delta\infty}?(u) \text{ then } P \text{ stands for } a^{\Delta\infty}?(u) \text{ then } P \text{ else } Q.$$

We consider that at each location l there is an agent $ATM(v)$ that allows a driver
to withdraw the amount v using a communication channel w, before returning
to its initial state:

$$ATM(v) = w^{\Delta\infty}!\langle v \rangle \text{ then } ATM(v).$$

and also an agent $Dest(l', v)$ for each arrow from l to l' indicating there is a
road between these two locations with cost v, that can be communicated to a
driver using the channel $dest$:

$$Dest(l, v) = dest^{\Delta\infty}!\langle l, v \rangle \text{ then } Dest(l, v).$$

A driver with cash amount $balance$, able to withdraw money using channel w
and reconfigure its travel plans by migrating to a destination received on channel
$dest$ if it has enough money to pay the cost of the road, is defined as:

$$Driver(balance) = w^{\Delta\infty}?(x) \text{ then } \overset{.}{dest}^{\Delta\infty}?(y, z) \text{ then}$$
$$\text{if } balance + x \geq z \text{ then go}^{\Delta 2}y \text{ then } Driver(balance + x - z)$$
$$\text{else } Driver'(balance + x) ,$$

where $Driver'(balance + x)$ denotes that the driver does not have enough money
to move to the destination received on channel $dest$ and gets stuck at current
location with cash amount $balance + x$.

Overall, the initial system of Fig. 1 with a driver residing in location a is described in rTiMo as the system:

$$ResEx = a[[ATM\,(100) \mid Dest\,(b, 70) \mid Dest\,(c, 100) \mid Driver\,(0)]]$$
$$\mid b[[ATM\,(50) \mid Dest\,(c, 50)]]$$
$$\mid c[[ATM\,(100) \mid Dest\,(d, 120)]]$$
$$\mid d[[\ ]].$$

Based on the operational semantics of rTiMo, there are two possible reachable systems: one after 2 time units in which the *Driver* reached location c but cannot move further to location d due to insufficient funds:

$$a[[ATM\,(100) \mid Dest\,(b, 70) \mid Dest\,(c, 100)]]$$
$$\mid b[[ATM\,(50) \mid Dest\,(c, 50)]]$$
$$\mid c[[ATM\,(100) \mid Dest\,(d, 120) \mid Driver'(100)]]$$
$$\mid d[[\ ]],$$

and one after 6 time units in which the *Driver* reached location d:

$$a[[ATM\,(100) \mid Dest\,(b, 70) \mid Dest\,(c, 100)]]$$
$$\mid b[[ATM\,(50) \mid Dest\,(c, 50)]]$$
$$\mid c[[ATM\,(100) \mid Dest\,(d, 120)]]$$
$$\mid d[[Driver\,(10)]].$$

3   Behavioural Equivalences in rTiMo

When studying distributed systems, bisimulations represent an useful instrument in comparing the behaviour of two systems [24]. Our current approach focuses on comparing the behaviours of the distributed real-time systems by taking into account multisets of actions executed in a parallel step followed by a migration, communication or time step. This represents a different approach from the classical one where two systems are said to be equivalent if they are able to execute the same actions and time steps of similar length in the same order [19,23].

Our approach considers a weaker version of bisimulation as we allow two systems to be equivalent if in each parallel step they can execute the same set of actions regardless of their order, followed by a migration, communication or time step.

Choosing an appropriate behavioural equivalence relation depends on the analyzed distributed system and what properties need to be preserved. By defining equivalence relations that are compositional with respect to the main constructs of rTiMo represents an advantage as we can substitute a system by an equivalent one without fearing that unwanted side-effects would appear as a result of the substitution.

In a similar way as it is presented in [4,6,10], we extend the standard notion of bisimilarity by taking into account multisets of actions executed in a parallel step followed by a migration, communication or time step. Before defining the bisimulations applicable to rTiMo systems, we recall some basic notions used in what follows. The identity relation over the set $\mathcal{N}$ of systems is defined as id $\overset{def}{=} \{(N,N) \mid N \in \mathcal{N}\}$. Given a relation $\mathcal{R}$, its inverse is defined as $\mathcal{R}^{-1} \overset{def}{=} \{(N_2, N_1) \mid (N_1, N_2) \in \mathcal{R}\}$. Given two relations $\mathcal{R}_1$ and $\mathcal{R}_2$ their composition is defined as $\mathcal{R}_1 \mathcal{R}_2 \overset{def}{=} \{(N, N'') \mid \exists N' \in \mathcal{N} \text{ s.t. } (N, N') \in \mathcal{R}_1 \text{ and } (N', N'') \in \mathcal{R}_2\}$.

Definition 1. *A binary relation $\mathcal{R}$ over $\mathcal{N}$ is a* **strong timed bisimulation** *(ST bisimulation) if $(N, M) \in \mathcal{R}$ implies, for all $\Lambda \in (\bigcup_{l \in Loc} \{call@l,\ \Delta 0@l,\ true@l,\ false@l\})^*$ and $t \in \mathbb{R}_+$:*

- *if $N \xrightarrow{\Lambda} \xrightarrow{l \triangleright l'} N'$ then $\exists M', M \xrightarrow{\Lambda} \xrightarrow{l \triangleright l'} M', (N', M') \in \mathcal{R}$;*
- *if $N \xrightarrow{\Lambda} \xrightarrow{\{v/u\}@l} N'$ then $\exists M', M \xrightarrow{\Lambda} \xrightarrow{\{v/u\}@l} M', (N', M') \in \mathcal{R}$;*
- *if $N \xrightarrow{\Lambda} \overset{t}{\rightsquigarrow} N'$ then $\exists M', M \xrightarrow{\Lambda} \overset{t}{\rightsquigarrow} M'$ and $(N', M') \in \mathcal{R}$;*
- *if $M \xrightarrow{\Lambda} \xrightarrow{l \triangleright l'} M'$ then $\exists N', N \xrightarrow{\Lambda} \xrightarrow{l \triangleright l'} N', (N', M') \in \mathcal{R}$;*
- *if $M \xrightarrow{\Lambda} \xrightarrow{\{v/u\}@l} M'$ then $\exists N', N \xrightarrow{\Lambda} \xrightarrow{\{v/u\}@l} N', (N', M') \in \mathcal{R}$;*
- *if $M \xrightarrow{\Lambda} \overset{t}{\rightsquigarrow} M'$ then $\exists N', N \xrightarrow{\Lambda} \overset{t}{\rightsquigarrow} N'$ and $(N', M') \in \mathcal{R}$.*

Two $\mathcal{N}$ systems N and M are **strongly timed bisimilar**, *written $N \sim M$, if exists a strong timed bisimulation $\mathcal{R}$ such that $(N, M) \in \mathcal{R}$. Formally:*

$$\sim = \bigcup \{\mathcal{R} \mid \mathcal{R} \text{ is a ST bisimulation}\}.$$

In the previous definition, action transitions and timed transitions are treated in the same way; thus, this bisimulation coincides with the original notion of bisimulation over a labelled transition system.

Proposition 2. $\sim$ *is an equivalence relation, and the largest ST bisimulation.*

A crucial result regarding the behaviour of rTiMo systems is that the above defined strong timed bisimularity is also useful in comparing the evolution of systems when complete computational steps are considered.

Proposition 3. $N \sim M$ *and* $N \xrightarrow{\Lambda} N_1 \overset{t}{\rightsquigarrow} N'$ *implies* $\exists M_1, M' \in \mathcal{N}$ *such that* $M \xrightarrow{\Lambda} M_1 \overset{t}{\rightsquigarrow} M'$ *and* $N' \sim M'$.

Definition 1 compares the evolution of whole systems, but does not provide means for reasoning about equivalence of compositionally defined systems. Consider, for example, two systems:

$$N_1 = l[[a^{\Delta \infty}!\langle 10 \rangle \text{ then } \mathbf{0}]] \text{ and } N_2 = l[[b^{\Delta \infty}?(x) \text{ then } \mathbf{0}]]$$

Clearly, $N_1 \sim N_2$ as both systems allow only transitions of the form $\overset{t}{\rightsquigarrow}$. However, when we compose them with $N = l[[a^{\Delta \infty}?(x) \text{ then } \mathbf{0}]]$ then:

$$N_1 \mid N \not\sim N_2 \mid N$$

as the first composition can execute transition $\xrightarrow{\{10/x\}@l}$ whereas the second one can only execute $\overset{t}{\rightsquigarrow}$.

Under certain constraints, the strong timed bisimilarity is compositional. In what follows, we denote by $Loc\,(N)$ the set of locations appearing in a system N.

Proposition 4. *If $N \sim M$, $N' \sim M'$ and $Loc\,(N) \cap Loc\,(N') = Loc\,(M) \cap Loc\,(M') = \emptyset$, then $N|N' \sim M|M'$.*

Requiring an exact matching between multisets of actions executed in a parallel step followed by a migration, communication or time step in strong timed equivalences might represent a too strong requirement. Since in Example 1 the observables are the costs and the change of locations, in what follows we define a bisimilarity in which two systems are deemed similar if they communicate the same values and move following the same routes between locations.

Definition 2. *A binary relation $\mathcal{R}$ over $\mathcal{N}$ is a **strong resource bisimulation** (SR bisimulation) if $(N, M) \in \mathcal{R}$ implies, for all $\Lambda \in (\bigcup_{l \in Loc} \{call@l, \Delta 0@l, true@l, false@l\})^*$ and $t \in \mathbb{R}_+$:*

- *if $N \xrightarrow{\Lambda, \ l \triangleright l'} N'$ then $\exists M', M \xrightarrow{\Lambda, \ l \triangleright l'} M', (N', M') \in \mathcal{R}$;*
- *if $N \xrightarrow{\Lambda, \ \{v/u\}@l} N'$ then $\exists M', u', M \xrightarrow{\Lambda, \ \{v/u'\}@l} M', (N', M') \in \mathcal{R}$;*
- *if $N \xrightarrow{\Lambda, \ t}{\rightsquigarrow} N'$ then $\exists M', t', M \xrightarrow{\Lambda, \ t'}{\rightsquigarrow} M'$ and $(N', M') \in \mathcal{R}$;*
- *if $M \xrightarrow{\Lambda, \ l \triangleright l'} M'$ then $\exists N', N \xrightarrow{\Lambda, \ l \triangleright l'} N', (N', M') \in \mathcal{R}$;*
- *if $M \xrightarrow{\Lambda, \ \{v/u\}@l} M'$ then $\exists N', u', N \xrightarrow{\Lambda, \ \{v/u'\}@l} N', (N', M') \in \mathcal{R}$;*
- *if $M \xrightarrow{\Lambda, \ t}{\rightsquigarrow} M'$ then $\exists N', t', N \xrightarrow{\Lambda, \ t'}{\rightsquigarrow} N'$ and $(N', M') \in \mathcal{R}$.*

*Two $\mathcal{N}$ systems N and M are **strong resource bisimilar**, written $N \approx M$, if exists a strong resource bisimulation $\mathcal{R}$ such that $(M, N) \in \mathcal{R}$. Formally:*

$$\approx = \bigcup \{\mathcal{R} \mid \mathcal{R} \text{ is a RS bisimulation}\}.$$

Proposition 5. *$\approx$ is an equivalence relation, and the largest SR bisimulation.*

Similar as for strong timed bisimularity, strong resource bisimilarity is useful in comparing the evolution of systems when complete computational steps are taken into account.

Proposition 6. *If $N \approx M$ and $N \xrightarrow{\Lambda} N_1 \overset{t}{\rightsquigarrow} N'$, then exist $M_1, M' \in \mathcal{N}$, Λ' a multiset of actions and $t' \in \mathbb{R}_+$, such that $M \xrightarrow{\Lambda'} M_1 \overset{t'}{\rightsquigarrow} M'$ and $N' \approx M'$.*

In a similar way as for strong timed bisimularity, the strong resource bisimilarity is compositional under certain constraints.

Proposition 7. *If $N \approx M$, $N' \approx M'$ and $Loc\,(N) \cap Loc\,(N') = Loc\,(M) \cap Loc\,(M') = \emptyset$, then $N|N' \approx M|M'$.*

Example 2. Inspired by the system *ResEx* already presented, we consider a different system $ResEx_1$ with a slight modified version of the *Driver*, namely:

$$Driver_1(balance\,) = w^{\Delta\infty}?(x_1)\text{ then }\ dest\ ^{\Delta\infty}?(y_1, z_1)\text{ then}$$
$$\text{if }\ balance\ + x_1 \geq z_1\text{ then go }^{\Delta 4}y_1\text{ then }Driver_1(balance\ + x_1 - z_1)$$
$$\text{else }Driver_1'(balance\ + x_1)$$

where $Driver_1'(balance\ +x_1)$ denotes the driver that does not have enough money to move to the destination received on channel $dest$, and so gets stuck at current location with cash amount $balance\ + x_1$.

Since $Driver_1$ uses different variables in communication and migration timers, then $ResEx \xrightarrow{\{100/x\}@l} ResEx'$ and $ResEx_1 \xrightarrow{\{100/x_1\}@l} ResEx_1'$ implies that $ResEx \not\sim ResEx_1$. However, after a run it holds that $ResEx \approx ResEx_1$.

Since $\sim$ is stricter than $\approx$, then the next result holds.

Proposition 8. *If $N \sim N'$, then $N \approx N'$.*

From the previous example it can be seen that the reverse implication does not hold; namely, if $N \approx N'$ then it is not the case that $N \sim N'$.

As noted in [15], what is depicted in Fig. 1 of Example 1 is an ordinary annotated graph describing what resources are needed, while the qualitative situation (when the money is not involved) requires a different approach as described in Fig. 2 of the next example.

Example 3. The double arrow of Fig. 2 from the arc a to c to the arc c to d signals that if the driver takes the road from a to c then the road from c to d gets closed and cannot be used anymore by the driver.

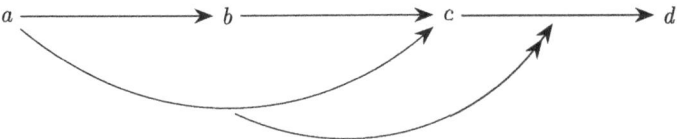

Fig. 2. A qualitative road system

In what follows, we show that the system of Fig. 2 can be modelled in rTiMo by using different agents than those needed to model the system of Fig. 1. Since the approach is qualitative, we no longer need the *ATM* agents.

The agent *Dest* has now a more complicated definition (with respect to the agent *Dest* of Example 1); it has to take into account if a road is open or closed, and if taking a certain road affects others by changing their status. Thus, in what follows we consider an agent $Dest\,(l, l', v)$, where l is the current location, l' is the next location and v marks a closed road (if its value is 0) or an open road (if its value is 1). If a road from l to l' is closed, then it will open after receiving a message on the channel $swap_{l,l'}$:

$$Dest\,(l, l', 0) = swap_{l,l'}^{\Delta\infty}?(x) \text{ then } Dest(l, l', 1).$$

On the other hand, if a road from l to l' is open, then it will be able to communicate a destination to the driver using the channel $dest$, change its state if it receives a message on the $swap_{l,l'}$ channel and also send messages to be communicated on the channel $swap_{c,d}$ to other locations to change the state of other roads:

$$Dest\,(l, l', 1) = dest^{\Delta 1}!\langle l'\rangle$$
$$\text{then if } (l == a \,\&\, l' == c) \text{ then } Dest(l, l', 1)$$
$$| \,go^{\Delta 0}c \text{ then } (swap_{c,d}^{\Delta 2}!\langle c\rangle \text{ then } \mathbf{0} \text{ else } \mathbf{0})$$
$$\text{else } Dest(l, l', 1)$$
$$\text{else } (swap_{l,l'}^{\Delta 1}?(x) \text{ then } Dest(l, l', 0) \text{ else } Dest(l, l', 1)).$$

However, the definition of a driver simplifies a lot as he does not use money anymore, but he only needs to reconfigure its travel plans after receiving its next destination:

$$Driver = dest^{\Delta\infty}?(y) \text{ then } go^{\Delta 2}y \text{ then } Driver.$$

In this case, the initial system of Fig. 2 with a driver residing at location a is described in rTIMO as:

$$ResEx_2 = a[[Dest\,(a, b, 1) \mid Dest\,(a, c, 1) \mid Driver\,]]$$
$$| \,b[[Dest\,(b, c, 1)]]$$
$$| \,c[[Dest\,(c, d, 1)]]$$
$$| \,d[[\,]].$$

Based on the operational semantics of rTIMO, there are two possible final configurations: one after 2 time units with the road from c to d blocked and the driver stuck at location c

$$a[[Dest\,(a, b, 1) \mid Dest\,(a, c, 1)]]$$
$$| \,b[[Dest\,(b, c, 1)]]$$
$$| \,c[[Dest\,(c, d, 0) \mid Driver\,]]$$
$$| \,d[[\,]],$$

and one after 6 time units with all roads open and the driver who reached location d

$$a[[Dest\,(a,b,1) \mid Dest\,(a,c,1)]]$$
$$\mid b[[Dest\,(b,c,1)]]$$
$$\mid c[[Dest\,(c,d,1)]]$$
$$\mid d[[Driver\,]].$$

Example 4. Inspired by the system $ResEx_2$, we consider a different system $ResEx_3$ with a slight modified version of the agent $Driver$, namely:

$Driver' = dest^{\Delta\infty}?(y')$ then $go^{\Delta 4}y'$ then $Driver'$.

Since the new $Driver'$ uses different variables in communication and migration timers, then $ResEx_2 \xrightarrow{\{c/y\}@l} ResEx_2'$ and $ResEx_3 \xrightarrow{\{c/y'\}@l} ResEx_3'$ implies that $ResEx_2 \not\approx ResEx_3$. However, after a run it holds that $ResEx_2 \approx ResEx_3$.

4 Conclusion

This paper considers a process calculus called rTiMo that uses timeouts to describe the migration and communication taking place in distributed real-time systems. This calculus models spatial reconfiguration through mobility of agents, and reconfiguration of connectivity through communication of channel names. A complete computational step consists in executing a multiset of actions followed by a time step. rTiMo is derived from TiMo [12] that was introduced with the purpose to connect (theoretical) process calculi and forthcoming realistic languages for multi-agent systems [11]. Over the years, an entire family of TiMo variants was defined and studied: e.g., PerTiMo [13] deals with access permissions, knowTiMo [5] deals with explicit knowledge for each agent, and BigTiMo [26] combines the bigraphs [20] with TiMo .

Our current approach focuses on comparing the behaviours of the distributed real-time systems by taking into account multisets of actions executed in a parallel step followed by a migration, communication or time step. By defining new types of bisimulations, we are able to consider as equivalent systems that otherwise would not be equivalent. This is done by considering weaker versions of bisimulation able to allow two systems to be equivalent.

References

1. Alrahman, Y.A., Nicola, R.D., Loreti, M.: A calculus for collective-adaptive systems and its behavioural theory. Inf. Comput. **268** (2019). https://doi.org/10.1016/J.IC.2019.104457
2. Alur, R., Dill, D.L.: A theory of timed automata. Theoret. Comput. Sci. **126**(2), 183–235 (1994). https://doi.org/10.1016/0304-3975(94)90010-8

3. Aman, B., Ciobanu, G.: Real-time migration properties of rTiMo verified in Uppaal. In: Hierons, R.M., Merayo, M.G., Bravetti, M. (eds.) Software Engineering and Formal Methods - 11th International Conference, SEFM 2013, Madrid, Spain, September 25-27, 2013. Proceedings. Lecture Notes in Computer Science, vol. 8137, pp. 31–45. Springer (2013). https://doi.org/10.1007/978-3-642-40561-7_3

4. Aman, B., Ciobanu, G.: Verification of critical systems described in real-time TiMo. Int. J. Softw. Tools Technol. Transfer **19**(4), 395–408 (2016). https://doi.org/10.1007/s10009-016-0439-9

5. Aman, B., Ciobanu, G.: Knowledge dynamics and behavioural equivalences in multi-agent systems. Mathematics **9**(22) (2021). https://doi.org/10.3390/math9222869

6. Aman, B., Ciobanu, G., Koutny, M.: Behavioural equivalences over migrating processes with timers. In: Giese, H., Rosu, G. (eds.) Formal Techniques for Distributed Systems - Joint 14th IFIP WG 6.1 International Conference, FMOODS 2012 and 32nd IFIP WG 6.1 International Conference, FORTE 2012. Lecture Notes in Computer Science, vol. 7273, pp. 52–66. Springer (2012). https://doi.org/10.1007/978-3-642-30793-5_4

7. Areces, C., Fervari, R., Hoffmann, G.: Relation-changing modal operators. Logic J. IGPL **23**(4), 601–627 (2015). https://doi.org/10.1093/JIGPAL/JZV020

8. van Benthem, J.: An essay on sabotage and obstruction. In: Hutter, D., Stephan, W. (eds.) Mechanizing Mathematical Reasoning, Essays in Honor of Jörg H. Siekmann on the Occasion of His 60th Birthday. Lecture Notes in Computer Science, vol. 2605, pp. 268–276. Springer (2005). https://doi.org/10.1007/978-3-540-32254-2_16

9. Cardelli, L., Gordon, A.D.: Mobile ambients. Theoret. Comput. Sci. **240**(1), 177–213 (2000). https://doi.org/10.1016/S0304-3975(99)00231-5

10. Ciobanu, G.: Behaviour equivalences in timed distributed pi-calculus. In: Wirsing, M., Banâtre, J., Hölzl, M.M., Rauschmayer, A. (eds.) Software-Intensive Systems and New Computing Paradigms - Challenges and Visions, Lecture Notes in Computer Science, vol. 5380, pp. 190–208. Springer (2008). https://doi.org/10.1007/978-3-540-89437-7_13

11. Ciobanu, G., Juravle, C.: Flexible software architecture and language for mobile agents. Concur. Comput. Practice Exp. **24**(6), 559–571 (2012). https://doi.org/10.1002/CPE.1854

12. Ciobanu, G., Koutny, M.: Modelling and verification of timed interaction and migration. In: Fiadeiro, J.L., Inverardi, P. (eds.) Fundamental Approaches to Software Engineering, 11th International Conference, FASE 2008, Held as Part of the Joint European Conferences on Theory and Practice of Software, ETAPS 2008, Budapest, Hungary, March 29-April 6, 2008. Proceedings. Lecture Notes in Computer Science, vol. 4961, pp. 215–229. Springer (2008). https://doi.org/10.1007/978-3-540-78743-3_16

13. Ciobanu, G., Koutny, M.: Timed migration and interaction with access permissions. In: Butler, M.J., Schulte, W. (eds.) FM 2011: Formal Methods - 17th International Symposium on Formal Methods, Limerick, Ireland, June 20-24, 2011. Proceedings. Lecture Notes in Computer Science, vol. 6664, pp. 293–307. Springer (2011). https://doi.org/10.1007/978-3-642-21437-0_23

14. Ciobanu, G., Prisacariu, C.: Timers for distributed systems. In: Pierro, A.D., Wiklicky, H. (eds.) Proceedings of the 4th International Workshop on Quantitative Aspects of Programming Languages, QAPL 2006. Electronic Notes in Theoretical

Computer Science, vol. 164, pp. 81–99. Elsevier (2006). https://doi.org/10.1016/J.ENTCS.2006.07.013

15. Gabbay, D.M.: Reactive Kripke Semantics. Cognitive Technologies, Springer (2013). https://doi.org/10.1007/978-3-642-41389-6

16. Groote, J.F.: Transition system specifications with negative premises (extended abstract). In: Baeten, J.C.M., Klop, J.W. (eds.) CONCUR '90, Theories of Concurrency: Unification and Extension, Amsterdam. Lecture Notes in Computer Science, vol. 458, pp. 332–341. Springer (1990). https://doi.org/10.1007/BFB0039069

17. Harel, D., Pnueli, A.: On the development of reactive systems. In: Apt, K.R. (ed.) Logics and Models of Concurrent Systems - Conference proceedings. NATO ASI Series, vol. 13, pp. 477–498. Springer (1984). https://doi.org/10.1007/978-3-642-82453-1_17

18. Hennessy, M.: A distributed Pi-calculus. Cambridge University Press (2007)

19. Milner, R.: Communicating and mobile systems - the Pi-calculus. Cambridge University Press (1999)

20. Milner, R.: The Space and Motion of Communicating Agents. Cambridge University Press (2009)

21. Milner, R., Parrow, J., Walker, D.: A calculus of mobile processes. I. Inf. Comput. **100**(1), 1–40 (1992). https://doi.org/10.1016/0890-5401(92)90008-4

22. Milner, R., Parrow, J., Walker, D.: A calculus of mobile processes. II. Inf. Comput. **100**(1), 41–77 (1992). https://doi.org/10.1016/0890-5401(92)90009-5

23. Park, D.M.R.: Concurrency and automata on infinite sequences. In: Deussen, P. (ed.) Theoretical Computer Science, 5th GI-Conference. Lecture Notes in Computer Science, vol. 104, pp. 167–183. Springer (1981). https://doi.org/10.1007/BFB0017309

24. Sangiorgi, D.: Introduction to Bisimulation and Coinduction. Cambridge University Press (2011)

25. Santiago, R., Martins, M.A., Figueiredo, D.: Introducing fuzzy reactive graphs: a simple application on biology. Soft. Comput. **25**(9), 6759–6774 (2021). https://doi.org/10.1007/S00500-020-05353-1

26. Xie, W., Zhu, H., Zhang, M., Lu, G., Fang, Y.: Formalization and verification of mobile systems calculus using the rewriting engine Maude. In: Reisman, S., et al., (eds.) 2018 IEEE 42nd Annual Computer Software and Applications Conference, COMPSAC 2018, Tokyo, Japan, 23-27 July 2018, Volume 1. pp. 213–218. IEEE Computer Society (2018). https://doi.org/10.1109/COMPSAC.2018.00034

Logics for Dynamic Graph Games

Johan van Benthem$^{(\boxtimes)}$

ILLC University of Amsterdam, Department of Philosophy Stanford University, and
Joint Research Center for Logic Tsinghua University, Amsterdam, The Netherlands
johan@stanford.edu
https://www.fnwi.uva.nl/j.vanbenthem

Abstract. With sabotage games on graphs that change during play
as a running example, we discuss logics designed for describing such
reactive systems, on which there is a growing literature – the collection
[12] has the relevant formal details. We consider three zoom levels for
these dynamic scenarios: graphs as game boards, extensive game trees,
and infinite dynamical systems. We compare these and discuss some of
the open problems concerning logic design that arise in this setting.

Keywords: Graph game · Modal logic · Game logic · Dynamical
system

1 Introduction

The *Sabotage Game* on graphs was proposed to model what happens to a standard computational task like path search in a perturbed environment, [8]. The
path-finding player now travels through a graph that changes during play:

> Starting from an initial position s, a *Traveler T* moves through a graph
> **G** toward a designated goal region (a set of points in the graph), from one
> position to the next via an available link, one at a time. However, in each
> round of the game, a *Demon D* first cuts one link, anywhere in the graph.
> Traveler wins, at any stage, when the goal region is reached.

More precisely, we stipulate that the game stops if (i) Traveler has reached the
goal region, or (ii) there is no more link to be cut in the graph, or (iii) there is
no link to move at Traveler's turn. In the latter two cases, we say that Demon
wins if Traveler is not already in the goal region.
  We discuss games on finite graphs, deferring the infinite case to Sect. 4.

Example 1 (A simple sabotage game).
Traveler starts at node 1 of the graph below, trying to reach the goal region {4}.
Demon has a winning strategy by first cutting one upper link between points
3 and 4, and then responding appropriately to whatever Traveler does. Note
that this requires global cutting anywhere in the graph – cutting locally at
Traveler's current positions does not yield a winning strategy in this particular
game (Fig. 1).

© The Author(s), under exclusive license to Springer Nature Switzerland AG 2026
J. Proença et al. (Eds.): SEFM 2024, LNCS 15551, pp. 22–35, 2026.
https://doi.org/10.1007/978-3-031-94748-3_2

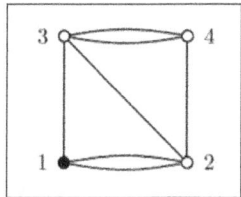

Fig. 1. A simple planar sabotage game.

This example used a planar graph, but higher dimensions also make sense.

Example 2 (Sabotage in grids).
Consider a cube with a goal region of three points. The following picture displays two of the three possible isomorphism types for this.

At each starting position for the Traveler, we have indicated the winning positions for players by 'T', 'D', As one illustration, for the lower left point * at the back in Graph (b) as Traveler's initial position, Demon must first cut the upward link, then Traveler can move right, Demon must then cut the forward link, and Traveler goes up to a point with two access links to the goal region (Fig. 2).

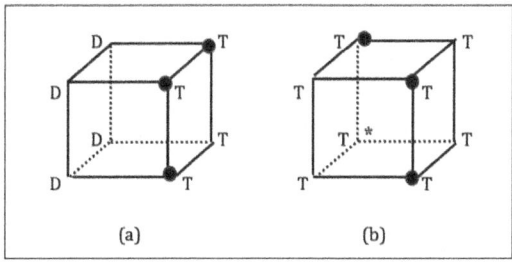

Fig. 2. Sabotage games on cubes.

The observations made in these examples have a more general background. It follows from *Zermelo's Theorem* about two-player finite-depth zero-sum games of perfect information, [22], that each sabotage game on a finite graph is *determined*: exactly one of the two players must have a winning strategy. On finite graphs this applies, since the total game length is bounded by the number of available edges. This simple but fundamental result allows us to concentrate on winning positions for Traveler in what follows without losing generality.

In addition to perturbed search, the Sabotage Game has many further useful interpretations. One can also think of players interacting with a graph-like transition system, one can allow adding links by deleting from the complement of the edge relation, and there are also benevolent interpretations in terms of teaching by removing unprofitable parts of a search space, [18]. One can even turn the scenario into a parlor game, say, with Traveler as a treasure hunter trying to escape from a pyramid where corridors collapse due to the Pharao's Curse.

It also makes sense to play on *directed* graphs, rather than the above undirected ones, since Traveler should never go back to an earlier position. For in that case, Traveler can only be worse off, since there are now fewer links in the graph. Stated positively, the following *monotonicity* property holds:

> If Traveler has a winning strategy at any location, then this location stays winning for Traveler when edges are added to the graph.

Such general features of the game have not yet been studied in their entirety, though the logic to be introduced in Sect. 2 can express some of them.

In sabotage games on directed graphs with a one-point goal region which Traveler has not yet reached, Demon always has a winning strategy by cutting directed links to that region. With larger goal regions, this changes, and Example 1 can be played on a similar directed graph by suitably duplicating the point 4.

Restricting to concrete graph classes can affect the Sabotage Game considerably. For instance, on *trees*, Demon's best moves always cut an immediate successor of Traveler's current location, as these make the largest subtrees inaccessible. Winning for Traveler can then be described recursively as having at least two successors to subtrees where Traveler has a winning strategy.

Another congenial graph game on a highly restricted model class is the famous *Angels-and-Devils* game, [14], where Angel tries to keep moving cell-by-cell in a $\mathbb{N} \times \mathbb{N}$-grid where Demon cancels one grid cell in each round. The rich combinatorial structure of this particular game and its finite versions suggests that much remains to be understood about specialized sabotage games.

There are many other graph games than the Sabotage Game: see [16] and for the special games relevant to this paper, [12]. For instance, goals need not be about reaching regions for individual players, they could also be correlated, and thus more interactive, as in Hide-and-Seek games where the purpose of one player is to force a meeting while the other player tries to avoid this.

In this broader setting, one can view 'dynamic graph games' where graphs change in the course of play in terms of *reactive systems* responding in various ways to agents accessing the system. This interpretation of our games may well come to generate new questions beyond those to be discussed in this paper.

2   Sabotage Modal Logic of Graphs

The moves for players in the Sabotage Game suggest links with two modalities.

First, a standard existential modality $\Diamond$ describes effects of available moves for Traveler, cf. [15] for basic modal logic. But we also need a new non-standard modality $\blacklozenge \varphi$ describing effects of the Demon's graph changes. This new modal statement holds at a point s in a modal model M on an underlying graph if,

> After some removal of an edge (t, u) from the current accessibility relation R, the formula φ is true at s in the new model $\mathsf{M}|R := R - \{(t, u)\}$.

Note how this dynamic modality refers to what is true in a model that is *different from the current one*. This cross-modal semantics is typical for many current modal logics that describe effects of model change, for instance, in scenarios of information update or opinion dynamics in social networks.

The resulting system SML of *Sabotage Modal Logic*, [8], [5], can express existence of a winning strategy for Traveler with a goal region defined by a formula γ in finite graphs ('WIN$_T$'). This game-theoretic statement is defined by a disjunction of finite iterations of the two-step modal combination $\blacksquare\Diamond$, from the 0-case (i.e., γ is true) to a finite number depending on the size of the graph:

$$\blacksquare\Diamond \ldots \blacksquare\Diamond\, \gamma$$

But the language can also express many other types of assertion. For instance, a modality $\Diamond\Diamond$ lets Traveler make two step, or a combination $\blacklozenge\blacklozenge\square\blacklozenge\square\varphi$ describes how the Demon can 'nudge' Traveler in three steps toward a region where property φ holds. For another illustration, the formula

$$\blacklozenge\text{WIN}_T \to \text{WIN}_T$$

expresses the earlier-mentioned Monotonicity principle for the Traveler.

Thus, SML is not just a game logic but a logic for quite general scenarios.

The dynamic character of this modal graph logic shows in various subtleties.

Example 3 (Valid and non-valid principles).

(i) The implication $\blacklozenge\Diamond\varphi \to \Diamond\blacklozenge\varphi$ is valid. After some edge cut (t, u), let the current point s still have a successor v where φ holds (in the new graph with one edge less). Then v is a successor of s in the initial model where one can cut a link, viz. (t, u), such that φ holds at v in the model with this link deleted.

(ii) The converse $\Diamond\blacklozenge\varphi \to \blacklozenge\Diamond\varphi$ is not valid. Take a model M with one reflexive point s. There is a successor, viz. s itself, such that the formula $\varphi = \square\bot$ will hold there after some edge cut. But the only available edge cut (s, s) in M leaves s without a successor, let alone one where $\square\bot$ is true.

Next, unlike in most standard logics, the valid principles of SML are not closed under substitution of arbitrary formulas for proposition letters.

Example 4 (Non-schematic validities).

(i) The formula $\square p \to \blacksquare(\Diamond\top \to \Diamond p)$ is valid. If some successor t of s remains after a link cut, and all successors were p, then t still witnesses $\Diamond p$ at s.

(ii) The schema $\square\varphi \to \blacksquare(\Diamond\top \to \Diamond\varphi)$ is not valid. The reason is that complex formulas φ containing modalities can change their truth values after a link cut. For instance, let model M have three points $\{1, 2, 3\}$ with $R = \{(1, 2), (2, 3)\}$. Let φ be $\Diamond\top$. In M, point 1 satisfies the formula $\square\Diamond\top$. But if we cut the link $(2, 3)$, 1 still has a successor ($\Diamond\top$ holds), but 1 has no successor satisfying $\Diamond\top$.

Still, some general features of modal logics persist.

Proposition 1. *The language of sabotage modal logic is* effectively translatable *into the language of first-order logic on graphs.*

This can be seen by inspecting the clauses in the above semantics. But the translation must maintain a growing finite memory of cuts already made, unlike the memory-free 'standard translation' from ML into first-order logic.

There are also model-theoretic characterizations, as for the basic modal logic, of the fragment of the above first-order language of graphs arising in this way, in terms of invariance for a suitable notion of *'sabotage bisimulation'.*

Next, by the completeness theorem for first-order logic, the effective translation implies that there must be an *effective axiomatization* for the validities of SML. Such axiomatisations have indeed been given in extensions of the SML-language with devices from *hybrid logic* such as nominals and a universal modality, but a complete purely modal axiomatization is still unknown. Likewise, we have no concrete axiomatization yet for the schematically valid formulas.

Note. Here and elsewhere, for details of the facts listed in this paper, we refer to the papers collected in the book [12] on logics for graph games.

To define winning positions for Traveler generically, we extend SML to the *sabotage μ-calculus* μSML, [5], using the following fixpoint formula:

$$\mu p \cdot (\gamma \vee \blacksquare \Diamond p)$$

This says that Traveler is either in the goal region or can reach it after some finite number of responses to Demon's challenges.

The system μSML is quite complex, and over abstract bimodal models, its language translates into that of μFO, the fixed-point extension of first-order logic whose theory is only partially understood.

The preceding fixed-point assertion may in fact look like one already available in a *propositional dynamic logic* μPDL, a simpler system suitable for describing the behavior of sabotaged labeled transition systems. However, the PDL-fragment of μSML can probably not define game solution statements like this, although a formal disproof seems an open problem. For an alternative approach to game solution statements, cf. the 'modal substitution logic' MSL in [11].

Next we briefly survey two issues of computational complexity.

The *model-checking complexity* of μSML is *Pspace*-complete, as opposed to the polynomial complexity for basic modal logic. This result already holds for checking existence of winning strategies at graph positions in sabotage games.

Moreover, the *SAT*-problem for μSML is *undecidable*. The reason here is a familiar one of expressive power. The modal language plus the new deletion modalities can define two-dimensional grids – and with a little more coding, existence of a *tiling* of the structure $\mathbb{N} \times \mathbb{N}$ by a given finite set of tiles can then be expressed as satisfiability of one μSML-formula constructed effectively.

Discussion. It is a moot point what this *SAT*-complexity means. First, it applies to a logic, i.e., a theory of reasoning, for sabotage games, not to the games themselves. But also, do the tiling statements in the complexity proof have any significance for sabotage games? One can indeed cast a tiling as a winning strategy in some suitably construed stepwise 'tiling game', but such a game does not appear to naturally support an analog for the edge removal or other grid-changing actions involved in the encoding formula.

In any case, the higher complexity suggests a line that has not been pursued systematically yet: the study of *fragments* of SML and its fixpoint extension. In particular, one might restrict attention to *guarded fragments* where link deletions can only occur when suitably guarded by parameter objects, as has been done to restore decidability for a related graph logic in [13]. But perhaps the most obvious open problem concerning modal sublanguages is this:

> What is the complexity of the graph logic with the basic modal syntax plus just one extra atom stating that Traveler has a winning strategy in the sabotage game over the graph starting at the current point?

Perhaps this logic is still decidable, though its smooth analysis might require some additional devices for describing the dynamic process, such as adding an explicit operator for *relativization* to definable subgraphs.

3 Sabotage Game Trees and Game Logics

So far, our logical analysis has concentrated on the graphs where sabotage games are played. But sabotage games themselves induce standard *extensive game trees* where nodes indicate turns for the players as well as a current state of the game board, i.e., the current graph marking Traveler's position.

Example 5 (Game trees for sabotage games).
Here is part of an extensive sabotage game, with Traveler's position at the dots. We suppressed isomorphic copies for different links between the same points. The general shape of the game trees should be clear from this special case (Fig. 3).

As already noted in Sect. 1, this standard game-theoretic perspective allows for applying general results to sabotage games such as Zermelo's Theorem. More precisely, the proof of this theorem, cf. [22], involves a Backward Induction argument which tells us that winning strategies are *memory-free*, requiring no reference to the history of the game leading up to a current game stage. This simplicity relates to the fact that winning was analyzed in the preceding section just in terms of a current board position, regardless of what had led there.

This is just a start, and studying further game structure makes sense. For instance, in actual graph games, we may prefer *optimal winning strategies* that lead to winning faster than others. These more refined outcomes can be represented in the *strategic form* of the games, [22], a preference structure for players beyond just recording winning and losing that we will not pursue further here.

Extensive games, and strategic form games, have long been studied using a variety of *game logics*, [9]. For the special case of sabotage games, the game trees support a system SGL of *sabotage game logic* with the following syntax which we present to make our discussion of logic design for graph games more concrete.

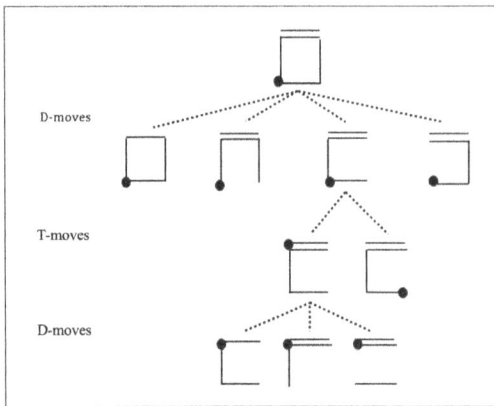

Fig. 3. Part of an extensive game tree for a sabotage game.

The language of SGL has proposition letters describing properties of graph positions, including a proposition letter γ for Traveler's goal region, as well as game indicators 'turn$_i$' marking a turn for player i, 'end' for when the game stops, and 'win$_i$' for when player i wins. In addition there are Boolean operations as well as two existential modalities $\langle T\rangle\varphi, \langle D\rangle\varphi$ intended to describe effects of the players' moves to a next stage of the game in terms of propositions φ true there.

In particular, as suggested by Example 5, sabotage game trees can be seen as models M with nodes $s = (s_1, s_2)$ where s_1 is the game part indicating whether the node is a turn for one of the players or an endpoint and where relevant, who has won, while s_2 is a pointed graph indicating the current position of Traveler. Moreover, for any node s, there is a connection: 'win$_T$' holds at s_1 if and only if γ holds at s_2. Next, players' moves can be seen as actions or events defined at nodes as follows. A move for Demon flips the turn (unless we reach a winning position, where the game stops) and removes one link from the current graph, a move for Traveler flips the turn (with the same proviso about winning positions) and moves the distinguished point in the graph along an available edge.

These models support a two-dimensional semantics, [23], for the above modal language, whose details should be obvious from the above description.

Excursion. This system can be seen as a special concrete case of an *abstract game logic* for extensive games, [9]. In terms of modal logic, winning positions for Traveler can be defined in the modal μ-calculus through the following recursion:

WIN$_T$ $\leftrightarrow$ (('end' $\wedge$ win$_T$) $\vee$ ('turn'$_T$ $\wedge \langle T\rangle$WIN$_T$) $\vee$ ('turn'$_D$ $\wedge [D]$WIN$_T$))

This formula also holds generally for arbitrary extensive games with abstract moves satisfying the Zermelo conditions, and thus, the modal μ-calculus encodes a decidable basic theory of such games. What is special in our case here is the particular choice of game states and moves.

The game logic SGL is still close to the graph logic SML, and this can be seen as follows. For each formula φ in the above two-dimensional game language, we define formulas $Tr_T(\varphi)$ (i), $Tr_D(\varphi)$ (ii) and $Tr_{end}(\varphi)$ (iii). Intuitively, these express in the graph what is expressed by the game formula φ at a node when (i) the turn is for Traveler, (ii) the turn is for Demon, and (iii) the game is at an endpoint. The definition uses the following mutual recursion:

(a1) $Tr_T(\text{p}) = \text{p}$ for all regular proposition letters p, $Tr_T(\text{'turn}_T\text{'}) = \top$,
  $Tr_T(\text{q}) = \bot$ for q one of 'turn$_D$', 'end', 'win$_T$', and 'win$_D$'.

(a2) Tr_T commutes with Boolean operations.

(a3) $Tr_T(\langle T \rangle \psi) = \lozenge Tr_D(\varphi)$, $Tr_T(\langle D \rangle \psi) = \bot$.

(b) The definition for Tr_D is completely analogous.

(c) Finally, Tr_{end} makes all subformulas headed by game modalities false, and treats the special proposition letters for game positions in the obvious way as $\top$ or $\bot$, thus delivering a purely propositional formula.

Now consider a finite extensive game model M for the sabotage game.

Proposition 2. *For all nodes s in* M *and formulas φ of* SGL:

(a) M$, s \models$ turn$_T$ *and* (M$, s \models \varphi$ *iff* $s_2 \models Tr_T(\varphi)$)*, or*
(b) M$, s \models$ turn$_D$ *and* (M$, s \models \varphi$ *iff* $s_2 \models Tr_D(\varphi)$)*, or*
(c) M$, s \models$ end *and* (M$, s \models \varphi$ *iff* $s_2 \models Tr_{end}(\varphi)$)*.*

Proof. The proof is by a straightforward induction on formulas in SGL. E.g., in Case (a), if M$, s \models \langle T \rangle \psi$, there is a move for Traveler in the game tree to a node t where turn$_D$ and ψ hold, and by the inductive hypothesis, $t_2 \models Tr_D(\psi)$. Given the definition of Traveler's moves, the distinguished point of t_2 is a graph successor of that for s_2, and therefore $s_2 \models \lozenge Tr_D(\psi) = Tr_T(\langle T \rangle \psi)$.

Conversely, still in Case (a), suppose that $s_2 \models Tr_T(\langle T \rangle \psi) = \lozenge Tr_D(\psi)$. So there is a graph successor for the distinguished point of s_2 which satisfies $Tr_D(\psi)$, and given that s_1 marked a turn for Traveler, there is a game move for Traveler to some node t with turn$_D$ and $t_2 \models Tr_D(\psi)$. By the inductive hypothesis then, M$, t \models \psi$, and therefore M$, s \models \langle T \rangle \psi$.

This analysis in terms of graph properties explains the earlier-noted memory-free character of winning strategies. It also shows how the game logic SGL is still close to the graph logic of Sect. 2. In fact, it may just be a fragment of the latter language, since the above translation produces SML-formulas of a special kind with alternating modalities $\lozenge, \blacklozenge$. For instance, it seems impossible to define even basic modal formulas like the iterated $\lozenge\lozenge p$ in this manner. This fragment of SML may well be undecidable, but this issue seems an open problem.

Discussion. The preceding issue may be surprising, as one might expect a direct SAT-embedding from SML into SGL. However, for this, we would need to add freely available standard modalities $\lozenge$ to our two-dimensional game language with their usual meaning in the second component of nodes in game trees.

What may also be surprising here in terms of complexity is the fact that the game structure seems richer than that of the graphs: the game boards. But this richer structure only comes into play with winning conditions unlike the earlier reachability. For instance, if we say that Traveler loses when *the same position in a graph is visited for a second time*, the histories in the extensive game matter, and a memory is needed that cannot be simply encoded in the graph.

It seems an interesting general question where the border-line lies between making do with logics for graphs (perhaps with suitable annotations at nodes) and having to move to richer logics of the actual game structure.

4   Infinite Games and Dynamical Systems

The Sabotage Game also allows infinite histories when the graph is infinite. Here are just a few thoughts on this natural extension of the earlier finite setting.

By our stipulation, Traveler still wins only when the goal region is reached, which must happen at some finite stage of game play. In this case, the relevant game-theoretic result extends Zermelo's Theorem. The *Gale-Stewart Theorem* says that each infinite two-player win-lose game with perfect information where one of the two players has a topologically open winning condition is determined, [22]. Here 'topologically open' means that, if an infinite history is winning, it has some finite initial segment all of whose continuations to total histories of the game are winning. Clearly, this property holds for Traveler.

The scenarios described by infinite games resemble non-deterministic dynamical systems where players' goals consist in producing some never-ending overall behavior through continuing moves. As for concrete interpretations of infinite sabotage games, one might think, for instance, of graph-based *cellular automata* or similar computational devices which incur some damage in each round of their computation. It would be of interest to determine which functions or predicates can still be correctly computed in this way 'with finite damage'.

Even when not determined, such infinite games still satisfy a condition of

Weak Determinacy   Either the 'open player' has a winning strategy, or the opponent has a strategy preventing the open player from ever getting to a position with a winning strategy.

In particular, this applies to infinite sabotage games: either Traveler has a winning strategy, or Demon has an 'obstruction strategy' of the sort just described.

A logic for describing powers of players in infinite games is found in [9], with 'forcing modalities' describing properties of histories that players can force by using one of their strategies. It would be of interest to compare this logic with SML on infinite graphs, continuing the analysis in the preceding section.

One especially interesting long-term behavior of sabotage games is this. What happens to the *probabilities of winning* for Traveler or Demon as we look at arbitrary finite pointed graphs with sizes going up to infinity?

A relevant result here is the *Zero-One Law* for first-order languages with a vocabulary of just predicates. For any sentence in such a language, its probability of being true goes to either 0 or 1 as finite graph size goes to infinity. It can even be decided effectively, for any formula, which of the two options occurs.

This result extends to μFO: first-order logic with operators for smallest or greatest fixed-points. Now, we expressed winning positions in the sabotage μ-calculus μSML which translates into μFO – and thus the Zero-One Law applies. But which player will prevail? [21] settles this by analyzing the sabotage game played on one single infinite structure: the *countable random graph*, as a generic representation for playing it on all finite graphs. The outcome is as follows:

The probability of winning for Traveler goes up to 1 as graph size increases.

Thus, the Sabotage Game is massively in favor of Traveler when played on arbitrary graphs. However, Zero-One laws for restricted classes do not always exist, and there are open problems for the special cases found in Sect. 1.

The preceding discussion shows how infinite sabotage games, or arbitrarily repeated finite sabotage games, display interesting further phenomena. However, a detailed analysis of the preceding probabilistic setting in terms of the above-mentioned forcing logics remains to be undertaken.

Finally, as noted, the infinite setting suggests a high-level global look at our games as *dynamical systems* with limit behavior over time. When choices are available as in our games, these systems are non-deterministic, but when we fix strategies for both players, a deterministic dynamical system results proceeding from graph state to graph state via a unique transition function.

There are some logics that describe general features of such dynamical system such as the topological temporal logic of [20], or the temporal dependence logic of [6], but these have not yet been applied to the study of games.

5   Further Directions

Finally, we list a few general issues suggested by the preceding games and logics.

Partial Observation and Knowledge. In many realistic graph games, players have limited observation from their current location. This might hold in particular for Traveler in sabotage games, and thus, knowledge and ignorance comes into play, depending on what has been observed so far. One source for this phenomenon is *'short sight'*: seeing only successors up to some specified depth, studied for exploring extensive game trees in [19]. Another interpretation of such restrictions might be limited attention. Either way, now Traveler's observation applies to the graph: the game board, instead of the game itself.

Example 6 (Sabotage game with limited sight).
Traveler can see only what happens at its current position and the links starting here, but has full knowledge of the total graph structure. Thus, cuts made by Demon outside of this field of vision may remain hidden, unless the game itself makes it clear where they occur. The following game tree shows a few steps of the resulting information dynamics for Traveler using epistemic uncertainty links.

After moving from position 1, Traveler cannot distinguish positions 2 and 3, since they have the same sight, and considers them epistemic alternatives for what has taken place. But while these positions also have the sight as 1,

Traveler will not see 1 as an alternative, as it is known that a move has been played. Without this information, even more complex scenarios might arise.

Next, if Traveler moves upwards, positions 4 and 5 have become distinguishable since the sight differs after the move. At this next level, position 5 has become visually indistinguishable from position 6, but this is not an epistemic uncertainty, since Traveler knows that their two histories are different (Fig. 4).

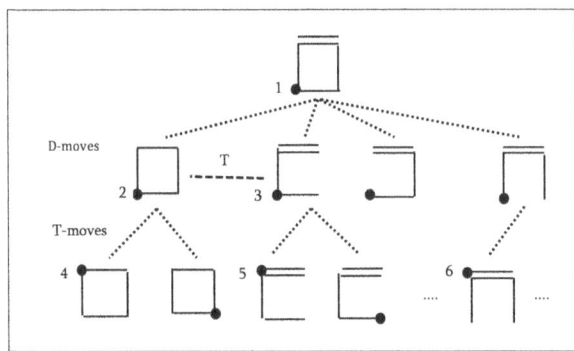

Fig. 4. Part of a sabotage game tree with imperfect information.

This example shows the subtlety of graph games with partial observation. As the game evolves, visual and epistemic indistinguishability can diverge, and players know more than just what they see. This calls for a logical analysis that combines our earlier systems with epistemic modalities. One candidate are *dynamic-epistemic game logics* for imperfect information games, [7], with graphs with various positions for Traveler and cuts made by Demon connected by epistemic uncertainty relations. But an interesting alternative working more directly on the graphs has been developed for Cops-and-Robbers games in [17]. It remains to be seen how this approach would work in the sabotage setting.

Dynamic-Epistemic Logics. The logic SML describes effects of cutting edges in graphs. But such transformations of models also occur in the already mentioned dynamic-epistemic logics where information updates can proceed by cutting epistemic links, thus removing uncertainty, [7]. This poses a prima facie challenge in understanding, since unlike SML, dynamic-epistemic logics tend to be decidable. The difference is that dynamic-epistemic edge deletions occur definably and uniformly, which validates 'recursion axioms' for new knowledge after update that lead to a decidable complete proof system. In contrast with this, the edge deletions in the sabotage game are arbitrary and *stepwise*.

These matters are clarified in [13] in terms of a new dynamic modal logic MLSR of stepwise removal of objects whose additional dynamic modality $\langle -\varphi \rangle \psi$ is true at a point s in a model M if

There is some point t different from s such that (i) $M, t \models \varphi$, and

(ii) the submodel $M - \{t\}$ resulting from M by deleting t satisfies ψ at s.
This can be viewed as a stepwise version of the basic 'public announcement logic' in the dynamic-epistemic realm, or as a general logic describing the effects of a dynamic notion of 'quantification without replacement'. It can also describe graph games where points are removed, or made inaccessible in some way.

MLSR is still first-order translatable, but its SAT problem is undecidable. This, 'going stepwise' can be computationally costly in logic design.

However, interestingly, illustrating a suggestion in Sect. 2, decidability is restored if we constrain object deletions in terms of earlier objects already removed, as we can then translate the system into the Loosely-Guarded Fragment of first-order logic. This suggests a study of graph games where players' choices are constrained in natural ways, something that has not been done yet.

The Bigger Picture: Translation and Tracking. A more general issue lies behind the topics in this paper. We can study graph games, and indeed any games, at *different levels of detail*. The extensive game tree offers the most information about what happens step by step in the process of play. The graph as a game board suppresses historical information, but may still suffice, as we saw, for important game-theoretic properties such as winning positions. In addition, we also mentioned strategic form games, powers in infinite games over time, and at a very high abstraction level, dynamical systems where the focus may be on global long-term patterns in the state space of the games.

Each of these levels suggests its own logical formalisms for describing the relevant structure of interest. But this mere coexistence seems unsatisfactory. One would like to see *connections* between these systems in the form of *translations* from more coarse-grained to more fine-grained logics, or even of *tracking* the dynamics of graph changes and their game effects at various levels, [10].

No comprehensive perspective exists yet on how the landscape of less or more fine-grained game logics coheres, and this seems one of the most urgent, and arguably also most profitable, topics for further study in the area.

6   Conclusion

In this short paper, we have discussed sabotage games, a variety of dynamic graph games that provides concrete instances of general reactive systems. Known results were surveyed describing their interfaces with logic at various levels, and in the process, a number of new open problems emerged. For further details of all topics discussed here, cf. the extensive forthcoming collection [12].

Our exploration has been quite modest, largely in modal logic style, and it by no means exhausted the available logic-games interfaces of which there are other major examples in the literature, such as alternating-temporal logic, [1]. We also did not go deeply into more general logical backgrounds, such as those offered by hybrid logics of graph change, [2], [3], or the 'atomic logics' of [4]. All these raise further interesting issues that are beyond our scope here.

Even so, we hope that the present case study offers some concrete scenarios, notions and issues for readers interested in logic design for reactive systems.

References

1. Alur, R., Henzinger, T., Kupferman, O.: Alternating-time temporal logic. J. ACM **49**(5), 672–713 (2002)
2. Areces, C., Fervari, R., Hoffmann, G.: Relation-changing modal operators. Logic J. IGPL **23**, 601–627 (2015)
3. Areces, C., Fervari, R., Hoffmann, G., Martel, M.: Relation-changing logics as fragments of hybrid logics. Electron. Proc. Theoretical Comput. Sci. 16–29 (2016)
4. Aucher, G.: On the Universality of atomic and molecular logics via proto- logics. Log. Univers. **16**(1), 285–322 (2022)
5. Aucher, G., van Benthem, J., Grossi, D.: Modal logics of sabotage revisited. J. Log. Comput. **28**(2), 269–303 (2017)
6. Baltag, A., van Benthem, J., Li, D.: Dependence logics in temporal settings. https://arxiv.org/abs/2204.07839 (2024)
7. van Benthem, J.: Logical Dynamics of Information and Interaction. Cambridge University Press, Cambridge UK (2011)
8. van Benthem, J.: An essay on sabotage and obstruction. In: Hutter, D., Werner, S., eds., Mechanizing Mathematical Reasoning, Essays in Honor of Jörg Siekmann on the Occasion of his 69th Birthday, Springer Verlag, pp. 268–276 (2005)
9. van Benthem, J.: Logic in Games. The MIT Press, Cambridge MA (2014)
10. van Benthem, J.: Game Levels, Game Logics, Translations, Tracking, and More. Working paper, Institute for Logic, Language and Computation, Amsterdam, and Joint Logic Center, Tsinghua University (2024)
11. van Benthem, J.: An abstract look at the fixed-point theorem for provability logic. In: Bezhanishvili, N., Iemhoff, R., Yang, F., Dick de Jongh on Intuitionistic and Provability Logics, Springer Science, pp. 75–88 (2024)
12. van Benthem, J., Liu, F.: Graph games and logic design. recent developments and future directions, Springer Asia, to appear (2025). In: Earlier programmatic paper appeared in Liu, F.H.O., Yu, J., eds., Knowledge, Proof and Dynamics, Springer Science, Singapore, 125–146, 2020.
13. J. van Benthem, C.M., Zaffora Blando, V.: A New Look at the Modal Logic of Stepwise Removal. In: van Benthem, J., Liu, F., eds. (2025)
14. Berlekamp, E., Conway, J., Guy, R.: Chapter 19: "The King and the Consumer", Winning Ways for your Mathematical Plays, Academic Press, 607–634 (1982)
15. Blackburn, P., de Rijke, M., Venema, Y.: Modal Logic. Cambridge University Press, Cambridge (2000)
16. Fijalkow, N., et al.: Games on Graphs. https://arxiv.org/abs/2305.10546 (2023)
17. Ghosh, S., Li, D., Liu, F.: Knowing is winning: an epistemic approach to the hide and seek game. In: van Benthem, J., Liu, F., eds., to appear (2025)
18. Gierasimczuk, N., Kurzen, L., Velázquez-Quesada, F.R.: Learning and Teaching as a Game: A Sabotage Approach. In: He, X., Horty, J., Pacuit, E. (eds.) LORI 2009. LNCS (LNAI), vol. 5834, pp. 119–132. Springer, Heidelberg (2009). https://doi.org/10.1007/978-3-642-04893-7_10
19. Grossi, D., Turrini, P.: Short Sight in Extensive Games. In: Proceedings AAMAS 12, Valencia, pp. 805–812 (2012)
20. Kremer, Ph., Mints, G.: Dynamic topological logic. In: Aiello, M., van Benthem, J., Pratt-Hartmann, I.: Handbook of Spatial Logics, Springer Science, Dordrecht, 565–606 (2017)

21. Mierzewski, Ch.: When random graphs are safe for travel: a note on the sabotage game. In: van Benthem, J., and Liu, F., eds., (2025)
22. Osborne, M., Rubinstein, A.: A Course in Game Theory. The MIT Press, Cambridge MA (1994)
23. Segerberg, K.: Two-dimensional modal logic. J. Philos. Log. $\mathbf{2}(1)$, 77–96 (1973)

Arbitrary Radical Upgrades

Raul Fervari[1,2] and Benjamin Icard[3(✉)]

[1] FAMAF, Universidad Nacional de Córdoba, Córdoba, Argentina
rfervari@unc.edu.ar
[2] Consejo Nacional de Investigaciones Científicas y Técnicas, Buenos Aires, Argentina
[3] LIP6, Sorbonne University, CNRS, Paris, France
benjamin.icard@lip6.fr

Abstract. This paper presents and investigates ARUL, a variant of dynamic belief revision logic in which revision policies, in particular radical, or lexicographic, upgrades, can be arbitrary. We discuss the motivations of having this kind of soft arbitrary operator, concretely for refining the analysis of agentivity and modelling classical epistemic paradoxes. We introduce a sound and complete axiomatic system over models whose accessibility relation is a reflexive, transitive and locally connected pre-order, following an approach parallel to Arbitrary Public Announcement Logic (APAL) for proving completeness.

Keywords: Dynamic Logics · Plausibility · Radical Upgrades · Arbitrary Upgrades · Epistemic Paradoxes

1 Introduction

Public Announcement Logic (PAL) [8,30,31] was tailored as an extension of Epistemic Logic [25] to reason about information change. Soon after its introduction, PAL was followed by logics for softer revision policies, such as the belief upgrades family of e.g. [11,12,16]. In the meantime, the expressivity of PAL increased substantially with the possibility to quantify over hard announcements, leading to Arbitrary Public Announcement Logic (APAL), introduced and axiomatized in [4]. The completeness argument was then fixed in [2], and improved in [5]. This paper proposes to make similar steps for dynamic belief revision theory by introducing ARUL, a logic for Arbitrary Radical Upgrades.

Arbitrary radical upgrades have been considered already in [28], not as syntactic primitive operators, but as defined notions to help analyze a Smullyan's deception puzzle on surprise [33] (see also [27]). In [28], arbitrary radical upgrades are used meta-logically to model two versions of deception in Smullyan's puzzle, the so-called deception by *commission* (i.e., false beliefs obtained by the existence of some radical upgrade) and deception by *omission* (i.e., false beliefs obtained by the lack of some radical upgrade). In this paper we aim to provide a formal and general treatment of these concepts, by defining and axiomatizing the logic ARUL.

J. Proença et al. (Eds.): SEFM 2024, LNCS 15551, pp. 36–49, 2026.
https://doi.org/10.1007/978-3-031-94748-3_3

The language of ARUL is based on dynamic epistemic languages divided into two parts. The static part elaborates on [34] by featuring modalities for "at least as plausible as" situations and for an agent's knowledge. In turn, the dynamic part of ARUL contains the standard radical upgrade modality on *specific* formulas of the language [12,16,19], but also incorporates an operator for arbitrary upgrades, authorizing quantification over *any* formulas of ARUL. The language of ARUL is interpreted over doxastic-plausibility models (see, e.g., [12,34]). Herein, the model's plausibility relation considered is a reflexive, transitive and locally connected pre-order. To our knowledge, the extension of arbitrariness to radical upgrades proposed by ARUL is novel. Regarding technical results, ARUL connects to standard modal logic by using tools designed to axiomatize APAL [5]. Regarding expressivity, the agentive definitions and distinctions that ARUL helps delineate find applications into the philosophical analysis of various paradoxes, such as e.g. Gerbrandy's formalization of the surprise examination paradox and variants, such as Fitch's paradox and Moore's paradox.

Outline of the Paper. In Sect. 2, we introduce the dynamic logic of arbitrary radical upgrades (ARUL), describing the syntax and semantic interpretation of the language. Section 3 presents an axiom system for ARUL, akin to the axiomatization of APAL, that we prove to be sound and complete with respect to doxastic plausibility models. We present our completeness argument in Sect. 4, following the strategy adopted by [5] for APAL. In Sect. 5, we show the expressivity strengths of ARUL regarding action theory and related epistemic paradoxes. We conclude in Sect. 6 and set the basis for future logical extensions to other belief revision policies, and to more general results.

2 Preliminaries

We present the logic ARUL, an extension of classic dynamic belief revision logic [11,12,16] incorporating arbitrary radical upgrades. Unlike the aforementioned approaches, the syntax of ARUL contains a modal plausibility operator as in [34], instead of a static modal operator for belief. Nevertheless, the belief operator is definable in our setting. In addition, ARUL features dynamic modal operators for plausibility upgrades with specific formulas, and a modality for upgrades with arbitrary formulas as a novelty.

Definition 1. *Let* Prop *be a countable set of propositional symbols. The set of all* ARUL-*formulas is given by the following Backus-Naur Form:*

$$\varphi, \psi ::= p \mid \neg\varphi \mid \varphi \vee \psi \mid [\leqslant]\varphi \mid \mathbf{K}\varphi \mid [\Uparrow\varphi]\psi \mid [\Uparrow]\psi,$$

where $p \in$ Prop. *On the one hand, the language contains the static modal formulas* $[\leqslant]\varphi$ *(standing for "φ holds in all worlds the agent considers at least as plausible as the current one"), and* $\mathbf{K}\varphi$ *(for "the agent knows that φ"). On the other hand, it contains dynamic formulas* $[\Uparrow\varphi]\psi$ *(standing for "after a radical upgrade* with formula φ, ψ holds"), and the arbitrary upgrade $[\Uparrow]\psi$ (read as "after any radical upgrade takes place, ψ holds"). Finally, a formula φ is called epistemic, if it does not contain any occurrence of $[\Uparrow\psi]$ or $[\Uparrow]$.

The simple language of ARUL defined above enables us to define several other notions, as shown hereafter.

Definition 2. *We define the possibility operator for knowledge as* $\hat{\mathbf{K}}\varphi := \neg\mathbf{K}\neg\varphi$, *and the existential modality for plausibility as* $\langle\leqslant\rangle\varphi := \neg[\leqslant]\neg\varphi$ *(standing for "there is at least a plausible world where φ holds"). Plain beliefs can be defined in terms of plausibility as* $\mathbf{B}\varphi := \langle\leqslant\rangle[\leqslant]\varphi$ *(see [34, Fact 1] for details), and read as "the agent believes that φ". We also define the existential radical upgrade as* $\langle\Uparrow\psi\rangle\varphi := \neg[\Uparrow\psi]\neg\varphi$, *and its arbitrary version as* $\langle\Uparrow\rangle\psi := \neg[\Uparrow]\neg\psi$ *(standing for "there exists a formula φ such that $[\Uparrow\varphi]\psi$ holds"). Additional connectives ($\top$, $\bot$, $\wedge$, $\rightarrow$, $\leftrightarrow$) are defined as usual.*

Formulas of ARUL are interpreted semantically by using (doxastic) plausibility models defined in [11,12,16,17]. Below we follow the presentation of [34].

Definition 3. *A plausibility model for ARUL is a tuple* $\mathfrak{S} = \langle\mathcal{S}, \leqslant, V\rangle$ *where:*

- $\mathcal{S}$ *is a countable non-empty set of "possible states" (or "worlds"),*
- $\leqslant \subseteq \mathcal{S} \times \mathcal{S}$, *the "plausibility relation" for the agent, is a locally connected pre-order, and*
- $V : \mathsf{Prop} \rightarrow \wp(\mathcal{S})$ *is a standard "valuation map", where $\wp(\mathcal{S})$ is the set of all subsets of $\mathcal{S}$.*

The conventional reading of the plausibility order is that in case $s \leqslant t$ (for all $s, t \in \mathcal{S}$), the agent considers state t to be "at least as plausible as" state s. Given $s \in \mathcal{S}$, we call $\mathfrak{S}, s$ a pointed model, with s being the "actual" state.

Definition 4. *Let* $\mathfrak{S} = \langle\mathcal{S}, \leqslant, V\rangle$ *be a plausibility model. We define the epistemic accessibility relation $\sim$ as* $\sim := \leqslant \cup \leqslant^{-1}$. *Notice that $\sim$ is an equivalence relation (i.e., reflexive, symmetric and transitive relation), thus for each $s \in \mathcal{S}$ we define its equivalence class* $[s]_\sim := \{t \mid s \sim t\}$.

Let $A \subseteq \mathcal{S}$. We define $\mathsf{Max}_{\leqslant}^A$ as the set of states in A that are maximal for the ordering $\leqslant$ restricted to states in A, i.e.,

$$\mathsf{Max}_{\leqslant}^A = \{u \in A \mid \text{for all } v \in A, \ v \leqslant u\}.$$

Recall that a *locally-connected pre-order* is a pre-order (i.e., it is reflexive and transitive), that is locally connected (for all $t, v \in [s]_\sim$ we have $t \sim v$). In e.g. [12,19,34], it is also required that the relation be *conversely well-founded* (i.e., it has a minimum element). However, as done in e.g. [16], we drop this condition as not being crucial in our logical presentation, and moreover, our completeness argument might no longer apply otherwise.

Definition 5. *The truth of a formula φ at the actual state s in the plausibility model $\mathfrak{S}$, denoted $\mathfrak{S}, s \models \varphi$, is defined inductively as follows:*

$$
\begin{array}{lll}
\mathfrak{S}, s \models p & \textit{iff} & s \in V(p) \\
\mathfrak{S}, s \models \neg\varphi & \textit{iff} & \mathfrak{S}, s \not\models \varphi \\
\mathfrak{S}, s \models \varphi \vee \psi & \textit{iff} & \mathfrak{S}, s \models \varphi \textit{ or } \mathfrak{S}, s \models \psi \\
\mathfrak{S}, s \models [\leqslant]\varphi & \textit{iff} & \textit{for all } t \in \mathcal{S}, \textit{if } s \leqslant t \textit{ then } \mathfrak{S}, t \models \varphi \\
\mathfrak{S}, s \models \mathbf{K}\varphi & \textit{iff} & \textit{for all } t \in \mathcal{S}, \textit{if } s \sim t \textit{ then } \mathfrak{S}, t \models \varphi \\
\mathfrak{S}, s \models [\Uparrow\varphi]\psi & \textit{iff} & \mathfrak{S}^{[\Uparrow\varphi]}, s \models \psi \\
\mathfrak{S}, s \models [\Uparrow]\psi & \textit{iff} & \textit{for all epistemic } \varphi, \; \mathfrak{S}, s \models [\Uparrow\varphi]\psi,
\end{array}
$$

where $[\![\psi]\!]^{\mathfrak{S}} := \{s \mid \mathfrak{S}, s \models \psi\}$, and $\mathfrak{S}^{[\Uparrow\varphi]} = \langle \mathcal{S}, \leqslant^{[\Uparrow\varphi]}, V \rangle$ is such that:

$$
\leqslant^{[\Uparrow\varphi]} := (\leqslant \cap (\mathcal{S} \times [\![\varphi]\!]^{\mathfrak{S}})) \; \cup \; (\leqslant \cap ([\![\neg\varphi]\!]^{\mathfrak{S}} \times \mathcal{S})) \; \cup \; (\sim \cap ([\![\neg\varphi]\!]^{\mathfrak{S}} \times [\![\varphi]\!]^{\mathfrak{S}})).
$$

A formula φ is said to be satisfiable if $\mathfrak{S}, s \models \varphi$ for some model $\mathfrak{S}$ and state s, and φ is valid in $\mathfrak{S}$ if $\mathfrak{S} \models \varphi$ for all states s of $\mathcal{S}$. Finally, φ is valid stricto sensu (notation: $\models \varphi$) if $\mathfrak{S} \models \varphi$ for all models $\mathfrak{S}$.

Following [16] and [12], the belief radical upgrade with respect to a formula φ defined above, written $[\Uparrow\varphi]$, induces a mapping of the following kind:

$$
[\Uparrow\varphi] : \mathfrak{S} \mapsto \mathfrak{S}^{[\Uparrow\varphi]}
$$

Here, $\mathfrak{S}$ is the initial plausibility model and $\mathfrak{S}^{[\Uparrow\varphi]}$ is the transformed model obtained once the operation $[\Uparrow\varphi]$ is performed on $\mathfrak{S}$. In this definition, $\mathcal{S}$ and V remain unchanged. The special feature of $\mathfrak{S}^{[\Uparrow\varphi]}$ is the plausibility order $\leqslant^{[\Uparrow\varphi]}$. The reordering of states defined by $\leqslant^{[\Uparrow\varphi]}$ ensures that the states where φ is true are promoted in plausibility. In the definition of $\leqslant^{[\Uparrow\varphi]}$, the first part ($\leqslant \cap (\mathcal{S} \times [\![\varphi]\!]^{\mathfrak{S}})$) states that the relative ordering of worlds where φ is true is the same as in the original order $\leqslant$. The second part ($\leqslant \cap ([\![\neg\varphi]\!]^{\mathfrak{S}} \times \mathcal{S})$) states that the relative ordering of worlds where φ is false is the same as in the original order $\leqslant$. Finally, the third part ($\sim \cap ([\![\neg\varphi]\!]^{\mathfrak{S}} \times [\![\varphi]\!]^{\mathfrak{S}})$) states that the worlds where φ is true become equally or more plausible than worlds where φ is false in the locally connected component.

Remark 1. Notice that, by Definition 5, the radical upgrade operator $[\Uparrow\psi]$ is self-dual, i.e., $[\Uparrow\psi]\varphi \leftrightarrow \langle\Uparrow\psi\rangle\varphi$ is valid, since $[\Uparrow\psi]$ can always be executed (its semantics does not involve a pre-condition) and the mapping $[\Uparrow\varphi] : \mathfrak{S} \mapsto \mathfrak{S}^{[\Uparrow\varphi]}$ always yields one and only one model.

Finally, we state that plain beliefs can be recovered from plausibility.

Proposition 1 ([34]). *Let $\mathfrak{S}$ be a plausibility model with s being one of its states, and let φ be an ARUL formula. Then,*

$$
\mathfrak{S}, s \models \mathbf{B}\varphi \textit{ iff for all } t \in \mathsf{Max}_{\leqslant}^{[s]_\sim}, \; \mathfrak{S}, t \models \varphi.
$$

3   Axiom System

In this section, we present an axiom system for ARUL. This puts together the axiomatization for the $[⇑φ]$-free fragment and reduction axioms to eliminate the occurrences of $[⇑φ]$ [11], plus axioms and rules for arbitrary announcements [4].

Our strategy closely follows the ideas introduced in [5] for APAL. In [4], it is noticed that single-agent APAL (over **S5** models) can be reduced into plain epistemic logic, while for $n > 1$ agents the expressive power of APAL is strictly greater than basic epistemic logic. For the case of ARUL, it has not been established whether this is also the case or not. Thus, to prove a completeness result for ARUL we will use the argument followed by [5] for multi-agent APAL.

Here we need to introduce the so-called *necessity forms* for ARUL. Necessity forms are crucial in axiomatizing the logic, as a mechanism for performing special restricted forms of substitution on certain formulas (see [1,5,24]).

Definition 6. *Let ♯ be a fresh propositional symbol. We define the set of* necessity forms *(whose members are notated $η(♯)$, $η'(♯)$, $η''(♯)$, etc.) of* ARUL *as:*

$$η(♯) ::= ♯ \mid φ → η(♯) \mid [≤]η(♯) \mid \mathbf{K}η(♯) \mid [⇑φ]η(♯),$$

where $φ$ is a formula of ARUL.

Our strategy to provide a sound and complete axiom system for ARUL consists in three parts. Firstly, we provide standard modal axioms for the epistemic fragment of ARUL, i.e., the fragment whose only modalities are $[≤]$ and $\mathbf{K}$, as in e.g. [34] (see also [18]). Secondly, we provide so-called *reduction axioms* for axiomatizing formulas containing the $[⇑ψ]$ modality. Reduction axioms enable us to eliminate occurences of $[⇑ψ]$, as done in [34]. Finally, a block should be introduced for axiomatizing arbitrary upgrades $[⇑]$. To achieve this, we provide basic modal axioms and a modal necessitation rule using a necessity form, similar to the ones for arbitrary public announcements described in [5].

Definition 7. *The axiom system $\mathcal{ARU}$ for* ARUL *is defined by the axioms and rules of Fig. 1. Precisely, $\mathcal{ARU}$ is the smallest set of formulas of* ARUL *that contains all the axioms of Fig. 1 and it is closed by its rules.*

Let us briefly discuss the list of axioms and rules of Fig. 1. The first block provides the propositional base of the system, as well as distribution axioms for each modality of ARUL. The second block axiomatizes the properties of knowledge (knowledge and factivity, and positive and negative introspection, respectively). In the third block, we introduce the axioms to capture the properties of the plausibility relation, as well as its connections with the knowledge modality $\mathbf{K}$. Then, axiom (LC) establishes that the plausibility relation is locally connected, whereas (Int) characterizes the interaction between arbitrary and non-arbitrary radical upgrades. Finally, blocks are provided for the inferences rules, including Modus Ponens and Necessitation rules for each modality (using a necessity form for $[⇑]$), and for the reduction axioms of $[⇑χ]$, including axiom (A5) which mimics every possible outcomes resulting from the application of a plausibility upgrade.

Basic Axioms	
CPL	All tautologies from propositional logic
$K_{[\leqslant]}$	$[\leqslant](\varphi \to \psi) \to ([\leqslant]\varphi \to [\leqslant]\psi)$
K_K	$\mathbf{K}(\varphi \to \psi) \to (\mathbf{K}\varphi \to \mathbf{K}\psi))$
$K_{\Uparrow\chi}$	$[\Uparrow\chi](\varphi \to \psi) \to ([\Uparrow\chi]\varphi \to [\Uparrow\chi]\psi)$
$K_\Uparrow$	$[\Uparrow](\varphi \to \psi) \to ([\Uparrow]\varphi \to [\Uparrow]\psi)$
T_K	$\mathbf{K}\varphi \to \varphi$
4_K	$\mathbf{K}\varphi \to \mathbf{K}\mathbf{K}\varphi$
5_K	$\neg\mathbf{K}\varphi \to \mathbf{K}\neg\mathbf{K}\varphi$
$T_{[\leqslant]}$	$[\leqslant]\varphi \to \varphi$
$4_{[\leqslant]}$	$[\leqslant]\varphi \to [\leqslant][\leqslant]\varphi$
Inc	$\mathbf{K}\varphi \to [\leqslant]\varphi$
LC	$\hat{\mathbf{K}}\varphi \wedge \hat{\mathbf{K}}\psi) \to \hat{\mathbf{K}}(\varphi \wedge \langle\leqslant\rangle\psi) \vee \hat{\mathbf{K}}(\psi \wedge \langle\leqslant\rangle\varphi)$
Int	$[\Uparrow]\varphi \to [\Uparrow\psi]\varphi$, for ψ epistemic

Inference Rules	
MP	from φ and $\varphi \to \psi$ infer ψ
$Nec_{[\leqslant]}$	from φ infer $[\leqslant]\varphi$
Nec_K	from φ infer $\mathbf{K}\varphi$
$Nec_{[\Uparrow\chi]}$	from φ infer $[\Uparrow\chi]\varphi$
$Nec_{[\Uparrow]}$	from $\eta([\Uparrow\psi]\varphi)$ infer $\eta([\Uparrow]\varphi)$, for ψ epistemic

Reduction Axioms	
(A1)	$[\Uparrow\chi]p \leftrightarrow p$
(A2)	$[\Uparrow\chi]\neg\varphi \leftrightarrow \neg[\Uparrow\chi]\varphi$
(A3)	$[\Uparrow\chi](\varphi \vee \psi) \leftrightarrow [\Uparrow\chi]\varphi \vee [\Uparrow\chi]\psi$
(A4)	$[\Uparrow\chi]\mathbf{K}\varphi \leftrightarrow \mathbf{K}[\Uparrow\chi]\varphi$
(A5)	$[\Uparrow\chi][\leqslant]\varphi \leftrightarrow [\leqslant]((\chi \to [\Uparrow\chi]\varphi) \wedge (\neg\chi \to [\leqslant][\Uparrow\chi]\varphi) \wedge$ $(\neg\chi \to \mathbf{K}(\chi \to [\Uparrow\chi]\varphi)))$

Fig. 1. Axiom system and inference rules $\mathcal{ARU}$ for ARUL.

Lemma 1 (Soundness). *The axiomatization $\mathcal{ARU}$ is sound, i.e., all the axioms are valid formulas, while inference rules preserve validity over formulas (on plausibility models).*

Proof. Soundness of most axioms and rules (or variants of them) has been shown in e.g. [12,19,34], and for arbitrary announcements in [2,3,5]. □

We list now a number of definitions and properties that are useful to establish completeness of the axiom system $\mathcal{ARU}$. These properties are mostly inspired by their analogues from [5] (some proofs and properties are omitted for space reasons). We start by defining the notion of a *theory*, which is our main ingredient for building a canonical model.

Definition 8. *Let Γ be a set of formulas. We call Γ a theory if: 1) Γ contains $\mathcal{ARU}$, and 2) Γ is closed under MP and $Nec_{[\Uparrow]}$.*

A theory Γ is consistent *if $\bot \notin \Gamma$, and it is* maximal *if for all φ in* ARUL, *we have either $\varphi \in \Gamma$ or $\neg\varphi \in \Gamma$. We denote as MCT the set of all theories that are both consistent and maximal.*

Notice that a theory is only required to be closed under rules MP and $\text{Nec}_{[\Uparrow]}$, as these rules preserve truth while the others preserve only validity. Next, we present classical properties which ensure that a theory behaves as expected.

Lemma 2. *Let Γ be a MCT. The following properties hold:*

1. $\bot \notin \Gamma$,
2. $\varphi \in \Gamma$ iff $\neg\varphi \notin \Gamma$,
3. $\varphi \vee \psi \in \Gamma$ iff either $\varphi \in \Gamma$ or $\psi \in \Gamma$.

Definition 9. *Let Γ be a theory. Define:*

$$[\Uparrow\psi]\Gamma = \{\varphi \mid [\Uparrow\psi]\varphi \in \Gamma\} \qquad \Gamma \oplus \varphi = \{\psi \mid \varphi \rightarrow \psi \in \Gamma\}$$
$$\mathbf{K}\Gamma = \{\varphi \mid \mathbf{K}\varphi \in \Gamma\} \qquad [\leqslant]\Gamma = \{\varphi \mid [\leqslant]\varphi \in \Gamma\}.$$

Lemma 3. *Let Γ be a theory, and let φ be a formula of* ARUL. *Then, $[\Uparrow\varphi]\Gamma$, $\Gamma \oplus \varphi$, $\mathbf{K}\Gamma$ and $[\leqslant]\Gamma$ are theories. Moreover, $\Gamma \cup \{\varphi\} \subseteq \Gamma \oplus \varphi$, and $\Gamma \oplus \varphi$ is consistent iff $\neg\varphi \notin \Gamma$.*

Lemma 4. *Each consistent theory can be extended to a MCT.*

Now, we provide some properties that are essential to guarantee that the canonical model is a proper plausibility model for ARUL.

Lemma 5. *Let Γ, Δ, Π be MCTs. Then,*

1. $\mathbf{K}\Gamma \subseteq \Gamma$, $[\leqslant]\Gamma \subseteq \Gamma$, and $\mathbf{K}\Gamma \subseteq [\leqslant]\Gamma$,
2. if $[\leqslant]\Gamma \subseteq \Delta$ and $[\leqslant]\Delta \subseteq \Pi$ then $[\leqslant]\Gamma \subseteq \Pi$,
3. if $\mathbf{K}\Gamma \subseteq \Delta$ and $\mathbf{K}\Delta \subseteq \Pi$ then $\mathbf{K}\Gamma \subseteq \Pi$,
4. if $\mathbf{K}\Gamma \subseteq \Delta$ then $\mathbf{K}\Delta \subseteq \Gamma$.

4   Completeness

We can now introduce our completeness argument for ARUL, following the standard methodology via a *canonical model*. To do so, we borrow the developments of [5] for proving completeness of APAL.

Definition 10 (Canonical Model). *The* canonical model *for $\mathcal{ARU}$ is defined as $\mathfrak{S}^c = \langle \mathcal{S}^c, \leqslant^c, V^c \rangle$, where:*

- $\mathcal{S}^c = \{\Gamma \mid \Gamma$ is a MCT $\}$,
- $\leqslant^c = \{(\Gamma, \Gamma') \mid [\leqslant]\Gamma \subseteq \Gamma'\}$,
- $V^c(p) = \{p \mid p \in \Gamma\}$, for all $p \in$ Prop.

Clearly, $\mathfrak{S}^c$ is a plausibility model (e.g. structural properties on $\leqslant^c$ are guaranteed by Lemma 5). We now introduce some definitions and syntactic properties, that are useful to properly treat formulas in our completeness proof.

Definition 11. *The size of a formula φ of* ARUL, *is written* $\mathrm{size}(\varphi)$ *and defined inductively as follows:*

$$\begin{aligned}
\mathrm{size}(p) &= 1 & \mathrm{size}(\varphi \vee \psi) &= 1 + \max\{\mathrm{size}(\varphi), \mathrm{size}(\psi)\} \\
\mathrm{size}(\delta\varphi) &= 1 + \mathrm{size}(\varphi) & \mathrm{size}([\Uparrow\psi]\varphi) &= 5.\mathrm{size}(\varphi) + \mathrm{size}(\psi),
\end{aligned}$$

with $\delta \in \{\neg, \mathbf{K}, [\leqslant], [\Uparrow]\}$. *The* $\Uparrow$-*depth of* φ, *written* $\mathrm{depth}^{\Uparrow}(\varphi)$, *is defined as:*

$$\begin{aligned}
\mathrm{depth}^{\Uparrow}(p) &= 0 & \mathrm{depth}^{\Uparrow}(\varphi \vee \psi) &= \max\{\mathrm{depth}^{\Uparrow}(\varphi), \mathrm{depth}^{\Uparrow}(\psi)\} \\
\mathrm{depth}^{\Uparrow}(\gamma\varphi) &= \mathrm{depth}^{\Uparrow}(\varphi) & \mathrm{depth}^{\Uparrow}([\Uparrow\psi]\varphi) &= \max\{\mathrm{depth}^{\Uparrow}(\varphi), \mathrm{depth}^{\Uparrow}(\psi)\} \\
\mathrm{depth}^{\Uparrow}([\Uparrow]\varphi) &= 1 + \mathrm{depth}^{\Uparrow}(\varphi),
\end{aligned}$$

with $\gamma \in \{\neg, \mathbf{K}, [\leqslant]\}$. *We write* $\varphi <_{\mathrm{d}}^{\mathrm{s}} \psi$ *iff either* $\mathrm{depth}^{\Uparrow}(\varphi) < \mathrm{depth}^{\Uparrow}(\psi)$, *or* $\mathrm{depth}^{\Uparrow}(\varphi) = \mathrm{depth}^{\Uparrow}(\psi)$ *and* $\mathrm{size}(\varphi) < \mathrm{size}(\psi)$.

Lemma 6. *The relation* $<_{\mathrm{d}}^{\mathrm{s}}$ *is a well-founded strict partial order over formulas.*

In Definition 11, we define $\mathrm{size}(\varphi \vee \psi)$ as $1 + \max\{\mathrm{size}(\varphi), \mathrm{size}(\psi)\}$. By contrast, in [5], $\mathrm{size}(\varphi \vee \psi)$ is defined as $1 + \mathrm{size}(\varphi) + \mathrm{size}(\psi)$. In addition, the "curious" factor of 3 in $\mathrm{size}([\Uparrow\psi]\varphi)$ becomes 5 here, the aim of which is to guarantee the application of the inductive hypothesis in the proof of Lemma 8. Below we prove the special property about the order $<_{\mathrm{d}}^{\mathrm{s}}$ that is not present in [5].

Lemma 7. *Let* χ, ψ *be* ARUL *formulas. Then,*

1) $[\leqslant](\neg\chi \vee [\Uparrow\chi]\psi) <_{\mathrm{d}}^{\mathrm{s}} [\Uparrow\chi][\leqslant]\psi$ 2) $[\leqslant](\chi \vee [\leqslant][\Uparrow\chi]\psi) <_{\mathrm{d}}^{\mathrm{s}} [\Uparrow\chi][\leqslant]\psi$
3) $[\leqslant](\chi \vee \mathbf{K}(\chi \rightarrow [\Uparrow\chi]\psi)) <_{\mathrm{d}}^{\mathrm{s}} [\Uparrow\chi][\leqslant]\psi$.

Proof. In all cases, the $\Uparrow$-depths coincide, so we need to check their sizes. Notice that by applying repeatedly Definition 11, we get:

$$\begin{aligned}
\mathrm{size}([\Uparrow\chi][\leqslant]\psi) &= 5.\mathrm{size}([\leqslant]\psi) + \mathrm{size}(\chi) \\
&= 5.(1 + \mathrm{size}(\psi)) + \mathrm{size}(\chi) \\
&= 5 + 5.\mathrm{size}(\psi) + \mathrm{size}(\chi)
\end{aligned}$$

Item 1 is shown below:

$$\begin{aligned}
\mathrm{size}([\leqslant](\neg\chi \vee [\Uparrow\chi]\psi)) &= 2 + \max\{1 + \mathrm{size}(\chi), \mathrm{size}([\Uparrow\chi]\psi)\} \\
&= 2 + \max\{1 + \mathrm{size}(\chi), 5.\mathrm{size}(\psi) + \mathrm{size}(\chi)\} \quad (\dagger) \\
&= 2 + 5.\mathrm{size}(\psi) + \mathrm{size}(\chi) < \mathrm{size}([\Uparrow\chi][\leqslant]\psi)
\end{aligned}$$

Step ($\dagger$) follows from the fact that the size is always at least 1. Using similar reasoning, we get $\mathrm{size}([\leqslant](\chi \vee [\leqslant][\Uparrow\chi]\psi)) = 3 + 5.\mathrm{size}(\psi) + \mathrm{size}(\chi) < \mathrm{size}([\Uparrow\chi][\leqslant]\psi)$, then item 2 follows. Finally, for item 3, we have:

$$\begin{aligned}
\mathrm{size}([\leqslant](\chi \vee \mathbf{K}(\chi \rightarrow [\Uparrow\chi]\psi))) = 2 + \max\{&\mathrm{size}(\chi), \\
&2 + \max\{1 + \mathrm{size}(\chi), 5.\mathrm{size}(\psi) + \mathrm{size}(\chi)\}\} \\
= 4 + 5.\mathrm{size}(\psi) &+ \mathrm{size}(\chi) < \mathrm{size}([\Uparrow\chi][\leqslant]\psi)
\end{aligned}$$

With this property at hand, in addition to those introduced in [5], we can proceed with the crucial result in this section.

Lemma 8. *Let φ be a formula, let conditions P and H be defined as follows:*

$P(\varphi)$**:** *for all MCT Γ, we have $\varphi \in \Gamma$ iff $\mathfrak{S}^c, \Gamma \models \varphi$;*
$H(\varphi)$**:** *for all formulas ψ, if $\psi <_{\mathrm{d}}^{\mathrm{s}} \varphi$, then $P(\varphi)$.*

Then, if $H(\varphi)$ then $P(\varphi)$.

Proof. The proof is by structural induction on φ. One interesting case is $\varphi = [\Uparrow\chi][\leqslant]\psi$. Assuming $H([\Uparrow\chi][\leqslant]\psi)$, we suppose $[\Uparrow\chi][\leqslant]\psi \in \Gamma$. By (A5), we get $[\leqslant]((\chi \to [\Uparrow\chi]\varphi) \wedge (\neg\chi \to [\leqslant][\Uparrow\chi]\varphi) \wedge (\neg\chi \to \mathbf{K}(\chi \to [\Uparrow\chi]\varphi))) \in \Gamma$. Then, we have $\{[\leqslant](\chi \to [\Uparrow\chi]\varphi), [\leqslant](\neg\chi \to [\leqslant][\Uparrow\chi]\varphi), [\leqslant](\neg\chi \to \mathbf{K}(\chi \to [\Uparrow\chi]\varphi))\} \subseteq \Gamma$. By CPL, $\{[\leqslant](\neg\chi \vee [\Uparrow\chi]\varphi), [\leqslant](\chi \vee [\leqslant][\Uparrow\chi]\varphi), [\leqslant](\chi \vee \mathbf{K}(\chi \to [\Uparrow\chi]\varphi))\} \subseteq \Gamma$. Thus, by Lemma 7, IH and (A5), we get $\mathfrak{S}^c, \Gamma \models [\Uparrow\chi][\leqslant]\psi$. Hence, $P([\Uparrow\chi][\leqslant]\psi)$ holds.

Lemma 9 (Truth Lemma). *Let φ be a formula of* ARUL, *and let Γ be a MCT. Then, $\varphi \in \Gamma$ iff $\mathfrak{S}^c, \Gamma \models \varphi$.*

Proof. By Lemmas 6 and 8.

Theorem 1. *The axiomatic system $\mathcal{ARU}$ from Fig. 1 is sound and complete for* ARUL *over the class of plausibility models from Definition 3.*

Proof. Soundness follows by Lemma 1. For completeness, we need to show that $\models \varphi$ implies $\varphi \in \mathcal{ARU}$. Aiming for a contradiction, suppose that $\models \varphi$ and that $\varphi \notin \mathcal{ARU}$. By Lemmas 3 and 4, there exists a MCT Γ such that $\neg\varphi \in \Gamma$. By Lemma 9, $\mathfrak{S}^c, \Gamma \models \neg\varphi$, thus $\mathfrak{S}^c, \Gamma \not\models \varphi$. Then, $\not\models \varphi$, a contradiction. Therefore, $\mathcal{ARU}$ is complete for ARUL over the class of plausibility models from Definition 3.

5   Applications

This section shows that our framework fruitfully paves the way to address some central philosophical issues. We first discuss the *surprise deception paradox* investigated from a dynamic doxastic logic perspective in [28],—a work that inspired the definition of our arbitrary upgrade notion. Then, we discuss *Fitch's knowability paradox* [22], and *Moore's paradox* (see e.g. [25,29]) in the context of logic ARUL.

Application 1 (Surprise Deception Paradox). ARUL elaborates on the arbitrary radical upgrade introduced meta-logically in [28] using standard radical upgrades. The goal in [28] is to analyze a Smullyan's puzzle on deception and surprise that can be summarized as follows: on the morning of April Fool's Day, an agent announces to an addressee that he or she would be deceived later on that day, but apparently nothing happened. Since the addressee waited all day to be deceived by some action, he or she was actually deceived, but by the lack of an action, i.e., by omission. This deception left the addressee strongly surprised.

In [28], such a deception-based surprise is modelled along the lines of Gerbrandy's formalization of the *three-day* Surprise Examination Paradox [23]. The difference is that exam days are replaced by types of deception, based on capturing the distinction between deception as a result of an action, or *deception by commission*, and deception by the lack of an action, or *deception by omission*.

The distinction between deception by commission versus by omission can be defined in ARUL using the plausibility operator $[\leqslant]$ to characterize deception, the existential radical upgrade $\langle \Uparrow \rangle$ to capture the existence of an action, or *commission*, and its negation $\neg \langle \Uparrow \rangle$ for the absence of such an action, or *omission*. We define the fact that the addressee is deceived on a formula ψ in case ψ is true but the addressee judges $\neg \psi$ as more highly plausible, i.e., as $(\psi \wedge [\leqslant] \neg \psi)$.

Definition 12. *Let ψ be an arbitrary formula of* ARUL, *we define the fact that the addressee is deceived by commission on formula ψ (written d_ψ^+), and that she is deceived by omission on ψ (written d_ψ^-), respectively as:*

$$d_\psi^+ := \langle \Uparrow \rangle (\psi \wedge [\leqslant] \neg \psi); \qquad d_\psi^- := \neg \langle \Uparrow \rangle (\psi \wedge [\leqslant] \neg \psi).$$

In [28], definitions of d_ψ^+ and d_ψ^- are used to express the fact that the agent's deception results in the addressee's surprise. Let d^+ and d^- be abbreviations for the complex formulas d_ψ^+ and d_ψ^-, respectively. Following [23], modulo minor adaptations to radical upgrades [10], the surprise aspect of the agent's announcement can be encoded by the formula D as follows:

$$\begin{aligned} D := &\, ((d^+ \wedge \neg d^-) \wedge \neg [\leqslant](d^+ \wedge \neg d^-)) \vee \\ &\, ((\neg d^+ \wedge d^-) \wedge [\Uparrow \neg (d^+ \wedge \neg d^-)] \neg [\leqslant](\neg d^+ \wedge d^-)) \vee \\ &\, ((d^+ \wedge d^-) \wedge [\Uparrow \neg (d^+ \wedge \neg d^-)][\Uparrow \neg(\neg d^+ \wedge d^-)] \neg [\leqslant](d^+ \wedge d^-)). \end{aligned}$$

The first disjunct of D states that in case addressees are deceived only by commission, i.e. $(d^+ \wedge \neg d^-)$, they will be surprised because they deny this possibility as being plausible: $\neg [\leqslant](d^+ \wedge \neg d^-)$. The second disjunct reflects an analogous situation in presence of deception by omission. The third disjunct of D states that in case addressees are deceived both by commission and by omission, i.e. $(d^+ \wedge d^-)$, they will be surprised because after rejecting deception only by commission and only by omission: $[\Uparrow \neg (d^+ \wedge \neg d^-)][\Uparrow \neg(\neg d^+ \wedge d^-)]$, they (still) deny option $(d^+ \wedge d^-)$ as being plausible: $\neg [\leqslant](d^+ \wedge d^-)$.

Following [10,23], though, [28] shows that any radical upgrade with D, or with a reinforced formula involving D, will result in the agent failing to surprise the addressee. But this failure is theoretical since in the puzzle at stake, the addressee is actually surprised as he fails to predict the type of deception he is preyed to, i.e. deception both by commission and by omission. The puzzle dynamics and interplay between deception and surprise can be modelled in ARUL. One noticeable difference is that arbitrary upgrades are defined externally in [28]. ARUL goes a step further by internalizing these upgrades as primitive operators of the syntax for which sound and complete axiomatization is proven.

Application 2 (Fitch's Paradox). Fitch's knowability paradox [20,22] is rooted in the verificationnist thesis according to which all truths are verifiable.

Following van Benthem's version in [15], this principle can be interpreted in terms of learnability and knowability as: *"what is true may come to be known"*. Accordingly, it can be expressed in APAL using the schema: {for all φ, $\varphi \rightarrow \langle ! \rangle \mathbf{K} \varphi$}, where φ is some given truth of the language, and $\langle ! \rangle$ is the arbitrary announcement modality. As shown in [15], paradox arises with the case of truths that are unknown by agents, expressed as $(\psi \wedge \neg \mathbf{K} \psi)$. It has been established in e.g. [6,7] that substituting $(\psi \wedge \neg \mathbf{K} \psi)$ to φ in the knowability principle with arbitrary announcements, leads to inconsistency and thus, to the necessary acceptance of the unrealistic omniscience conclusion that all truths are already known: $\varphi \rightarrow \mathbf{K} \varphi$.

It turns out that a variant of Fitch's paradox with plausibility operator $[\leqslant]$ and arbitrary upgrade $\langle \Uparrow \rangle$ applies to ARUL. Let $\mathfrak{S} = \langle \mathcal{S}, \leqslant, V \rangle$ be a plausibility model with $s \in \mathcal{S}$. Aiming for a contradiction, suppose that the learnability principle transfers to the ARUL operators $[\leqslant]$ and $\langle \Uparrow \rangle$, stating that all truth ψ of ARUL will be considered plausible by the agent after some arbitrary upgrade: {for all φ, $\varphi \rightarrow \langle \Uparrow \rangle [\leqslant] \varphi$)}. Suppose that a given truth ψ of ARUL is judged implausible by the agent: $(\psi \wedge \neg [\leqslant] \psi)$. By instantiating the learnability principle with this formula, substituting $(\psi \wedge \neg [\leqslant] \psi)$ to φ, we have: $\mathfrak{S}, s \models (\psi \wedge \neg [\leqslant] \psi) \rightarrow \langle \Uparrow \rangle [\leqslant] (\psi \wedge \neg [\leqslant] \psi)$. By modus ponens: $\mathfrak{S}, s \models \langle \Uparrow \rangle [\leqslant] (\psi \wedge \neg [\leqslant] \psi)$. By Definition 5, for some epistemic φ, $\mathfrak{S}, s \models \langle \Uparrow \varphi \rangle [\leqslant] (\psi \wedge \neg [\leqslant] \psi)$, iff $\mathfrak{S}^{[\Uparrow \varphi]}, s \models [\leqslant] (\psi \wedge \neg [\leqslant] \psi)$. Observe that $\mathfrak{S}^{[\Uparrow \varphi]}, s \models [\leqslant] (\psi \wedge \neg [\leqslant] \psi)$ leads to contradiction since, by distributing $[\leqslant]$ over $\wedge$, we have $\mathfrak{S}^{[\Uparrow \varphi]}, s \models [\leqslant] \psi \wedge [\leqslant] \neg [\leqslant] \psi$. So, in particular $\mathfrak{S}^{[\Uparrow \varphi]}, s \models [\leqslant] \psi$. But we also have $\mathfrak{S}^{[\Uparrow \varphi]}, s \models [\leqslant] \neg [\leqslant] \psi$. By instantiating axiom $\mathsf{T}_{[\leqslant]}$, it holds that $\mathfrak{S}^{[\Uparrow \varphi]}, s \models [\leqslant] \neg [\leqslant] \psi \rightarrow \neg [\leqslant] \psi$. Then, $\mathfrak{S}^{[\Uparrow \varphi]}, s \models \neg [\leqslant] \psi$, a contradiction.

Application 3 (Moore's Paradox). Hidden behind Fitch's paradox are so-called *"unsuccessful formulas"* [21], i.e. formulas φ that do not necessarily hold after an update with φ. As noticed in e.g. [14,26], this phenomenon is at the heart of Moore's paradox [29], since announcing a true formula ψ that is not believed by the agent, i.e. a formula of the form $\psi \wedge \neg \mathbf{B} \psi$, leads to contradiction. This concerns **KD45** belief modalities, as well as **S5** knowledge modalities.

In ARUL, arbitrary upgrades $[\Uparrow]$ on formula $(\psi \wedge \neg [\leqslant] \psi)$ give rise to such a Moorean phenomenon. Let $\mathfrak{S}$ be a plausibility model with a state $s \in \mathcal{S}$. Let $(\psi \wedge \neg [\leqslant] \psi)$ be the formula stating that ψ is true but not judged as plausible by the agent, and suppose that $\mathfrak{S}, s \models (\psi \wedge \neg [\leqslant] \psi)$. As a way towards a contradiction, suppose that $[\leqslant] (\psi \wedge \neg [\leqslant] \psi)$ holds after any universal arbitrary radical upgrade, i.e., that $\mathfrak{S}, s \models [\Uparrow][\leqslant](\psi \wedge \neg [\leqslant] \psi)$. By Definition 5, it is the case that $\mathfrak{S}, s \models [\Uparrow][\leqslant](\psi \wedge \neg [\leqslant] \psi)$ if and only if $\mathfrak{S}, s \models [\Uparrow \varphi][\leqslant](\psi \wedge \neg [\leqslant] \psi)$ for all epistemic $\varphi \in$ ARUL. So this applies in particular for $\varphi \equiv (\psi \wedge \neg [\leqslant] \psi)$, i.e. $\mathfrak{S}, s \models [\Uparrow (\psi \wedge \neg [\leqslant] \psi)][\leqslant](\psi \wedge \neg [\leqslant] \psi)$. A contradiction ensues since in presence of Moorean formulas, the formula $[\Uparrow \varphi][\leqslant] \varphi$ is not valid (see e.g., [34]).

Accordingly, $(\psi \wedge \neg [\leqslant] \psi)$ is an unsuccessful formula of ARUL. Actually, there is no escaping the Moore's paradox with the arbitrary variation of the learnability principle holding, as shown above with the instantiation of $(\psi \wedge \neg [\leqslant] \psi)$. As for APAL, this issue also concerns the more classical version of Moore's paradox involving plain beliefs **B**, now with the version: {for all φ, $\varphi \rightarrow \langle \Uparrow \rangle \mathbf{B} \varphi$)}.

6   Conclusion

This paper introduces ARUL, a variant of dynamic belief revision logic that incorporates arbitrary radical upgrades, a concept not previously formalized in the literature. The syntax and semantics of ARUL extend the standard belief revision logics by allowing arbitrary quantification of radical upgrades. We present a sound and complete axiomatization for ARUL, operating over doxastic plausibility models characterized by a reflexive, transitive, and locally connected plausibility relation. Our completeness result relies on the proof for arbitrary announcements presented in [5]. Interestingly, ARUL complements extant logical frameworks by helping analyze classical epistemic paradoxes, such as the surprise examination paradox, Fitch's paradox, and Moore's paradox.

As pointed out in [5], the argument therein inspires a new realm of logics featuring information quantification, and our work should be seen as a first step towards the understanding of quantified upgrades in general. In this regard, many other dynamic belief revision policies exist that are weaker than radical upgrades [9,32]. A classical example is the "conservative upgrade" [11,16] with respect to φ, in which *only the best* φ-states increase in plausibility to reach the top of the plausibility ordering, leaving the rest of the ordering unchanged. Preliminary results obtained for ARUL could be extended to conservative upgrades. Also interesting would be to deal with arbitrary upgrades over different classes of models, including conversely well-founded orders as in [12,34]. Moreover, we would like to characterize the exact expressivity of ARUL, for instance to determine whether single-agent ARUL is already more expressive than its [⇑]-free fragment or not. In fact, this would help adjudicate on the robustness of the puzzles analyzed with ARUL, showing whether Fitch's and Moore's paradoxes still hold in case of increased expressivity. Finally, this framework can be used to investigate agentive notions tied to commission versus omission and related notions (see, e.g. [13,35]). We leave those investigations for future work.

Acknowledgements. We thank three anonymous reviewers for helpful comments and feedback, and Fernando R. Velázquez-Quesada for his advice. RF is supported by the IRP-SINFIN, the EU Grant 101008233 (MISSION), the CONICET project PIBAA-28720210100165CO and the ANPCyT project PICT-2021-00400. BI thanks the programs THEMIS (DOS0222794/00 and DOS0222795/00) and HYBRINFOX (ANR-21-ASIA-0003).

References

1. Ågotnes, T., Alechina, N., Galimullin, R.: Logics with group announcements and distributed knowledge: completeness and expressive power. J. Logic Lang. Inf. **31**(2), 141–166 (2022)
2. Balbiani, P.: Putting right the wording and the proof of the truth lemma for APAL. J. Appl. Log. **25**(1), 2–19 (2015)

3. Balbiani, P., Baltag, A., van Ditmarsch, H., Herzig, A., Hoshi, T., de Lima, T.: What can we achieve by arbitrary announcements?: A dynamic take on Fitch's knowability. In: Samet, D. (ed.) Proceedings of the 11th Conference on Theoretical Aspects of Rationality and Knowledge (TARK-2007), pp. 42–51 (2007)
4. Balbiani, P., Baltag, A., van Ditmarsch, H., Herzig, A., Hoshi, T., de Lima, T.: knowable' as 'known after an announcement. Rev. Symb. Logic 1(3), 305–334 (2008)
5. Balbiani, P., van Ditmarsch, H.: A simple proof of the completeness of APAL. CoRR arxiv:1409.2612 (2014)
6. Balbiani, P., Baltag, A., Van Ditmarsch, H., Herzig, A., Hoshi, T., De Lima, T.: What can we achieve by arbitrary announcements? A dynamic take on Fitch's knowability. In: Proceedings of the 11th Conference on Theoretical Aspects of Rationality and Knowledge, pp. 42–51 (2007)
7. Balbiani, P., Baltag, A., Van Ditmarsch, H., Herzig, A., Hoshi, T., De Lima, T.: Knowable'as 'known after an announcement. Rev. Symb. Logic 1(3), 305–334 (2008)
8. Baltag, A., Moss, L.S., Solecki, S.: The logic of public announcements, common knowledge, and private suspicions. In: Proceeding TARK '98 Proceedings of the 7th Conference on Theoretical Aspects of Rationality and Knowledge (1998)
9. Baltag, A., Rodenhäuser, B., Smets, S.: Doxastic attitudes as belief-revision policies. In: Proceedings of the ESSLLI Workshop on Strategies for Learning, Belief Revision and Preference Change (2012)
10. Baltag, A., Smets, S.: Surprise?! an answer to the hangman, or how to avoid unexpected exams! In: Logic and Interactive Rationality Seminar (LIRA), Slides (2009)
11. Baltag, A., Smets, S.: Dynamic belief revision over multi-agent plausibility models. In: Proceedings of LOFT, vol. 6, pp. 11–24 (2006)
12. Baltag, A., Smets, S.: A qualitative theory of dynamic interactive belief revision. Logic Found. Game Decis. Theory (LOFT 7) 3, 9–58 (2008)
13. Belnap, N.: Before refraining: concepts for agency. Erkenntnis 34(2), 137–169 (1991). https://doi.org/10.1007/BF00385718
14. van Benthem, J.: Logical Dynamics of Information and Interaction. Cambridge University Press, Cambridge (2011)
15. van Benthem, J.: What one may come to know. Analysis 64(282), 95–105 (2004)
16. van Benthem, J.: Dynamic logic for belief revision. J. Appl. Non-Classical Logics 17(2), 129–155 (2007)
17. van Benthem, J., Smets, S.: Dynamic logics of belief change. In: Handbook of Logics for Knowledge and Belief, pp. 299–368. College Publications (2015)
18. Blackburn, P., de Rijke, M., Venema, Y.: Modal Logic, Cambridge Tracts in Theoretical Computer Science, vol. 53. Cambridge University Press (2001)
19. Board, O.: Dynamic interactive epistemology. Games Econ. Behav. 49(1), 49–80 (2004)
20. Brogaard, B., Salerno, J.: Fitch's paradox of knowability (2002)
21. van Ditmarsch, H.P., Kooi, B.: The secret of my success. Synthese 153(2), 339–339 (2006)
22. Fitch, F.B.: A logical analysis of some value concepts1. J. Symb. Logic 28(2), 135–142 (1963)
23. Gerbrandy, J.: The surprise examination in dynamic epistemic logic. Synthese 155(1), 21–33 (2007)
24. Goldblatt, R.: Axiomatising the Logic of Computer Programming. Springer, Heidelberg (1982)

25. Hintikka, J.: Knowledge and Belief. Cornell University Press, Ithaca (1962)
26. Holliday, W.H., Icard, T.F., III.: Moorean phenomena in epistemic logic. Adv. Modal Logic **8**(8), 178–199 (2010)
27. Icard, B.: Lying, deception and strategic omission: definition and evaluation. Ph.D. thesis, Université Paris sciences et lettres (2019)
28. Icard, B.: The Surprise Deception Paradox (2024). https://hal.science/hal-04647404
29. Moore, G.E.: A reply to my critics. In: Schilpp, P.A. (ed.) The Philosophy of G. E. Moore. Tudor Pub. Co. (1942)
30. Plaza, J.: Logics of public communications. In: Emrich, M.L., Pfeifer, M.S., Hadzikadic, M., Ras, Z.W. (eds.) Proceedings of the 4th International Symposium on Methodologies for Intelligent Systems, pp. 201–216 (1989)
31. Plaza, J.: Logics of public communications. Synthese **158**(2), 165 (2007)
32. Rodenhäuser, B.: A matter of trust: dynamic attitudes in epistemic logic. Universiteit van Amsterdam [Host] (2014)
33. Smullyan, R.M.: What is the Name of this Book? The Riddle of Dracula and Other Logical Puzzles: Mysteries, Paradoxes, Gödel's Discovery. Prentice-Hall, Upper Saddle River (1978)
34. Velázquez-Quesada, F.R.: Dynamic epistemic logic for implicit and explicit beliefs. J. Logic Lang. Inf. **23**(2), 107–140 (2014)
35. Xu, M.: Doing and refraining from refraining. J. Phil. Log. **23**, 621–632 (1994)

Binders for Switch Graphs Specification

Daniel Figueiredo[(✉)] and Alexandre Madeira

CIDMA – Center for Research and Development in Mathematics and Applications,
University of Aveiro, Aveiro, Portugal
daniel.figueiredo@ua.pt

Abstract. Switch graphs, as proposed by Marcelino and Gabbay are
relation-changing state transition structures which make use of higher-
level directed edges (edges connecting edges) to represent how the accessibility relation changes. In previous work, the same authors propose an
hybrid logic to describe such systems. In this work we consider a variant of hybrid logic that excludes nominals and considers state-variables,
and we explore how this logic can be used to describe these structures,
in particular, higher-level edges. Afterwards, we define two classes of
behavioural equivalence and discuss their utility and limitation with
some examples.

Keywords: Relation-changing · Switch graph · Binding operator

1 Introduction

When one thinks about a state transition system, the most common structure
used is a graph like model (W, R) where W is a set of states/nodes and $R \subseteq
W \times W$ is a set of (directed) edges. The notion of relation-changing models
admits that the accessibility relation R is not fixed and can change through
some determined process. Some examples of such formalisms can be found in
the work of van Benthem [1,2] and Areces, Fervari & Hoffmann [3,4], and also
in epistemic logics with public announcements [5]. The approach used by these
authors consider the use of a proper operator which cause the relation-changing
dynamics. Another approach consists of moving the cause for relation-changing
from syntax to semantics. Marcelino & Gabbay [6], proposed switch graphs as
semantical models for these relation-changing systems, by adding "higher-level"
edges to regular Kripke frames. These higher-level edges link two other edges
representing the process of (temporarily) removing/restore edges. In this work,
we focus on switch graphs and study how logic can be used to formally reason
about such structures.

The study of such structures has been gradually gaining some attention for
model design, with concepts such as reactive automata (automata whose structure is based on a switch graph) being introduced in [7]. These structures can
be useful, for instance, in biological contexts, being used to represent the effect
of an unknown component on a systems dynamics [8,9].

Diverse kinds of modal logics have been proposed and studied to reason about
switch graphs. In [6], a bimodal logic is proposed over a path-induced model.

J. Proença et al. (Eds.): SEFM 2024, LNCS 15551, pp. 50–61, 2026.
https://doi.org/10.1007/978-3-031-94748-3_4

In [9] the concept of plain representation is introduced, in order to retrieve a regular Kripke model from a switch graph model. Paraconsistent [10], weighted [11] and fuzzy [12,13] variants are also proposed. A common strategy found on these works is to approach reactivity by considering an equivalent Kripke model and using (multi-)modal logic. As opposition, in [14], hybrid logic is employed and nominals were shown useful to specify the existence of higher-level edges, responsible for the relation changing dynamics. Hybrid logic, as an extension of modal logic, has an increased expressiveness by making use of nominals to refer states of a model and adding proper operators (check [15,16] for details).

In this work we propose an intermediary approach, by introducing $M^{\downarrow}$, a logic obtained by enriching modal logic with the $\downarrow$ and @ operators. Instead of considering a set of nominals (where each nominal is already assigned to a state), the $\downarrow$ operator is used to assign a variable x to the state of the model where it is evaluated. This fragment of hybrid logic is then used to explore the relation-changing properties of these structures. Afterwards, we explore behavioural equivalence and study how it relates with logic satisfiability. Finally, we note that the logic proposed in this paper is based on the one introduced in [17]. Thus, this logic will retrieve the operator $\downarrow$ and @ from hybrid logic but omits nominals.

Outline. In Sect. 2, we formally introduce switch graphs and introduce the syntax and semantics of modal logic enriched with the $\downarrow$ operator. We explore the expressiveness of this language to describe switch graphs. In Sect. 3 we introduce two kinds of behavioural equivalence and show their capacities and limitations regarding $M^{\downarrow}$. Finally, Sect. 4 concludes with a brief discussion and ideas to follow as future work.

2   A Logic to Relation-Changing Structures with the Binding Operator

Switch graphs are relation-changing structures whose accessibility relation can change whenever an edge is crossed. these changes are directed by *higher-level edges*, which connect to other edges. In [14], Marcelino and Gabbay make use of hybrid logic and nominals to the specification of switch graphs, which encode relation-changing dynamics. While they explore this logic and obtain an axiomatization for it, this is done considering a nominal for each state. Let us start by recalling the notion of switch graph.

Definition 1. *Let W be a non-empty set of states. A switch graph is a pair (W, S) satisfying:*

- $S_0 \subseteq W \times W$;
- $S_n \subseteq S_0 \times S_{n-1} \times \{\circ, \bullet\}$, for $n \geq 1$;
- $S = \bigcup_{n \geq 0} S_n$

Moreover, we define a function $I : S \to \{0, 1\}$ as an instantiation. If $s \in S - S_0$, it is called a higher-level edge.

Together with the instantiation function higher-level edges are responsible for describing the changes in the usual accessibility relation S_0. Contrarily to edges contained on S_0, higher-level edges cannot be crossed and are solely responsible for describing the relation-changing dynamics. Given a switch graph S and an instantiation I, an edge s is said to be *active* if $I(s) = 1$ and is said to be *inactive* if $I(s) = 0$. In a semantical perspective, an *inactive* edge $s \in S_0$ cannot be crossed because it is considered to be *temporarily removed* from the structure. Only *active* or *restored* edges $s \in S_0$, which verify $I(s) = 1$, can be crossed.

Given a switch graph (W, S) and an instantiation I, the effect of crossing an active edge $s \in S_0$ in the accessibility relation is described by updating the function I to $I^s : S \to \{0, 1\}$, which is defined as follows:

$$I^s(t) = \begin{cases} 1, & \text{if } (s, t, \bullet) \in S \text{ and } I((s, t, \bullet)) = 1 \\ 0, & \text{if } (s, t, \circ) \in S \text{ and } I((s, t, \circ)) = 1 \\ I(t), & \text{otherwise.} \end{cases}$$

Thus, an edge $(s, t, \bullet) \in S$ is called an activator edge and $(s, t, \circ) \in S$ is called a deactivator edge.

We say that $M = (W, S, I)$ is a switch graph at the instantiation I whenever (W, S) is a switch graph and $I : S \to \{0, 1\}$ is an instantiation. Moreover, the notation M^s can be used as an abbreviation of (W, S, I^s) for an active edge $s = (v, w) \in S_0$.

Example 1. Consider (W, S, I), a switch graph at the instantiation I, such that $W = \{w_1, w_2\}$, $S = S_0 \cup S_1$ with $S_0 = \{(w_1, w_2), (w_2, w_2)\}$ and $S_1 = \{((w_1, w_2), (w_2, w_2), \bullet), ((w_2, w_2), (w_2, w_2), \circ)\}$, $I((w_2, w_2)) = 0$ and $I(s) = 1$ for $s \in S - \{(w_2, w_2)\}$.

This switch graph is illustrated in Fig. 1. Note that activator edges are depicted with black head and deactivator ones with white heads. Moreover, inactive/temporarily removed edges are pictured with a dashed line.

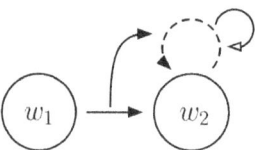

Fig. 1. Example of a switch graph.

Given the present switch graph and instantiation, when the edge (w_1, w_2) is crossed, the activator edge $((w_1, w_2), (w_2, w_2), \bullet)$ is triggered and the edge (w_2, w_2) – which was temporarily removed – is restored. Hence, the updated instantiation $I^{(w_1, w_2)}$ is a function whose image is constant and equal to 1. If (w_2, w_2) is crossed afterwards, $((w_2, w_2), (w_2, w_2), \circ)$ is triggered, temporally removing the edge (w_2, w_2). Thus $\left(I^{(w_1, w_2)}\right)^{(w_2, w_2)} = I$.

As mentioned, a wide variants of modal logic have been proposed to reason about these structures and a hybrid logic was already proposed. In this paper we consider $M^{\downarrow}$, a modal logic enriched with the binder operator $\downarrow$ as well as @ to recall marked states, but without using nominals.

Definition 2. *Let X be an infinite set of variables. The set $Fm^{M^{\downarrow}}$ of $M^{\downarrow}$ formulas is defined by:*

$$\varphi ::= \mathbf{tt} \mid \mathbf{ff} \mid x \mid \downarrow x.\varphi \mid @x\varphi \mid \Diamond\varphi \mid \Box\varphi \mid \neg\varphi \mid \varphi \vee \varphi \mid \varphi \wedge \varphi$$

where $x \in X$. Moreover, let $FVar(\varphi) \subseteq X$ be the set of free variables of $\varphi \in Fm^{M^{\downarrow}}$, defined as usual. φ is a sentence of $M^{\downarrow}$ if $FVar(\varphi) = \{\}$. We denote the set of sentences of $M^{\downarrow}$ by $Sen^{M^{\downarrow}}$. We denote by $Fm^{M^{\Box}}$ the fragment of $Fm^{M^{\downarrow}}$ that excludes formulas with occurrences of variables and of operators $\downarrow$ and @.

Additionally, we say that φ is a subformula of ψ whenever $\varphi \in SubFm^{M^{\downarrow}}(\psi)$, which is defined as the least set containing ψ and such that $\phi \in SubFm^{M^{\downarrow}}(\psi)$ whenever $\{\downarrow x.\phi, @x\phi, \Diamond\phi, \Box\phi, \neg\phi, \phi\vee\eta, \eta\vee\phi, \phi\wedge\eta, \eta\wedge\phi\} \bigcap SubFm^{M^{\downarrow}}(\psi) \neq \{\}$, for every $\eta \in Fm^{M^{\downarrow}}$.

Complementarily, to define the satisfiability of formulas, one needs to define a satisfaction relation "$\vDash$" for $M^{\downarrow}$. For this, we need a valuation function which records the state $w \in W$ bound to each variable $x \in X$. With this purpose, we define a valuation $g : X \to$ and represent by $g[x \mapsto w]$ the function such that $g[x \mapsto w](x) = w$ and $g[x \mapsto w](y) = g(y)$ for every $y \in X - \{x\}$.

Definition 3. *Given a switch graph $M = (W, S)$, $w \in W$, an instantiation $I : S \to \{0,1\}$ and a valuation $g : X \to W$. The satisfaction relation "$\vDash$" is defined recursively as:*

- $M, g, w \vDash \mathbf{tt}$
- $M, g, w \nvDash \mathbf{ff}$
- $M, g, w \vDash x$ *iff* $g(x) = w$
- $M, g, w \vDash\downarrow x.\varphi$ *iff* $M, g[x \mapsto w], w \vDash \varphi$
- $M, g, w \vDash @x\varphi$ *iff* $M, g, g(x) \vDash \varphi$
- $M, g, w \vDash \Diamond\varphi$ *iff there is a $w' \in W$ such that $(w, w') \in S$, $I(w, w') = 1$ and* $M^{(w,w')}, g, w' \vDash \varphi$
- $M, g, w \vDash \Box\varphi$ *iff for every $w' \in W$ such that $(w, w') \in S$ and $I(w, w') = 1$,* $M^{(w,w')}, g, w' \vDash \varphi$
- $M, g, w \vDash \neg\varphi$ *iff* $M, g, g(x) \nvDash \varphi$
- $M, g, w \vDash \varphi \vee \psi$ *iff* $M, g, w \vDash \varphi$ *or* $M, g, w \vDash \psi$
- $M, g, w \vDash \varphi \wedge \psi$ *iff* $M, g, w \vDash \varphi$ *and* $M, g, w \vDash \psi$

for formulas $\varphi, \psi \in Fm^{M^{\downarrow}}$ and $x \in X$.

We simply write $M, w \vDash \varphi$ if $M, g, w \vDash \varphi$ for every valuation $g : X \to W$. We say that φ is valid on M and write $M \vDash \varphi$ if $\forall w \in W; M, w \vDash \varphi$

To conclude this section, let us explore the expressiveness of the modal logic introduced. In [14], hybrid logic is shown to be able to describe the existence of higher-level edges.

Consider the following formula of $Fm^{M^{\downarrow}}$:

$$\downarrow x.\Diamond @x\Box\mathbf{ff}$$

By analysing this formula, one can note that it is only satisfiable at a state w if there is a reachable state, say w'. Moreover, w' must satisfy $@x\Box\mathbf{ff}$, *i.e.*, when returning to $g(x) = w$, $\Box\mathbf{ff}$ holds. This means that there is no reachable state from w. While this is a contradiction for regular Kripke frames, in switch graphs it mean that there must be an inhibitor higher level edge which is triggered whenever we move from w to w' and temporarily removes (w, w'). Thus, if the formula is satisfied at a state w, then there is a reachable state w' with (w, w') and $\{(w, w'), (w, w'), \circ\}$ being active edges.

Let us now consider the switch graph $M = (W, S)$ and the instantiation I from Example 1, illustrated in Fig. 1. One can check that all the following formulas are valid on this switch graph (*i.e.*, they hold at every state):

(1) $\Box\Box\Box\mathbf{ff}$
(2) $\downarrow x.(\Box\neg x)$
(3) $\Box \downarrow x.(\Diamond x \wedge \Box x)$

These formulas state that, whichever state we start: (1) "it is not possible to cross more than two edges"; (2) that "there are no loops in the initial instantiation of the switch graph"; and (3) "whenever we cross an edge there is a loop in the reached state and no other edge". Due to this, it is implied that each state of the switch graph either admits no edge coming out of it or that there are at least two higher level edges in the switch graph. This is because when it is possible to cross an edge at the initial instance of the model, one moves to other edge and activates a loop in the reached state, which did not existed before due to (2) and (3). Moreover, whenever we cross this loop it fades away due to (1).

Note that we can have multiple switch graphs were the formulas (1), (2) and (3) are valid. In addition to having several states with no active edges, we can add w_3 as a "replica" of w_1. w_3 would be added to W and S would include all edges already existing in S where w_1 occur, by replacing w_1 for w_3. Indeed, we can repeat this process and add w_4, w_5, and so on. Indeed, due to the absence of nominals, this logic only distinguishes states of a switch graph due to their reachability properties.

3   Behavioural Equivalences

When mentioning classes of indistinguishable states, one can recall concepts such as bisimulation. In this work, we continue to follow an approach closer to [17] and use an approach using bijective functions to define two kinds of behavioural equivalence. For this, if $M = (W, S, I)$ is a switch graph at the instantiation

I, we denote by $r^*(M) \subseteq W \times \{0,1\}^W$ the least set that contains (w, I) for every $w \in W$; and that $(v, J) \in r^*(M)$ implies $(v', J^{(v,v')}) \in r^*(M)$, whenever $(v, v') \in S$ and $J(v, v') = 1$.

Definition 4 (Weak and Strong Behavioural Equivalences).
    Let $M = (W, S, I)$ and $M' = (W', S', I')$ be switch graphs at the respective instantiation. We say that M and M' are weakly behavioural equivalent *whenever it is possible to define a bijective function $b : r^*(M) \to r^*(M')$ such that:*

(1) For every $w \in W$ and $b((u, I)) = (u', I')$:
    If $(u, w) \in S$ and $I(u, w) = 1$, then $\exists w' \in W'$ such that $(u', w') \in S'$, $I'(u', w') = 1$ and $b((w, I^{(u,w)})) = (w', I'^{(u',w')})$;
(2) For every $w' \in W$ and $b((u, I)) = (u', I')$:
    If $(u', w') \in S'$ and $I'(u', w') = 1$, then $\exists w \in W$ such that $(u, w) \in S$, $I(u, w) = 1$ and $b((w, I^{(u,w)})) = (w', I'^{(u',w')})$;

We say that M and M' are strongly behavioural equivalent *whenever is possible to define a bijective function $b : r^*(M) \to r^*(M')$ satisfying (1), (2) and such that:*

(3) for every $p, q \in r^*(M)$, $\pi_1(p) = \pi_1(q) \Leftrightarrow \pi_1(b(p)) = \pi_1(b(q))$, where π_1 is the projection function that returns the first element of the tuple.

Moreover, for each case, if $b(w, I) = (w', I')$, we say that w and w' are weakly (respectably strongly) behavioural equivalent.

Proposition 1. *Let $M = (W, S, I)$ and $M' = (W', S', I')$ be switch graphs at the respective instantiation such that $w \in W$ is weakly behavioural equivalent to $w' \in W'$. Then $M, w \vDash \varphi \Leftrightarrow M', w' \vDash \varphi$ for every formula $\varphi \in Fm^{M^\square}$.*

Proof. The proof is obtained by induction over formulas.

- The property trivially holds for **tt** and **ff**;
- $M, w \vDash \Diamond\varphi$ iff there is a $v \in W$ such that $(w, v) \in S$, $I((w, v)) = 1$ and $M^{(w,v)}, w \vDash \varphi$. Since w and w' are weakly-behavioural equivalent, then there is $v' \in W'$ such that $(w', v') \in S$, $I'(w', v') = 1$ and $b((v, I^{w,v})) = (v', I^{w',v'})$. Thus, this implies that v and v' also are two weakly-behavioural equivalent states of the switch graphs $M^{(w,v)}$ and $M^{(w',v')}$. Hence, by induction hypothesis, $M^{(w,v)}, v \vDash \varphi$ iff $M^{(w',v')}, v' \vDash \varphi$ iff $M, w' \vDash \Diamond\varphi$;
- $M, w \vDash \square\varphi$ iff for every $v \in W$ such that $(w, v) \in S$ and $I((w, v)) = 1$, $M^{(w,v)}, w \vDash \varphi$. Since w and w' are weakly-behavioural equivalent, for éach $v \in W$ such that $(w, v) \in S$ and $I((w, v)) = 1$, there is $v' \in W'$ such that $(w', v') \in S$, $I'(w', v') = 1$ and $b((v, I^{w,v})) = (v', I^{w',v'})$. Thus, this implies that for each v such that $(w, v) \in S$ and $I((w, v)) = 1$, there exists $v' \in W'$ such that both are weakly-behavioural equivalent states of the switch graphs $M^{(w,v)}$ and $M^{(w',v')}$. Hence, by induction hypothesis, for each v such that $(w, v) \in S$ and $I((w, v)) = 1$, $M^{(w,v)}, v \vDash \varphi$ iff for each v' such that $(w', v') \in S$ and $I'((w', v')) = 1$, $M^{(w',v')}, v' \vDash \varphi$ iff $M, w' \vDash \square\varphi$;

- $M, w \vDash \neg \varphi$ iff $M, w \nvDash \varphi$ iff, by induction hypothesis, $M, w' \nvDash \varphi$ iff $M, w' \vDash \neg \varphi$;
- $M, w \vDash \psi \vee \varphi$ iff $M, w \vDash \psi$ or $M, w \vDash \varphi$ iff, by induction hypothesis, $M, w' \vDash \psi$ or $M, w' \vDash \varphi$ iff $M, w' \vDash \psi \vee \varphi$;
- $M, w \vDash \psi \wedge \varphi$ iff $M, w \vDash \psi$ and $M, w \vDash \varphi$ iff, by induction hypothesis, $M, w' \vDash \psi$ and $M, w' \vDash \varphi$ iff $M, w' \vDash \psi \wedge \varphi$.

□

Fig. 2. Weak behavorial equivalent switch graphs M (left) and M' (right).

Example 2. Consider the switch graphs $M = (W, S, I)$ and $M' = (W', S', I')$ at the respective instantiations, depicted in Fig. 2. Both these graphs contain two states but a different set of edges.

In this example, we have:

$$r^*(M) = \{(w_1, I), (w_2, I^{(w_1, w_2)}), (w_2, (I^{(w_1, w_2)})^{(w_2, w_2)}), (w_2, I), (w_2, I^{(w_2, w_2)})\}$$
$$r^*(M') = \{(w_1', I'), (w_1', I'^{(w_1, w_1)}), (w_2', (I'^{(w_1, w_1)})^{(w_1, w_2)}), (w_2', I'), (w_2', I'^{(w_2, w_2)})\}$$

Then, M and M' present a weak behavioural equivalence with the witness $b : r^*(M) \to r^*(M')$ defined by $b((w_1, I)) = (w_1', I')$, $b((w_2, I^{(w_1, w_2)})) = (w_1', I'^{(w_1, w_1)})$, $b((w_2, (I^{(w_1, w_2)})^{(w_2, w_2)})) = (w_2', (I'^{(w_1, w_1)})^{(w_1, w_2)})$, $b((w_2, I)) = (w_2', I')$ and $b((w_2, I^{(w_2, w_2)})) = (w_2', I'^{(w_2, w_2)})$.

Note that the previous proposition is not valid for the full set $Fm^{M^{\downarrow}}$ of formulas. Despite w_1 and w_1' being weakly-behavioural equivalent, $M, w_1 \vDash_{\downarrow} x.\lozenge \neg x$ but $M', w_1' \nvDash_{\downarrow} x.\lozenge \neg x$.

Note 1. One can note that the notion of weak-behavioural equivalence introduced in this papers may resemble a function-version of the bisimulation from [10]. There, the notion of bisimulation is defined in a similar way but considering b as a relation instead of as a function. Since there are no hybrid-logic operators but rather a paraconsistent framework, they were able to obtain that the validity of formulas is invariant for bisimilar states.

Proposition 2. *Let $M = (W, S, J)$ and $M' = (W', S', J')$ be switch graphs at the respective instantiation such that $w \in W$ is strongly behavioural equivalent to $w' \in W'$. Then $M, w \vDash \varphi \Leftrightarrow M', w' \vDash \varphi$ for every formula $\varphi \in Sen^{M^{\downarrow}}$.*

Proof. The proof is obtained by induction over formulas. Since the result holds only for sentences, we start by noting that if the same sentence is evaluated in two strongly behavioural equivalent states, variables are bound to the behavioural equivalent states. Note that if $(w, I) \in r^*(M)$, with $b((w, I)) = (w', I')$, then w and w' also are two strongly behavioral equivalent states of M and M' at instantiations I and I'. This is important when evaluation subformulas of a sentence and using the inductive hypothesis.

Thus, we start by proving by induction over the structure of formulas that, when evaluating a sentence at two strongly behavioural equivalent states, free variables of the subformulas generated due to the course of the valuation are assign to strongly behavioural equivalent states.

- It trivially holds for any sentence φ, because there is no free variables
- Let us suppose that the hypothesis holds for a subformula ϕ, which has the form $\downarrow x.\psi$. Let w and w' be two behavioral equivalent states of M and M', respectively. Then, $M, w \models \downarrow x.\psi \Leftrightarrow M', w' \models \downarrow x.\psi$ iff $M, g[x \mapsto w], w \models \psi \Leftrightarrow M', g'[x' \mapsto w'], w' \models \psi$, for any $g : X \rightarrow W$, $g' : X \rightarrow W'$. Hence, if x is a free variable of ψ, it is thus assigned to two strongly behavioural equivalent states;
- Using the same reasoning for the remaining operators, the result trivially holds.

We can now proceed with the main proof using induction over the strcuture of formulas.

- $M, w, g \models x \Leftrightarrow M', w', g' \models x$ iff $g(x) = w \Leftrightarrow g'(x) = w'$, which holds because x is now free a variable of the subformula x and, due to the definition of strong behavioural equivalence, b is a bijection that guaranties that w' is the only strongly behavioural equivalent state from W' to $w \in W$ at the respective instantiation;
- For binded formulas, we observe that

$$M, w \models \downarrow x.\varphi \Leftrightarrow M', w' \models \downarrow x.\varphi$$

$\equiv \quad \{ \models \text{defn}\}$

for any $g : X \rightarrow W$. $M, g, w \models \downarrow x.\varphi \Leftrightarrow$ for any $g' : X \rightarrow W'$.
$M', g', w' \models \downarrow x.\varphi$

$\equiv \quad \{ \text{since } g \text{ and } g' \text{ are independent}\}$

for any $g : X \rightarrow W, g' : X \rightarrow W'$
$M, g, w \models \downarrow x.\varphi \Leftrightarrow M', g', w' \models \downarrow x.\varphi$

$\equiv \quad \{ \models \text{defn}\}$

for any $g : X \rightarrow W, g' : X \rightarrow W'$
$M, g[x \mapsto w], w \models \varphi \Leftrightarrow M', g'[x \mapsto w'], w' \models \varphi$

and this is true since, by induction hypothesis, $M, h, w \models \varphi \Leftrightarrow M', h', w' \models \varphi$ holds for any $h : X \to W$ and $h' : X \to W'$. Moreover if x is a free variable of φ, strongly behavioural equivalent states are assigned to it, as guaranteed by the functions $g[x \mapsto w]$ and $g'[x \mapsto w']$.

– $M, w \models @x\varphi \Leftrightarrow M', w' \models @x\varphi$ iff $M, g(x) \models \varphi \Leftrightarrow M', g'(x) \models \varphi$, which holds by inductive hypothesis because $g(x)$ and $g'(x)$ are strongly behavioural equivalent.

– For the remaining operator, please refer to the proof of Proposition 1 since it is analogous.

□

As shown this notion of behavioural equivalence is able to identify states from switch graph satisfying the same set of $Fm^{M^\downarrow}$ formulas. However, the reciprocal of the Proposition 2 is not true, *i.e.* it is possible to find switch graphs where states which satisfy the same formulas are not strongly behavioural equivalent. This is illustrated by Example 3.

Example 3. Consider the switch graphs $M = (W, S, I)$ and $M' = (M', S', I')$ at the respective instantiations, depicted in Fig. 3.

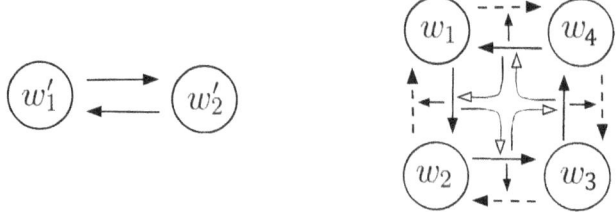

Fig. 3. Two switch graphs M (right) and M' (left).

It is easy to analyse M' since it is a usual graph without higher-level edges and, thus, no edges will be temporarily removed/restored. On its turn, M is harder to analyze with four states which only admit a transition at the initial instantiation. Moreover, one can check that, independently on the initial state, after crossing an edge, the higher-level edges act in such a way that the only possible move is to return and afterwards one is basically trapped within a M'-like graph. Consider, for instance, the state w_1 from M. After crossing (w_1, w_2), the only active edges that leaves w_1, the edge (w_2, w_3) is temporarily removed and (w_2, w_1) is restored. If we move back to w_1 through the new edge, no higher-level edges acts and we are trap on keeping moving between w_1 and w_2 since the instantiation will not change anymore.

While one can trivially prove that, for any $\varphi \in Sen^{M^\downarrow}$, $M, w_1 \models \varphi \Leftrightarrow M, w_1' \models \varphi$, it can also be noted that there are no strong behavioural equivalence between M and M' because $\#r^*(M) \neq \#r^*(M')$, thus not being possible to find any bijection between these sets.

4   Discussion and Future Work

In this work we introduced a fragment of hybrid logic to reason about switch graphs. With this fragment, which we denote by $M^{\downarrow}$ we are able to describe some structural properties of switch graphs such as the existence of higher-level edges. This logical language was based on the one presented in [17] and adapted for relation-changing structures.

By recalling [17], where the authors were able to obtain a formula to fully describe a model by following an algorithm (Table 1 of that paper), one can think about whether a similar result is possible to obtain for these relation-changing structures. Shortly, on that work, the authors develop an algorithm to generate formulas that, given an initial state, can fully describe the reachable part of the model. However, in this paper we conclude that a analogous process cannot be obtained on our scenario for $M^{\downarrow}$. Note that, due to the changing of the instantiation function, each bounded variable of X does not capture the full picture of a graph at all marked states. Consider the switch graph 1 and that $x \in X$ marks w_2. One cannot distinguish whether w_2 was marked while the loop is active or not.

Despite this, we still can describe some relation changing properties of a switch graph such as the existence of specific higher-level edges, by using the binding operator. Moreover, we were able to define two kinds of behavioural equivalence for switch graphs and noted that while the weak one is able to preserve validity of formulas from $M^{\downarrow}$ where $\downarrow$ do not occur, the strong one attains this objective. However, even this strong behavioural equivalence is not able to establish a perfect correspondence between states which satisfy the same set of $M^{\downarrow}$ formulas.

As expected, one can understand that due to admitting different instantiations, the satisfaction of formulas at each state of a switch graph is able to change. In this scenario, we believe that it would be interesting to consider a second class of binding operator, which would be able to assign instantiations to variables in addition to the already existing binding operator.

There are other proposals of behavioural equivalences in literature, including the bisimulation-based purpose within the team in [10,18]. As expected, as happens with standard bisimulation in Kripke models, the modal invariance property does not holds for formulas with binders (cf. [19]). Is this context, the property can be recovered by enriching the bisimulation with some additional properties; or by relaxing the satisfaction relation, as done in observational logic of [20]. The exploration of behavioural semantics for switch graphs seems to be an interesting line to pursue.

The implementation of computational support to interpret hybrid formulas in reactive graphs is currently being developed in the animator Marge [21], a tool that illustrates graphically the accessibility relation changes (activation and deactivation of edges) occurring on a switch graph while other edge is crossed.

Other ideas for future work include to explore additional features of this logic such as axiomatizations and proof calculus. The inclusion of labels (or actions) to edges was done in [8] and we plan to enrich the logic proposed in the present paper with labels/actions (such as it is done in [17]).

Acknowledgment. This work is supported by FCT – Fundação para a Ciência e a Tecnologia through projects UIDB/04106/2025 at CIDMA and by National and European Funds through SACCCT- IC&DT - Sistema de Apoio à Criação de Conhecimento Científico e Tecnológico, as part of COMPETE2030, within the project BANSKY with reference number 15253.

References

1. van Benthem, J.: An essay on sabotage and obstruction. In: Mechanizing Mathematical Reasoning, pp. 268–276. Springer, Heidelberg (2005)
2. van Benthem, J., Li, L., Shi, C., Yin, H.: Hybrid sabotage modal logic. J. Log. Comput. **33**(6), 1216–1242 (2023)
3. Areces, C., Fervari, R., Hoffmann, G.: Swap logic. Logic J. IGPL **22**, 309–332 (2013)
4. Areces, C., Fervari, R., Hoffmann, G.: Relation-changing modal operators. Logic J. IGPL **23**(4), 601–627 (2015)
5. Balbiani, P., Baltag, A., Van Ditmarsch, H., Herzig, A., Hoshi, T., De Lima, T.: Knowable'as 'known after an announcement. Rev. Symb. Logic **1**(3), 305–334 (2008)
6. Gabbay, D.M., Marcelino, S.: Modal logics of reactive frames. Studia Logica **93**(2), 405–446 (2009)
7. Crochemore, M., Gabbay, D.M.: Reactive automata. Inf. Comput. **209**(4), 692–704 (2011)
8. Figueiredo, D., Barbosa, L.S.: Reactive models for biological regulatory networks. In: Chaves, M., Martins, M.A. (eds.) MLCSB 2018. LNCS, vol. 11415, pp. 74–88. Springer, Cham (2019). https://doi.org/10.1007/978-3-030-19432-1_5
9. Figueiredo, D.: Logical foundations and computational tools for synthetic biology. PhD thesis, Universities of Minho, Aveiro and Porto joint doctoral program (2020)
10. Costa, D., Figueiredo, D., Martins, M.A.: Relation-changing models meet paraconsistency. J. Logical Algebraic Methods Program. **133**, 100870 (2023)
11. Figueiredo, D., Rocha, E., Martins, M.A., Chaves, M.: rPrism -a software for reactive weighted state transition models. In: HSB 2019 - 6th International Workshop, Hybrid Systems Biology, pp. 165–174 (2019)
12. Campos, S., Santiago, R., Martins, M.A., Figueiredo, D.: Reversal fuzzy switch graphs. In: Carvalho, G., Stolz, V. (eds.) SBMF 2020. LNCS, vol. 12475, pp. 137–154. Springer, Cham (2020). https://doi.org/10.1007/978-3-030-63882-5_9
13. Campos, S., Santiago, R., Martins, M.A., Figueiredo, D.: Introduction to reversal fuzzy switch graph. Sci. Comput. Program. **216**, 102776 (2022)
14. Gabbay, D., Marcelino, S.: Global view on reactivity: switch graphs and their logics. Ann. Math. Artif. Intell. **66**(1–4), 131–162 (2012)
15. Areces, C., ten Cate, B.: 14 hybrid logics. In: Studies in Logic and Practical Reasoning, vol. 3, pp. 821–868. Elsevier (2007)
16. Blackburn, P., Seligman, J.: Hybrid languages. J. Logic Lang. Inf. **4**(3), 251–272 (1995)

17. Madeira, A., Barbosa, L.S., Hennicker, R., Martins, M.A.: A logic for the stepwise development of reactive systems. Theor. Comput. Sci. **744**, 78–96 (2018)
18. Santiago, R., Martins, M.A., Figueiredo, D.: Introducing fuzzy reactive graphs: a simple application on biology. Soft Comput. **25**(9), 6759–6774 (2021)
19. Braüner, T.: Hybrid Logic and its Proof-Theory. Springer, Dordrecht and New York (2010)
20. Hennicker, R., Madeira, A.: Observational semantics for dynamic logic with binders. In: James, P., Roggenbach, M. (eds.) WADT 2016. LNCS, vol. 10644, pp. 135–152. Springer, Cham (2017). https://doi.org/10.1007/978-3-319-72044-9_10
21. Tinoco, D., Madeira, A., Martins, M.A., Proença, J.: Reactive graphs in action. In: Marmsoler, D., Sun, M. (eds.) International Conference on Formal Aspects of Component Software, vol. 15189 of Lecture Notes in Computer Science, pp. 97–105. Springer, Heidelberg (2024). https://doi.org/10.1007/978-3-031-71261-6_6

Higher-Order Arrows for Path-Dependent Many-Valued Systems

Sérgio Marcelino(✉)

Departamento de Matemática, IST, SQIG – Instituto de Telecomunicações,
Lisbon, Portugal
smarcel@math.tecnico.ulisboa.pt

Abstract. As our reliance on critical automated systems grows, the ability to model and analyze their complex behaviors becomes increasingly important. Dov Gabbay's idea of representing path-dependency on reactive graphs through higher-order arrows – the *switches* – offers a unified framework for modelling and understanding a wide range of reactive systems.

Building on previous work, this paper revisits and extends this approach to a wider context, allowing for many-valued base relations. This means that the base relation, which changes as an effect of crossing arrows, can take values on an arbitrary set instead of simply *on* and *off*. We report on the expressivity of many-valued switch graphs in capturing reactivity and how these can concisely represent important classes of reactive systems, including those with fuzzy or probabilistic elements.

Keywords: Reactivity · Higher-Order Arrows · Many-Valuedness · Fuzzy Logic · Probabilistic Models · Path-Dependency · Switch Graphs · Higher-Order Markov Chains

1 Introduction

We explore a concept of reactivity rooted in Gabbay's idea of extending traditional Kripke frames by incorporating path dependency into the accessibility relation [7,8]. This extension allows the set of accessible worlds to be influenced not only by the current world but also by the history of transitions leading up to it. Additionally, Gabbay proposed that higher-order arrows should represent the effects of traversing these transitions.

The systematic exploration of these ideas led to the development of abstract concepts like reactive graphs, where relationships between nodes evolve dynamically as transitions occur, and switch graphs, which generate these dynamics by locally encoding path dependency. The primary advantage of these frameworks is their ability to represent complex dynamics more concisely, making dependencies on hidden variables explicit through higher-order conditions, rather than merely expanding the state space.

In [9,10], it was shown that switches with two distinct effects – turning on and turning off – are sufficient to represent every reactive behavior when

J. Proença et al. (Eds.): SEFM 2024, LNCS 15551, pp. 62–76, 2026.
https://doi.org/10.1007/978-3-031-94748-3_5

the underlying accessibility relation is Boolean, meaning each arrow between nodes is either active or inactive. To illustrate this, consider the switch graphs in Figs. 1 and 2. Open headed arrows represent the base relation. White and black triangle-headed arrows represent switches that turn off and on the target arrows, respectively. Arrows or switches that are inactive are depicted with dotted lines.

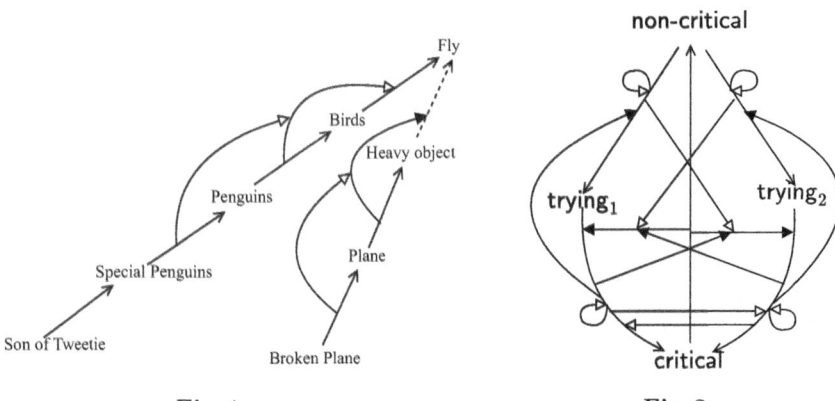

Fig. 1. .   Fig. 2. .

Figure 1 depicts an inheritance network, extending a motivational example from [7,8]. The left-hand indicates that: birds fly; penguins are birds that do not fly; and that Tweetie's son is a special penguin – one that, despite being a penguin and thus a bird, does indeed fly. As expressed in Fig. 3, the right-hand side reflects that: planes are heavy objects that fly and that broken planes, while still planes and heavy objects, do not fly.

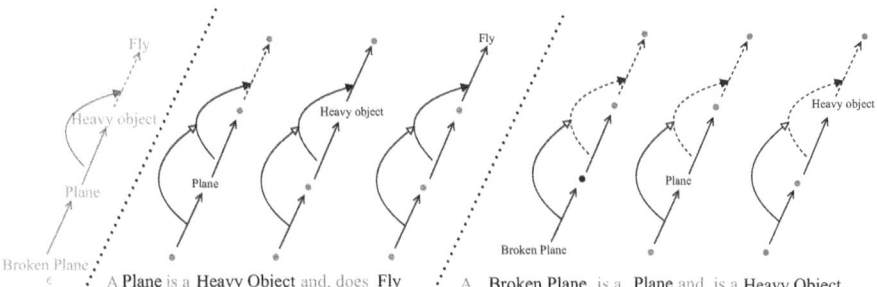

Fig. 3. .

Figure 2 depicts a system regulating processes access to a shared critical area, while Fig. 4 illustrates its underlying dynamics. The chosen switches ensure safety (preventing simultaneous critical area access), liveness (guaranteeing eventual access) and no strict sequencing (allowing processes to enter the critical area in any order), see [9,10] for more details.

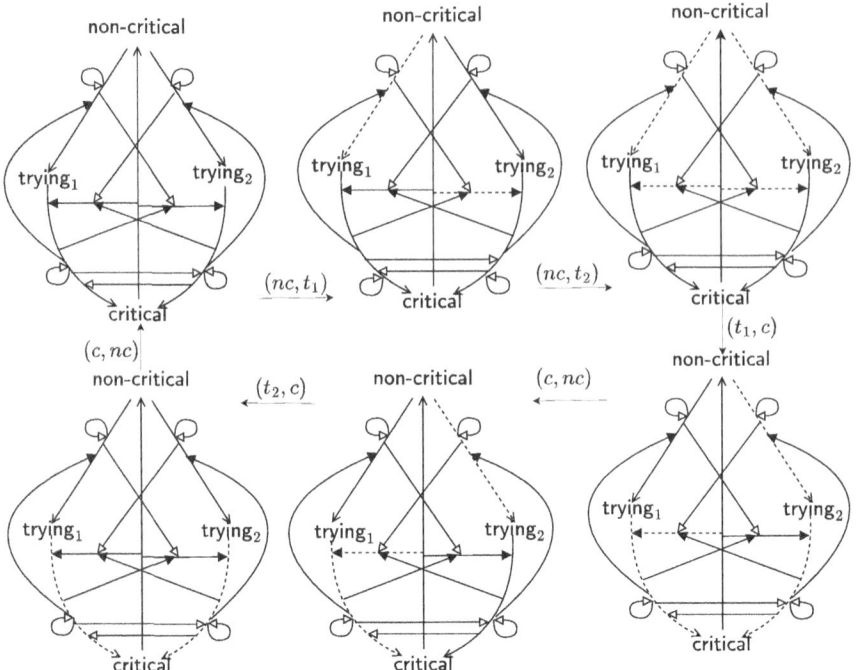

Fig. 4. Interleaved access to a critical area by two processes. Transitions are labeled with abbreviated state pairs, using initials for conciseness.

We will extend the concept of reactive graphs to a general many-valued context. This means that the base relation, which evolves as arrows are traversed, can assume values from any arbitrary set. In order to cover the extra richness we will have to go beyond considering switches that turn arrows on and off. We allow switches to be labeled with values from the same set as the arrows and introduce an additional structure known as the *switch interpretation*. An interpretation determines how the updated values of target arrows depend on current values. Each switch is associated with a function that relies on a finite number of parameters.

While this setting allows for a wide range of choices, we identify a particularly simple one: the *blind* interpretation, where the effect of firing a switch is to impose its current value on the target arrow.

We generalise the results for the 2-valued case showing that any many-valued reactive graph can be represented by a switch graph by using the blind interpretation. Further, we show that under the blind interpretation, it suffices to consider switches of order at most n to represent reactive graphs whose configuration depends only on the last n arrows crossed. The potential benefits of considering non-blind dynamics include achieving smaller representations or representing systems with unbounded memory.

2   Reactive Many-Valued Graphs

Let W be a set of points, the pairs $a = (w_1, w_2) \in W^2$ are called arrows. For a given arrow a, we denote its *origin* as $o(a) = w_1$ and *target* as $t(a) = w_2$.

We refer to finite sequences of arrows as *paths* and denote them by $paths(W)$, the empty sequence is denoted by ϵ. The concatenation of two paths α and β is written as $\alpha\beta$. The length of a path is denoted by $size(\alpha)$, where $size(\epsilon) = 0$ and $size(\alpha a) = size(\alpha) + 1$. A path $a_1 \ldots a_k \in paths(W)$ is *connected* if $t(a_i) = o(a_{i+1})$ for every $1 \leq i < k$.

We say that a set $\Lambda \subseteq paths(W)$ is *closed for prefixes* if $\epsilon \in \Lambda$, and if $\alpha a \in \Lambda$ then $\alpha \in \Lambda$. We have $paths(W)$ is closed for prefixes but also its subset $Cpaths(W)$, consisting only on the connected paths over W.

Consider fixed a set of values V and a partition $\langle on, off \rangle$ of V.

A *reactive many-valued graph* is a tuple

$$\mathcal{G} = \langle W, \{R_\alpha\}_{\alpha \in \Lambda} \rangle$$

where W is a set, $\Lambda \subseteq paths(W)$ is closed for prefixes, for each $\alpha \in \Lambda$, $R_\alpha : W^2 \to V$ satisfies $\alpha a \in \Lambda$ if, and only if, $R_\alpha(a) \in on$. The set Λ is the set of paths allowed by $\mathcal{G}$ which we denote by $paths(\mathcal{G})$.

Intuitively, many-valued reactive graphs capture the possible dynamics of edge values along permitted paths, where the behavior depends on which edges are assigned a value in on at any given moment. For simplicity, we will often refer to them as reactive graphs, omitting the 'many-valued' attribute.

Example 1. In [13], a reactive many-valued graph is proposed to model the binding capacity of a hemoglobin protein with oxygen molecules, using fuzzy values within the unit interval.

The accessibility relation corresponds to the addition of a new oxygen molecule. Initially, the binding capacity is low (0.2). However, it increases with each successive binding $(0.6, 0.8, 0.9)$ until a maximum of four oxygen molecules are bound. Beyond this point, the binding capacity reaches 0, and no further oxygen molecules can bind. This process is illustrated in Fig. 5.

Formally, let $\mathcal{G}_h = \langle W_h, \{R_\alpha\}_{\alpha \in \Lambda} \rangle$ with $W_h = \{h\}$, $\lambda = paths(\mathcal{G}_h) = \{\epsilon, a, aa, aaa, aaaa\}$, $V = [0, 1]$, $off = \{0\}$, $on =]0, 1]$, $W = \{h\}$, $a = (h, h)$, $R_\epsilon(a) = 0.2$, $R_a(a) = 0.6$, $R_{aa}(a) = 0.8$, $R_{aaa}(a) = 0.9$ and $R_{aaaa}(a) = 0$.   △

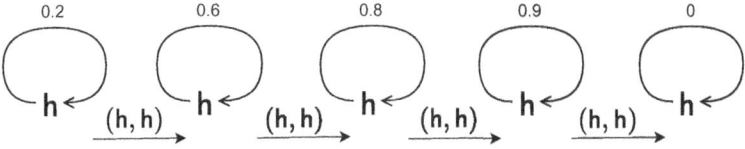

Fig. 5. The behavior of $\mathcal{G}_h$ along its finite set of paths.

Given $\Lambda \subseteq \mathsf{paths}(W)$, we write $\alpha_1 \sim_\Lambda \alpha_2$ for $\alpha_1, \alpha_2 \in \mathsf{paths}(W)$ whenever, for every $\beta \in \mathsf{paths}(W)$, $\alpha_1 \beta \in \Lambda$ if, and only if, $\alpha_2 \beta \in \Lambda$.

We write $\alpha_1 \sim_{\mathcal{G}} \alpha_2$ when $\alpha_1 \sim_\Lambda \alpha_2$ for $\Lambda = \mathsf{paths}(\mathcal{G})$ and for every $\beta \in \mathsf{paths}(W)$, if $\alpha_1 \beta \in \Lambda$ then $\mathsf{R}_{\alpha_1 \beta} = \mathsf{R}_{\alpha_2 \beta}$. Note that in the 2-valued these notions coincide and we have $\sim_\Lambda = \sim_{\mathcal{G}}$.

Given $\alpha \in \mathsf{paths}(W)$ and $k \in \mathbb{N}$, we denote sequence consisting in the first/last k arrows of α by

$$\mathsf{First}_k(\alpha) = \mathsf{Last}_k(\alpha) = \alpha \quad \text{for } \mathsf{size}(\alpha) \leq n$$
$$\mathsf{First}_k(\alpha) = \beta \quad \text{for } \alpha = \beta\gamma \text{ with } \mathsf{size}(\beta) = k$$
$$\mathsf{Last}_k(\alpha) = \gamma \quad \text{for } \alpha = \beta\gamma \text{ with } \mathsf{size}(\gamma) = k$$

We say $\mathcal{G}$ has *memory n* whenever $\mathsf{Last}_n(\alpha_1) = \mathsf{Last}_n(\alpha_2)$ implies $\alpha_1 \sim_{\mathcal{G}} \alpha_2$, for $\alpha_1, \alpha_2 \in \mathsf{paths}(W)$.

In $\mathcal{G}_\mathsf{h}$ introduced in Example 1, for every $\alpha_1 \neq \alpha_2 \in \Lambda = \mathsf{paths}(\mathcal{G}_\mathsf{h}) = \{\epsilon, a, aa, aaa, aaaa\}$ we have that $\alpha_1 \not\sim_\Lambda \alpha_2$ and thus also $\alpha_1 \not\sim_{\mathcal{G}} \alpha_2$. In fact, $\mathcal{G}_\mathsf{h}$ has memory 4.

In the following example we show how a 1st-order Markov can be modeled by a reactive graph of memory 1.

Example 2. Consider $x, y, z \in [0, 1]$, $x' = 1 - x$, $y' = 1 - y$ and $z' = 1 - z$, and a two state 1st order Markov chain (see [12]) with the transition probability given by

$$\begin{pmatrix} P(X_{i+1} = \mathsf{A}|X_i = \mathsf{A}) & P(X_{i+1} = \mathsf{B}|X_i = \mathsf{A}) \\ P(X_{i+1} = \mathsf{A}|X_i = \mathsf{B}) & P(X_{i+1} = \mathsf{B}|X_i = \mathsf{B}) \end{pmatrix} = \begin{pmatrix} x' & x \\ y & y' \end{pmatrix}$$

and initial probability given by $P(X_0 = \mathsf{A}) = z$ and $P(X_0 = \mathsf{B}) = z'$. Letting

$$x_1 = z' \times x' \qquad x_2 = z' \times y' \qquad x_3 = z \times x \qquad x_4 = z \times y$$

we have that $x_1 = P(X_0 = \mathsf{A}|X_1 = \mathsf{A})$, $x_2 = P(X_0 = \mathsf{A}|X_1 = \mathsf{B})$, $x_3 = P(X_0 = \mathsf{B}|X_1 = \mathsf{A})$, $x_4 = P(X_0 = \mathsf{B}|X_1 = \mathsf{B})$.

Let us show how the Markov chain's dynamic behavior can be seen as a $[0, 1]$-valued[1] reactive graph. Consider $W_\mathsf{m} = \{\mathsf{A}, \mathsf{B}\}$, $V = [0, 1]$, $\mathsf{off} = \{0\}$, $\mathsf{on} =]0, 1]$. In the initial state the arrows in $a \in W_\mathsf{m}^2$ take values in $\{x_1, \ldots, x_4\}$ corresponding to the probability of the starting with $\mathsf{o}(a)$ followed by $\mathsf{t}(a)$. In this encoding, if in the $i+1$-step the arrow (A, B) is crossed it means that $X_i = \mathsf{A}$ and $X_{i+1} = \mathsf{B}$. For every arrow crossing, the arrows coming out of that arrow's target will take values in $\{x, y, x', y'\}$. Only connected paths have meaning in this encoding, thus the arrows not coming out of that arrow's target will take value 0.

---

[1] In this concrete case it would be enough to consider $V = \{0, x_1, x_2, x_3, x_4, x, x', y, y'\}$.

Formally, $\mathcal{G}_m = \langle W_m, \{R_\alpha\}_{\alpha \in \Lambda} \rangle$, where Λ is the subset of $\mathsf{paths}(W_m)$ satisfying $\epsilon \in \Lambda$, and $\alpha a \in \Lambda$ if, and only if, $\alpha \in \Lambda$ and $R_\alpha(a) \in$ on with

$$R_\epsilon(a) = \begin{cases} x_1 & \text{if } a = (\mathsf{A}, \mathsf{A}) \\ x_2 & \text{if } a = (\mathsf{A}, \mathsf{B}) \\ x_3 & \text{if } a = (\mathsf{B}, \mathsf{A}) \\ x_4 & \text{if } a = (\mathsf{B}, \mathsf{B}) \end{cases} \qquad R_{\alpha b}(a) = \begin{cases} 0 & \text{if } \mathsf{o}(a) \neq \mathsf{t}(b) \\ x' & \text{if } \mathsf{t}(b) = \mathsf{o}(a) = \mathsf{t}(a) = \mathsf{A} \\ x & \text{if } \mathsf{t}(b) = \mathsf{o}(a) = \mathsf{A}, \mathsf{t}(a) = \mathsf{B} \\ y & \text{if } \mathsf{t}(b) = \mathsf{o}(a) = \mathsf{B}, \mathsf{o}(a) = \mathsf{A} \\ y' & \text{if } \mathsf{t}(b) = \mathsf{o}(a) = \mathsf{t}(a) = \mathsf{B} \end{cases}$$

Note that $R_\epsilon(a) = P(X_0 = \mathsf{o}(a)) \times P(X_1 = \mathsf{t}(a)|X_0 = \mathsf{o}(a))$ and for every $\alpha b \in \mathsf{Cpaths}(W)$ we have for $\mathsf{size}(\alpha b) = k > 0$

$$R_{\alpha b}(a) = \begin{cases} P(X_{k+2} = \mathsf{t}(a)|X_{k+1} = \mathsf{o}(a)) & \text{if } \mathsf{t}(b) = \mathsf{o}(a) \\ 0 & \text{if } \mathsf{t}(b) \neq \mathsf{o}(a) \end{cases}$$

Hence, $\mathsf{paths}(\mathcal{G}_m) = \Lambda \subseteq \mathsf{Cpaths}(W_m)$ and the equality holds whenever $x, y, z \in \,]0,1[$. Assume that $x, y, z \in \,]0,1[$ and $\alpha_1 a, \alpha_2 b \in \Lambda$. We have that $\alpha_1 a \sim_{\mathcal{G}_m} \alpha_2 b$ if, and only if, $\mathsf{t}(a) = \mathsf{t}(b)$.   △

Typically, we are not concerned with every admissible sequence of arrows, but rather with those that follow certain patterns. Depending on the specific application, we may focus solely on connected paths, and/or paths where the first arrow originates from a particular node. For instance, in Fig. 1, we are interested in the connected paths. In Fig. 2, our focus is on meshes of connected paths that begin in the non-critical state.

Lemma 1. *Let* $\mathcal{G} = \langle W, \{R_\alpha\}_{\alpha \in \Lambda} \rangle$, $0 \in$ *off and* $\Lambda' \subseteq \mathsf{paths}(W)$ *be closed for prefixes. Let* $\mathcal{G}' = \langle W, \{R'_\alpha\}_{\alpha \in \Lambda'} \rangle$, *where* $R'_\alpha(a) = \begin{cases} R_\alpha(a) & \text{if } \alpha a \in \Lambda' \\ 0 & \text{otherwise} \end{cases}$.
$\mathcal{G}'$ *is a reactive many-valued graph and* $\mathsf{paths}_\Lambda(\mathcal{G}') = \mathsf{paths}(\mathcal{G}) \cap \Lambda'$.

Proof. We easily obtain that $\epsilon \in \mathsf{paths}(\mathcal{G}')$, and that $\alpha a \in \mathsf{paths}(\mathcal{G}')$ if, and only if, $\alpha \in \mathsf{paths}(\mathcal{G}')$ and $R'_\alpha(a) \in$ on.   □

For $\mathcal{G} \in \{\mathcal{G}_h, \mathcal{G}_m\}$ from Examples 1 and 2, and $\Lambda' = \mathsf{Cpaths}(W)$ we have $\mathcal{G} = \mathcal{G}_{\Lambda'}$, however, often it is easier to describe a reactive graph $\mathcal{G}$ and restrict the reading to the paths in Λ' as we illustrate further ahead in Example 5.

3   Path-Dependences via Switches

In this section, we introduce the concept of higher-order arrows, which can be used to represent the dynamic configurations of a reactive graph, referred to as *switches*. Fixed a set of nodes W, the set of arrows at the base level, or switches of order 0, is denoted by $S_0 = W^2$. For $n > 0$, the switches of order n are defined recursively as $S_n = S_0 \times S_{n-1}$. We also let $S_{\leq n} = \bigcup_{k \leq n} S_k$, $S_\omega = \bigcup_{k \in \mathbb{N}} S_k$ and $S_{>0} = S_\omega \setminus S_0$.

A *many-valued switch graph* is a tuple $\mathcal{S} = \langle W, \mathsf{S} \rangle$ where $\mathsf{S} : S_\omega \rightharpoonup V$ is a partial function such that[2] $S_0 \subseteq \mathsf{dom}(\mathsf{S})$ and if $(a, b) \in \mathsf{dom}(\mathsf{S})$ then $b \in \mathsf{dom}(\mathsf{S})$. We say that switches in $\mathsf{dom}(\mathsf{S})$ are *active* in $\mathcal{S}$.

In the original 2-valued formulation in [9], switches were represented as higher-order arrows with black or white heads, indicating connecting or disconnecting actions. This meant that *parallel* switches (with different effects) were allowed. The current approach forbids this by defining a switch as a pair of origin and target arrows/switches. However, these switches now take values in an arbitrary set and as we shall see this will suffice to capture every reactive graph's behavior, including those represented by switch graphs using parallel switches as in [9] or fuzzy reversal switch graphs [6].

The goal is to encode the dynamics of a reactive graph on the 0-order arrows by establishing how the values depend on the paths taken. The key idea is that when an arrow a is traversed, all switches of the form (a, b) are fired, thereby altering the value of b. The effect of triggering a switch is determined by extra structure called the interpretation.

An *interpretation* over $\mathcal{S}$ is a tuple $\mathcal{I} = \langle \mathcal{P}, \mathcal{F} \rangle$, where:

- For each $c \in \mathsf{dom}(\mathsf{S}) \cap S_{>0}$,

$$\mathcal{P}(c) = \overrightarrow{x}_c \in \mathsf{dom}(\mathsf{S})^{m_c}$$

  selects a finite tuple of parameters ($m_c \in \mathbb{N}$) among the values stored in switches that are relevant when c is fired.
- The family of trigger/firing functions

$$\mathcal{F} = \{\mathsf{fire}_c : V^{m_c} \to V\}_{c \in \mathsf{dom}(\mathsf{S}) \cap S_{>0}}$$

  describes the effect of triggering c.

An interpretation $\mathcal{I} = \langle \mathcal{P}, \mathcal{F} \rangle$ over a many-valued switch graph $\mathcal{S} = \langle W, \mathsf{S} \rangle$ *induces a set of paths* $\mathsf{paths}(\mathcal{S}, \mathcal{I})$ over W, along which S evolves yielding, for each $\alpha \in \mathsf{paths}(\mathcal{S}, \mathcal{I})$, a potentially different switch graph $\mathcal{S}_\alpha = \langle W, \mathsf{S}_\alpha \rangle$, called the *configuration* of $\mathcal{S}$ after α, which is defined recursively:

- $\epsilon \in \mathsf{paths}(\mathcal{S}, \mathcal{I})$, and $\mathcal{S}_\epsilon = \mathcal{S}$,
- for every $\alpha \in \mathsf{paths}(\mathcal{S}, \mathcal{I})$, $a \in S_0$ with $\alpha(a) \in \mathsf{on}$, then $\alpha a \in \mathsf{paths}(\mathcal{S}, \mathcal{I})$ and for every $b \in \mathsf{dom}(\mathsf{S})$ let

$$\mathsf{S}_{\alpha a}(b) = \begin{cases} \mathsf{S}_\alpha(b) & \text{if } c \notin \mathsf{dom}(\mathsf{S}) \\ \mathsf{fire}_c(\overrightarrow{y}) & \text{if } c \in \mathsf{dom}(\mathsf{S}) \end{cases}$$

with $c = (a, b)$, $\overrightarrow{x} = \mathcal{P}(c) \in \mathsf{dom}(\mathsf{S})^{n_c}$ and $\overrightarrow{y} = \mathsf{S}_\alpha(\overrightarrow{x}) \in V^{n_c}$.

We denote the reactive graph *represented* by an interpretation $\mathcal{I}$ over $\mathcal{S} = \langle W, \mathsf{S} \rangle$ by $\mathcal{G}_{\mathcal{S}, \mathcal{I}} = \langle W, \{\mathsf{R}_\alpha\}_{\alpha \in \Delta} \rangle$ where $\Delta = \mathsf{paths}(\mathcal{S}, \mathcal{I})$ and $\mathsf{R}_\alpha(a) = \mathsf{S}_\alpha(a)$ for any $a \in W^2 = S_0$.

---

[2] As usual for a partial function $f : X \to Y$ we denote by $\mathsf{dom}(f)$ the subset of X for which f is defined.

Example 3. Recall $\mathcal{G}_h = \langle W_h, R \rangle$ from Example 1 and consider the switch graphs $\mathcal{S}_h = \langle \{h\}, S \rangle$ and $\mathcal{S}'_h = \langle \{h\}, S' \rangle$, interpreted respectively by $\mathcal{I} = \langle \mathcal{P}, \mathcal{F} \rangle$ and $\mathcal{I}' = \langle \mathcal{P}', \mathcal{F}' \rangle$ with $S(a) = S'(a) = R(a)$ for $a = (h, h)$, and

- $\text{dom}(S) = S_4$ and for any $c = (a, b) \in S_4$, $\mathcal{P}(c) = \langle c, b \rangle$ and $\text{fire}_c(y_1, y_2) = \min\{y_2, \frac{y_1+y_2}{2}\}$.
- $\text{dom}(S') = \{a, (a, a)\} = S_1$ and for $b = (a, a)$ we have $\mathcal{P}(b) = \langle a \rangle$ and $\text{fire}'_b = f(y)$ where f is any function such that $f(0.2) = 0.6$, $f(0.6) = 0.8$, $f(0.8) = 0.9$ and $f(0.9) = 0$.

Figure 6 shows that $\mathcal{G}_h = \mathcal{G}_{\mathcal{S}_h, \mathcal{I}}$ as seen in [13].

Clearly, $\mathcal{G}_h = \mathcal{G}_{\mathcal{S}_h, \mathcal{I}} = \mathcal{G}_{\mathcal{S}'_h, \mathcal{I}'}$. We have that $\mathcal{S}'_h$ is more concise than $\mathcal{S}_h$ and having a single switch of order 1 whose interpretation directly captures the dynamics through fire' that depends solely on a single parameter - the current value of the arrow (h, h). △

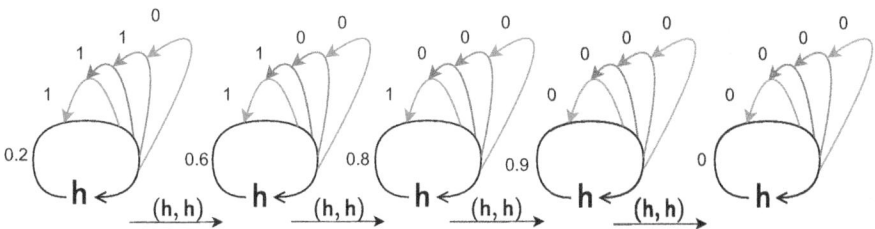

Fig. 6. The behaviour of $\mathcal{S}_h$ under $\mathcal{I}$.

The generalization of switch graphs to the many-valued context, as presented here, fits well with the notion of fuzzy switch graph [13], but does not directly subsume the original definition of switch graphs [9] or of fuzzy reversal switch graphs [6]. In these last two notions, switches are embedded with their actions. For instance, for every arrow $a, b \in W^2$ two 1-level switches with the same origin and target are allowed: $(a, b, \bullet)$ and $(a, b, \circ)$. These represent b being activated (or deactivated, respectively) when a is traversed. The same happens with higher-order switches that have as target switches with that also include their actions. Thus switches that start in the active state can later be deactivated. An inactive switch, however, has no effect when triggered. Such behavior can be captured by assigning it a (possibly fresh) value that ensures it behaves like the identity on the target's value in the chosen interpretation. As a result, by considering a flexible notion of many-valued interpretations, allowing switches to become disconnected becomes less crucial, and we can safely work with a fixed domain of active switches. While we could have incorporated multiple parallel switches, this would have unnecessarily complicated the notation. As we demonstrate next, the adopted formulation is sufficiently expressive to capture all possible behaviors without this added complexity.

3.1   The Blind Interpretation

Given a $\mathcal{S} = \langle W, S \rangle$ we call *blind* the interpretation $\mathcal{I}_{\text{blind}} = \langle \mathcal{P}, \mathcal{F} \rangle$ over $\mathcal{S}$ when for every $a \in \text{dom}(S)$, $\mathcal{P}(a) = \langle a \rangle$ and $\text{fire}_a = \text{Id}_V$. The value of the switch being fired is passed on to its target.

Example 4. In Example 3, we introduced two distinct switch graphs, $\mathcal{S}_h$ and $\mathcal{S}_h'$, that when coupled with the interpretations $\mathcal{I}$ and $\mathcal{I}'$, give two different representations of $\mathcal{G}h$ from Example 1. Neither $\mathcal{I}$ nor $\mathcal{I}'$ are blind. Now, we consider a third switch graph $\mathcal{S}_h''$ that coupled with the blind interpretation also represents $\mathcal{G}h$.

Let $\mathcal{S}_h'' = \langle W_h, S'' \rangle$ with $\text{dom}(S'') = S_4$, $S''(a) = 0.2$, $S''(b) = 0.6$, $S''(b) = 0.8$, $S''(d) = 0.9$ and $S''(e) = 0.9$ for $a = (h, h)$, $b = (a, a)$, $c = (a, b)$, $d = (a, c)$ and $e = (a, e)$.

Using $\mathcal{I}_{\text{blind}}$ we obtain the cascading effect represented in Fig. 7, showing that $\mathcal{G}_{\mathcal{S}_h'', \mathcal{I}_{\text{blind}}} = \mathcal{G}_{\mathcal{S}_h, \mathcal{I}} = \mathcal{G}_{\mathcal{S}_h', \mathcal{I}'}$. △

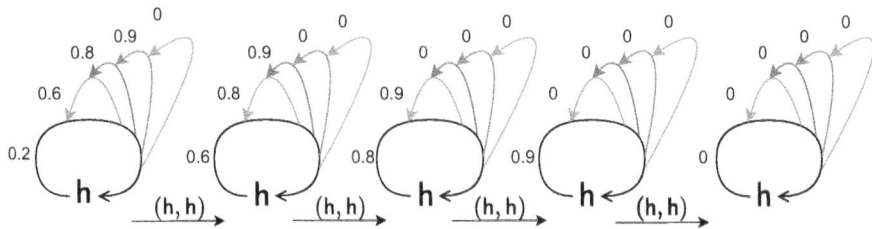

Fig. 7. The behaviour of $\mathcal{S}_h''$ under $\mathcal{I}_{\text{blind}}$.

Let us introduce a convenient abbreviation for switches: given a path α and a switch a, $\text{Switch}(\alpha, a)$ represents a switch whose effect can only be felt at a after traversing every arrow in α. Let $\text{Switch} : \text{paths}(W) \times S_\omega \to S_\omega$ where for $a \in S_n$ is defined inductively on $\alpha \in \text{paths}(W)$ as

$$\text{Switch}(\alpha, a) = \begin{cases} a & \text{if } \alpha = \epsilon \\ \text{Switch}(\beta, (b, a)) & \text{if } \alpha = \beta b \end{cases}$$

Note that if $\text{size}(\alpha) = k$ and $a \in S_n$, then $\text{Switch}(\alpha, a) \in S_{n+k}$. Further, $\text{Switch}(b\beta, a) = (b, \text{Switch}(\beta, a))$.

Lemma 2. *If* $\text{Switch}(\alpha, a) \in \text{dom}(S)$ *then* $a \in \text{dom}(S)$.

Proof. By induction on α. For the base case $\alpha = \epsilon$ and thus $\text{Switch}(\alpha, a) = a \in \text{dom}(S)$. For the step, letting $\alpha = b\beta$ we obtain that $\text{Switch}(\alpha, a) = (b, \text{Switch}(\beta, a))$. Since $\mathcal{S}$ is a switch graph we have that $\text{Switch}(\beta, a) \in \text{dom}(S)$. By induction hypothesis we conclude that $a \in \text{dom}(S)$. □

The evolution of a switch graph S under the blind interpretation can now be concisely formulated.

Lemma 3. *For every* $\alpha \in \mathsf{Paths}(\mathcal{S}, \mathcal{I}_{\mathsf{blind}})$ *and* $a \in S_n$ *such that* $b = \mathsf{Switch}(\alpha, a) \in \mathsf{dom}(S)$ *we have that* $\mathsf{S}_\alpha(a) = \mathsf{S}(b)$.

Proof. By induction on α.

In the base case $\alpha = \epsilon$ then $a = b$ thus $\mathsf{S}_\alpha(a) = \mathsf{S}_\epsilon(b) = \mathsf{S}(b)$.

For the step let $\alpha = \alpha'c$ and $b' = \mathsf{Switch}(c, a)$. Hence, $b = \mathsf{Switch}(\alpha', b')$. Since $b \in \mathsf{dom}(S)$ then $b' \in \mathsf{dom}(S)$ by Lemma 2.

By induction hypothesis $\mathsf{S}_{\alpha'}(b') = \mathsf{S}(b)$. Since $\mathcal{I}_{\mathsf{blind}}$ is the blind interpretation, we have that $\mathcal{P}(b') = \langle b' \rangle$ and $\mathsf{fire}_{b'} = \mathsf{Id}_V$.

Hence, $\mathsf{S}_\alpha(a) = \mathsf{S}_{\alpha'c}(a) = \mathsf{fire}_{b'}(\mathsf{S}_{\alpha'}(b')) = \mathsf{S}_{\alpha'}(b') = \mathsf{S}(b)$. $\square$

We can finally show that this formulation of switch graphs is enough to represent every reactive graph, and, furthermore, blind interpretations suffice.

Theorem 1. *For every reactive many-valued graph* $\mathcal{G} = \langle W, \{R_\lambda : \lambda \in \Lambda\} \rangle$ *there is* $\mathcal{S} = \langle W, \mathsf{S} \rangle$ *such that* $\mathcal{G}$ *is represented by the blind interpretation over* $\mathcal{S}$.

Proof. We let $\mathsf{S} = \langle W, \mathsf{S} \rangle$ with

$$\mathsf{dom}(\mathsf{S}) = \{\mathsf{Switch}(\alpha, a) : \alpha \in \mathsf{paths}(\mathcal{G}), a \in S_0\}$$

and for every $\alpha \in \mathsf{paths}(\mathcal{G})$ and $b = \mathsf{Switch}(\alpha, a)$ we set

$$\mathsf{S}(b) = \mathsf{R}_\alpha(a).$$

We will show by induction on the size of $\alpha \in \mathsf{paths}(W)$ that

(i) $\alpha \in \mathsf{paths}(\mathcal{G})$ if, and only if, $\alpha \in \mathsf{paths}(\mathcal{S}, \mathcal{I}_{\mathsf{blind}})$
(ii) if $\alpha \in \mathsf{paths}(\mathcal{G})$, $\mathsf{S}_\alpha(a) = \mathsf{R}_\alpha(a)$ for $a \in S_0$.

For the base case we consider $\alpha = \epsilon$. By definition $\epsilon \in \mathsf{paths}(\mathcal{S}, \mathcal{I}_{\mathsf{blind}})$ and $\epsilon \in \mathsf{paths}(\mathcal{G})$, thus (i) holds. Since $\mathsf{S}_\epsilon(a) = \mathsf{S}(a) = \mathsf{R}_\epsilon(a)$ then (ii) also holds.

For the step we let $\alpha = \beta b$. By induction hypothesis we have that: (i) $\beta \in \mathsf{paths}(\mathcal{G})$ if, and only if $\beta \in \mathsf{paths}(\mathcal{S}, \mathcal{I}_{\mathsf{blind}})$; and (ii) if $\beta \in \mathsf{paths}(\mathcal{G})$ then $\mathsf{S}_\beta(d) = \mathsf{R}_\beta(d)$ for $d \in S_0$.

Therefore, $\mathsf{S}_\beta(d) \in \mathsf{on}$ if, and only if, $\mathsf{R}_\beta(d) \in \mathsf{on}$. Hence $\beta b \in \mathsf{paths}(\mathcal{G})$ if, and only if, $\beta b \in \mathsf{paths}(\mathcal{S}, \mathcal{I}_{\mathsf{blind}})$, and (i) holds.

Assuming that $\alpha = \beta b \in \mathsf{paths}(\mathcal{G})$ we have that $c = \mathsf{Switch}(\alpha, a) \in \mathsf{dom}(S)$ for every $a \in S_0$. Thus, by Lemma 3 we obtain that $\mathsf{S}_\alpha(a) = \mathsf{S}(c)$. Finally, since by definition $\mathsf{S}(c) = \mathsf{R}_\alpha(a)$ we conclude that $\mathsf{S}_\alpha(a) = \mathsf{R}_\alpha(a)$, and (ii) holds. $\square$

This result is analogous to Theorem 2.8 in [9], stating that every 2-valued reactive graph can be represented by the original switch graphs, however the proof is much simpler. In the original context, swapping a switch's effect from connecting to disconnecting required deactivating that switch and activating the parallel one with the opposite effect. Nonetheless, as in the original result, there is no upper bound on the level of switches required, as each path of size k introduces switches of level k. Characterizing reactive graphs by the level of switches necessary for their representation remains a non-trivial task, heavily dependent on both the structure of the active switches and the specific interpretation employed.

In the concrete case of the blind interpretation, if every switch of level below a fixed natural n, is active then the memory of the represented reactive graph is bounded by n. Furthermore, every bounded memory reactive graph can be represented by such a switch graph.

Proposition 1. *Assume* $S = \langle W, \mathsf{S} \rangle$ *is such that* $\mathsf{dom}(\mathsf{S}) = S_{\leq n}$. *Given* $\alpha \in$ $\mathsf{paths}(\mathsf{S}, \mathcal{I}_{\mathsf{blind}})$ *if* $\beta = \mathsf{Last}_n(\alpha)$ *then* $\mathsf{S}_\alpha = \mathsf{S}_\beta$. *Hence,* $\mathcal{G}_{\mathsf{S}, \mathcal{I}_{\mathsf{blind}}}$ *has memory* n.

Proof. Since $S_{\leq n} = \bigcup_{0 \leq k \leq n} S_{n-k}$, it is enough to show that for every $0 \leq k \leq n$ and $a \in S_{n-k}$, if $\gamma = \mathsf{First}_k(\alpha)$ and $b = \mathsf{Switch}(\gamma, a)$ then $\mathsf{S}_\alpha(a) = \mathsf{S}_\gamma(b) = \mathsf{S}_\beta(a)$. By induction on $0 \leq k \leq n$.

For the base case let $k = 0$. Since for $m > n$ we have $S_m \cap \mathsf{dom}(\mathsf{S}) = \emptyset$ we conclude that for every $a \in S_{n-0} = S_n \subseteq \mathsf{dom}(\mathsf{S})$, we have that $\gamma = \mathsf{First}_0(\alpha) = \epsilon$ and $\mathsf{S}_\alpha(a) = \mathsf{S}_\epsilon(a) = \mathsf{S}(a)$.

For the step let $k = k' + 1$, $\gamma' = \mathsf{First}_{k'}(\alpha)$, $\beta = \beta'c$ and $b' = \mathsf{Switch}(c, a) = (c, a)$.

Since $a \in S_{n-k}$ we have that $b' \in S_{n-k'}$. By induction hypothesis we have that $\mathsf{S}_\alpha(a) = \mathsf{S}_{\beta'}(b') = \mathsf{S}(a)$. Since $\mathcal{I}_{\mathsf{blind}}$ is the blind interpretation, $\mathcal{P}(b') = \{b'\}$ and $\mathsf{fire}_{b'} = \mathsf{Id}_V$. Thus $\mathsf{S}_\beta(a) = \mathsf{S}_{\beta'c}(a) = \mathsf{fire}_{b'}(a) = \mathsf{S}_{\beta'}(b')$ and $\mathsf{S}_\alpha(a) = \mathsf{S}_\beta(b) = \mathsf{R}(a)$. □

Theorem 2. *If* $\mathcal{G} = \langle W, \{\mathsf{R}_\alpha : \alpha \in \Lambda\} \rangle$ *has memory* n *then exists* $\mathcal{S} = \langle W, \mathsf{S} \rangle$ *with* $\mathsf{dom}(\mathcal{S}) \subseteq S_{\leq n}$ *such that* $\mathcal{I}_{\mathsf{blind}}$ *over* $\mathcal{S}$ *represents* $\mathcal{G}$.

Proof. Consider $\Lambda_{\leq n} = \{\alpha \in \Lambda : \mathsf{size}(\alpha) \leq n\}$, $\mathcal{S} = \langle W, \mathsf{S} \rangle$ with

$$\mathsf{dom}(\mathsf{S}) = \{\mathsf{Switch}(\alpha, a) : \alpha \in \Lambda_{\leq n}, a \in S_0\} \subseteq S_{\leq n}$$

and for every $\alpha \in \Lambda_{\leq n}$ and $b = \mathsf{Switch}(\alpha, a)$ we set $\mathsf{S}(b) = \mathsf{R}_\alpha(a)$.

The rest of the proof follows as in Theorem 1, using Lemma 3 plus the extra assumption that for $\beta = \mathsf{Last}_n(\alpha)$ we have $\mathsf{S}_\beta(b) = \mathsf{S}_\alpha(b)$. □

Note that for a switch graph $\mathcal{S}$ with a finite number of nodes W and $\mathsf{dom}(\mathsf{S}) \subseteq S_{\leq n}$, then $\mathcal{G}_{\mathcal{S}, \mathcal{I}_{\mathsf{blind}}}$ uses only a finite subset of V. However, $\mathsf{dom}(\mathcal{S}) \subseteq S_{\leq n}$ does not imply that $\mathcal{G}_{\mathcal{S}, \mathcal{I}_{\mathsf{blind}}}$ has memory n.

Example 5. Recall $\mathcal{G}_{\mathsf{m}}$ from Example 2, and let $\mathcal{S}$ and $\mathcal{S}'$ be as shown in the top part of Fig. 8. We have that $\mathcal{G}_{\mathsf{m}} = \mathcal{G}_{\mathcal{S}', \mathcal{I}_{\mathsf{blind}}}$ and $\mathsf{paths}(\mathcal{G}_{\mathsf{m}}) = \mathsf{paths}(\mathcal{S}', \mathcal{I}_{\mathsf{blind}}) = \mathsf{paths}(\mathcal{S}, \mathsf{blind}) \cap \mathsf{Cpaths}(W_{\mathsf{m}})$.

Bellow, in Fig. 8 is depicted the behaviour of $\mathcal{S}$ under the blind interpretation along $\mathsf{paths}(\mathcal{G}_{\mathsf{m}})$. Note that $\mathcal{G}_{\mathsf{m}} \neq \mathcal{G}_{\mathcal{S}, \mathcal{I}_{\mathsf{blind}}}$ and let $\mathcal{G}'_{\mathsf{m}} = \mathcal{G}_{\mathcal{S}, \mathcal{I}_{\mathsf{blind}}}$. We have that $(\mathsf{B}, \mathsf{B}) \sim_{\mathcal{G}'_{\mathsf{m}}} (\mathsf{A}, \mathsf{A})(\mathsf{B}, \mathsf{B})$ only if $x_1 = x'$ or $x_2 = x$. Thus $\mathcal{G}'_{\mathsf{m}}$ does not need to have memory 1 which is acceptable since $\mathcal{S}$ under $\mathcal{I}_{\text{blind}}$ is not exactly captur-ing $\mathcal{G}_{\text{m}}$. Non-connected paths in $\mathcal{S}$, such as $(A, A)(B, B)$, are not consistent with the expected Markov chain behavior, so arrows breaking connectedness could be disregarded as in Lemma 1. This allows us to use $\mathcal{S}$ instead of $\mathcal{S}'$, avoiding the complexity of enforcing connectedness. While $\mathcal{S}$ quickly converges to a fixed configuration, $\mathcal{S}'$ forbids non-connected paths and alternates between two config-urations based on the last arrow's target, which we omit due to space constraints. A similar encoding of an nth-order Markov chain with the blind interpretation would require n-level switches and also display more complex behavior.

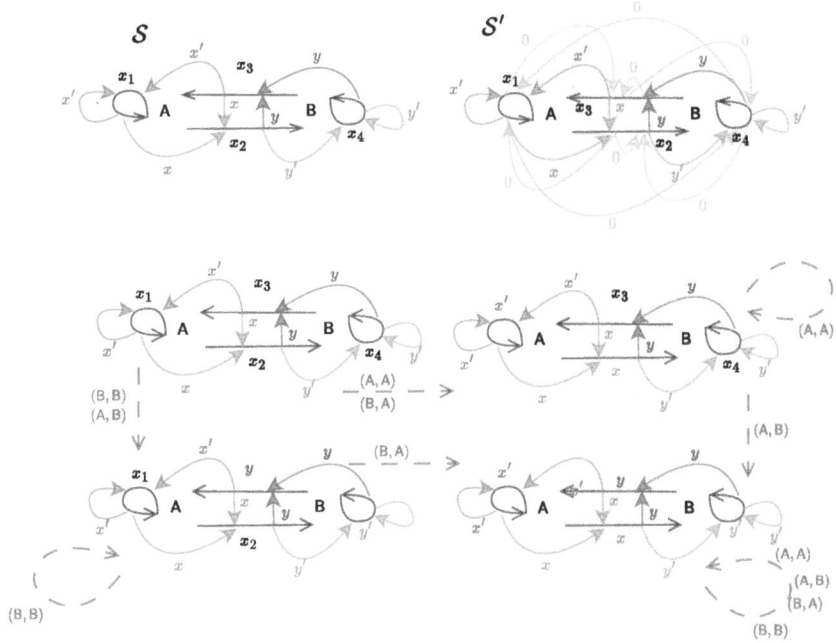

Fig. 8. Above: the switch graphs $\mathcal{S}$ and $\mathcal{S}'$. Below: the behavior of $\mathcal{S}$ under the blind interpretation along $\mathsf{paths}(\mathcal{G}_{\text{m}})$, assuming $x, y, z \in \,]0, 1[$.

There are several alternative ways to encode the considered Markov chain as a reactive graph. For instance, allowing for non-connected paths and interpreting each arrow crossing as a new pairs of consecutive events. In this case, a path $a_1 \ldots a_k \in \mathsf{paths}(W_{\text{m}})$ could represent the sequence where $X_{2i-2} = \mathsf{o}(a_i)$ and $X_{2i-1} = \mathsf{t}(a_i)$ for $1 \leq i \leq k$. The values on the arrows of the reactive graph would also need to be adjusted accordingly. While R_ϵ would remain unchanged, we would consider

$$\mathsf{R}_{ab}(a) = P(X_{i+1} = \mathsf{o}(a)|X_i = \mathsf{t}(b)) \times P(X_{i+1} = \mathsf{t}(a)|X_i = \mathsf{o}(a)).$$

Still another alternative would be to have the reactive graph encoding additional information. For instance, we might as values pairs $(x, y) \in [0, 1]^2$, where the first component x could work as before, while the second component y could carry some relevant aggregated value accumulated along the path. Although the blind interpretation is sufficient to represent any behavior, more nuanced interpretations are likely to prove useful in representing richer dynamics.   △

These illustrative examples show that reactive graphs can capture the arrow-level dynamics encoding the behavior of the system being described, and how switch graphs, along with their interpretations, can be used to locally implement these dynamics. Understanding when two switch graphs together with respective switch interpretations represent the same reactive graph is a non-trivial task and points to a general study of homomorphisms and bisimulations between these structures.

4   Concluding Remarks

We have adapted the concepts of reactive and switch graphs to a general many-valued setting. Given their roots in modal logic, can we leverage its machinery to reason about these structures?

A promising strategy involves adapting the approach in [9], which employs hybrid logic resources to describe the switch dynamics, to the many-valued case, particularly for lattice-based logics that have natural modal operator interpretations. As a first step, we should consider a base logic given by logical matrices [5] whose truth values contain V, and whose connectives should be able to express the functions used to interpret the switches. For instance, the firing functions considered in Example 4 could easily be expressed in a variety of fuzzy logics. Namely, if f of $\mathcal{I}'$ is piecewise linear with integer coefficients it can be expressed by a Łukasiewicz formula [11].

There is a rich literature on modal logics whose semantics involve graph-changing operations or path-dependency. For instance, in sabotage logics [1], the basic language of modal logics is extended with a black diamond operator, which non-deterministically deactivates a single arrow in the current state of the accessibility relation. In contrast, memory logics [2] allow models to retain information about previously visited nodes, though not necessarily the order in which they were visited. It would be very interesting to establish formal bridges between these frameworks, and reactive graphs and their representations by switch graphs.

In [8], Gabbay considered that switches that could non-deterministically fire or not, leading to non-deterministic reactive graphs where each step results in a set of possible configurations. This branching behavior in the many-valued case could be modelled by interpreting switches using multi-functions. At that point we may find out that picking logics given by non-deterministic matrices may also be helpful given their compositional advantages [3] while maintaining much of the algebraic flavor [4].

Besides the possibility of parallel switches and non-deterministic effects, there are various other features of potential interest that were left out in an effort to strike a balance between generality and simplicity. It is only natural that such features will be included also under the umbrela of reactive graphs. An immediate possibility is to go beyond sharp nodes, and allow nodes to take values from the same arbitrary set, which can also vary along the paths. Such dynamics could be represented, for example, by further allowing switches to have nodes as targets.

Acknowledgment. This work was supported by FCT - Fundação para a Ciência e Tecnologia, I.P. by project reference UIDB/50008/2020, https://doi.org/10.54499/UIDB/50008/2020.

Disclosure of Interests. The author has no competing interests to declare that are relevant to the content of this article.

References

1. Aucher, G., Benthem, J., van Grossi, D.: Modal logics of sabotage revisited. J. Logic Comput. **28**(2), 269–303 (2017). https://doi.org/10.1093/logcom/exx034
2. Areces, C., Figueira, S., Mera, S.: Completeness results for memory logics. Ann. Pure Appl. Logic **163**(7), 961–972 (2012). https://doi.org/10.1016/j.apal.2011.09.005
3. Caleiro, C., Marcelino, S., Rivieccio, U.: some more theorems on structural entailment relations and non-deterministic semantics. In: Malinowski, J., Palczewski, R. (eds.) Janusz Czelakowski on Logical Consequence. Outstanding Contributions to Logic, vol. 27, Springer, Cham (2024). https://doi.org/10.1007/978-3-031-44490-6_12
4. Caleiro, C., Marcelino, S.: Modular many-valued semantics for combined logics. J. Symb. Logic, 1–54 (2023). https://doi.org/10.1017/jsl.2023.22
5. Font, J.: Abstract Algebraic Logic. Studies in Logic. Mathematical Logic and Foundation, vol. 60. College Publications, London (2016)
6. Campos, S., Santiago, R., Martins, A.M., Figueiredo, D.: Reversal fuzzy switch graphs. In: Carvalho, S.V. (ed.) Formal Methods: Foundations and Applications, SBMF 2020, LNCS, vol. 12475, pp. 137–154. Springer, Cham (2020). https://doi.org/10.1007/978-3-030-63799-4_9
7. Gabbay, D.: Reactive Kripke semantics and arc accessibility. In: Carnielli, W., Dionisio, F.M., Mateus, P. (eds.) Proceedings of CombLog 2004, Centre for Logic and Computation, University of Lisbon, pp. 7–20 (2004)
8. Gabbay, D.M.: Introducing reactive kripke semantics and arc accessibility. In: Avron, A., Dershowitz, N., Rabinovich, A. (eds.) Pillars of Computer Science. LNCS, vol. 4800, pp. 292–341. Springer, Heidelberg (2008). https://doi.org/10.1007/978-3-540-78127-1_17
9. Gabbay, D., Marcelino, S.: Global view on reactivity: switch graphs and their logics. Ann. Math. Artif. Intell. **66**(1), 131–162 (2012). https://doi.org/10.1007/s10472-012-9316-8

10. Marcelino, S.: Modal logic for changing systems. PhD thesis, University of London (2011)
11. McNaughton, R.: A theorem about infinite-valued sentential logic. J. Symb. Logic **16**, 1–13 (1951). https://doi.org/10.2307/2268660
12. Wang, Y.H.: Approximating kth-order two-state Markov chains. J. Appl. Probab. **29**(4), 861–868 (1992). https://doi.org/10.2307/3214718
13. Santiago, R., Martins, A.M., Figueiredo, D.: Introducing fuzzy reactive graphs: a simple application on biology. Soft. Comput. **25**, 6759–6774 (2021). https://doi.org/10.1016/j.scico.2022.102776

Towards Resolving Distributed Beliefs

John Lindqvist[1]([✉]), Fernando R. Velázquez-Quesada[1] [ID],
and Thomas Ågotnes[1,2]

[1] Department of Information Science and Media Studies, University of Bergen,
Bergen, Norway
{John.Lindqvist,Fernando.VelazquezQuesada,Thomas.Agotnes}@uib.no
[2] Institute of Logic and Intelligence, Southwest University, Chongqing, China

Abstract. In multi-agent systems, a particularly important action is that through which some agents share information with some others. Within epistemic logic and its relational semantics, this action has been represented as a model operation that assigns to every agent in the communicating group the relation describing the group's distributed knowledge in the initial model, leaving the relation of all other agents as before. While this approach works well when the shared information is knowledge, it has some issues when the shared information is beliefs: consistent agents might be turned into inconsistent ones. This manuscript explores an approach that relies on maximally consistent subgroups of agents, discussing also how to modify it to guarantee that all the relevant properties of beliefs are preserved.

1 Introduction

Epistemic logic (*EL*; [13, 22]) is a framework for representing and reasoning about the information different agents have not only about the world but also about their own and other agents' information. Its 'dynamic' extensions (*DEL*; [6, 8, 11]) deal with representing and reasoning about different informational events. As such, *EL* and *DEL* are useful tools for reasoning about knowledge, belief and information change, an important topic for areas where multi-agent interaction is of interest (e.g., A.I., Computer Science, Economics, Philosophy).

A particularly interesting informational action is that through which some agents share information with some others to combine it. This general idea has been studied from different perspectives, depending of the kind of information and how it is represented. One example is *preferences* represented by ordering relations, which lead to the study of voting systems (e.g., Part 1 of [10]); another is beliefs represented syntactically as finite belief bases, which lead to belief merging/fusion (e.g., [23, 24]) as well as judgment aggregation (e.g., [17, 26]). Within *EL* (a semantic representation of the agents' knowledge/beliefs about facts as well as one anothers' knowledge/beliefs), this communication act is closely related to the concept of *distributed knowledge* [18, 19, 21], which intuitively describes the logical consequences of the combination of the individual knowledge of a group of agents. When *EL*'s semantics are given by relational

J. Proença et al. (Eds.): SEFM 2024, LNCS 15551, pp. 77–91, 2026.
https://doi.org/10.1007/978-3-031-94748-3_6

'Kripke' models, it is said that a group of agents has distributed knowledge of φ at a world w if and only if φ holds in all the situations that *no member of the group* can distinguish from w. Most (if not all) *EL*-based studies of this action rely on this concept.

There are several variations of the described communication action (e.g., [1,5,7,15,31]). The focus here will be that in which every agent in a group shares *all* her information with *everybody in the group*, with all other agents sharing and receiving nothing. The case in which the shared information is knowledge (i.e., truthful information) is studied in [1]. There it is represented by a model operation whose input is the model representing the agents' initial situation, and whose output is the model representing the agents' information *after* the action's execution. This model operation "resolves" the distributed knowledge of a group by assigning, to every agent in the communicating group, the relation describing the group's distributed knowledge, leaving the relation of all other agents as before. This 'simple' strategy works well in the knowledge case: the to-be-combined information is truthful, and thus it is impossible to have an agent that knows some φ while another knows $\neg\varphi$. In other words, the to-be-combined information is *consistent*, and thus it can be put together through this *knowledge resolution* operation within any additional consideration. But when the to-be-merged information are beliefs, a consistent agent might believe p, and another might believe $\neg p$. In such cases, one needs some method to make decisions, to guarantee that the result is of the required type (in this case, consistent beliefs). This issue has been already discussed in the *DEL* literature (albeit not in the context of agents communicating, but rather in the context of *public announcements* [16,27]), with some proposals advocating ignoring the conflicting information [29] and some others updating only when the resulting model has the required properties [4].

This manuscript uses the idea of *maximally consistent subgroups of agents* for defining a more general version of the knowledge-based operation of [1]. Rather than looking at the intersection relation for the entire group, the new accessibility relation of an agent is based on the maximal consistent subgroups she is part of.[1] The resulting operation is called *cautious belief resolution*, which preserves consistency. However, other belief properties, namely positive and negative introspection, might still be lost. For that reason, a further *patched* cautious belief resolution is introduced. This patched version can be seen as adding extra restrictions to the information accepted by the agents, to guarantee that their initially 'rational' beliefs remain that way.

Outline. Section 2 covers preliminaries, including the knowledge resolution of [1] and how it performs without the truthfulness assumption. Section 3 starts with the *cautious belief resolution*, showing that it preserves belief consistency. Still, as it does not preserve introspection, a further *patched cautious belief resolution* is presented and studied. It is shown not only that it preserves the properties of belief but also that, while in some cases an agent might 'forget'/'ignore' the

---

[1] Maximal consistency is a well known approach to dealing with conflicting information in different areas of logic (e.g., [9,12,20,25,28]).

information she is receiving, she will not not forget information that she had before. Section 4 summarises the contents, pointing to work to be done and suggesting that representing a belief sharing event requires more than what the intersection approach can do, even when using caution and patching.

2 Basic Definitions

In this text, P is a countable set of atoms and $A \neq \varnothing$ is a finite set of agents.

Definition 1. A model is a tuple $\langle W, \{R_i \mid i \in A\}, V \rangle$ where $W \neq \varnothing$ is a domain whose elements are called (possible) worlds, each $R_i \subseteq W \times W$ is a binary indistinguishability relation (for a non-empty $G \subseteq A$, define G's distributed information relation as $R_G := \bigcap_{b \in G} R_b$) and $V : P \to \wp(W)$ is an atomic valuation. Take a model $\langle W, \{R_i \mid i \in A\}, V \rangle$ and a world $w \in W$. For an agent $i \in A$, define $R_i(w) := \{v \in W \mid R_i wv\}$ as i's conjecture set (sometimes referred to in the literature as i's belief state); for a non-empty $G \subseteq A$, define $R_G(w) := \{v \in W \mid R_G wv\}(= \bigcap_{b \in G} R_b(w))$ as G's conjecture set. If all relations $\{R_i \mid i \in A\}$ in a given model have certain property (e.g., reflexivity, transitivity, Euclidicity, seriality), the model is said to have the property. A *pointed model* is a pair $(\mathcal{M}, w)$ with $\mathcal{M}$ a model and w a world in it. ◀

Pointed models can be described by languages with different operators. Besides the Boolean ones (including constants $\top$ and $\bot$, all of them with the standard semantics), the most relevant for us are those for the information of individuals as well as the distributed information of groups.

Definition 2. Let $(\mathcal{M}, w)$ be a pointed model. The semantics for the modalities $\Box_i$ (for $i \in A$) and D_G (for a non-empty $G \subseteq A$) are as follows.

$$\mathcal{M}, w \vDash \Box_i \varphi \qquad \text{iff} \qquad \mathcal{M}, v \vDash \varphi \text{ for all } v \in R_i(w)$$
$$\mathcal{M}, w \vDash D_G \varphi \qquad \text{iff} \qquad \mathcal{M}, v \vDash \varphi \text{ for all } v \in R_G(w)$$

If $(\mathcal{M}, w) \vDash \varphi$ then φ is true at $(\mathcal{M}, w)$. A formula φ is valid (notation: $\vDash \varphi$) when it is true in every pointed model (i.e., in every world of every model). ◀

The concept of consistency plays an important role in this text; let's make it precise. An agent i (a group G) is *consistent* at $(\mathcal{M}, w)$ iff $\mathcal{M}, w \vDash \neg \Box_i \bot$ ($\mathcal{M}, w \vDash \neg D_G \bot$). Otherwise, i (G) is inconsistent. Thus, semantically, i (G) is *inconsistent* at $(\mathcal{M}, w)$ iff $R_i(w) = \varnothing$ ($R_G(w) = \varnothing$). Note: consistency is a local property, defined not at a model but rather at a *pointed* model.

When the information is taken as knowledge, the modality $\Box_i$ is replaced by K_i (so $K_i \varphi$ is read as "*agent i knows that φ holds*"). More importantly, each agent's relation is required to be reflexive, transitive and Euclidean (i.e., an equivalence relation). Under such conditions, each agent's knowledge is truthful ($\vDash K_i \varphi \to \varphi$), and each agent is both positively and negatively introspective ($\vDash K_i \varphi \to K_i K_i \varphi$ and $\vDash \neg K_i \varphi \to K_i \neg K_i \varphi$). When the information is taken as beliefs, the modality $\Box_i$ is replaced by B_i (so $B_i \varphi$ is read as "*agent i believes that* *φ holds"*). More importantly, each agent's relation is required to be serial, transitive and Euclidean. Under such conditions, each agent's beliefs are consistent ($\models B_i\varphi \to \neg B_i\neg\varphi$ is valid[2]), and each agent is both positively and negatively introspective ($\models B_i\varphi \to B_iB_i\varphi$ and $\models \neg B_i\varphi \to B_i\neg B_i\varphi$ are valid, respectively).

Individual information can change through different actions. Within *DEL*, the change is represented by taking the (pointed) model depicting the agents' initial information, then returning the one depicting the information they have after the specific action. Since the individual information of the agents is potentially different, a natural action to consider is one through which some agents share information with some others. There are variations of this, depending on who shares, what is being shared, who receives and what is learnt (if anything) by agents not receiving (see, e.g., [1,5,7,15,31]). One of the simplest (and still interesting) scenarios is that in which every agent in a group $G \subseteq A$ shares all her information with everybody in the group, with all other agents sharing and receiving nothing (yet noticing that communication within G happens). When the shared information is knowledge, the action is represented as follows.

2.1 Communicating Knowledge

The knowledge resolution operator from [1] deals with agents and their knowledge (thus, equivalence relations are assumed, and modalities K_i are used). It represents the effect of a form of communication through which all agents in $G \subseteq A$ share all their knowledge among themselves, with agents not in G neither receiving nor sharing (but noticing that communication happens).

Definition 3 (Knowledge G-resolution). Let $\mathcal{M} = \langle W, \{R_i \mid i \in A\}, V\rangle$ be a model; take $G \subseteq A$. The *knowledge G-resolved update* of $\mathcal{M}$ is the model $\mathcal{M}^G = \langle W, \{R_i^G \mid i \in A\}, V\rangle$ (so, domain and valuation remain the same) where each R_i^G is given by

$$R_i^G := \begin{cases} R_G(= \bigcap_{b \in G} R_b) & i \in G; \\ R_i & \text{otherwise.} \end{cases}$$

For describing the effects of this operation, add to the language an operator $\mathbf{R}_G$ for every $G \subseteq A$, with its semantic interpretation given by

$$\mathcal{M}, w \models \mathbf{R}_G\varphi \qquad \text{iff} \qquad \mathcal{M}^G, w \models \varphi$$

◄

Note: while the operation leaves the indistinguishability relation for agents not in G untouched (they do not 'hear' what agents in G share), it assigns to

---
[2] Modulo the $\Box_i/B_i$ difference, this formula is, in this setting, equivalent to the earlier $\neg\Box_i\bot$.

every agent in G the group's distributed information relation (i.e., the intersection of the agents in G's initial relations, as only they communicate).[3] Note also how the operation preserves equivalence relations: if every R_i in the initial model is an equivalence relation, so are all relations R_i^G in the new model. So, the properties of knowledge are preserved. The following validities make precise what the individual knowledge of the agents (those in G and those not in G) is after this form of communication takes place:

$$\vDash \mathbf{R}_G K_i \varphi \leftrightarrow D_G \mathbf{R}_G \varphi \text{ for } i \in G \qquad\qquad \vDash \mathbf{R}_G K_i \varphi \leftrightarrow K_i \mathbf{R}_G \varphi \text{ for } i \notin G$$

Thus, agents in G get to know φ after the action iff, before the action, the group G knew, distributively, that the action will make φ true. Agents not in G need a stronger requirement to know φ after the action: they need to know, on their own, that the action will make φ true.

Now, suppose the agents' information is not knowledge but rather beliefs. First, each agent's relation is now required to be serial, transitive and Euclidean. But, even though transitivity and Euclidicity are preserved by the operation (i.e., by intersections), seriality is not. Thus, the same operation might yield inconsistent agents, even when there were none before. More to the point: when consistent agents resolve their beliefs with those of consistent agents they disagree with, they will turn inconsistent.

Example 1. Consider the serial, transitive and Euclidean model $\mathcal{M}_1$ (below left). Its $\{a, b\}$-resolved update $\mathcal{M}_1^{\{a,b\}}$ (below right) is not serial: at w neither a nor b has any world accessible.

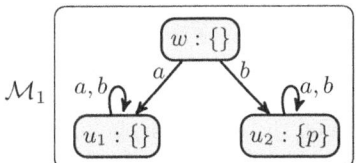 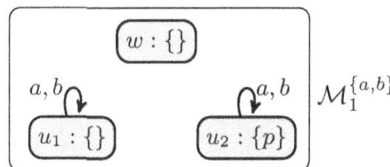

So, resolving makes a, b inconsistent: $\mathcal{M}_1, w \vDash \neg B_a \bot \wedge \neg B_b \bot \wedge \mathbf{R}_G (B_a \bot \wedge B_b \bot)$. ◀

3   Using Maximal Consistency

In the knowledge case, the fact that intersections preserve the required relational properties is crucial for both distributed information as well as the G-resolution

---

[3] Still, because of the nature of the (relational) models, under this definition the information of agents not in G changes too: they get to know that agents in G have shared information. Note that *secret* forms of communication (some agents exchange information without the others noticing it) can be also represented: see [7] for this in the context of 'taking' rather than 'sharing', and [6] for this in the context of announcements/observations (i.e., agents receiving information from an *external* source).

update. For the first, it makes this distributed information (given as normal modality working on the relation R_G) a proper notion of knowledge; for the latter, it guarantees that the properties of knowledge are preserved. However, intersections do not preserve seriality, a property typically required for a model representing beliefs. Thus, the distributed belief of a group of consistent agents might end up not being consistent [2], and a resolution update might turn previously consistent agents into inconsistent ones Example 1.

To avoid ascribing inconsistent beliefs to a group of consistent agents, [25] proposes two forms of distributed beliefs: cautious and bold. These notions, related to the *sceptical* and *credulous* consequence in default logic [28], rely on the idea of maximally consistent subsets from a given group of consistent agents G. First, recall: $H \subseteq G$ is consistent at a world w iff $R_H(w) \neq \varnothing$; then, $H \subseteq G$ is maximally consistent at w within G (notation: $H \subseteq_w^{max} G$) iff it is consistent and adding any agent in $G \setminus H$ makes the resulting set inconsistent. Thus, at a given world there might be several sets of agents that are maximally consistent within G. With this, cautious and bold distributed beliefs are defined as follow. On a given w, while a group G has *cautious* distributed belief on φ (in the language: $D_G^\forall \varphi$) iff *every* maximally consistent subset of G has distributed belief on φ, the group has *bold* distributed belief on φ (in the language: $D_G^\exists \varphi$) iff *some* maximally consistent subset of G has distributed belief on φ.

Definition 4 (Cautious & bold distributed belief). Take a pointed model $(\mathcal{M}, w)$ and a group $G \subseteq A$. Then,

$$\mathcal{M}, w \vDash D_G^\forall \varphi \qquad \text{iff} \qquad \forall H \subseteq_w^{max} G : \mathcal{M}, w \vDash D_H \varphi$$
$$\mathcal{M}, w \vDash D_G^\exists \varphi \qquad \text{iff} \qquad \exists H \subseteq_w^{max} G : \mathcal{M}, w \vDash D_H \varphi$$

◀

Cautious and bold beliefs deal better with potential inconsistencies (see [25]). The ideas behind them can be also used for defining the effects on the individual beliefs of members of G upon an action through which the agents in G communicate their beliefs among themselves.

3.1   A 'Cautious' Approach for Communicating Beliefs

Take a group G and an agent $i \in G$. Following the idea of cautious distributed belief, a "cautious" version of the G-resolution action will, intuitively, ascribe a belief to i iff this belief is held distributively by *every* maximally consistent subset of G she belonged to. In this *EL* setting, this means defining the new relation for i, at each possible world w, as reaching those worlds that are reachable by *at least one* maximally consistent subset of G to which i belongs.[4]

---

[4] One might also consider a "bold" version, intuitively ascribing a belief to i iff this belief was held distributively by *some* maximally consistent subset of G she belonged to. However, while this preserves seriality when i belongs to a single maximally consistent subset, in general an agent might belong to more than one such a set. A further discussion of this alternative is left for future work.

Definition 5 (Cautious belief G-resolution). Let $\mathcal{M} = \langle W, \{R_i \mid i \in A\}, V \rangle$ be a model; take $G \subseteq A$. The *cautious G-resolved update* of $\mathcal{M}$ is the model $\mathcal{M}^{\forall|G} = \langle W, \{R_i^{\forall|G} \mid i \in A\}, V \rangle$ (so, domain and valuation remain the same) where each $R_i^{\forall|G}$ is given by

$$R_i^{\forall|G} := \begin{cases} \{(w,v) \in W \times W \mid v \in \bigcup_{\{H \mid i \in H \subseteq_w^{max} G\}} R_H(w)\} & i \in G; \\ R_i & \text{otherwise.} \end{cases}$$

Thus, while relations for agents in $A \setminus G$ are untouched, for agents in G are s.t.

$$R_i^{\forall|G} wv \qquad \text{iff} \qquad v \in R_H(w) \text{ for some } H \text{ such that } i \in H \subseteq_w^{max} G.$$

◀

To see better the relationship between this operation and that for knowledge resolution (Definition 3), here is an equivalent 'point-wise' version of the latter:[5]

$$R_i^G := \begin{cases} \{(w,v) \in W \times W \mid v \in R_G(w)\} & i \in G; \\ R_i & \text{otherwise.} \end{cases}$$

The difference is that, at each w, cautious belief resolution takes as i's successors not the worlds in $R_G(w)$, but rather those in the union of the sets $R_H(w)$, for H a maximal consistent subgroup of G to which i belongs.

Preserving Properties? The cautious belief resolution does not create inconsistent agents, as it preserves seriality.

Proposition 1. *If $\mathcal{M}$ is a serial model, then $\mathcal{M}^{\forall|G}$ is also a serial model.*

Proof. Take any serial model $\mathcal{M} = \langle W, \{R_i \mid i \in A\}, V \rangle$ and any $G \subseteq A$. Take $i \in A$. If $i \notin G$, then $R_i^{\forall|G}$ is R_i and hence serial. Otherwise, $i \in G$, so $R_i^{\forall|G} = \{(w,v) \in W \times W \mid v \in \bigcup_{\{H \mid i \in H \subseteq_w^{max} G\}} R_H(w)\}$. Since R_i is serial, for every $w \in W$ there is at least one consistent subgroup of G that i belongs to (namely, $\{i\}$), which can then be extended into an $H \subseteq_w^{max} G$ to which i belongs; being such H consistent at w, we have $R_H(w) \neq \varnothing$. Hence, for every $w \in W$ there is some $v \in W$ such that $R_i^{\forall|G} wv$; thus, $R_i^{\forall|G}$ is serial. But i is arbitrary, so every $R_i^{\forall|G}$ is serial, and thus so is $\mathcal{M}^{\forall|G}$. ∎

However, consistency is not the only property required for beliefs, and thus not the only property a communication operation should preserve.

Example 2. First, consider the serial, transitive and Euclidean model $\mathcal{M}_2$ (below left). Its cautious $\{a,b\}$-resolved update $\mathcal{M}_2^{\forall|\{a,b\}}$ (below right) is not Euclidean: e.g., both $R_a w u_2$ and $R_a w u_1$ hold, and yet $R_a u_2 u_1$ fails.

---

[5] In Definition 5 the 'point-wise' definition is needed, as group consistency is local.

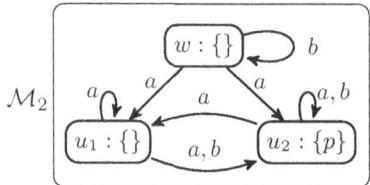
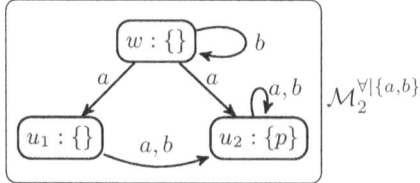

Note how a loses negative introspection: after cautious belief resolution a does not believe p, yet she believes that she believes it ($\mathcal{M}_2^{\forall|\{a,b\}}, w \vDash \neg B_a p \wedge B_a B_a p$).

Then, consider the serial, transitive and Euclidean model $\mathcal{M}_3$ (below left). Its cautious $\{a, b, c\}$-resolved update $\mathcal{M}_3^{\forall|\{a,b,c\}}$ (below right) is not transitive (neither Euclidean): both $R_a w u_1$ and $R_a u_1 u_2$ hold, and yet $R_a w u_2$ fails ($R_a u_1 u_2$ and $R_a u_1 u_1$ hold, yet $R_a u_2 u_1$ fails).

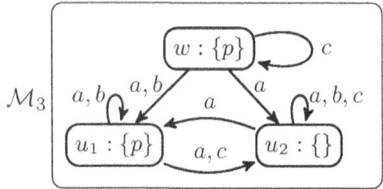
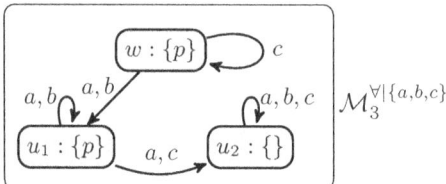

Note how a loses positive (and negative) introspection: after cautious communication a believes p, but does not believe that she believes it ($\mathcal{M}_3^{\forall|\{a,b,c\}}, w \vDash B_a p \wedge \neg B_a B_a p$).   ◀

3.2 Patching Cautious Belief Resolution

While cautious resolution preserves seriality (consistency), it fails to preserve the other properties for a relation representing beliefs, namely transitivity (positive introspection) and Euclidicity (negative introspection). To deal with this, one can look at the natural ways for a relation to (re)gain these properties: the transitive and Euclidean closures (i.e., the smallest transitive/Euclidean relation that contains the original). Note how this idea does not work for the issue of not preserving seriality: there is not such a thing as 'the serial closure' because, in general, there is no single smallest serial relation containing the original.

Definition 6 (Closure operations). Let $R \subseteq W \times W$ be a binary relation.

- Its transitive closure, $R^+ \subseteq W \times W$, is defined as

$$R^+ := \bigcup_{n \geq 1} R^n \qquad \text{with} \begin{cases} R^1 := R \\ R^{k+1} := R^k \circ R \end{cases}$$

for $\circ$ the relational composition. It is well-known that R^+ is *the* smallest transitive relation containing R.

- Its Euclidean closure, $R^E \subseteq W \times W$, is defined as

$$R^E := R \cup (\bar{\mathfrak{K}} \circ (R \cup \mathfrak{K})^* \circ R) \qquad \text{with} \begin{cases} R^* := \{(w,w) \mid w \in W\} \cup R^+ \\ \mathfrak{K} := \{(v,w) \mid Rwv\} \end{cases}$$

As proved in [14, Lemma 3.1], R^E is indeed *the* smallest Euclidean relation containing R.

For a model $\mathcal{M}$, use $\mathcal{M}^+$ and $\mathcal{M}^E$ to denote, respectively, its transitive and Euclidean closure (the model resulting from applying transitive/Euclidean closure to every R_i in it). ◀

There are some aspects to consider before using these operations. First, both closures are needed. On the one hand, transitive closure alone is not enough: there are models (e.g., $\mathcal{M}_2|_{\{a,b\}}^{\forall}$ in Example 2) that are transitive (so, transitive closure will not modify anything) but not Euclidean. On the other hand, Euclidean closure alone is not enough: there are models (e.g., the Euclidean closure of $\mathcal{M}_3^{\forall|\{a,b,c\}}$ in Example 2, shown below) that are Euclidean (so, Euclidean closure will not modify anything) but not transitive.

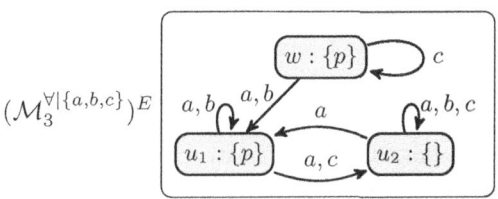

Second, the order in which the closures are applied matters for the preservation of both properties, as Euclidean closure does not preserve transitivity. The model $\mathcal{M}_4$ (below on the left) is transitive but not Euclidean (e.g., Rwu and Rww hold, yet Ruw fails); yet, while its Euclidean closure (below on the right) is Euclidean, it is not transitive ($R^E vu$ and $R^E uw$ hold, yet $R^E vw$ fails).

Still, as it is shown below, transitive closure preserves Euclidicity.

Proposition 2. *Let $R \subseteq W \times W$ be a binary relation. If R is Euclidean, so is R^+.*

Proof. Assume R is Euclidean. Take any $w, u_1, u_2 \in W$ with $R^+ w u_1$ and $R^+ w u_2$. By the construction of R^+, while the first implies there are $n \geq 1$ and $\{x_i \mid 1 \leq i \leq n\}$ such that Rwx_1, $Rx_i x_{i+1}$ for $i \in [1 .. n-1]$ and $x_n = u_1$, the second implies there are $m \geq 1$ and $\{y_i \mid 1 \leq i \leq m\}$ such that Rwy_1, $Ry_i y_{i+1}$ for $i \in [1 .. m-1]$ and $y_m = u_2$. It will be shown that $Ru_1 u_2$, which implies the required $R^+ u_1 u_2$. The fact that $Rx_n y_m$ and $Ry_m x_n$ is shown by induction on the length of $n + m$. For the base case $(n + m = 2)$, Rwx_1 and Rwy_1. By R's Euclidicity, Rwx_1 and Rwy_1 imply Rx_1y_1 and Ry_1x_1. Without loss of generality, assume $n > 2$, and assume as inductive hypothesis (for $n - 1 + m$) that $Rx_{n-1}y_m$ and Ry_mx_{n-1}. Then, since $Rx_{n-1}x_n$ and by the Euclidicity of R, Rx_ny_m and Ry_mx_n. Thus Ru_1u_2. ∎

This leads to the following 'patched' cautious belief G-resolution.

Definition 7 (Patched cautious belief G-resolution). Let $\mathcal{M} = \langle W, \{R_i \mid i \in A\}, V\rangle$ be a model; take $G \subseteq A$. The *patched cautious G-resolved update* of $\mathcal{M}$ is the model $\mathcal{M}^{\forall \odot | G} = \langle W, \{R_i^{\forall \odot | G} \mid i \in A\}, V\rangle$ where each $R_i^{\forall \odot | G}$ is given by

$$R_i^{\forall \odot | G} := ((R_i^{\forall | G})^E)^+$$

with $R_i^{\forall | G}$ as in Definition 5. ◀

This new operation preserves the three belief relational properties.

Proposition 3. *If $\mathcal{M}$ is a serial, transitive and Euclidean model, then so is $\mathcal{M}^{\forall \odot | G}$.*

Proof. Each relation in $\mathcal{M}^{\forall \odot | G}$ is given by $R_i^{\forall \odot | G} := ((R_i^{\forall | G})^E)^+$. For seriality recall that, if $\mathcal{M}$ is serial, so is $R_i^{\forall | G}$ Proposition 1. Hence, so are $(R_i^{\forall | G})^E$ and then $((R_i^{\forall | G})^E)^+$, as the operations do not erase edges (and the domain does not change). Transitivity follows from the construction's last step, transitive closure. For Euclidicity, $(R_i^{\forall | G})^E$ is Euclidean, and thus Proposition 2 so is $((R_i^{\forall | G})^E)^+$. ∎

Properties of Patched Cautious Belief Resolution. The just defined operation preserves the relational properties of belief (and thus preserves consistent as well as positively and negatively introspective agents). Now let's look at its effects. This is useful/important as, while the first step in the model construction process can only remove edges (so the agent can lose uncertainty), both Euclidean and transitive closure might add them (so the agent can gain uncertainty).

First, there are belief cases in which the edges added by the closure operations still leave the agent with new information.

Example 3. Consider the serial, transitive and Euclidean model $\mathcal{M}_5$ below on the left. In w, agent a considers u_3 (where p and q are both true), u_1 (p is true and q false) and u_2 (both p and q are false). Thus, a is uncertain about both atoms: $\mathcal{M}_5, w \vDash (\neg B_a\, p \wedge \neg B_a\, \neg p) \wedge (\neg B_a\, q \wedge \neg B_a\, \neg q)$. Yet, b considers only u_1 (so $\mathcal{M}_5, w \vDash B_b\, p \wedge B_b\, \neg q$)) and c considers only u_3 (so $\mathcal{M}_5, w \vDash B_c\, p \wedge B_c\, q$)). Thus, a is consistent with both b and c, but b and c are mutually inconsistent.

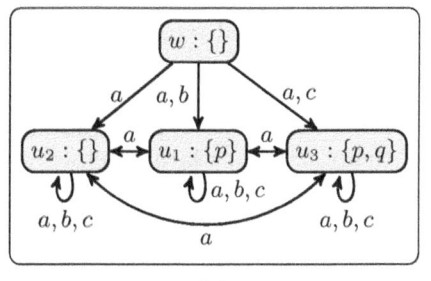

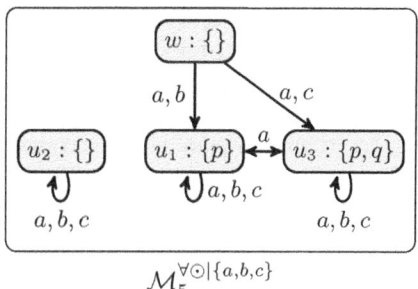

$$\mathcal{M}_5 \qquad\qquad \mathcal{M}_5^{\forall\odot|\{a,b,c\}}$$

In the patched cautious resolved update $\mathcal{M}_5^{\forall\odot|\{a,b,c\}}$ (above right), the worlds a considers from w are now $\{u_1, u_3\}$. Hence, a now believes p, but maintains uncertainty about q: in symbols, $\mathcal{M}_5^{\forall\odot|\{a,b,c\}}, w \models B_a\, p \wedge (\neg B_a\, q \wedge \neg B_a\, \neg q)$. ◄

Then, there are cases in which the additional work the closure operations makes an agent 'forget'/'ignore' the information she received.

Example 4. Consider the non-Euclidean model $\mathcal{M}_2^{\forall|\{a,b\}}$ below on the left, which resulted from applying cautious belief resolution to $\mathcal{M}_2$ (both from Example 2). Completing the patched cautious G-resolved update yields $\mathcal{M}_2^{\forall\odot|\{a,b\}}$ below on the right, which is identical to the original $\mathcal{M}_2$.

$$\mathcal{M}_2^{\forall|\{a,b\}}$$ 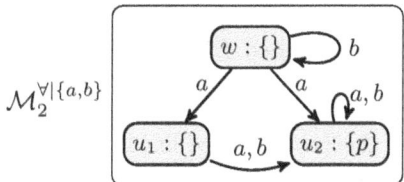 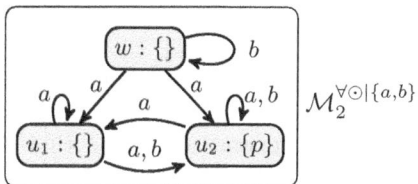 $$\mathcal{M}_2^{\forall\odot|\{a,b\}}$$

The same happens when the patched cautious $\{a, b, c\}$-resolved update is applied to $\mathcal{M}_3$ (again, in Example 2): $\mathcal{M}_3$ and $\mathcal{M}_3^{\forall\odot|\{a,b,c\}}$ are the same. ◄

On arbitrary models, the patched operation can clearly add brand new edges. Still, when working with Euclidean and transitive relations, 'no learning' is this operation's 'worst' possible scenario: the agent might not learn anything new, but she will not forget either. In relational terms, the agent will not have, after the operation, more uncertainty than what she initially had.

Proposition 4. *Let $\mathcal{M}$ be a transitive and Euclidean model; take $i \in A$ and $G \subseteq A$. Then, $R_i^{\forall\odot|G} \subseteq R_i$.*

Proof. The case for $i \notin G$ is trivial. For the interesting one, take $i \in G$. Then, $R_i^{\forall|G} \subseteq R_i$. In the rest, use $S = R_i$, $S' = R_i^{\forall|G}$, $S'^E = (R_i^{\forall|G})^E$ and $S'^{E+} = ((R_i^{\forall|G})^E)^+$. First, it will be shown that $S'^E \setminus S' \subseteq S$: any edge in S'^E but not in S' should have been in the original S. So, take any $(u_1, u_2) \in S'^E \setminus S'$; by definition, $(u_1, u_2) \in (\breve{S} \circ (S' \cup \breve{S})^* \circ S')$. Then, there are $n \geq 0$ and $\{x_k \mid 0 \leq k \leq n\}$ such that $S'x_0u_1$, $S'x_nu_2$, and $S'x_kx_{k+1}$ or $S'x_{k+1}x_k$ for $k \in [0 .. n-1]$.

Since $S' \subseteq S$, the $n \geq 0$ and $\{x_k \mid 0 \leq k \leq n\}$ are such that Sx_0u_1, Sx_nu_2, and Sx_kx_{k+1} or $Sx_{k+1}x_k$ for $k \in [0..n-1]$. Now, note how Sx_ku_1 for every $k \in [0..n]$. The base case of this is the given Sx_0u_1. For the inductive case, suppose Sx_ku_1 for $k < n$ (so x_{k+1} exists). If Sx_kx_{k+1} then $Sx_{k+1}u_1$ as S is Euclidean; if $Sx_{k+1}x_k$ then $Sx_{k+1}u_1$ as S is transitive. Hence, Sx_nu_1, which together with Sx_nu_2 imply Su_1u_2, as S is Euclidean. Thus, $S'^E \setminus S' \subseteq S$; from which $S'^E \subseteq S$ follows. Now, it will be shown that $S'^{E+} \setminus S'^E \subseteq S$: any edge in S'^{E+} but not in S'^E should have been in the original S. So, take any $(u, u') \in S'^{E+} \setminus S'^E$. By definition, there are $m \geq 1$ and $\{y_k \mid 1 \leq k \leq m\}$ such that $S'^E uy_1$, $S'^E y_ky_{k+1}$ for $k \in [1..m-1]$, and $y_m = u'$. Since $S'^E \subseteq S$, the $m \geq 1$ and $\{y_k \mid 1 \leq k \leq m\}$ are such that Suy_1, Sy_ky_{k+1} for $k \in [1..m-1]$, and $y_m = u'$. Then, Suu' as S is transitive. Thus, $S'^{E+} \setminus S'^E \subseteq S$, from which $S'^{E+} \subseteq S$ follows. This is the required $((R_i^{\forall \mid G})^E)^+ \subseteq R_i$. ∎

Finally, it can be shown that this operation generalises the knowledge case of [1] (Definition 3).

Proposition 5. *Let $\mathcal{M}$ be a reflexive, transitive and Euclidean model; take $i \in A$ and $G \subseteq A$. Then, $R_i^{\forall \odot \mid G} = R_i^G$.* ∎

4   Conclusions and Further Work

This text has discussed, within the relational-model-based *EL* and *DEL* frameworks, communication actions through which some agents share their information with some others. When the information is taken to be knowledge, there is a straightforward operation that preserves the properties of knowledge (the resolution of [1]). However, as it has been observed in the literature, the same strategy does not work when information is taken to be beliefs: consistent beliefs might be turned into inconsistent ones. Using the idea of maximally consistent subgroups of agents, this manuscript has proposed a *cautious belief resolution*, through which an agent updates her information only when it comes from *every* maximally consistent subset she belonged to. Still, while this operation does not create inconsistent agents (technically: it preserves seriality), it might turn introspective agents into non-introspective ones (technically: it does not preserve transitivity and Euclidicity). A further operation, *patched cautious belief resolution*, solves this, as it preserves the three properties typically required for a relational structure representing beliefs, while being also a generalisation of the original knowledge resolution. As it has been shown, while through this action an agent might 'forget'/'ignore' the information she is receiving, she will not forget information that she had before.

There are still several questions to answer. Some of them concern the two defined operations: once a modality is added for describing their effects (as $\mathbf{R}_G$ from Definition 3 does for knowledge resolution), one can look for an axiomatisation of the resulting languages, and also investigate whether the added 'dynamic' modality increases the respective languages' expressivity. One can also look at more general scenarios, such as those in which there is some form of 'priority' on the doxastic relations to be merged (see, e.g., [3,30]). Depending on the properties of this 'priority' (capturing expertise/reputation), one might still need to combine potentially conflicting equally important information, but there will be cases in which priority would simplify the work.

Finally, one can also wonder about whether the standard 'intersection approach', which works properly in the knowledge case, is doing everything one wants in the beliefs scenario. If the goal of the action is only to combine the shared information (while preserving the 'essential' properties of the concept under discussion), the proposed patched cautious belief resolution does the job. However, to maintain belief properties, conflicting information is ignored (by using only maximal consistency), and so is information that would break positive and negative introspection (through the patching). As a consequence, agents might not learn everything they can learn from the action: when a receives information from b, she can not only incorporate b's information to her own, but also learn what b's information was. Thus, to capture fully the effects of these belief communication acts, additional ways of capturing higher-order belief sharing will be needed.

References

1. Ågotnes, T., Wáng, Y.N.: Resolving distributed knowledge. Artif. Intell. **252**, 1–21 (2017). https://doi.org/10.1016/j.artint.2017.07.002
2. Ågotnes, T., Wáng, Y.N.: Group belief. J. Log. Comput. **31**(8), 1959–1978 (2021). https://doi.org/10.1093/logcom/exaa068
3. Andréka, H., Ryan, M.D., Schobbens, P.Y.: Operators and laws for combining preference relations. J. Log. Comput. **12**(1), 13–53 (2002). https://doi.org/10.1093/logcom/12.1.13
4. Balbiani, P., van Ditmarsch, H., Herzig, A., de Lima, T.: Some truths are best left unsaid. In: Bolander, T., Braüner, T., Ghilardi, S., Moss, L. (eds.) Advances in Modal Logic (AiML 2012), Copenhagen, 22–25 Aug 2012, vol. 9, pp. 36–54. College Publications (2012). http://www.irit.fr/~Andreas.Herzig/P/Aiml12.html
5. Baltag, A.: What is del good for? (2010). http://ai.stanford.edu/~epacuit/lograt/esslli2010-slides/copenhagenesslli.pdf. Workshop on Logic, Rationality and Intelligent Interaction
6. Baltag, A., Moss, L.S., Solecki, S.: The logic of public announcements, common knowledge, and private suspicions. In: Proceedings of the 7th Conference on Theoretical Aspects of Rationality and Knowledge, TARK 1998, pp. 43–56. Morgan Kaufmann Publishers Inc., San Francisco (1998)
7. Baltag, A., Smets, S.: Learning what others know. In: Albert, E., Kovács, L. (eds.) LPAR 2020. EPiC Series in Computing, vol. 73, pp. 90–119. EasyChair (2020). https://doi.org/10.29007/plm4
8. van Benthem, J.: Logical Dynamics of Information and Interaction. Cambridge University Press (2011)
9. van Benthem, J., Pacuit, E.: Dynamic logics of evidence-based beliefs. Stud. Log. **99**(1), 61–92 (2011). https://doi.org/10.1007/s11225-011-9347-x
10. Brandt, F., Conitzer, V., Endriss, U., Lang, J., Procaccia, A.D. (eds.): Handbook of Computational Social Choice. Cambridge University Press, USA (2016)

11. van Ditmarsch, H., van der Hoek, W., Kooi, B.: Dynamic Epistemic Logic. Springer, Dordrecht (2007)
12. Dung, P.M.: On the acceptability of arguments and its fundamental role in non-monotonic reasoning, logic programming and n-person games. Artif. Intell. **77**(2), 321–358 (1995). https://doi.org/10.1016/0004-3702(94)00041-X
13. Fagin, R., Halpern, J.Y., Moses, Y., Vardi, M.Y.: Reasoning About Knowledge. The MIT Press, Cambridge (1995)
14. Fervari, R., Velázquez-Quesada, F.R.: Introspection as an action in relational models. J. Log. Algebraic Methods Program. **108**, 1–23 (2019). https://doi.org/10.1016/j.jlamp.2019.06.005
15. Galimullin, R., Velázquez-Quesada, F.R.: Topic-based communication between agents. Stud. Log. (2024). https://doi.org/10.1007/s11225-024-10119-z
16. Gerbrandy, J., Groeneveld, W.: Reasoning about information change. J. Log. Lang. Inform. **6**(2), 147–169 (1997). https://doi.org/10.1023/A:1008222603071
17. Grossi, D., Pigozzi, G.: Judgment Aggregation: A Primer. No. 27 in Synthesis Lectures on Artificial Intelligence and Machine Learning. Morgan & Claypool Publishers (2014). https://doi.org/10.2200/S00559ED1V01Y201312AIM027
18. Halpern, J.Y., Moses, Y.: A guide to the modal logics of knowledge and belief: preliminary draft. In: Joshi, A.K. (ed.) Proceedings of the 9th International Joint Conference on Artificial Intelligence, Los Angeles, CA, USA, pp. 480–490. Morgan Kaufmann (1985). http://ijcai.org/Proceedings/85-1/Papers/094.pdf
19. Halpern, J.Y., Moses, Y.: Knowledge and common knowledge in a distributed environment. J. ACM **37**(3), 549–587 (1990). https://doi.org/10.1145/79147.79161
20. Herzig, A., Lorini, E., Perrotin, E., Romero, F., Schwarzentruber, F.: A logic of explicit and implicit distributed belief. In: ECAI 2020 - 24th European Conference on Artificial Intelligence. Frontiers in Artificial Intelligence and Applications, vol. 325, pp. 753–760. IOS Press (2020). https://doi.org/10.3233/FAIA200163
21. Hilpinen, R.: Remarks on personal and impersonal knowledge. Can. J. Philos. **7**(1), 1–9 (1977). https://doi.org/10.1080/00455091.1977.10716173
22. Hintikka, J.: Knowledge and Belief: An Introduction to the Logic of the Two Notions. Cornell University Press, Ithaca (1962)
23. Konieczny, S., Pino Pérez, R.: Propositional belief base merging or how to merge beliefs/goals coming from several sources and some links with social choice theory. Eur. J. Oper. Res. **160**(3), 785–802 (2005)
24. Konieczny, S., Pino Pérez, R.: Logic based merging. J. Philos. Log. **40**(2), 239–270 (2011). https://doi.org/10.1007/s10992-011-9175-5
25. Lindqvist, J., Velázquez-Quesada, F.R., Ågotnes, T.: Cautious distributed belief. In: Areces, C., Costa, D. (eds) DaLí 2022. LNCS, vol. 13780, pp. 106–124. Springer, Heidelberg (2023). https://doi.org/10.1007/978-3-031-26622-5_7
26. List, C., Polak, B.: Introduction to judgment aggregation. J. Econ. Theory **145**(2), 441–466 (2010). https://doi.org/10.1016/j.jet.2010.02.001
27. Plaza, J.A.: Logics of public communications. In: Emrich, M.L., Pfeifer, M.S., Hadzikadic, M., Ras, Z.W. (eds.) Proceedings of the 4th International Symposium on Methodologies for Intelligent Systems, pp. 201–216. Oak Ridge National Laboratory, ORNL/DSRD-24, Tennessee (1989)
28. Reiter, R.: A logic for default reasoning. Artif. Intell. **13**(1–2), 81–132 (1980). https://doi.org/10.1016/0004-3702(80)90014-4
29. Steiner, D.: A system for consistency preserving belief change. In: Artemov, Sergei; Parikh, R. (ed.) Proceedings of Workshop on Rationality and Knowledge. 18th European Summer School of Logic, Language and Information, pp. 133–144 (2006)

30. Velázquez-Quesada, F.R.: Reliability-based preference dynamics: lexicographic upgrade. J. Log. Comput. **27**(8), 2341–2381 (2017). https://doi.org/10.1093/logcom/exx019
31. Velázquez-Quesada, F.R.: Communication between agents in dynamic epistemic logic. arXiv CoRR abs/2210.04656 (2022). https://doi.org/10.48550/arXiv.2210.04656

A New Fuzzy Approach to Transition and Bisimulation Systems

Benjamin Bedregal[1]([✉])[iD] and Claudio Callejas[2][iD]

[1] Universidade Federal do Rio Grande do Norte, Natal, RN 59078-970, Brazil
`bedregal@dimap.ufrn.br`
[2] Universidade Federal Rural do Semi-Árido, Pau dos Ferros, RN 59900-000, Brazil
`claudio.callejas@ufersa.edu.br`
`http://www.dimap.ufrn.br/, https://detec.ufersa.edu.br/`

Abstract. Just as there are many non-equivalent structures called transition systems, there are also different notions of fuzzy transition systems. However, the idea is the same: generalize a notion of transition by considering at least the fuzziness in transitions. In this paper we propose a fuzzy version of transition systems with a set of initial and final states. Concepts such as tracking, accessibility and bisimulation are also introduced.

Keywords: Transition systems · Fuzzy transition systems · α-cuts · α-Bisimulation

1 Introduction

Transition systems are a simple notion consisting of a set of states and a transition relation between states which are useful in theoretical computer science to describe the potential behaviour of discrete systems. When they were introduced by Edmund Lien in [6] and besides states and transition relations they considered an initial state. There are currently several variants of the original concept that are also termed "transition systems": some do not include an initial state (as in [15]), some require a set of initial states (e.g. [20]), other approaches considered labels in the transitions (cf. [14]) and in [8] they incorporate both a set of initial states as well as a set of final states.

A bisimulation in theoretical computer science is a binary relation between transition systems that associates those that perform the same action [2]. The bisimulation for several structures, such as unlabeled directed graphs, Kripke structures, labeled transition systems, etc. have been defined and investigated in [16,18].

On the other hand, Lotfi Zadeh, the founder of fuzzy logic, observed that in everyday life people naturally deal with expressions such as "warm temperature", "low inflation", "elderly", "around 5 kilos", etc. In a fuzzy set each objects of the discourse universe belong to the set with some degree in the interval $[0,1]$ in

J. Proença et al. (Eds.): SEFM 2024, LNCS 15551, pp. 92–98, 2026.
https://doi.org/10.1007/978-3-031-94748-3_7

contrast to classical set theory in which there are only two possibilities: an object belongs (1) to a set or it does not (0).

Since the appearance of fuzzy set theory, several mathematical concepts, structures and theories have been "fuzzyfied", as for example, the concepts of real numbers, partial orders, metrics, entropy, etc., and several algebraic structures and theories like graph, category, computability, topology, chaos, etc. [12,13, 19]. In particular, several notions of transition systems also were fuzzyfied, as for example in [2,5,7,17,21]. The common characteristic between versions of fuzzy transition systems is the underlying fuzzy transition, that is, the set of transitions is fuzzy. Nevertheless, none of those notions of transition systems considers fuzziness in the initial and final sates of the transition systems as proposed here.

The rest of the paper is organized as follows: Sect. 2 fixes some notation and concepts. In Sect. 3 we propose a notion of fuzzy transition system as well as the notions of trace, reachability and bisimulation. Section 4 provides some final remarks.

2   Fuzzy Transition Systems

First, recall that a fuzzy set A on a set X is a function $A : X \to [0,1]$, A is called crisp if $A(x) \in \{0,1\}$ for each $x \in X$, and the α-cut of A for a given $\alpha \in (0,1]$ is the set $A^{[\alpha]} = \{x \in X \mid A(x) \geq \alpha\}$.

Based on the notion of Transition System by John Lygeros [8], a new notion of Fuzzy Transition System and some related concepts are introduced in this section.

Definition 1. *A Fuzzy Transition System, FTS in short, is a quadruple $\mathcal{T} = \langle S, \varrho, \mathcal{S}_0, \mathcal{S}_F \rangle$ where S is a nonempty set of states, $\varrho \in \mathfrak{F}(S \times S)$ is the fuzzy transition relation, $\mathcal{S}_0 \in \mathfrak{F}(S)$ the fuzzy set of initial states; and $\mathcal{S}_F \in \mathfrak{F}(S)$ the fuzzy set of final states.*

Each FTS $\mathcal{T} = \langle S, \varrho, \mathcal{S}_0, \mathcal{S}_F \rangle$ where $\mathcal{S}_0$ and $\mathcal{S}_F$ are crisp sets, and $\varrho(s,t) \in \{0,1\}$ for each $s,t \in S$, is called a crisp transition system because it is equivalent to a transition system as defined by Lygeros.

Proposition 1. *Let $\alpha \in (0,1]$ and a FTS $\mathcal{T} = \langle S, \varrho, \mathcal{S}_0, \mathcal{S}_F \rangle$. Then $\mathcal{T}^{[\alpha]} = \langle S, \varrho^{[\alpha]}, \mathcal{S}_0^{[\alpha]}, \mathcal{S}_F^{[\alpha]} \rangle$ where $\varrho^{[\alpha]} : S \to \wp(S)$ defined by $\varrho^{[\alpha]}(s) = \{t \in S \mid \varrho(s,t) \geq \alpha\}$, is a transition system. $\mathcal{T}^{[\alpha]}$ is called the alpha-cut of $\mathcal{T}$.*

Example 1. *Let the FTS $\mathcal{T} = \langle S, \varrho, \mathcal{S}_0, \mathcal{S}_F \rangle$ where $S = \{s_0, \ldots, s_5\}$, $\mathcal{S}_0(s_0) = \mathcal{S}_F(s_5) = 0.8$, $\mathcal{S}_F(s_2) = 0.6$, $\mathcal{S}_0(s_2) = \mathcal{S}_F(s_4) = 0.2$, and the remaining cases are 0. The fuzzy transition relation ϱ is illustrated in Table 1(a). Empty positions indicate that the membership of the respectives pairs of states is 0. Observe that s_4 is a useless state in $\mathcal{T}^{[0.6]}$.*

The interpretation of the membership degree of an edge from a state s to a state t is similar to the given in fuzzy digraphs [4,12], i.e. when the current

Table 1. Fuzzy transition relations ϱ of Example 1 and $\widehat{\varrho}$ generated from ϱ and partition $\{S_0, S_1, S_2, S_3\}$

ϱ	s_0	s_1	s_2	s_3	s_4	s_5
s_0		0.6	0.8			
s_1	0.8			0.7	0.5	
s_2	0.7			0.3	0.5	
s_3						0.9
s_4						0.9
s_5				0.4	0.4	0.9

(a)

$\widehat{\varrho}$	S_0	S_1	S_2	S_3
S_0		0.6	0.8	
S_1	0.8	0.7		0.9
S_2	0.7	0.3		0.5
S_3		0.4		0.9

(b)

state is s, the possibility (not probability) to change for the state t is $\varrho(s,t)$. On the other hand, the meaning of $\mathcal{S}_0(s)$ and $\mathcal{S}_F(s)$ is similar to the given in fuzzy automata and variants [3,11], i.e. the degree of possibility that s is an initial state and a final state, respectively.

Let $\alpha \in (0,1]$. A finite α-trajectory (also called trace) of an FTS $\mathcal{T}$ is a finite sequence of states $(t_i)_{i=0}^n$ of S, such that $\mathcal{S}_0(t_0) \geq \alpha$ and $\varrho(t_i, t_{i+1}) > 0$ for each $i = 0, \ldots, n-1$ and a countable trajectory of $\mathcal{T}$ is a sequence of states $(t_i)_{i \in \mathbb{N}}$ of S, such that $\mathcal{S}_0(t_0) \geq \alpha$ and $\varrho(t_i, t_{i+1}) > 0$ for each $i \in \mathbb{N}$. For the sake of simplicity, we will use $(t_i)_{i \in I}$ for both cases, $(t_i)_{i=0}^n$ and $(t_i)_{i \in \mathbb{N}}$. Furthermore, we denote by I^- the set $\{0, \ldots, n-1\}$ in the first case and I in the second one. For example, in the case of the FTS $\mathcal{T}$ from Example 1, the sequence $(s_0, s_1, s_0, s_2, s_3, s_5, s_5, s_3)$ is a finite α-trajectory for any $\alpha \leq 0.8$ and the sequence $(s_2, s_3, s_5, s_3, s_5, \ldots, s_3, s_5, \ldots)$ is an enumerable α-trajectory for any $\alpha \leq 0.2$.

Proposition 2. *Let* $\mathcal{T} = \langle S, \varrho, \mathcal{S}_0, \mathcal{S}_F \rangle$ *be an FTS and* $\widehat{S} = \{S_j \subseteq S \mid j \in J\}$ *be a partition of* S. *Then,* $\widehat{\mathcal{T}} = \langle \widehat{S}, \widehat{\varrho}, \widehat{\mathcal{S}_0}, \widehat{\mathcal{S}_F} \rangle$ *such that* $\widehat{\varrho}(S_j, S_k) = \sup\limits_{(s,t) \in S_j \times S_k} \varrho(s,t)$, $\widehat{\mathcal{S}_0}(S_j) = \sup\limits_{s \in S_j} \mathcal{S}_0(s)$, *and* $\widehat{\mathcal{S}_F}(S_j) = \sup\limits_{s \in S_j} \mathcal{S}_F(s)$, *is also an FTS. Furthermore, if* $(t_i)_{i \in I}$ *is an* α-trajectory of $\mathcal{T}$ for some $\alpha \in (0,1]$ then there is a unique α-trajectory $(T_i)_{i \in I}$ in $\widehat{\mathcal{T}}$ such that $t_i \in T_i$ for each $i \in I$.*

Example 2. *Let* $\mathcal{T}$ *be the FTS from Example 1 and the partition* $\widehat{S} = \{S_0, S_1, S_2, S_3\} = \{\{s_0\}, \{s_1, s_3\}, \{s_2\}, \{s_4, s_5\}\}$ *of* S. *Then, the FTS generated from* $(\mathcal{T}, \widehat{S})$ *is* $\widehat{\mathcal{T}} = \langle \widehat{S}, \widehat{\varrho}, \widehat{\mathcal{S}_0}, \widehat{\mathcal{S}_F} \rangle$, *where* $\widehat{S} = \{S_0, S_1, S_2, S_3\}$; $\widehat{\varrho}$ *is defined in Table 1(b);* $\widehat{\mathcal{S}_0}(S_0) = 0.8$, $\widehat{\mathcal{S}_0}(S_1) = 0$, $\widehat{\mathcal{S}_0}(S_2) = 0.2$ *and* $\widehat{\mathcal{S}_0}(S_3) = 0$; *and* $\widehat{\mathcal{S}_F}(S_0) = 0$, $\widehat{\mathcal{S}_F}(S_1) = 0$, $\widehat{\mathcal{S}_F}(S_2) = 0.6$ *and* $\widehat{\mathcal{S}_F}(S_3) = 0.8$. *Observe that, since* $(s_0, s_1, s_0, s_2, s_3, s_5, s_5, s_3)$ *is an* α-trajectory in $\mathcal{T}$, for $\alpha \leq 0.8$, then by Proposition 2, $(S_0, S_1, S_0, S_2, S_1, S_3, S_3, S_1)$ *is an* α-trajectory of $\widehat{\mathcal{T}}$.

An important aspect of this technique is the possibility of obtaining a finite FTS from an infinite FTS.

Example 3. Let $\mathcal{T}_{\mathbb{R}} = \langle S, \varrho, S_0, S_F \rangle$ be the FTS where $S = \mathbb{R}$ and for each $s, t \in S$,

$$S_0(s) = \begin{cases} \frac{1}{-s} & \text{if } s \in \mathbb{Z}^- \\ 0.5 & \text{if } s = 0 \\ 0 & \text{otherwise} \end{cases} \qquad S_F(s) = \begin{cases} \frac{1}{4s} & \text{if } s \in \mathbb{Z}^+ \\ 1 & \text{if } s = 0 \\ 0 & \text{otherwise} \end{cases}$$

$$\varrho(s, t) = \begin{cases} \frac{1}{t-s} & \text{if } s < t \text{ and } s, t \in \mathbb{Z} \\ 0.7 & \text{if } s \in \mathbb{Z}, \ s \neq 0 \text{ and } t \in \mathbb{R} \setminus \mathbb{Z} \\ 0.3 & \text{if } s \in \mathbb{R} \setminus \mathbb{Z} \text{ and } t \neq 0 \\ 0 & \text{otherwise} \end{cases}$$

Let $S_1 = \mathbb{Z}^-$, $S_2 = \{0\}$, $S_3 = \mathbb{Z}^+$ and $S_4 = \mathbb{R} \setminus \mathbb{Z}$. Then, $\widehat{S} = \{S_1, S_2, S_3, S_4\}$ is a partition of S. So, $\widehat{\mathcal{T}} = \langle \widehat{S}, \widehat{\varrho}, \widehat{S_0}, \widehat{S_F} \rangle$, where

$$\widehat{S_0}(T) = \begin{cases} 1 & \text{if } T = S_1 \\ 0.5 & \text{if } T = S_2 \\ 0 & \text{otherwise} \end{cases} \qquad \widehat{S_F}(T) = \begin{cases} 0.25 & \text{if } T = S_3 \\ 1 & \text{if } T = S_2 \\ 0 & \text{otherwise} \end{cases}$$

$$\widehat{\varrho}(S, T) = \begin{cases} 1 & \text{if } (S, T) \in \{(S_1, S_1), (S_1, S_2), (S_2, S_3), (S_3, S_3)\} \\ 0.7 & \text{if } (S, T) \in \{(S_1, S_4), (S_3, S_4)\} \\ 0.5 & \text{if } S = S_1 \text{ and } T = S_3 \\ 0.3 & \text{if } S = S_4 \text{ and } T \neq S_2 \\ 0 & \text{otherwise} \end{cases}$$

2.1 (α, β)-Reachable Fuzzy Transition Systems

Let $\alpha, \beta \in (0, 1]$ and let $\mathcal{T} = \langle S, \varrho, S_0, S_F \rangle$ be an FTS. S_F is (α, β)-reachable in $\mathcal{T}$ if there is a finite α-trajectory $(t_i)_{i \in I}$ such that $S_F(t_i) \geq \beta$ for some $i \in I$. First define the predecessor operator for $\mathcal{T}$ as the map $Pred : \wp(S) \to \wp(S)$ such that $Pred(X) = \{s \in S \mid \varrho(s, t) > 0 \text{ for some } t \in X\}$ for each $X \in \wp(S)$.

Algorithm 1 determines the (α, β)-reachability of an FTS.

2.2 Bisimulation for Fuzzy Transition Systems

Bisimulation techniques were introduced in [9] as a tool to determine behavioural equivalences between concurrent processes. Since then, the bisimulation of several structures, like event systems, Petri nets, state machines, etc. have been investigated as well as different versions of fuzzy transition systems [17]. Bisimulation, in the context of fuzzy transition systems, establish a way to reduce the states of an FTS preserving some aspects of their behaviours. The main difference of the following bisimulation for FTS is that it considers the α-cuts of the initial and final fuzzy sets.

Definition 2. Let $\mathcal{T} = \langle S, \varrho, S_0, S_F \rangle$ be an FTS. A partition $\widehat{S} = \{S_j \subseteq S | j \in J\}$ of S is a bisimulation of $\mathcal{T}$ if for some $\alpha, \beta \in (0, 1]$, there is $K_0, K_F \subseteq J$ such that $S_0^{[\alpha]} = \bigcup_{k \in K_0} S_k$ and $S_F^{[\beta]} = \bigcup_{k \in K_F} S_k$; and for each $j, k \in J$ and $s, t \in S_j$ there is $v \in S_k$ such that $\varrho(t, v) > 0$ whenever there is $u \in S_k$ such that $\varrho(s, u) > 0$.

Algorithm 1. Algorithm to determine if an FTS is (α, β)-reachable.

Require: FTS $\mathcal{T} = \langle S, \varrho, \mathcal{S}_0, \mathcal{S}_F \rangle$
Ensure: (α, β)-reachability of $\mathcal{T}$
1: **if** $\mathcal{S}_F^{[\beta]} \cap \mathcal{S}_0^{[\alpha]} = \emptyset$ **then**
2:      $W_0 = \emptyset$, $W_1 = \mathcal{S}_F^{[\beta]}$, $i = 1$, $F =$"not (α, β)-reachable"
3:      **while** $W_i \not\subseteq W_{i-1}$ and $F =$"not (α, β)-reachable" **do**
4:          $i = i + 1$
5:          $W_i = W_{i-1} \cup Pred(W_{i-1})$
6:          **if** $W_i \cap \mathcal{S}_0^{[\alpha]} \neq \emptyset$ **then**
7:              $F =$"(α, β)-reachable"
8:          **end if**
9:      **end while**
10: **else**
11:      $F =$ "(α, β)-reachable"
12: **end if**
13: **return** F

Theorem 1. *Let $\alpha, \beta \in (0, 1]$, $\mathcal{T} = \langle S, \varrho, \mathcal{S}_0, \mathcal{S}_F \rangle$ be an FTS and $\widehat{S} = \{S_j \subseteq S \mid j \in J\}$ be a bisimulation of $\mathcal{T}$ and $\widehat{\mathcal{T}}$ the FTS construct in Proposition 2. Then,*

1. *If $\mathcal{S}_F$ is (α, β)-reachable in $\mathcal{T}$ then $\widehat{\mathcal{S}_F}$ is (α, β)-reachable in $\widehat{\mathcal{T}}$;*
2. *If $\widehat{\mathcal{S}_F}$ is (α, β)-reachable in $\widehat{\mathcal{T}}$ then $\mathcal{S}_F$ is (α', β')-reachable in $\mathcal{T}$ for some $0 < \alpha' \leq \alpha$ and $0 < \beta' \leq \beta$.*

3   Final Remarks

The proposed variant of FTS widens the potential use of other variants of fuzzy transition systems by incorporating a fuzzy set of initial and final states. Furthermore, various fuzzy dynamic systems, such as fuzzy Petri nets and fuzzy discrete event structures, are tools for obtaining formal descriptions of fuzzy systems that are not FTS, they can be translated into an FTS that represents their behavior [2]. In this way, the new elements of the FTS proposed in this article allow the FTS to be closer to fuzzy automata [11], fuzzy tree automata [10], fuzzy Petri nets for computing with words [1], among others, and in this way better preserve the original structure of this translation cited by Yongzhi Cao. Furthermore, the use of α-cuts of the fuzzy set of initial states in trajectories is new and offers greater possibilities for using this concept. This also applies to the concept of reachability, where the α-cut is also considered in the final states. Finally, a notion of bisimulation for FTS is given considering these α-cuts.

Acknowledgments. This work has been supported by the National Council for Scientific and Technological Development (CNPq-Brazil) within the project 311429/2020-3.

Disclosure of Interests. The authors have no competing interests to declare that are relevant to the content of this article.

A   Graphical Representations of Examples

An FTS $\mathcal{T}$ with finite S can be represented graphically, like a fuzzy automaton [11], in the following way: we draw a circle where we inscribe $(s, S_0(s), S_F(s))$. We omit $S_0(s)$ when $S_0(s) = 0$ and likewise for $S_F(s)$. If s is such that $S_0(s) > 0$, then we add an arrow incoming from the word "start"; in case $S_F(s) > 0$, we use a double circle. Finally, for each pair $(s, t) \in S \times S$ such that $\varrho(s, t) > 0$, an edge from s to t labeled with $\varrho(s, t)$ is added to the graphical representation (Figs. 1 and 2).

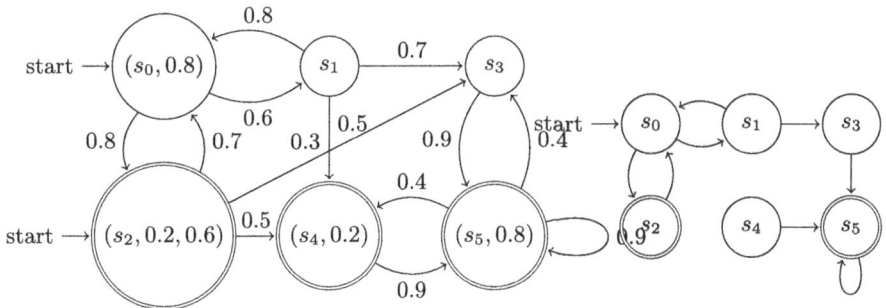

Fig. 1. Graphical representations of the FTS $\mathcal{T}$ and $\mathcal{T}^{[0.6]}$ from Example 1.

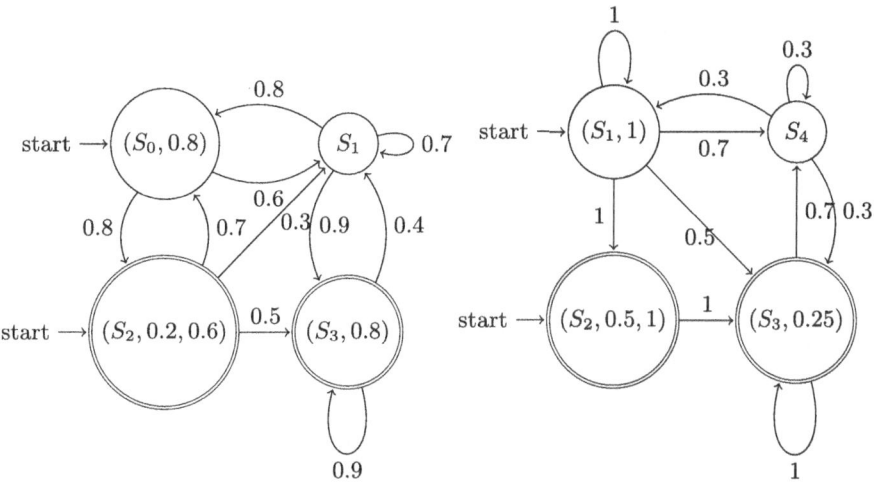

Fig. 2. Graphical representations of the FTS generated from Examples 2 and 3.

References

1. Cao, Y., Chen, G.: A fuzzy petri-nets model for computing with words. IEEE Trans. Fuzzy Syst. **18**(3), 486–499 (2010)
2. Cao, Y., Chen, G., Kerre, E.E.: Bisimulations for fuzzy-transition systems. IEEE Trans. Fuzzy Syst. **19**(3), 540–552 (2011)
3. Costa, V.S., Bedregal, B.C.: On typical hesitant fuzzy automata. Soft. Comput. **24**(12), 8725–8736 (2020). https://doi.org/10.1007/s00500-020-04896-7
4. Enriquez, E., Estrada, G., Loquias, C., Bacalcio, R.J., Ocampo, L.: Domination in fuzzy directed graphs. Mathematics **9**(17), 2143 (2021)
5. Jain, M., Madeira, A., Martins, M.A.: A fuzzy modal logic for fuzzy transition systems. Electron. Notes Theoret. Comput. Sci. **348**, 85–103 (2020)
6. Lien, Y.E.: A note on transition systems. Inf. Sci. **10**(2), 347–362 (1976)
7. Lizasoain, I., Gómez, M.: Products of lattice-valued fuzzy transition systems and induced fuzzy transformation semigroups. Fuzzy Sets Syst. **317**, 133–150 (2017)
8. Lygeros, J.: Lecture notes on hybrid systems. ENSIETA 2–6/2/2004, p. 82 (2004)
9. Milner, R.: A Calculus of Communicating Systems. In: Goos, G., Hartmanis, J., (eds.), Lecture Notes in Computer Science, vol. 92, p. 169 (1980)
10. Moghari, S.: Synthesizing fuzzy tree automata. RAIRO-Theor. Inf. Appl. **56**, 6 (2022)
11. Mordeson, J.N., Malik, D.S.: Fuzzy Automata and Languages: Theory and Applications. Chapman and Hall/CRC, New York (2002)
12. Mordeson, J., Nair, P.: Successor and source of (fuzzy) finite state machines and (fuzzy) directed graphs. Inf. Sci. **95**, 113–124 (1996)
13. Mordeson, J.; Nair, P.: Fuzzy Mathematics: An Introduction for Engineers and Scientists. Physica-Verlag (2010)
14. Nielsen, M.; Rozenberg, G., Thiagarajan, P.S.: Elementary Transition Systems. DAIMI PB, 310, p. 43 (1990)
15. Nygaard, M.; Schmidt, E.M. : Transition Systems: Algorithms and Data Structures. DAIMI FN., Del 64, p. 81 (2004)
16. Pous, D., Sangiorgi, D.: Bisimulation and coinduction enhancements: a historical perspective. Formal Aspects Comput. **12**, 1–17 (2019). https://doi.org/10.1007/s00165-019-00497-w
17. Qiao, S., Zhu, P., Pedrycz, W.: Approximate bisimulations for fuzzy-transition systems. Fuzzy Sets Syst. **472**, 108533 (2023)
18. Sangiorgi, D.: Origins of bisimulation and coinduction. In: Sangiorgi, D., Rutten, Jan J. M.M., (eds.), Advanced Topics in Bisimulation and Coinduction, Cambridge Tracts in Theoretical Computer Science, vol. 52, pp. 1–37, Cambridge University Press, Cambridge (2012)
19. Syropoulos, A., Grammenos, T.: A Modern Introduction to Fuzzy Mathematics. Wiley, Hoboken (2020)
20. Tripakis, S.: Formal System Modeling: Transition System. In System Specification, Verification and Synthesis (SSVS) – CS 4830/7485, Fall (2019)
21. Wu, H., Chen, T., Han, T., Chen, Y.: Bisimulations for fuzzy transition systems revisited. Int. J. Approx. Reason. **99**, 1–11 (2018)

Pivotal Rules Consequence in Action Model Logic

Valentin Cassano[1,2(✉)] and Sabine Frittella[3]

[1] Consejo Nacional de Investigaciones Científicas y Técnicas (CONICET),
Buenos Aires, Argentina
[2] Universidad Nacional de Río Cuarto (UNRC), Río Cuarto, Argentina
valentin@dc.exa.unrc.edu.ar
[3] Institut National des Sciences Appliquées Centre Val de Loire (INSA-CVL),
Bourges, France

Abstract. We take the internalization of the concept of Pivotal Rules Consequence (PRC) into Public Announcement Logic (PAL) in [2] and rework it into Action Model Logic (AML) [5]. PRC is introduced in [9] as a way of building a "bridge" from monotonic to nonmonotonic consequence using so called *pivotal rules*. Particularly interesting is how PRC leads gradually to consequence in Default Logic (DL) [11]. In [2], drawing inspiration from the dynamic take on consequence proposed in [3,4], it is shown how PRC can be captured into PAL [10] by encoding pivotal rules as announcements. Here we rework the ideas in [2] into AML by casting pivotal rules into action models. We consider action models provide a more accurate way of modeling the semantics of pivotal rules as standalone elements of PRC; therefore providing a better account of the dynamic effect of pivotal rules. More interesting, we consider the internalization of pivotal rules as action models to open the door to a way for thinking about agent-dependent pivotal rules, i.e., pivotal rules associated to individual agents. This would allow, for instance, to model exceptions to general rules but from the viewpoint of a particular agent rather than the global nature of exceptions to rules found in Default Logics.

Pivotal Rules Consequence. The operation Cn of consequence in Classical Propositional Logic (CPL) satisfies, among other familiar properties, *monotonicity*, i.e.: $\Phi \subseteq \Psi$ implies $\text{Cn}(\Phi) \subseteq \text{Cn}(\Psi)$. The concept of Pivotal Rules Consequence (PRC) introduced in [9] can briefly be understood as a consequence operation akin to Cn with the distinguishing characteristic that in addition to the rule of *modus ponens* it makes use of *pivotal rules* for drawing consequences. Pivotal rules capture general statements that are not necessarily obtained as derived rules of CPL. The argument put forth in [9] is that PRC naturally bridges the gap between monotonic and nonmonotonic consequence. In particular, it is shown how if we impose some "consistency" conditions on the use of pivotal rules we obtain a notion of consequence in Default Logic, one of the major topics in nonmonotonic reasoning [1,11]. Below, we make precise the concept of PRC and

J. Proença et al. (Eds.): SEFM 2024, LNCS 15551, pp. 99–104, 2026.
https://doi.org/10.1007/978-3-031-94748-3_8

its connection to consequence in Default Logic. Once this is done, we comment on how PRC can be thought of in the setting of AML [5].

We begin with Definition 1 where we introduce what we mean by a *pivotal rule*.

Definition 1. *Let* $\mathbf{F}_0$ *be the set of formulas of* CPL. *Moreover, let* $\{\pi, \chi\} \subseteq \mathbf{F}_0$. *A pivotal rule is an expression* (π/χ) *where:* π *is called* prerequisite, *and* χ *is called* consequent. *If* Φ *is a subset of formulas of* $\mathbf{F}_0$, *and* P *be a set of pivotal rules, then, the* image *of* P *under* Φ *is the set* $P(\Phi) = \{\chi \mid (\pi/\chi) \in P \text{ and } \pi \in \Phi\}$.

We will restrict our attention to finite sets P of pivotal rules. Intuitively, pivotal rules can be understood as non-admissible rules of inference, i.e., rules which extend the set of CPL-consequences of a set of formulas. From a modeling perspective, pivotal rules capture general rules which are not logical. PRC refers to a consequence operation extending Cn with pivotal rules. A first take on the definition of a PRC consequence operation is given in Definition 2.

Definition 2. *Let* $\Phi \subseteq \mathbf{F}_0$ *and* P *be a set of pivotal rules. Define*

$$C_P(\Phi) = \bigcap\{\Psi \mid \Phi \subseteq Cn(\Psi) \subseteq \Psi \text{ and } P(\Psi) \subseteq \Psi\}.$$

We call $\varphi \in \mathbf{F}_0$ *a* pivotal-rule consequence *of* Φ *iff* $\varphi \in C_P(\Phi)$.

In words, $C_P(\Phi)$ is the smallest superset of Φ closed under Cn and the application of pivotal rules in P. Unless it is strictly necessary, we will drop the subscript P from C_P. It is worth noting that: (a) each set of pivotal rules gives rise to a particular operation C, (b) different sets of pivotal rules may give rise to the same operation C, and (c) Cn is a particular case of an operation C, i.e., $Cn = C_\emptyset$. In Definition 3, we present a more constructive way of looking at C_P.

Definition 3. *Let* $\bar{P}$ *be a total ordering of a set* P *of pivotal rules, and* (π_i/χ_i) *be the i-th element in* $\bar{P}$. *Moreover, let* $\Phi \subseteq \mathbf{F}_0$. *Define* $C_{\bar{P}}(\Phi) = \bigcup\{C_{\bar{P}}^i(\Phi) \mid i \geq 0\}$ *where:*

$$C_{\bar{P}}^0(\Phi) = Cn(\Phi) \quad and \quad C_{\bar{P}}^{(i+1)}(\Phi) = \begin{cases} Cn(C_{\bar{P}}^i(\Phi) \cup \{\chi_i\}) & \text{if } \pi_i \in C_{\bar{P}}^i(\Phi) \\ C_{\bar{P}}^i(\Phi) & \text{otherwise.} \end{cases}$$

We write $\bar{C}$ when there is no need to make the set P of pivotal rules explicit.

Proposition 1. *It follows that* $\varphi \in C_P(\Phi)$ *iff exists* $\bar{P}$ *s.t.* $\varphi \in C_{\bar{P}}(\Phi)$.

Proposition 1 tells us that φ is a pivotal consequence of Φ iff we can obtain φ from Φ using the pivotal rules in P in some particular order. Just as Cn, C satisfies monotonicity. However, we will see that imposing some natural constraints on the use of pivotal rules gives us a PRC operation which fails to satisfy monotonicity.

Definition 4. *Let* P *be a set of pivotal rules, and* $\bar{P}$ *be a total ordering on* P. *Moreover, let* $\Phi \subseteq \mathbf{F}_0$. *Define* $D_{\bar{P}}(\Phi) = \bigcup \{D_{\bar{P}}^i(\Phi) \mid i \geq 0\}$ *where:*

$$D_{\bar{P}}^0(\Phi) = \mathrm{Cn}(\Phi) \quad and \quad D_{\bar{P}}^{(i+1)}(\Phi) = \begin{cases} \mathrm{Cn}(D_{\bar{P}}^i(\Phi) \cup \{\chi_i\}) & \textit{if } \pi_i \in D_{\bar{P}}^i(\Phi) \textit{ and} \\ & \qquad \neg\chi_i \notin D_{\bar{P}}^i(\Phi) \\ D_{\bar{P}}^i(\Phi) & \textit{otherwise.} \end{cases}$$

We use $\bar{D}$ instead of $D_{\bar{P}}$. In contrast to $\bar{C}$, the operation $\bar{D}$ requires a "consistency check" before applying a pivotal rule. This constraint appears in settings where inference rules capture 'typicality judgements' or 'jumps to conclusions' and are pervasive in the literature on nonmonotonic reasoning [6,9]. The rationale behind them hinges on the consideration that a contradiction to a typicality judgement is an exception to the rule, and that we would not apply the rule in such situations. Such a simple "consistency check" causes $\bar{D}$ to *fail* monotonicity. To see why, let $P = \{(p/q)\}$; we have $D_{\bar{P}}(\{p\}) = \mathrm{Cn}(\{p,q\})$ and $D_{\bar{P}}(\{p,\neg q\}) = \mathrm{Cn}(\{p,\neg q\})$; i.e., $\{p\} \subseteq \{p,q\}$ and $D_{\bar{P}}(\{p\}) \not\subseteq D_{\bar{P}}(\{p,q\})$.

The operation $\bar{D}$ is in itself of interest. In some cases, however, we may want to steer away from choosing a particular ordering for pivotal rules. Instead, we may wish to reason *credulously* knowing that there is one such possible ordering from which we can obtain our conclusions. We make this idea precise in Definition 5.

Definition 5. *Define* D_P *s.t.* $\varphi \in D_P(\Phi)$ *iff exists* $\bar{P}$ *s.t.* $\varphi \in D_{\bar{P}}(\Phi)$.

We write D instead of D_P. The operation D coincides with *credulous* consequence for the case of *normal* defaults in Default Logic [9,11]. The point made in [9] is that this way of reaching the notion of credulous consequence presents itself in a way such that is more amicable for the traditional logician. The argument is that we can understand nonmonotonic logics via **PRC** by showing first how to extend consequence in **CPL** with the use of pivotal rules, and then showing how to restrict the use of pivotal rules with a simple consistency check. In the following section, we comment on how **PRC** can be captured in Action Model Logic [5].

Pivotal Rules Consequence in Action Model Logic. In this section we take some steps to show how **PRC** operations can be cast into Action Model Logic (AML). The key is to capture the application of a pivotal rule as an action model. This enables us to internalize pivotal rules and the definition of pivotal rules consequence in the object language of the logic.

Action Model Logic. We briefly recall the language and semantics of **AML** [5].

Definition 6. *An* action model *on a set* $\mathbf{F}$ *is a tuple* $\alpha = \langle A, T, \mathrm{pre} \rangle$ *where:* A *is a non-empty finite of action points,* $T \subseteq A \times A$, *and* $\mathrm{pre} : A \to \mathbf{F}$ *is a* precondition *function. For* $a \in A$, *we call the pair* α, a *a* pointed action model. *We use* $\varphi! = \langle \{a\}, \{(a,a)\}, \mathrm{pre}(a) = \varphi \rangle$ *for the* truthful public announcement *of* $\varphi \in \mathbf{F}$.

It turns out that internalizing PRC into AML needs of a single modality $\Diamond$.

Definition 7. *The set of* formulas *of* AML *is the set* $\mathbf{F}_1 = \bigcup\{\mathbf{F}_1^i \mid i \geq 0\}$ *where:*

$$\mathbf{F}_1^0 = \mathbf{F}_0 \quad \mathbf{F}_1^{(i+1)} = \mathbf{F}_1^i \cup \{\chi \mid \chi \in \{\neg\varphi, \varphi \rightarrow \psi, \Diamond\varphi\} \subseteq \mathbf{F}_1^i\} \cup$$
$$\{\langle\alpha, \mathsf{a}\rangle\varphi \mid \varphi \in \mathbf{F}_1^i \text{ and } \alpha, \mathsf{a} \text{ is a pointed action model on } \mathbf{F}_1^i\}$$

We use $\Box\varphi$ *and* $[\alpha, \mathsf{a}]\varphi$ *as abbreviations of* $\neg\Diamond\neg\varphi$, *and* $\neg\langle\alpha, \mathsf{a}\rangle\neg\varphi$, *respectively.*

The semantics of AML is given using Kripke models and product updates [5].

Definition 8. *A* Kripke model *is a tuple* $\mathfrak{M} = \langle W, R, V \rangle$ *where:* W *is a non-empty set of* worlds, $R \subseteq W \times W$ *is an* accessibility relation, *and* $V : \mathsf{Prop} \rightarrow 2^W$ *is a* valuation function. *A* pointed *Kripke model is a pair* $\mathfrak{M}, w$ *where* $w \in W$.

Definition 9. *Let* $\mathfrak{M} = \langle W, R, V \rangle$ *be a Kripke model, and* $\varphi \in \mathbf{F}_1$. *The* truth set *of* φ *is defined as expected if* φ *is a propositional formula, or if it is of the form* $\Diamond\psi$; *for the case in which* φ *is of the form* $\langle\alpha, \mathsf{a}\rangle\psi$, *we have:*

$$\llbracket\langle\alpha, \mathsf{a}\rangle\psi\rrbracket^{\mathfrak{M}} = \{w \mid w \in \llbracket\mathsf{pre}(\mathsf{a})\rrbracket^{\mathfrak{M}} \text{ and } (w, \mathsf{a}) \in \llbracket\psi\rrbracket^{\mathfrak{M}\otimes\alpha}\}$$

where $\mathfrak{M} \otimes \alpha$ *is the* product update *of* $\mathfrak{M}$ *with* α *[5].*

Internalizing PRC *into* AML. Of particular interest for our purposes is the Kripke model $\mathfrak{C} = \langle W, R, V \rangle$ where: $W = 2^{\mathsf{Prop}}$, $R = W \times W$, and $V(p) = \{w \mid p \in w\}$. Intuitively, $\mathfrak{C}$ is the model whose worlds are all possible valuations in CPL. In $\mathfrak{C}$, a formula $\Box\varphi$ can be understood as "φ holds in every valuation" and a formula $\Diamond\varphi$ as "φ holds in some valuation". We make use of this view of worlds, and $\Box$ and $\Diamond$, in $\mathfrak{C}$ in the formulation of PRC in AML. In particular, we use $\Box$ to determine the provability of the prerequisite of a pivotal rule in semantic terms, and use $\Diamond$ to check for consistency in the use of pivotal rules. Crucial in our internalization of PRC into AML is how to capture the application of a pivotal rule –with and without a consistency check– as an action model. We make this precise below.

We begin with the straightforward –i.e., no consistency check– application of a pivotal rule as an action model.

Definition 10. *To every pivotal rule* (π/χ) *we associate a pointed action model* ρ, a *where* $\rho = \langle\{a, b\}, \{(a, b), (b, b)\}, \mathsf{pre} = \{a \mapsto \Box\pi, b \mapsto (\pi \wedge \chi)\}, a\rangle$.

Intuitively, the action model associated to a pivotal rule captures the effect of applying a pivotal rule at a semantic level. This effect can be explained as follows. Let $\Phi \subseteq \mathbf{F}_0$. To apply a pivotal rule (π/χ) w.r.t. Φ we need $\pi \in \mathsf{Cn}(\Phi)$. The result of the application amounts to adding χ to Φ. Semantically, to apply a pivotal rule we need every model of Φ to be also a model of π. If we restrict our attention to the models of Φ, we can check this condition with the formula $\Box\varphi$. This corresponds to the state a of the action model for the pivotal rule. Also, semantically, the result of applying a pivotal rule will correspond to updating the models being considered by eliminating those that are not models of χ. This corresponds to the state b in the action model for the pivotal rule. The relation between the states a and b corresponds to the scenarios before and after applying the pivotal rule. These ideas are summarized in Proposition 2.

Proposition 2. *Let $\rho = (\pi/\chi)$ be a pivotal rule, and $\{\varphi, \psi\} \subseteq \mathbf{F}_0$; the following are equivalent:*

1. $[\![\varphi!]\Box\psi]\!]^{\mathfrak{C}} = 2^{\mathsf{Prop}}$ *or* $[\![\varphi!]\langle\rho, a\rangle\Box\psi]\!]^{\mathfrak{C}} = 2^{\mathsf{Prop}}$
2. $\psi \in C_{\{(\pi/\chi)\}}(\{\varphi\})$

The following definition captures the application of a pivotal rule with a consistency check.

Definition 11. *To every pivotal rule (π/χ) we associate a pointed action model δ, a where $\delta = \langle\{a, b\}, \{(a, b), (b, b)\}, \mathrm{pre} = \{a \mapsto (\Box\pi \wedge \Diamond\chi), b \mapsto (\pi \wedge \chi)\}, a\rangle$.*

Intuitively, the action model in Definition 11 captures the consistency check with the formula $\Diamond\chi$ in the state a. Notice that, intuitively, we can read this formula as: there is a model of χ. This definition enables us to obtain the following result.

Proposition 3. *Let (π/χ) be a pivotal rule, and $\{\varphi, \psi\} \subseteq \mathbf{F}_0$; the following are equivalent:*

1. $[\![\varphi!]\psi]\!]^{\mathfrak{C}} = 2^{\mathsf{Prop}}$ *or* $[\![\varphi!]\langle\delta, a\rangle\Box\psi]\!]^{\mathfrak{C}} = 2^{\mathsf{Prop}}$
2. $\psi \in D_{\{(\pi/\chi)\}}(\{\varphi\})$.

Final Remarks and Future Work. We began a semantic exploration of PRC [8,9] using the standard machinery of AML [5]. Building on the results in [2], our main goal is to construct a more general framework for exploring the concept of PRC. We are particularly interested in exploring notions related to situations in which pivotal rules are not omniscient, but they are seen from the point of view of a particular agent, in a multi-agent setting. In this respect, it becomes interesting to explore how the notion of belief interacts with pivotal rules; understood both as in the operation C and as in the operation D. More precisely, we would like to explore what happens with formulas of the form $\mathsf{B}\langle\rho, a\rangle\psi$ and $\langle\rho, a\rangle\mathsf{B}\psi$, or $\mathsf{B}\langle\delta, a\rangle\psi$ and $\langle\delta, a\rangle\mathsf{B}\psi$ where B is a belief modality. In this line of research it would also be interesting to find connections with works such as [7]. Finally, continuing and completing the work in [2], we are also interested in an internalization of the sequential application of pivotal rules as a form of composition of action models.

Acknowledgments. The research of Sabine Frittella was funded by the grant ANR JCJC 2019, project PRELAP (ANR-19-CE48-0006). This research is part of the MOSAIC project financed by the European Union's Marie Sklodowska-Curie grant No. 101007627. The research of Valentin Cassano was funded by the Laboratoire

International Associé SINFIN, the EU Grant Agreement 101008233 (MISSION), the ANPCyT projects PICT-2021-00675, and PICTO-2022-CBA-00088, and the CON-ICET project PIBAA-28720210100165CO.

References

1. Antoniou, G., Wang, K.: Default logic. In: Gabbay and Woods [6], pp. 517–555
2. Areces, C., Cassano, V., Fervari, R.: Non-monotonic reasoning via dynamic consequence. In: Proceedings of WoLLIC 2022. LNCS, vol. 13468, pp. 395–410. Springer (2022)
3. van Benthem, J.: Logical dynamics meets logical pluralism? Australas. J. Logic **6**, 182–209 (2008)
4. Cordón-Franco, A., van Ditmarsch, H., Nepomuceno-Fernández, Á.: Dynamic consequence and public announcement. Rev. Symbolic Logic **6**(4), 659–679 (2013)
5. van Ditmarsch, H., Hoek, W., Kooi, B.: Dynamic Epistemic Logic, Synthese Library, vol. 337. Springer, Cham (2008)
6. Gabbay, D., Woods, J.: The Many Valued and Nonmonotonic Turn in Logic, Handbook of the History of Logic, vol. 8. North-Holland, Dutch (2007)
7. Gómez Álvarez, L., Rudolph, S.: Standpoint logic: Multi-perspective knowledge representation. In: Proceedings of FOIS 2021. Frontiers in Artificial Intelligence and Applications, vol. 344, pp. 3–17. IOS Press (2021)
8. Makinson, D.: Bridges between classical and nonmonotonic logic. Logic J. IGPL **11**(1), 69–96 (2003)
9. Makinson, D.: Bridges from Classical to Nonmonotonic Logic, Texts in Computing, vol. 5. College Publications, London (2005)
10. Plaza, J.: Logics of public communications. Synthese **158**(2), 165–179 (2007)
11. Reiter, R.: A logic for default reasoning. Artif. Intell. **13**(1–2), 81–132 (1980)

Paraconsistent Reactive Graphs

Juliana Cunha[1,2](✉), Alexandre Madeira[1], and Luís S. Barbosa[2]

[1] CIDMA, Dep. Mathematics, Aveiro University, Aveiro, Portugal
{juliana.cunha,madeira}@ua.pt
[2] INESC TEC and Dep. Informatics, Minho University, Braga, Portugal
lsb@di.uminho.pt

Abstract. This paper introduces *Paraconsistent Reactive Graphs*, as an extension of Reactive graphs that incorporates paraconsistency into the ground edges to address vagueness and inconsistency within dynamic systems. By assigning pairs of truth values to ground edges, this framework captures the uncertainty and contradictions stemming from incomplete or conflicting information. We explore the semantics of these graphs and provide a practical example to illustrate the proposed approach.

Keywords: Reactive systems · Paraconsistency · Contradictions

1 Introduction

Dov Gabbay introduced *reactive graphs* as structures where the accessibility relation can be modified by prior transitions [15]. This dynamic behavior is achieved through higher-order edges, or hyper-edges, which update the accessibility relation when traversed. Hyper-edges connect one edge to another, acting as switches that either activate (➤➤) or deactivate (➤✗) the connected edge [14]. Although reactive graphs are a powerful tool, it is natural to seek extensions that allow the representation of information that may not always adhere to classical reasoning. Such extensions are particularly relevant in nuanced applications where certain factors may reinforce or contradict one another.

A fuzzy approach to reactive graphs, initially limited to activating higher-order edges, was proposed in [17], where both ground and higher-order edges could take values in the closed interval $[0, 1]$. This approach also introduced a modal logic to verify properties of such systems and demonstrated its potential application through an example in biology. Subsequently, this framework was extended in [4,5] to allow hyper-edges to act as switches, either activating or deactivating edges.

We propose a paraconsistent extension to this framework by incorporating inconsistency and vagueness into the ground edges of the graph, while hyper-edges remain bivalent—they either activate or deactivate other edges. Similarly to fuzzy reasoning [17], which uses a spectrum of values between 0 and 1 to measure the certainty of an event's occurrence, our paraconsistent framework assigns two truth values that gauge certainty in contrasting ways. Unlike fuzzy

J. Proença et al. (Eds.): SEFM 2024, LNCS 15551, pp. 105–111, 2026.
https://doi.org/10.1007/978-3-031-94748-3_9

reasoning, which only addresses vagueness, our framework accommodates both vague and inconsistent information by using a pair of truth values to measure the certainty of occurrence and non-occurrence of an event. Vagueness arises when the sum of these values is less than the unit, indicating incomplete information. Inconsistency, on the other hand, is reflected when the sum exceeds the unit, suggesting conflicting information from multiple sources. For further details on this framework, see previous work [13].

While fuzzy approaches allow the representation of vague information, our paraconsistent approach extends this capability to encompass both vague and inconsistent information. Other paraconsistent approaches, such as [6], introduce paraconsistency into reactive graphs by employing four-valued propositional variables. These values represent truth, falsehood, absolute contradiction, and a complete lack of information. Furthermore, [6] proposes a paraconsistent logic and explores additional topics, such as measuring inconsistencies, as seen in [7,8]. In contrast, our work maintains the binary switching nature of hyperedges but incorporates paraconsistency into the ground edges, allowing them to exhibit both vague and inconsistent information.

Introducing reactivity to paraconsistent models is a natural approach, as contradictions often stem from different sources, beliefs, or even lies, leading to an ever-evolving model as more information is received. This paper introduces *Paraconsistent Reactive Graphs*, their semantics, and a concrete application example.

2   Paraconsistent Reactive Graphs

2.1   Paraconsistent Graphs

Before introducing Paraconsistent Graphs, we first establish the underlying framework. Similar to research on many-valued Kripke frames [2], we use a specific class of residuated lattices $\mathbf{A}$ over a set A representing the set of possible truth values.

We focus on Heyting algebras [1], structures $\mathbf{A} = \langle A, \wedge, \vee, 1, 0, \rightarrow \rangle$ where $\wedge$ has $\rightarrow$ as its residuum. Examples of Heyting algebras include the Boolean algebra $\mathbf{2} = \langle 0, 1, \wedge, \vee, 1, 0, \rightarrow \rangle$ and the Gödel algebra $\mathbf{G} = \langle [0, 1], \min, \max, 0, 1, \rightarrow_G \rangle$, with $a \rightarrow b = \{ \begin{smallmatrix} 1 & \text{if } a \leq b \\ b & \text{otherwise} \end{smallmatrix}$. In our paraconsistent framework, events are represented as pairs of weights $(t\!t, f\!f) \in A \times A$, with $t\!t$ measuring the evidence of occurrence and $f\!f$ the evidence of not occurrence.

The product of $\mathbf{A}$ and its order dual $\mathbf{A}^\partial$ forms a residuated lattice known as a twist-structure [3], which will be discussed in the concluding remarks (Sect. 3). This structure enables the joint computation of pairs $A \times A$, which is crucial for this framework (see [11,12]).

Definition 1. *[10] Given an Heyting algebra $\mathbf{A}$ over a set A, an $\mathbf{A}$-twist structure $\mathcal{A} = \langle A^2, \overset{\wedge}{\wedge}, \overset{\vee}{\vee}, /\!/, (1, 0), (0, 1) \rangle$ is defined for any pair A^2 as:*

$$/\!/ \, (a, b) = (b, a) \qquad (a, b) \overset{\wedge}{\wedge} (c, d) = (a \wedge c, b \vee d) \qquad (a, b) \overset{\vee}{\vee} (c, d) = (a \vee c, b \wedge d)$$

Finally, we present the definition of a Paraconsistent Graph whose transitions are labeled by a pair of weights taken from a set A of possible truth values.

Definition 2. *Let* **A** *be a Heyting algebra over a set A and* Act *a set of actions. An (A, Act)-Paraconsistent transition system is a tuple $M = (W, w_0, R)$ where W is a non-empty set of states, $w_0 \in W$ is the initial state and $R \subseteq W \times \text{Act} \times \mathbf{A}^2 \times W$ is a paraconsistent relation, i.e., if $(w, a, \mathfrak{t}, \mathfrak{f}, w') \in R$ then, $\mathfrak{t}$ measures the evidence of the transition from w to w' occurring via action a and $\mathfrak{f}$ measures the evidence of the transition being prevented from occurring.*

Example 1. The structure $(\{w_0, w_1, w_3\}, w_0, R)$ depicted below is a $(\mathbf{G}, \{a, b\})$-paraconsistent graph.

The pair of weights $(0.3, 0.4)$ represents vague information, while $(1, 1)$ represents contradictory information. Additionally, transitions that are consistently known not to occur, such as $(w_2, a, 0, 1, w_3)$, are omitted from the diagram.

2.2 Paraconsistent Reactive Graphs

The definitions in this Section are adapted from recent work on reactive graphs [18]. We introduce *Paraconsistent Reactive Graphs*, which extend Paraconsistent Graphs by embedding hyper-edges that activate ($\twoheadrightarrow$) or deactivate ($\rightarrow\!\!\times$) other edges. Although not traversable, these hyper-edges capture the model's reactive behavior by showing how edges change when a ground edge ($\rightarrow$) is traversed. We then present the semantics and a concrete example of these graphs.

Definition 3. *Let* **A** *be an Heyting algebra and* Act *a set of actions. A (A, Act)-Paraconsistent Reactive Graph is a tuple $M = (W, w_0, \alpha_0, E, \rightarrow, \twoheadrightarrow, \rightarrow\!\!\times, \vdots)$ where:*

- *W is a set of states and $w_0 \in W$ is the* initial *state;*
- *E is the set of all edge names and $\alpha_0 \subseteq E$ is the set of* initially active edges;
- *$\rightarrow \subseteq W \times \text{Act} \times \mathbf{A}^2 \times W$*
  is the set of ground edges, $\twoheadrightarrow \subseteq E \times E$ is the set of activating edges and $\rightarrow\!\!\times \subseteq E \times E$ is the set of deactivating edges;
- *$\vdots : E \longrightarrow (\rightarrow \cup \twoheadrightarrow \cup \rightarrow\!\!\times)$ is a bijective function that maps edges in E to their internal details*

Example 2. The following model is a $([0, 1], \{a, b\})$-Paraconsistent Reactive graph with $E = \{e_1, e_2, e_3, e_a, e_d\}$ and initial active edges $\alpha_0 = E \setminus \{e_2\}$. To illustrate $\vdots$, for the ground edge e_3 and the hyper edge e_d the function takes values $(w_2, a, 1, 0, w_3)$ and (e_a, e_3), respectively.

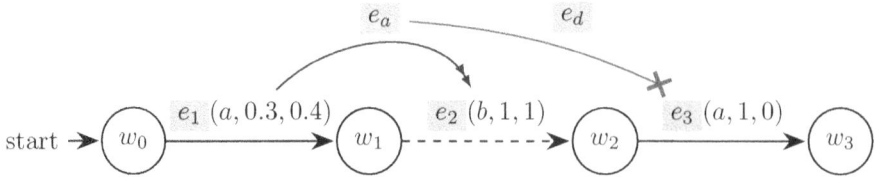

Definition 4. *Given a* (A, Act)*-Paraconsistent Reactive Graph with a set of active edges* $\alpha \subseteq E$ *and an edge* $e \in E$. *The set of edges activated by* e *(resp. deactivated by* e*), written* $\mathrm{on}(e, \alpha)$ *(resp.*$\mathrm{off}(e, \alpha)$*) are defined as follows.*

$$\mathrm{from}(e_s) = \{e \mid \exists e_t \cdot \overline{e} = (e_s, e_t)\}$$
$$\mathrm{from}^*(e, \alpha) = \bigcup_{r \in (\mathrm{from}(e) \cap \alpha)} \mathrm{from}^*(r, \alpha \backslash \{e\}) \cup \{r\}$$
$$\mathrm{on}(e, \alpha) = \{e_t \mid e_{trg} \in \mathrm{from}^*(e, \alpha) \wedge \exists e_s \cdot \overline{e_{trg}} = (e_s, e_t) \in \twoheadrightarrow\}$$
$$\mathrm{off}(e, \alpha) = \{e_t \mid e_{trg} \in \mathrm{from}^*(e, \alpha) \wedge \exists e_s \cdot \overline{e_{trg}} = (e_s, e_t) \in \rightarrow\!\!\!\times\}$$

Intuitively, $\mathrm{from}(e_s)$ returns the hyper-edges originating from e_s. from^* recursively traverses from to gather all (active) hyper-edges triggered from a given edge. Additionally, $\mathrm{on}(e, \alpha)$ (resp. $\mathrm{off}(e, \alpha)$) collect all the targets triggered from e by an activating (resp. deactivating) edge.

Example 3. Recall the Paraconsistent Reactive graph in Ex. 2. The edge e_1, represents a transition from state w_0 to w_1 via action a with occurrence and non-occurrence evidence of 0.3 and 0.4, respectively, that triggers hyper-edges e_a and e_d, which activate e_2 and deactivate e_3, respectively. Thus, $\mathrm{from}(e_1) = \{e_a\}$ returns the hyper edges that start from e_1, $\mathrm{from}^*(e_1, \alpha_0) = \{e_a, e_d\}$ returns the hyper edges triggered by e_1, $\mathrm{on}(e_1, \alpha_0) = \{e_2\}$ and $\mathrm{off}(e_1, \alpha_0) = \{e_3\}$ return the edges triggered from e_1 by activation and deactivation, respectively.

Definition 5. *The semantics of a* (A, Act)*-Paraconsistent Reactive Graph* P *is given by evolving a configuration* $\langle w, \alpha \rangle$, *with* $w \in W$ *and* $\alpha \subseteq E$, *starting from* $\langle w_0, E_0 \rangle$, *as defined by the following rule.*

$$\frac{\exists e \in \alpha \cdot \overline{e} = (w, a, t\!t, f\!\!f, w') \wedge \alpha' = (\alpha \cup \mathrm{on}(e, \alpha)) \backslash \mathrm{off}(e, \alpha)}{\langle w, \alpha \rangle \xrightarrow{(a, t\!t, f\!\!f)}_P \langle w', \alpha' \rangle}$$

Applying the semantics above to Ex. 2 yields the Paraconsistent Graph in Ex. 1.

Example 4. (Liar's Coin) Two players are engaged in a game called *Liar's Coin*, which is adapted from work on epistemic logic [16]. Player 1 bets on heads, while Player 2 bets on tails. Player 1 tosses a coin and announces either heads or tails, but keeps the actual outcome hidden from Player 2. If Player 1 announces tails

($\dagger t$), Player 2 wins, and the game ends. If Player 1 announces heads ($\dagger h$), Player 2 has two options: pass (p)—in which case Player 1 wins—or challenge (c), forcing Player 1 to show the coin (h or t). The player with the correct bet then wins. From Player 2's perspective, the game can be represented by the following model.

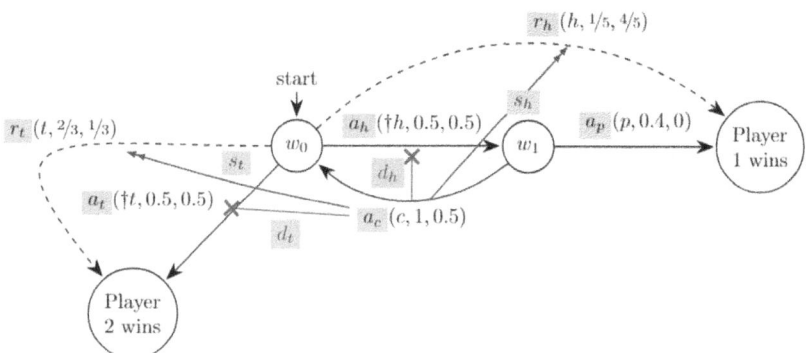

Initially, Player 2's belief about the outcome (heads or tails) mirrors the probability of a fair coin toss (0.5 for each). When deciding whether to pass or challenge, Player 2 can rely on various vague indicators—such as Player 1's behavior when lying or knowledge from past rounds—to assess how confident they are about their decision. If Player 2 challenges, the game resets: the announcement edges (a_h and a_t) are deactivated, and the reveal edges (r_h and r_t) are activated, with their weights reflecting Player 1's likelihood of lying.

3   Conclusions

This work is part of a research agenda on paraconsistent transition structures [9,11–13]. We combine this agenda with Reactive Graphs [15] by allowing ground edges to represent consistent, vague, or inconsistent information. Consequently, we can model paraconsistent systems where beliefs, lies, incomplete information, and contradictions arise naturally and evolve as the system acquires more information.

Future research will focus on replacing bivalent hyper-edges with pairs of weights for each hyper-edge that convey evidence for activation or deactivation. These paraconsistent hyper-edges may represent different sources, with varying trust levels that may sometimes be even doubtful. As with fuzzy systems [5,17], we anticipate that this will require incorporating aggregation functions based on operators from the twist-structure. Potential applications include adjusting the impact of hyper-edges on the system based on the degree of vagueness or inconsistency and prioritizing hyper-edges with fewer inconsistencies or greater overall certainty.

Acknowledgement. This work was financed by PRR - Plano de Recuperação e Resiliência under the Next Generation EU from the European Union within Project Agenda ILLIANCE C644919832-00000035 - Project n 46, as well as by National Funds through

FCT, the Portuguese Foundation for Science and Technology, within the project IBEX, with reference PTDC/CCI-COM/4280/2021.

References

1. Borceux, F.: Locales, Encyclopedia of Mathematics and its Applications, p. 1–86. Cambridge University Press, Cambridge (1994). https://www.cambridge.org/core/books/handbook-of-categorical-algebra/A0B8285BBA900AFE85EED8C971E0DE14

2. Bou, F., Esteva, F., Godo, L., Rodríguez, R.O.: On the minimum many-valued modal logic over a finite residuated lattice. J. Logic Comput.**21**(5), 739–790 (2009). https://doi.org/10.1093/logcom/exp062

3. Busaniche, M., Cignoli, R.: The subvariety of commutative residuated lattices represented by twist-products. Algebra Univers. **71**(1), 5–22 (2014). https://doi.org/10.1007/s00012-014-0265-4

4. Campos, S., Santiago, R., Martins, M.A., Figueiredo, D.: Introduction to reversal fuzzy switch graph. Sci. Comput. Program. **216**, 102776 (2022)

5. Campos, S., Santiago, R., Martins, M.A., Figueiredo, D.: Aggregation-based operations for reversal fuzzy switch graphs. Fuzzy Sets Syst. **466**, 108273 (2023)

6. Costa, D., Figueiredo, D., Martins, M.A.: Relation-changing models meet paraconsistency. J. Logical Algebraic Methods Program. **133**, 100870 (2023)

7. Costa, D., Martins, M.A.: Paraconsistency in hybrid logic. J. Logic Comput. **27**(6), 1825–1852 (10 2016). https://doi.org/10.1093/logcom/exw027

8. Costa, D., Martins, M.A.: Measuring inconsistent diagnoses. In: 2018 IEEE 20th International Conference on e-Health Networking, Applications and Services (Healthcom), pp. 1–4 (2018). https://doi.org/10.1109/HealthCom.2018.8531146

9. Cruz, A., Madeira, A., Barbosa, L.S.: Paraconsistent transition systems. In: Nantes-Sobrinho, D., Fontaine, P. (eds.) Proceedings 17th International Workshop on Logical and Semantic Frameworks with Applications, LSFA 2022, Belo Horizonte, Brazil (hybrid), 23-24 September 2022. EPTCS, vol. 376. pp. 3–15 (2022). https://doi.org/10.4204/EPTCS.376.3

10. Cunha, J., Madeira, A., Barbosa, L.S.: Paraconsistent relations as a variant of kleene algebras. - - (2024)

11. Cunha, J., Madeira, A., Barbosa, L.S.: Stepwise development of paraconsistent processes. In: David, C., Sun, M. (eds.) TASE 2023. LNCS, vol. 13931, pp. 327–343. Springer, Cham (2023). https://doi.org/10.1007/978-3-031-35257-7_20

12. Cunha, J., Madeira, A., Barbosa, L.S.: Structured specification of paraconsistent transition systems. In: Hojjat, H., Ábrahám, E. (eds.) FSEN 2023. LNCS, vol. 14155, pp. 1–17. Springer, Cham (2023). https://doi.org/10.1007/978-3-031-42441-0_1

13. Cunha, J., Madeira, A., Barbosa, L.S.: Specification of paraconsistent transition systems, revisited. Sci. Comput. Program. **240**, 103196 (2025)

14. Gabbay, D., Marcelino, S.: Global view on reactivity: switch graphs and their logics. Ann. Math. Artif. Intell. **66**(1), 131–162 (2012). https://doi.org/10.1007/s10472-012-9316-8

15. Gabbay, D.M.: Introducing reactive kripke semantics and arc accessibility. In: Avron, A., Dershowitz, N., Rabinovich, A. (eds.) Pillars of Computer Science. LNCS, vol. 4800, pp. 292–341. Springer, Heidelberg (2008). https://doi.org/10.1007/978-3-540-78127-1_17

16. Mousavi, M.R., Varshosaz, M.: Telling lies in process algebra. In: Pang, J., Zhang, C., He, J., Weng, J. (eds.) 2018 International Symposium on Theoretical Aspects of Software Engineering, TASE 2018, Guangzhou, China, August 29-31, 2018, pp. 116–123. IEEE Computer Society (2018). https://doi.org/10.1109/TASE.2018.00023

17. Santiago, R., Martins, M.A., Figueiredo, D.: Introducing fuzzy reactive graphs: a simple application on biology. Soft. Comput. **25**(9), 6759–6774 (2021). https://doi.org/10.1007/s00500-020-05353-1

18. Tinoco, D., Martins, M.A., Proença, J.: Reactive graphs in action. In: Marmsoler, D., Sun, M. (eds.) FACS 2024. LNCS, vol. 15189, pp. 97–105. Springer, Cham (2024). https://doi.org/10.1007/978-3-031-71261-6_6

Reconfiguring Staggered Quantum Walks with ZX

Bruno Jardim[(✉)], Jaime Santos, and Luís S. Barbosa

HASLab INESC TEC and Universidade do Minho, Campus de Gualtar,
4710-057 Braga, Portugal
bruno.f.jardim@inesctec.pt

Abstract. The staggered model is a recent, very general variant of discrete-time quantum walks which, avoiding the use of a coin to direct the walker evolution, explores the underlying graph structure to build an evolution operator based on local unitaries induced by adjacent vertices. Optimising their implementation to increase resilience to decoherence phenomena motivates their analysis with the ZX-calculus. The whole optimisation can be seen as a graph reconfiguration process along which the original circuit is rewrote, significantly reducing the number of (expensive) gates used. The exercise identified an underlying pattern leading to an alternative, potentially more efficient evolution operator.

1 Introduction

Thought of as the quantum counterpart to classical random walks, quantum walks [VA12] provide an interesting technique in algorithmic design, with applications in unstructured search, graph algorithmics and communication protocols.

Differently from the classical case, where the walker's next move follows the result of some sort of random choice, in a quantum setting evolution typically proceeds in an equally weighed superposition of possible moves through the iteration of a unitary operator, without resorting to intermediate measurements. This results in a very rich dynamics, in which the design of the evolution operator, and even seemingly innocent differences in its phase and in the initial state, determine complex 'walking patterns' which differ greatly both from each other and from the classical setting.

The relevance of quantum walks as a tool for algorithmic design justifies both a better understanding of their behaviour and the optimisation of their implementation, namely to increase resilience to decoherence phenomena. This paper resorts to the ZX-calculus [CD08, vdW20, CHKW22] for such a purpose.

Optimisation of quantum circuits can be seen as a *reconfiguration* process. Indeed the interpretation of such circuits as ZX-diagrams provides a flexible description of quantum computations graphically. Then, the rules of the ZX-calculus guide through a simplification strategy which corresponds to sequences

---

This work was supported by FCT, the Portuguese Foundation for Science and Technology, within the project IBEX, with reference PTDC/CCI-COM/4280/2021.

J. Proença et al. (Eds.): SEFM 2024, LNCS 15551, pp. 112–119, 2026.
https://doi.org/10.1007/978-3-031-94748-3_10

of graph transformations. Finally, the reconfigured circuit is extracted from the transformed graph. The process is illustrated here in a closed setting. However, it extends smoothly to the dynamic case where algorithms reconfigure themselves as a result of the (classical) evaluation of measurement results. This is particularly relevant in the context of variational algorithms [CAB+21] currently used in quantum machine learning [DTB16].

The exercise reported here focuses on a recent, very general variant of discrete-time quantum walks—the *staggered* model [PdOM17, PSFG16], briefly revisited in Appendix A—which, avoiding the use of a coin to direct the walker evolution, explores the underlying graph structure to build an evolution operator based on local unitaries induced by adjacent vertices. Section 2 discusses how its standard circuit implementation is translated and rewritten in ZX, supported by the *PyZX* tool [KvdW20a]. This process leads in Sect. 3 to the identification of a diagrammatic pattern providing an interesting approximation to, and in some cases more efficient version of, the underlying evolution operator.

2 Bringing ZX into the Picture

A circuit implementation of the staggered model can be found in [San21]. For the example discussed in the Appendix, it yields

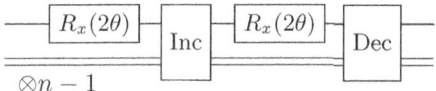

where $R_x(\theta) = e^{\frac{-i\theta X}{2}}$ and the Inc(rement) and Dec(rement) circuits have the usual implementation through generalised Toffoli gates. When the walker reaches the limit of the state space it cycles back. An implementation for a 3 qubit staggered quantum walk, and taking $\theta = \frac{\pi}{3}$, which maximizes[1] propagation, is represented in a ZX diagram as

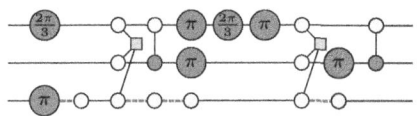

using ZH-calculus H-box notation for a concise representation of Toffoli gates. Advanced techniques, described in [KvdW20b] and directly implemented in *PyZX* [KvdW20a] as the full_reduce method, may reduce the circuit T-count in about 50% [KvdW20b]. Although this is not the case for our small example, when we start applying such simplifications to staggered models with larger amounts of steps the T-count reduction can reach approximately 60-70%. Back to the example, this simplification yields

---

[1] For this specific graph $\theta = \frac{\pi}{3}$ maximizes propagation, however $\frac{\pi}{2}$ is the optimal parameter for a complete graph.

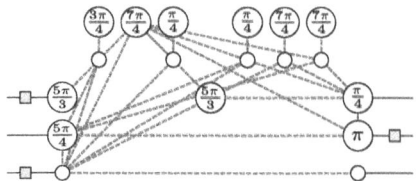

This diagram no longer resembles a circuit, making a comparison with the original one difficult. The circuit extracted [dBKvdW22] by *PyZX* has more gates than the one obtained from simple optimisations one can perform, although the T-count is indeed smaller. In fact, the `full_reduce` method introduces several additional Hadamard gates. The subsequent circuit extraction 'preserves' the nature of the *graph-like* ZX-diagram. Following the extraction with a small set of simplifications, basically resorting to fusion rewrite rules followed by a color-change, we get a much smaller circuit. This fully-simplified circuit now surpasses the original one in both the total amount of gates and T-count. Although this reduction is not outstanding in this example, it becomes most relevant when the number of steps in an example increases. The following tables show, respectively, the total number of gates and the T-count value induced by the different optimisation procedures for the same 3-qubit implementation.

	Number of steps in the staggered quantum walk:			
Optimizations used:	1	2	4	8
None	39	77	153	305
Full-reduce + fusion/id/to_rg	37	47	72	118
	Number of steps in the staggered quantum walk:			
Optimizations used:	1	2	4	8
None	16	32	64	128
Full-reduce + fusion/id/to_rg	10	16	28	52

3   An Alternative Evolution Operator

When analysing the ZX diagram for a long staggered quantum walk (i.e. with more than 5 steps) a pattern starts to emerge, repeating itself as many times as the number of steps considered. Depicted in ZX below, it seems able to approximate, both the increment and decrement layers of the evolution operator.

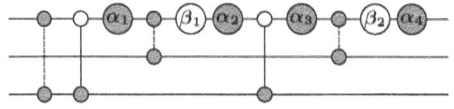

where $\alpha_n = \pm\frac{\pi}{4}$ and $\beta_n = \frac{2\pi}{3} + m\pi$, with $m = 0$ or $m = 1$. There is also a slight variation of this operator, where a CNOT gate between the first and last qubit appears right after the β_1 Z-spider. This diagram does not fully capture the staggered model we started with, but, once suitably enveloped, it captures the exact same tensor as the original circuit. The set of gates to be placed as an envelope, in the beginning and the end of the diagram, does not exhibit a specific structure. This construction appeared when optimising the 3 qubit staggered quantum walk. However, it can be generalised for an n qubit implementation, yielding the following operator, in the form of a ZX-diagram:

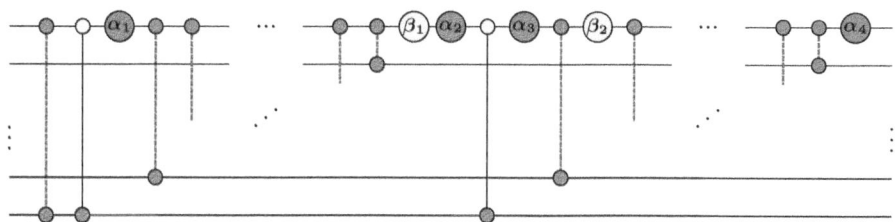

The rationale behind this operator is easy to explain: it creates a uniform distribution over a certain number of states, applies a rotation that makes some states more likely than others and then spreads these probabilities over the remaining states using CNOT gates. This also explains why the pattern only shows up in staggered quantum walks over a certain length. The classical evolution operator needs to be repeated a number of times to be able to spread the probability distributions over the whole state space. This is exactly what this version does on the first layer.

In any case, it has a number of advantages. First and foremost it reduces the total amount of gates needed to represent the evolution of the quantum walk. With the number of qubits increasing so does the cost of the increment and decrement layers, as a n qubit staggered quantum walk needs to implement MCX gates with $n - 1$ controls. The alternative operator uses gates controlled by at most 1 qubit. Moreover, to go from an n-qubit to an $n + 1$ qubit quantum walk, all that needs to be done is to add two more XCX-gates, one to each ladder of XCX-gates.

In general, this makes the alternative operator much more efficient with respect to the total number of gates used, leading to lower depth and, therefore, potentially less error-prone circuits.

As mentioned above, just by itself this operator can approximate the evolution of a staggered quantum walk. Although the approximation is not perfect it can yield results which are quite similar to the ones obtained with the original implementation of the staggered model, as shown in the graph below, where the original operator is represented in red and the alternative in blue.

One particular advantage of this alternative evolution operator is that it can work quite well on a quantum processor with limited connectivity. This is due to the fact that all the qubits used in the staggered quantum walk only need to be strongly connected to the first qubit. However, a number of challenges remain, requiring further investigation. These concern the most suitable choice of parameters for α_n and β_n, as well as whether and how they depend on the number of qubits used in a particular staggered walk. Actually, when optimising the 4 qubit implementation of this circuit the resulting parameters did not seem to follow any regular pattern.

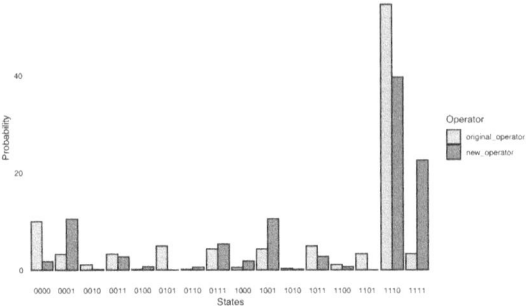

4   Conclusions and Future Work

This exercise showed that the original, 'intuitive' implementation of a staggered quantum walk can be heavily optimised with respect to both the total number of gates and the T-count value. It also lead to the identification of an alternative formulation of the evolution operator with a significant reduction in the number of gates involved and thus suitable for running on more limited quantum processing units. However, a number of issues, related to determining the suitable parametrisation scheme and better understanding the structure of the initial and final stages in the resulting circuit, still require further investigation. Similarly, it is not completely clear how the choice of the initial state influences how well the operator approximates the model evolution. Comparison of our results with other work on graph reconfiguration in ZX reported in recent references [DKPvdW20, UPR+23] is being carried out.

From another perspective, this exercise regards algorithmic optimisation in quantum programming as a *graph reconfiguration* process. This has a huge potential in the development of hybrid quantum-classical algorithms, which are the ones that can actually run in current quantum devices [Pre18]. They are essentially dynamic in the sense that, depending on a measurement carried over the quantum state, the quantum code running in the quantum device acting as a co-processor is transformed on-the-fly. The connection to suitable logic methods to reason about such transformations at a higher level of abstraction is a main direction for future work. The whole area of quantum machine learning and variational algorithms [DTB16, CAB+21] emerges as a main testbed for this research.

A   Staggered Quantum Walks

Staggered walks [PSFG16] explore partitions of graph cliques (subsets of vertices in which every two distinct vertices are adjacent) over the graph structure of the walking space. Each partition forms a tesselation whose elements do not overlap. The set of cliques in each tesselation must cover all vertices of the graph, and the set of tessellations $\{T_1, T_2, \ldots, T_k\}$ chosen must cover all the edges. Then a unit vector, typically encoding a uniform superposition, is associated to each clique so that the vector belongs to the subspace spanned by the corresponding vertices; i.e., $|u_j^k\rangle = \frac{1}{\sqrt{|\alpha_j^k|}} \sum_{l \in \alpha_j^k} |l\rangle$, where α_j^k is the jth polygon in the kth tessellation. This way each tessellation k gives rise to an operator $H_k = 2 \sum_{j=1}^{p} |u_j^k\rangle\langle u_j^k| - I$. which propagates the probability amplitude locally, in each clique. The composition of all such operators defines the evolution operator, which, by solving the the time-independent Schrödinger equation, is equivalent to

$$U = e^{i\theta_k H_k} \ldots e^{i\theta_2 H_2} e^{i\theta_1 H_1}, \text{ where } e^{i\theta_k H_k} = \cos(\theta_k) I + i \sin(\theta_k) H_k$$

since $H_k^2 = I$, meaning that the Hamiltonian is a reflection operator that, when expanded in a Taylor series, generates a local operator.

As an elementary example consider a line where the following two tessellations (depicted in red and blue below) are defined

$$T_\alpha = \{\{2x, 2x + 1\} : x \in \mathbb{Z}\} \text{ and } T_\beta = \{\{2x + 1, 2x + 2\} : x \in \mathbb{Z}\}.$$

Thus,

$$|\alpha_x\rangle = \frac{|2x\rangle + |2x + 1\rangle}{\sqrt{2}} \text{ and } |\beta_x\rangle = \frac{|2x + 1\rangle + |2x + 2\rangle}{\sqrt{2}},$$

yielding Hamiltonians

$$H_\alpha = 2 \sum_{x=-\infty}^{+\infty} |\alpha_x\rangle\langle\alpha_x| - I \text{ and } H_\beta = 2 \sum_{x=-\infty}^{+\infty} |\beta_x\rangle\langle\beta_x| - I.$$

Therefore, $U = e^{i\theta H_\beta} e^{i\theta H_\alpha}$ is the evolution operator. The probability distribution on a line after 50 steps, starting at $|+\rangle$, for different values of θ, is depicted below, noticing that the walker is more likely to be found further away from the origin as the angle increases.

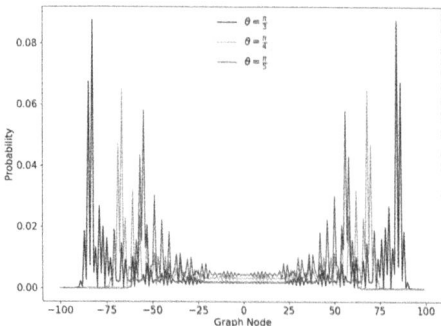

References

[CAB+21] Cerezo, M., et al.: Variational quantum algorithms. Nature Rev. Phys. **3**(9), 625–644 (2021)

[CD08] Coecke, B., Duncan, R.: Interacting Quantum Observables. In: Aceto, L., Damgård, I., Goldberg, L.A., Halldórsson, M.M., Ingólfsdóttir, A., Walukiewicz, I. (eds.) ICALP 2008. LNCS, vol. 5126, pp. 298–310. Springer, Heidelberg (2008). https://doi.org/10.1007/978-3-540-70583-3_25

[CHKW22] Coecke, B., Horsman, D., Kissinger, A., Wang, Q.: Kindergarden quantum mechanics graduates ...or how I learned to stop gluing LEGO together and love the ZX-calculus. Theor. Comput. Sci. **897**, pp. 1–22, (2022)

[dBKvdW22] de Beaudrap, N., Kissinger, A., van de Wetering, J.: Circuit extraction for ZX-diagrams can be #p-hard. In: 49th International Colloquium on Automata, Languages, and Programming (ICALP 2022). Schloss Dagstuhl ? Leibniz-Zentrum für Informatik, (2022)

[DKPvdW20] Duncan, R., Kissinger, A., Perdrix, S., van de Wetering, J.: Graph-theoretic simplification of quantum circuits with the ZX-calculus. Quantum **4**, 279 (2020)

[DTB16] Dunjko, V., Taylor, J.M., Briegel, H.J.: Quantum-enhanced machine learning. Phys. Rev. Lett. **117**(13), (2016)

[KvdW20a] Kissinger, A., van de Wetering, J.: PyZX: Large scale automated diagrammatic reasoning. In: Electronic Proceedings in Theoretical Computer Science, 318, pp. 229–241, (2020)

[KvdW20b] Kissinger, A., van de Wetering, J.: Reducing the number of non-Clifford gates in quantum circuits. Phys. Rev. A, **102**(2), (2020)

[PdOM17] Portugal, R., de Oliveira, M.C., Moqadam, J.K.: Staggered quantum walks with hamiltonians. Phys. Rev. A, **95**(1), (2017)

[Pre18] Preskill, J.: Quantum computing in the NISQ era and beyond. Quantum **2**, 79 (2018)

[PSFG16] Portugal, R., Santos, R. A. M., Fernandes, T.D., Gonçalves, D.N.: The staggered quantum walk model. Quantum Inf. Process. **15**(1), pp. 85–101 (2016)

[San21] Santosm, J.: Quantum random walks: simulations and physical realizations. MSc Thesis in Engineering Physics, DI, Universidade do Minho, 2021

[UPR+23] Ufrecht, C., Periyasamy, M., Rietsch, S., Scherer, D.D., Plinge, A., Mutschler, C.: Cutting multi-control quantum gates with ZX calculus. Quantum **7**, 1147 (2023)

[VA12] Venegas-Andraca, S.E.: Quantum walks: a comprehensive review. Quantum Inf. Process. **11**(5), 1015–1106 (2012)

[vdW20] van de Wetering, J.: ZX-calculus for the working quantum computer scientist, (2020)

Many-Logic Modal Structures Based on the Lattice $L6$: A First Look

Abilio Rodrigues[1(✉)], Marcelo E. Coniglio[2], and Alfredo Freire[3]

[1] Federal University of Minas Gerais, Belo Horizonte, Brazil
abilio.rodrigues@gmail.com
[2] University of Campinas, Campinas, Brazil
coniglio@unicamp.br
[3] University of Brasília, Brasília, Brazil

Abstract. We propose an approach to information-based logics using *many-logic modal structures* (*MLMS*). These structures can express accessibility relations between worlds with different underlying logics by anchoring them to a common lattice, which contains the semantics of each logic as a sublattice. The common lattice allows us to transfer semantic information between different logics in a natural way. *MLMS* are suitable for representing connections between information states (i.e., configurations of databases) and the evolution of information states over time. We will illustrate the application of *MLMS* by means of the six-valued logic of evidence and truth LET_K^+, related to the lattice $L6$, and some four-, three-, and two-valued logics related to sublattices of $L6$. These logics are capable of representing paracomplete, paraconsistent, and classical contexts with six, four, three, and two scenarios. *MLMS* are able to represent connections between databases, users with different types of access (expressed by different logics) to a common database, and the evolution of databases over time.

1 Introduction

In 1977 Belnap published a very influential paper with the suggestive title 'How a computer should think' [2]. His motivation was to provide an account of logical consequence appropriate for a computer dealing with possibly inconsistent and incomplete information. The underlying idea was that of an information-based logic: a computer answers questions based on inferences that take as premises the information stored in its database, and such database may be inconsistent and incomplete. The idea of a computer obtaining information from multiple sources can be expressed in terms of different configurations of a database over time. Each configuration is an *information state* that can be represented by a world in a Kripke model. In this context, a world is essentially the set of sentences that hold within it.

Here we propose an account of information states based on *many-logic modal structures* (*MLMS*), a paradigm for Kripke semantics introduced by Freire and Martins in [7]. As we will see, *MLMS* are capable of expressing the connections

J. Proença et al. (Eds.): SEFM 2024, LNCS 15551, pp. 120–125, 2026.
https://doi.org/10.1007/978-3-031-94748-3_11

between information states conceived as different databases, the evolution of databases over time, and different types of access to databases. This framework integrates worlds in different environments, which are different formal systems related to sublattices of a given lattice. These modal structures can express connections between these formal systems – and thus between worlds in the corresponding many-logic structure – by anchoring them to a common lattice that contains the semantics of each formal system as a sublattice. In this framework, the notion of necessity is redefined, and the common lattice allows the transfer of semantic information between different logics in a natural way.

We will explore some applications of many-logic modal structures based on sublattices of the lattice *L6*, defined by the six-valued semantics of the logic of evidence and truth LET_K^+ [4]. Logics of evidence and truth (*LETs*) are equipped with a classicality operator ∘ that recovers classical logic for sentences in its scope. When ∘A holds, the sentence A is subjected to classical logic, otherwise the underlying logic of A is *FDE* (the Belnap-Dunn 4-valued logic [2,6,9]), or an extension of *FDE*. *LETs* can be interpreted in terms of information, and in this case a sentence ∘A means that the information conveyed by A, positive or negative, is reliable. The connective ∘ can thus be thought of as a kind of *certification*.

2   Many-Logic Modal Structures

The language $\mathcal{L}$ is composed of the set of denumerably many sentential letters $Var = \{p_1, p_2, \dots\}$, the unary connectives ∘ and ¬, the binary connectives ∧, ∨, and →, and parentheses. The set of formulas of $\mathcal{L}$ is inductively defined in the usual way. Roman capitals $A, B, C, \dots$ will be used as metavariables for the formulas of $\mathcal{L}$, while Greek capitals $\Gamma, \Delta, \Sigma, \dots$ will be used as metavariables for sets of formulas. The language $\mathcal{L}^{\square}$ is obtained just by extending $\mathcal{L}$ with the unary connective $\square$.

A *filtered $\mathcal{L}$-lattice* is a matrix logic $\langle \mathbf{L}, \mathrm{D} \rangle$, where

- $\mathbf{L} = \langle L, ., +, -, \odot, \Rightarrow \rangle$ such that $\langle L, ., + \rangle$ is a lattice $-, \odot$ are unary operations over L and $\Rightarrow$ is a binary operation over L
- $\mathrm{D} \subseteq L$.

We denote by $SubLat(\langle L, ., + \rangle)$ the set of all complete sublattices of $\langle L, ., + \rangle$. Let $LAT \subseteq SubLat(\langle L, ., + \rangle)$.

Definition 1. A *many-logic modal structure M* (over LAT and $\mathcal{L}^{\square}$) is a tuple $\langle W, R, I, v \rangle$ such that:

1. $I : W \to LAT$ assigns a lattice to each world. We denote the lattice $I(w)$ by L_w.
2. R is a relation from worlds to worlds, i.e. $R \subseteq W \times W$.
3. v is a *valuation function* from the set Var to values in $I(w)$, i.e. $v : W \times Var \longrightarrow L_w$ such that $v(w, p) \in L_w$, for each world $w \in W$ and $p \in Var$.

To extend a valuation $v_w := v(w, -)$ to all formulas of $\mathcal{L}^\square$ we need to define a way to interpret in a complete sublattice $L' \subseteq L$ elements not necessarily in L'.

Definition 2. Let L be a lattice and L' a complete sublattice of L.

The *down-interpretation* of value $x \in L$ in a lattice L' is defined as follows: $x_{dn}^{L'} = \bigvee_{L'} \{y \in L' : y \leqslant x\}$ (if $\{y \in L' : y \leqslant x\} = \emptyset$, then $x^{L'}$ is the least value in L').

Note that if $a \in L'$ then $a_{dn}^{L'} = a$. In the sequel, we just write $a^{L'}$ for $a_{dn}^{L'}$. For each world w in a many-logic modal structure M, the valuation v_w is extended to all formulas of $\mathcal{L}^\square$.

Definition 3. Let M be a many-logic modal structure $M = \langle W, R, I, v \rangle$. For each $w \in W$, the valuation v_w induced by M is the function $v_w : \mathcal{L}^\square \longrightarrow L_w$ such that:

1. $v_w(p) = v(w, p)$, where p is an atom,
2. $v_w(\neg A) = (-v_w(A))^{L_w}$,
3. $v_w(\circ A) = (\odot v_w(A))^{L_w}$,
4. $v_w(A \vee B) = (v_w(A) + v_w(B))^{L_w}$,
5. $v_w(A \wedge B) = (v_w(A).v_w(B))^{L_w}$,
6. $v_w(A \rightarrow B) = (v_w(A) \Rightarrow v_w(B))^{L_w}$,
7. $v_w(\square A) = \bigwedge_{L_w} \{(v_u(A))^{L_w} \mid wRu\}$,

The operations 2 to 6 above in L_w are defined within the specific lattice L_w (the co-domain of v_w is L_w). They correspond to the connectives of the logic related to L_w.

3   The Lattices and the Logics

Now we define, over the language $\mathcal{L}$, a family of logics that extend the logic FDE. One of them is the logic of evidence and truth LET_K^+. All these logics can be interpreted in terms of information and admit semantics whose related lattices are sublattices of $L6$, the lattice defined by LET_K^+ [4, Sect. 4.1]. These lattices and the respective logics will be used to instantiate the many-logic modal structures defined above.

Although in LET_K^+ the principles of explosion and excluded middle are not valid, for every A and B, $\circ A, A, \neg A \vdash B$ and $\circ A \vdash A \vee \neg A$. LET_K^+ extends the four scenarios of FDE to six in a natural way, by adding two more scenarios, of reliable positive and reliable negative information:

- When $\circ A$ does not hold:
    (i) $v(A) = T_0$: only positive information A (A holds, $\neg A$ does not hold);
    (ii) $v(A) = F_0$: only negative information A ($\neg A$ holds, A does not hold);
    (iii) $v(A) = \mathsf{b}$: contradictory information about A (both A and $\neg A$ hold);
    (iv) $v(A) = \mathsf{n}$: no information at all about A (neither A nor $\neg A$ hold).

– When $\circ A$ holds:
   (v) $v(A) = T$: reliable positive information A;
   (vi) $v(A) = F$: reliable negative information A.

The lattice $L6$ extends the lattice $L4$, the logical order defined by the semantics of FDE [2, pp. 40ff.], with a new top and a new bottom, represented below by T and F respectively:

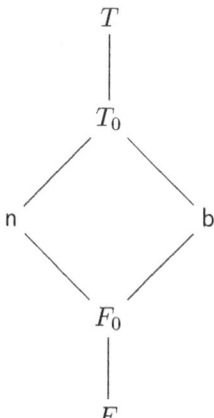

The logic FDE is extended to obtain logics with a lattice-based semantics related to sublattices of $L6$ intuitively interpreted in terms of the corresponding subsets of the six scenarios of LET_K^+. $FDE_\perp^\rightarrow$ extends FDE with a bottom particle and a material implication. It admits a semantics with the values T_0, n, b, F_0, corresponding to the scenarios (i)–(iv). $LP_\perp^\rightarrow$ extends the logic of paradox LP with a material implication and a bottom particle. It admits a semantics with the values T_0, b, F_0, scenarios (i), (ii), and (iii). $K3^\rightarrow$ extends $K3$ with a material implication. It admits a semantics with the values T_0, n, F_0, corresponding to the scenarios (i), (ii), and (iv). CL_w, which is classical logic with the semantic values T_0 and F_0. The lattices related to the logics above are sublattices of $L6$. We call them, respectively, $L4^w$, $B3^w$, $N3^w$, and $C2^w$, where the superscript w indicates that they are a *weak* interpretation of the corresponding scenarios.

The following logics admit semantics based on sublattices of $L6$, but with the strong values T and F instead of the values T_0 and F_0. $LJ4$, a four-valued logic with the values T, F, b, n (scenarios (iii) to (vi)). $J3$, the three-valued paraconsistent logic introduced in [5], admits a three-valued semantics with the values T, b, F (scenarios (iii), (v), (vi)). $L3$ is the three-valued Łukasiewicz's logic, which admits a semantics with the values T, n, F (scenarios (iv), (v), (vi)). CL_s, classical logic interpreted with the semantic values T, F. We call the lattices related to the logics above, respectively, $L4^s$, $B3^s$, $N3^s$, and $C2^s$, where the superscript s indicates that they are a *strong* interpretation of the corresponding scenarios, in the sense that there is certified (reliable) information being expressed.

The multi-valued semantics of all the logics mentioned above are defined by means of twist structures, adapting the semantics of LET_K^+ (see [8, Sect. 3] and [4, Sect. 3.2]). The logic $J3$ is equivalent to the logic $LFI1$, investigated in [3] as a paraconsistent logic suitable for closed-world databases. *J3* is presented in [5] in a language with $\neg$, $\lor$, and ∇ (∇A holds when A is assigned a designated value). *LFI1* is presented in [1] in the same language of LET_K, with $\circ$ as a primitive connective.

4   Examples and What's Next

Many-logic model structures can be constructed based on the filtered $\mathcal{L}$-lattice $\langle \mathbf{L}, D \rangle$ where $\mathbf{L} = \langle L6, \tilde{\land}, \tilde{\lor}, \tilde{\neg}, \tilde{\circ}, \tilde{\rightarrow} \rangle$ and $D = \{T, T_0, \mathsf{b}\}$, and making $LAT = \{L6, L4^w, L4^s, B3^w, B3^s, N3^w, N3^s, C2^w, C2^s\}$. An illustrative example is given by the model below.

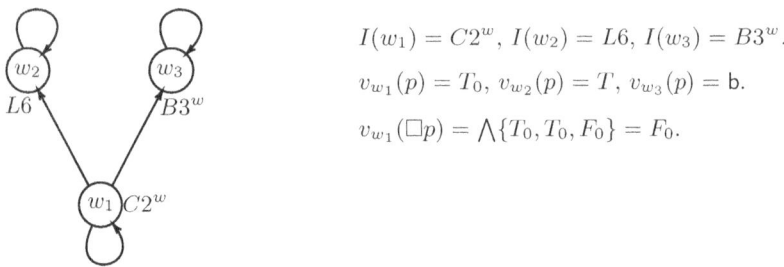

$$I(w_1) = C2^w, \; I(w_2) = L6, \; I(w_3) = B3^w.$$

$$v_{w_1}(p) = T_0, \; v_{w_2}(p) = T, \; v_{w_3}(p) = \mathsf{b}.$$

$$v_{w_1}(\Box p) = \bigwedge\{T_0, T_0, F_0\} = F_0.$$

Note that w_1 is a $C2^w$-world, so it sees $v_{w_2}(p) = T$ as T_0 and $v_{w_3}(p) = \mathsf{b}$ as F_0, i.e. $(v_{w_2}(p))^{L_{w_1}} = T_0$ and $(v_{w_3}(p))^{L_{w_1}} = F_0$. The model above can be thought of as representing three databases with different underlying logics, each of which accesses itself, but only w_1 is able to access the other two (w_2 and w_3).

More examples of *MLMS* with the set *LAT* above representing connections between databases, users with different types of access to a common database, and the evolution of databases over time are provided in [8, Sect. 4]. Some issues that arise in this context are (i) merging of data bases, (ii) temporal operators and the evolution of databases over time, (ii) inconsistency measures, and (iv) data certification. The authors are currently investigating these and other related topics.

Acknowledgements. The first author acknowledges support from the National Council for Scientific and Technological Development (CNPq, Brazil), grants 310037/2021-2 and 408040/2021-1, and from Minas Gerais State Agency for Research and Development (FAPEMIG, Brazil), grant APQ-02093-21. The second author acknowledges support from the National Council for Scientific and Technological Development (CNPq, Brazil), grants 309830/2023-0 and 408040/2021-1. He was also supported by the São Paulo Research Foundation (FAPESP, Brazil), thematic project *Rationality, logic and probability – RatioLog*, grant 2020/16353-3.

References

1. Antunes, H.: Contradictions for free: towards a nominalistic interpretation of contradictory theories. Ph.D. thesis, University of Campinas (2019)
2. Belnap, N.: How a computer should think. In: Ryle, G. (ed.) Contemporary Aspects of Philosophy. Oriel Press (1977). Reprinted in New Essays on Belnap-Dunn Logic. Springer (2019)
3. Carnielli, W., Marcos, J., de Amo, S.: Formal inconsistency and evolutionary databases. Logic Log. Philos. 8(8), 115–152 (2000)
4. Coniglio, M., Rodrigues, A.: From Belnap-Dunn four-valued logic to six-valued logics of evidence and truth. Stud. Log. 112(3), 561–606 (2024)
5. D'Ottaviano, I., da Costa, N.: Sur un probléme de Jaśkowski. Comptes Rendus l'Acad. Sci. 270(A), 1349–1353 (1970). https://gallica.bnf.fr/ark:/12148/bpt6k480298g/f1359.item
6. Dunn, J.M.: Intuitive semantics for first-degree entailments and 'coupled trees'. Philos. Stud. 29, 149–168 (1976). Reprinted in New Essays on Belnap-Dunn Logic. Springer (2019)
7. Freire, A., Martins, M.: Modality across different logics. Log. J. IGPL (2024). https://doi.org/10.1093/jigpal/jzae082
8. Martins, M., Rodrigues, A., Coniglio, M., Freire, A.: On many-logic modal structures based on the lattice $L6$. Manuscript (2024). https://www.researchgate.net/publication/383455863_On_many-logic_modal_structures_based_on_the_lattice_L6
9. Omori, H., Wansing, H. (eds.): New Essays on Belnap-Dunn Logic. Springer (2019)

CIFMA 2024

CIFMA 2024 Organizers' Message

CIFMA 2024, the *6th International Workshop on Cognition: Interdisciplinary Foundations, Models and Applications* took place on 5 November 2024, at the University of Aveiro, Aveiro, Portugal, co-located with SEFM 2024.

Cognition encompasses many aspects of intellectual functions and processes such as attention, knowledge, memory, judgment, reasoning, problem solving, decision making, and comprehension and production of language. Although it originated from the field of psychology, it goes beyond the individual human mind and behaviour, and involves and affects interaction with the environment in which humans act. The increasing complexity of the environment with which humans interact is no longer restricted to their natural living environment and the other humans populating it, but includes a large technological support consisting of physical and computational systems, virtual worlds, and robots.

At the workshop, cognitive processes were analysed from different perspectives within different contexts, notably in the fields of linguistics, neuroscience, psychiatry, psychology, education, philosophy, anthropology, linguistics, biology, systemics, logic, and computer science.

We received a total of 12 submissions; 9 of these papers were accepted for presentation and elaborated versions of these presentations are included in the present proceedings. The program was completed by an invited talk of João Gama (Inesc Tec and FEP, University of Porto) entitled A New Spring for Artificial Intelligence. We are grateful to the Program Committee for their dedication to the critical task of reviewing the submissions. We are also grateful to members of the Organizing Committee of SEFM and the local staff in Aveiro for making the necessary arrangements. Finally, we thank the keynote speaker and the authors for their efforts in writing their papers and for the excellent presentations.

February 2025

Reinhard Kahle
Graham Pluck

CIFMA 2024 Organization

Program Committee Chairs

Reinhard Kahle   NOVA University Lisbon, Portugal and University
                                  of Tübingen, Germany
Graham Pluck   Chulalongkorn University, Thailand

Program Committee

Pierluigi Graziani   University of Urbino, Italy
Antonio Cerone   Nazarbayev University, Kazakhstan
Oana Andrei   University of Glasgow, UK
Giuseppe Primiero   University of Milan, Italy
Paolo Milazzo   University of Pisa, Italy
Edoardo Datteri   Università degli Studi di Milano-Bicocca, Italy
Giuseppe Sergioli   University of Cagliari, Italy
Samuel Alexander   Ohio State University, USA
Mirko Tagliaferri   University of Urbino, Italy
Pedro Quaresma   University of Coimbra, Portugal
Ulrich Kohlenbach   TU Darmstadt, Germany
Francesco Bianchini   University of Bologna, Italy
Giorgia Troiani   Nazarbayev University, Kazakhstan
Heather Winskel   James Cook University Singapore, Singapore
Suphasiree Chantavarin   Chulalongkorn University, Thailand
Davide Grossi   University of Groningen, The Netherlands
Gianluca Curzi   University of Gothenburg, Sweden

On Group Secrets
and the Metacommunicative Aspects
of Revealing a True Secret

Alessandro Aldini[1] , Davide Fazio[2(✉)] , Pierluigi Graziani[1] ,
Raffaele Mascella[2] , and Mirko Tagliaferri[1]

[1] University of Urbino, Urbino, Italy
{alessandro.aldini,pierluigi.graziani,mirko.tagliaferri}@uniurb.it
[2] University of Teramo, Teramo, Italy
{dfazio2,rmascella}@unite.it

Abstract. This research paper explores the logical foundations of group
secrets, focusing on their preservation and the interplay of belief, knowledge, and intention inherent in secrecy among agents. Key findings establish the logical conditions under which group secrets are maintained and
examine how various logical operations influence these secrets. Additionally, the paper offers insights into certain metacommunicative aspects of
secret revelation, specifically when the goal is leaving the secret unknown
to a targeted nescient. In particular, we provide a formal analysis of
intentions crucial in communicative acts.

Keywords: Logic of Secret · Group Secret · Common Knowledge ·
Metacommunicative dimension · Secrets' disclosure

1 Introduction

Secrets are integral to private and public aspects of our lives, encompassing information we wish to remain confidential. Whether it's keeping a secret recipe from
competitors or protecting home banking credentials from hackers, the essence of
a secret lies in the separation between those who hold the information (secret
keepers) and those from whom it is hidden (nescients).

Studies on secrecy span multiple disciplines, including psychology [9,11,13],
philosophy [2], computer science [6], management science [4,10], and semiotics
[14]. Additionally, there has been significant research on secrecy from the perspective of formal logic [8,15], which is where our contribution lies. While previous studies have formalized key aspects of secrecy, such as the distinction between

---

The Italian Ministry of Education, University, and Research, through the PRIN 2022
project 'Developing Kleene Logics and their Applications' (DeKLA), project code:
2022SM4XC8, supported the work of A. Aldini and P. Graziani. The European Union
has funded the work of D. Fazio and R. Mascella - NextGenerationEU under the
Italian Ministry of University and Research (MUR) National Innovation Ecosystem
grant ECS00000041 - VITALITY - CUP C43C22000380007.

J. Proença et al. (Eds.): SEFM 2024, LNCS 15551, pp. 131–147, 2026.
https://doi.org/10.1007/978-3-031-94748-3_12

knowing a secret [15] and *(intending) to keep a secret*[1], further exploration is required.

In a recent paper [1], the authors aimed to logically investigate the concept of *keeping a true secret*, focusing on its modal and intentional components. Specifically, [1] sought to formalize propositions like "Agent *a intends* to keep φ *secret* from agent *b*," along with related notions. The approach carried out in [1] aligns with existing research, such as [11,12], where secrecy is broadly defined as "an intention to keep some piece of information, known to oneself, unknown from one or more others" (cf. [12, p. 542]). However, the investigation of [1] adopted a static and descriptive perspective, deliberately excluding dynamic aspects like belief revision or interactions between secret keepers. The research outcome was a formal system bridging the existing frameworks in the literature by introducing a new tool for investigating secrecy-related intentions. Furthermore, [1] focused on secrecy involving only two agents, the nescient and the secret keeper, without favouring any specific nature of the agents. However, in many cases, the nescient and secret keepers are not individual agents but groups of agents. They can be companies, computer networks, or people. An example is represented by a national intelligence agency that intends to keep a piece of particular national security information, such as a covert operation or a strategic plan, secret from unauthorized individuals to protect the country's security and prevent internal or external threats. Or consider a division of a technology company that intends to keep a research and development project, a patented formula, or a market strategy secret from potential competitors to maintain a competitive advantage and protect intellectual property.

The concept of a group secret has attracted great attention over the past years due to its importance for understanding social dynamics within groups of agents. Processes underpinning secrecy are associated with creating boundaries, with the impacts of secrecy among the in-group often traced to the formation of strong interpersonal ties and collective identities (cf., e.g. [4]), which accounted for higher levels of social interaction and social trust. The concept of a group secret is significant within the framework of managerial sciences, with organizational secrets being subjects in point.

To provide a formal framework capable of dealing with group secrets, the system proposed by [1] can be easily extended to sets of agents as it does not presuppose any postulation about the nature of agents involved: they can stand for either individuals or collective entities whatsoever. However, members of a group of secret keepers might be related to each other through relationships and internal rules concerning the *sharing* of knowledge and secrets that a suitable system should consider. Among them, we recognize the following[2]:

S1 All members of the secret keepers' group *know* the secret φ;
S2 All members of the secret keepers' group believe that outsiders (nescients) do not know φ;

---

[1] See Slepian [13] for a thorough analysis of this distinction in psychology.
[2] Cf. [4] for examples in managerial contexts.

S3 All members of the secret keepers' group intend to ensure that nescients do not know/have access to φ;

S4 All secret keepers' group members do not intend to destroy/make false the information to be kept hidden.[3]

However, if we confine ourselves to S1-S4 above, we would only be considering extremely general situations as, for example, when a group of individuals intends to keep a piece of information secret from any member from another group independently, possibly not knowing that members from the same group are doing the same. However, in concrete social scenarios, it often happens that the group's members are *aware* to be part of the group of secret keepers. This fact means that:

S5 They share the common belief they all *know* the proposition to be kept secret;

S6 They share the common belief about with whom they have to keep the secret;

S7 They share the common belief that nescients do not know the secret;

S8 They share the common intention/commitment not to reveal the secret to the nescients and, at the same time, to preserve its truth as long as it aligns with theirs goals.

As previously mentioned, several studies have explored the concept of secrecy. In particular, some of them focus on the act of revealing (sharing) a secret. From Bellman [2] to Slepian [11], these analyses have shed light on various aspects of this process. An exciting aspect of the formal study of secret-keeping is the consideration of how the group of secret-keepers can expand when a secret is disclosed with the intent that it remains confidential among the original and newly informed parties while still being kept secret from those not included in the communication.

Following Bellman [2], the act of revealing a secret introduces a *metacommunicative element*; beyond the content of the secret itself, there is an implicit communication that the information should not be shared further and that the source must be protected. However, suppose agent a reveals φ to agent b with the intent that φ remains a secret from everyone except a and b. In that case, this does not necessarily mean that a and b now constitute a group of secret keepers in the above sense as its internal dynamics might fail to fulfil S8.[4]

---

[3] Imagine I intend to keep the statement *"there is* a secret laboratory in Raffaello Street" secret from a targeted group of nescients. If, to keep this information concealed, I decided to destroy the laboratory, the object of the secret would no longer exist. Therefore, the secret would be missing or even pointless.

[4] Imagine a tech company developing a new product. Alice, a senior engineer, discovers a critical vulnerability in the software. She shares this information with Bob, another engineer, asking him to keep it secret. Alice intends to keep the vulnerability secret from everyone outside their circle, including others in the company. Bob agrees to keep it secret, but *does not internalize the intention of secrecy*, e.g. although he intends not to reveal the secret himself, he intends to push Alice to disclose it. Therefore, they do not reach a shared commitment to secrecy, and so they do not form a group of secret keepers under condition S8.

The present article aims to extend [1] for investigating the group and meta-communicative dimensions of secrecy intentions and revelations. To this end, the paper will be structured as follows: in Sect. 2, we introduce an expansion of the formal system presented in [1] aimed at providing a formal treatment of group secret; in Sect. 3, we attempt a formal analysis of the metacommunicative dimension of revealing a true secret; we conclude in Sect. 4 with a summary and suggestions for future works.

2   Formalizing Group Secrets

The formalization of keeping true secrets given in [1] considers the presence of at least two agents: agent a, the secret keeper, and agent b, the nescient, from whom the secret must be kept. Moreover, the definition of secrecy in [1] is based on the following key assumptions from agent a's perspective:

1. Agent a knows the object of the secret, referred to as the *secretum*. Since knowledge is assumed to be factive, the content of a's secret must be true, which justifies the term *true secret* used in [1].
2. Agent a believes that agent b does not know the *secretum*. We use belief rather than knowledge because agent a cannot directly access agent b's mental states.
3. Agent a intends to act so that the truth of the *secretum* is preserved and agent b remains unaware of the *secretum* as long as it aligns with agent's goals.

Following [1], to capture these assumptions, we will use three modal operators: knowledge (K), belief (B), and intentionality (I), applied to multiple agents. The formal definition of a true secret, denoted by $S_{a,b}\varphi$, is expressed as follows (cf. [1, p. 3]):

$$S_{a,b}\varphi := K_a\varphi \wedge B_a \neg K_b \varphi \wedge I_a(\varphi \wedge \neg K_b \varphi).$$

It is worth observing that, by (3), we assume that the concept of a true secret involves the intention of preserving the truth of its content. Indeed, it might look quite strong, at first sight. After all, it is intuitively reasonable to argue that secrets might be preserved also e.g. by "destroying" their content. However, as we are dealing with intentions of secrecy concerning propositions that are *known*, making a proposition false, and so unknown to the secret keeper would inevitably result in the elimination of the main motivation to keep it secret.

2.1   A Logical System for Group Secrets

To provide a basic axiomatization of the primitive operators employed to formalize the notion of a group secret, we introduce the formal system SC as an expansion of the system S of multi-agent normal modal logic introduced in [1] using modal operators and inference rules for common belief, common knowledge and common commitment. To this aim, we enrich the alphabet of S employing new symbols $\mathbb{B}_C$, $\mathbb{I}_C$ and $\mathbb{K}_C$ (for any set C of agents) such that $\mathbb{B}_C\varphi$ will stand for "the group C has the common belief that φ", $\mathbb{I}_C\varphi$ will mean "the group C has the common commitment of intending to bring about a state of affairs in which φ is true as long as it aligns with group's goals" and, of course, $\mathbb{K}_C\varphi$ will be short for "The group C has the common knowledge that φ". Indeed, the above statements will be codified within our framework using the *infinite* conjunction of formulas of the form $(E_C^B)^n\varphi$, $(E_C^I)^n\varphi$, and $(E_C^K)^n\varphi$ $(n \geq 1)$, respectively, where e.g. $(E_C^K)^n\varphi$ is to be meant as the n-th composition of the "every-member-of-C-knows-that" operator E_C^K. Consequently, saying that φ is a common belief (knowledge) among members of C will be equivalent to asserting that any member of C believes (knows) that φ, any member of C believes (knows) that any member of C believes (knows) that φ, and so on. Similarly, the common commitment of C towards φ will amount to say that all members of C intend to bring about a state of affairs in which φ is true as long as it aligns with group's goals, all members of C intend to bring about a state in which any member of C intends to bring about a state of affair in which φ is true as long as it aligns with group's goals, and so on.

A presentation of the system SC comes next. Let Ag be a non-empty, finite set of agents, and let Var be an infinite, countable set of variables. Let $\mathrm{Fm_{SC}}$ be the smallest set of formulas generated by the following grammar:

$$\varphi := p \mid \neg\varphi \mid \varphi \wedge \psi \mid I_a\varphi \mid K_a\varphi \mid B_a\varphi \mid \mathbb{K}_C\varphi \mid \mathbb{B}_C\varphi \mid \mathbb{I}_C\varphi.$$

where $p \in Var$ and $C \cup \{a\} \subseteq Ag$. As customary, we set $\varphi \vee \psi := \neg(\neg\varphi \wedge \neg\psi)$ and $\varphi \to \psi := (\neg\varphi \vee \psi)$. Following customary conventions, for any $C \subseteq Ag$ and $\varphi \in \mathrm{Fm_S}$, we set:

$$E_C^\star\varphi := \bigwedge_{a\in C} \star_a\varphi,$$

where $\star \in \{K, B, I\}$. In other words, $E_C^K\varphi, E_C^I\varphi$, and $E_C^B\varphi$ encode the statement "all agents from C know that φ", "all agents from C intend to bring about a state of affairs in which φ is true as long as it aligns with their goals"[5], and "all members form C believe that φ", respectively.

The logic $\mathsf{SC} = \langle \mathrm{Fm_{SC}}, \vdash_{\mathsf{SC}} \rangle$ is the *derivability* relation (to be defined as customary) induced by the axiom and inference rule schemes, for any $C \cup \{a\} \subseteq Ag$, illustrated in Table 1.

We remark that $(RI)_I$, $(RI)_B$ and $(RI)_K$ mean that if the premise of (an instance of) the rule is a theorem, then the conclusion is.

The epistemic part of the axiomatization (A1–A7) contains nothing new and is, therefore, standard. However, we remark that we do not assume negative introspection for knowledge operators. This is motivated by the need of keeping our system as "basic" as possible and investigating secrecy without endorsing more assumption than those accepted by almost all researchers in epistemic logic. Focusing on the intentionality operator I, axiom A8 states that any agent a is

---

[5] For brevity, we will omit the clause "as long as it aligns with agents' goals" where no ambiguity or misunderstanding arises.

Table 1. Axioms and rules of SC.

A1	All tautologies of classical propositional logic
A2	$\star(\varphi \rightarrow \psi) \rightarrow (\star\varphi \rightarrow \star\psi)$ for any $\star \in \{B_a, K_a, I_a\}$
A3	$K_a\varphi \rightarrow \varphi$
A4	$K_a\varphi \rightarrow K_a K_a\varphi$
A5	$B_a\varphi \rightarrow \neg B_a \neg\varphi$
A6	$K_a\varphi \rightarrow B_a\varphi$
A7	$B_a\varphi \rightarrow K_a B_a\varphi$
A8	$I_a\varphi \rightarrow \neg I_a \neg\varphi$
A9	$I_a\varphi \rightarrow K_a I_a\varphi$
A10	$I_a\varphi \rightarrow I_a K_a\varphi$
A11	$I_a\varphi \rightarrow I_a I_a\varphi$
A12	$\mathbb{I}_C\varphi \rightarrow E_C^I(\varphi \wedge \mathbb{I}_C\varphi)$
A13	$\mathbb{B}_C\varphi \rightarrow E_C^B(\varphi \wedge \mathbb{B}_C\varphi)$
A14	$\mathbb{K}_C\varphi \rightarrow E_C^K(\varphi \wedge \mathbb{K}_C\varphi)$

$$\frac{\varphi \qquad \varphi \rightarrow \psi}{\psi} \text{ RMP} \quad \text{and} \quad \frac{\varphi}{\star\varphi} \text{ RN}_\star \quad \text{where } \star \in \{I_a, K_a, B_a\}$$

$$\frac{\varphi \rightarrow E_C^I(\psi \wedge \varphi)}{\varphi \rightarrow \mathbb{I}_C\psi} \text{ (RI)}_I \qquad \frac{\varphi \rightarrow E_C^B(\psi \wedge \varphi)}{\varphi \rightarrow \mathbb{B}_C\psi} \text{ (RI)}_B \qquad \frac{\varphi \rightarrow E_C^K(\psi \wedge \varphi)}{\varphi \rightarrow \mathbb{K}_C\psi} \text{ (RI)}_K$$

$$\text{for any } C \subseteq Ag$$

consistent with her intentions, axioms A9 and A10 express the transparency and awareness conditions (see [1] for details), respectively, and axiom A11 represents a *persistence* condition for intentionality. Having the intention to bring about a state of affairs in which φ is true entails that such an intention is preserved in all states of affairs reachable through it. This assumption does not make any commitment from a *tense* perspective, as we are concerned with a static tenseless framework. Therefore, the operator I should not be regarded as a *tense* operator. Also, it is worth observing that I, like B, is not factive and, differently from B, is not implied by K. The interested reader is referred to [1] for a thorough discussion of A1–A11. Axioms A12–A13 as well as inference rules $(\text{RI})_I$, $(\text{RI})_B$, and $(\text{RI})_K$ are nothing but axioms and inference rules for common knowledge (straightforwardly extended to common belief and common intention) provided by [5]. Of course, an operator of "common intention" might look quite nonstandard at first sight. However, it has a quite natural motivation. Indeed, as we are interested in group secrets, a natural desideratum is dealing with situation in which one has not only common knowledge/belief among members of a group, but also a sort of joint commitment, to be meant as an intention to preserve group's intentions (of secrecy, in our case) – see p. 2.1. Therefore, we have endowed the system SC with a common intention operator to make reason of statements like "everyone intends to bring about a state of affairs in which φ is true, everyone intends to bring about a state of affairs in which everyone intends that φ, and so on ...."

We can now introduce the semantics for SC. Let A be a non-empty set. Recall that a binary relation $R \subseteq A \times A$ is said to be *serial* provided that, for any $i \in A$, there exists $j \in A$ such that $R(i, j)$.

Definition 1. *An $\mathcal{S}$-frame (a frame, for short) is a tuple*

$$\mathcal{F} = (W, \{R_a^I\}_{a \in Ag}, \{R_a^K\}_{a \in Ag}, \{R_a^B\}_{a \in Ag})$$

such that:

1. *W is a non-empty set of worlds (or states);*
2. *$R_a^B \subseteq W \times W$ is serial;*
3. *For any $a \in Ag$, $R_a^I \subseteq W \times W$ is serial and transitive;*
4. *For any $a \in Ag$, $R_a^K \subseteq W \times W$ is reflexive and transitive;*
5. *For any $i, j, w \in W$, and any $a \in Ag$, if $R_a^K(i, j)$ and $R_a^I(j, w)$, then $R_a^I(i, w)$.*
6. *For any $a \in Ag$, $R_a^B \subseteq R_a^K$;*
7. *For any $i, j, w \in W$ and $a \in Ag$, if $R_a^K(i, j)$ and $R_a^B(j, w)$, then $R_a^B(i, w)$;*
8. *For any $i, j, w \in W$ and $a \in Ag$, $R_a^I(i, j)$ and $R_a^K(j, w)$ imply $R_a^I(i, w)$.*

Note that, for any $\mathcal{S}$-frame $\mathcal{F} = (W, \{R_a^I\}_{a \in Ag}, \{R_a^K\}_{a \in Ag}, \{R_a^B\}_{a \in Ag})$, R_a^B is transitive. This is an immediate consequence of Definition 1(6), (7). Moreover, we observe that items 1(5), (7), (8) mirror semantically axioms (A9), (A7) and (A10), respectively.

Definition 2. *An $\mathcal{S}$-model (a model, in brief) is a tuple*

$$\mathcal{M} = (W, \{R_a^I\}_{a \in Ag}, \{R_a^K\}_{a \in Ag}, \{R_a^B\}_{a \in Ag}, v)$$

such that

1. *$(W, \{R_a^I\}_{a \in Ag}, \{R_a^K\}_{a \in Ag}, \{R_a^B\}_{a \in Ag})$ is an $\mathcal{S}$-frame, and*
2. *$v : Var \rightarrow \mathcal{P}(W)$ is a mapping, called an evaluation.*

Given an $\mathcal{S}$-model $\mathcal{M} = (W, \{R_a^I\}_{a \in Ag}, \{R_a^K\}_{a \in Ag}, \{R_a^B\}_{a \in Ag}, v)$, $i \in W$, $\varphi \in \text{Fms}$ the notion of truth in i ($\mathcal{M}, i \models \varphi$), truth in $\mathcal{M}$ ($\mathcal{M} \models \varphi$) and truth in any $\mathcal{S}$-model ($\models_\mathcal{S} \varphi$) are quite standard, so we refer e.g. to [5,7] for details. For the reader's convenience, we recap the semantic definitions of common belief, common knowledge, and common commitment (intention).

Let $\star \in \{I, B, K\}$, $C \subseteq Ag$, and $\varphi \in \text{Fm}_{\text{SC}}$. We define the formula $(E_C^\star)^n \varphi$, for any $n \geq 1$ as follows:

- $(E_C^\star)^1 \varphi := E_C^\star \varphi$;
- $(E_C^\star)^{n+1} \varphi := E_C^\star (E_C^\star)^n \varphi$

Let $\mathcal{F} = (W, \{R_a^I\}_{a \in Ag}, \{R_a^K\}_{a \in Ag}, \{R_a^B\}_{a \in Ag})$ be an $\mathcal{S}$-model. For any $C \subseteq Ag$ and $\star \in \{I, B, K\}$, we define:

$$R_C^\star := \bigcup_{a \in C} R_a^\star.$$

Note that, for any $C \subseteq Ag$, and any $\varphi \in \mathrm{Fm}_{\mathsf{SC}}$, the reading o R_C^B and R_C^K is the standard one, as they express nothing but general belief and general knowledge about φ, respectively, among members of C. As regards R_C^I, it expresses that all members of C share the intention of bringing about a state of affairs in which φ is true.

Moreover, given a non-empty set A and $R \subseteq A \times A$, we will denote by R^+ its transitive closure, i.e. the *smallest* transitive relation over A containing R. It is easily seen that, for any $x, y \in A$, xR^+y iff there exist $n > 1$, $x_1, \ldots, x_n \in A$ such that $x_1 = x$, $x_n = y$ and $x_i R x_{i+1}$, for any $1 \le i < n$.

Let $\mathcal{M} = (W, \{R_a^I\}_{a \in Ag}, \{R_a^K\}_{a \in Ag}, \{R_a^B\}_{a \in Ag}, v)$ be an $\mathcal{S}$-model, the clauses of satisfaction in $i \in W$ for common belief, common knowledge and common intention are defined, for any $C \subseteq Ag$, $i \in W$, as:

- $\mathcal{M}, i \models \mathbb{I}_C \varphi$ iff, for any $j \in W$ such that $(R_C^I)^+(i, j)$, $\mathcal{M}, j \models \varphi$;
- $\mathcal{M}, i \models \mathbb{B}_C \varphi$ iff, for any $j \in W$ such that $(R_C^B)^+(i, j)$, $\mathcal{M}, j \models \varphi$;
- $\mathcal{M}, i \models \mathbb{K}_C \varphi$ iff, for any $j \in W$ such that $(R_C^K)^+(i, j)$, $\mathcal{M}, j \models \varphi$.

The proof of the following proposition is straightforward.

Proposition 1. *Let* $\mathcal{M} = (W, \{R_a^I\}_{a \in Ag}, \{R_a^K\}_{a \in Ag}, \{R_a^B\}_{a \in Ag}, v)$, $C \subseteq Ag$, $\varphi \in \mathrm{Fm}_{\mathsf{SC}}$, *the following are equivalent:*

1. $\mathcal{M}, i \models \mathbb{I}_C \varphi$;
2. $\mathcal{M}, i \models (E_C^I)^n \varphi$, *for any* $n \ge 1$;
3. *If* $j \in W$ *and there are* $x_1, \ldots, x_n \in W$ $(n > 1)$ *such that* $x_1 = i, x_n = j$ *and, for any* $1 \le k < n$, $R_{a_i}^I(x_k, x_{k+1})$, $a_i \in C$, *then* $\mathcal{M}, j \models \varphi$.

Moreover, the same holds upon replacing $\mathbb{I}$ *by* $\mathbb{B}$ *(*$\mathbb{K}$*),* E_C^I *by* E_C^B *(*E_C^K*), and* R_C^I *by* R_C^B *(*R_C^K*).*

The next result can be proven through customary arguments already thoroughly discussed in the literature. See [5,7] for details.

Theorem 1. *For any* $\varphi \in \mathrm{Fm}_{\mathsf{SC}}$:

$$\vdash_{\mathsf{SC}} \varphi \text{ iff } \models_{\mathcal{S}} \varphi.$$

Obviously, SC is a *conservative expansion* of the system S from [1].

Following [1], we have started from a notion of "keeping a true secret" involving only two agents: a secret keeper and a (alleged) nescient.

Nevertheless, a natural question arises. Is it possible to generalize such a notion to express that a *group* C of agents keeps φ secret from a group D of agents such that $C \cap D = \emptyset$? A tentative answer is relatively easy to obtain. It suffices to set:

$$S_{C,D}\varphi := \bigwedge_{a \in C, b \in D} S_{a,b}\varphi.$$

Note that, by virtue of $\vdash_S \star(\varphi \wedge \psi) \leftrightarrow \star\varphi \wedge \star\psi$ with $\star \in \{K_a, B_a, I_a\}$ $(a \in Ag)$, one has

$$\vdash_{SC} S_{C,D}\varphi \leftrightarrow \bigwedge_{a \in C} K_a\varphi \wedge \bigwedge_{a \in C} B_a(\bigwedge_{b \in D} \neg K_b\varphi) \wedge \bigwedge_{a \in C} I_a((\bigwedge_{b \in D} \neg K_b\varphi) \wedge \varphi) \quad (1)$$

or, using the more streamlined notation introduced above,

$$\vdash_{SC} S_{C,D}\varphi \leftrightarrow E_C^K\varphi \wedge E_C^B(\bigwedge_{b \in D} \neg K_b\varphi) \wedge E_C^I((\bigwedge_{b \in D} \neg K_b\varphi) \wedge \varphi). \quad (2)$$

Indeed, such a notion of group secret turns out to preserve many important features of secrecy between pairs of agents, as it can be seen that, e.g., results from [1, Propositions 2 and 3] holding for $S_{a,b}$ are still valid once $S_{C,D}$ (for some non-empty $C, D \subseteq Ag$ such that $C \cap D = \emptyset$) is considered. However, an easy check shows that, e.g. agents from C need not know that other members of C intend to keep a proposition φ secret from a given agent $b \in D$ or there need not be *agreement* on secrecy intentions. A striking example is given by the fact that easy buildable Kripke models allow one to show that, for any $a, b, c \in Ag$

$$\nvdash_{SC} S_{\{a,b\},\{c\}}\varphi \rightarrow \neg(S_{a,b}\varphi \vee S_{b,a}\varphi). \quad \text{(A)}$$

or

$$\nvdash_{SC} S_{\{a,b\},\{c\}}\varphi \rightarrow B_b S_{a,c}\varphi, \quad \text{(B)}$$

Therefore, such a notion of a group secret falls short of capturing S5–S8. This remark suggests that a much more sophisticated definition of secrecy is needed to cope with more complex forms of secrecy.

The notion of a group secret formalized by (1) reveals certain limitations when it comes to encoding the full complexity of secret-sharing phenomena, e.g. in organizational contexts where a group of agents is explicitly "designated" to keep certain information secret. An example is given by company members who are requested to keep a piece of information of strategic relevance secret from outsiders. One notable issue is that (1) fails to capture whether any agent within the group is aware of the secrecy intentions of the other agents. In other words, while the formalism ensures that a group of agents collectively holds a secret, it does not guarantee that each agent understands that the other group's members are intentionally keeping the secret. Put another way, (1) does not capture the idea that secret keepers recognize that the group they are members of is the group of secret keepers.

Furthermore, (1) does not address the idea of a joint or common commitment to preserving the group's intention to keep a secret. Indeed, suppose secret keepers are aware of being part of a group designated to keep information concealed and intend to preserve the group's "mission". In that case, each member has not only the intention of keeping the information secret, but she also has the intention of preserving other members' intention of doing the same, e.g. by preserving conditions making intentions of concealment possible[6]. Without such a joint commitment, the group's "agreement" to preserve the secret need not hold, as individual agents may fail to realize the importance of maintaining the secrecy from the perspective of the group as a whole.

These shortcomings suggest that a slightly more sophisticated approach is required. In this venue, we propose a notion of *true group secret with common commitment* upon setting, for any $\varphi \in \mathrm{Fm_{SC}}$, $C, D \subseteq Ag$:

$$\mathbb{S}_{C,D}\varphi := \mathbb{B}_C S_{C,D}\varphi \wedge \mathbb{I}_C S_{C,D}\varphi \wedge S_{C,D}\varphi. \tag{$\mathbb{S}$}$$

Whenever no danger of confusion will be impending, if $a, b \in Ag$, $C = \{a\}$ and $D = \{b\}$, we will write simply $\mathbb{S}_{a,b}$, $\mathbb{I}_a$ and $\mathbb{B}_a$, instead of $\mathbb{S}_{\{a\},\{b\}}$, $\mathbb{I}_{\{a\}}$ and $\mathbb{B}_{\{a\}}$, respectively.[7]

Proposition 2. *For any $\varphi \in \mathrm{Fm_{SC}}$ it holds that*

$$\vdash_{\mathsf{SC}} \mathbb{S}_{a,b}\varphi \leftrightarrow S_{a,b}\varphi.$$

In other words, the concept of "intending to keep a true" secret outlined in [1] is a limit case of the concept of a group secret once only two agents, a secret keeper and a nescient, are considered. The next proposition can be proven by exploiting well-known techniques.

Proposition 3. *Let $\varphi \in \mathrm{Fm_{SC}}$, $C \subseteq Ag$:*

1. $\vdash_{\mathsf{SC}} \mathbb{B}_C\varphi \to \mathbb{B}_C\mathbb{B}_C\varphi$;
2. $\vdash_{\mathsf{SC}} \mathbb{I}_C\varphi \to \mathbb{I}_C\mathbb{I}_C\varphi$
3. $\vdash_{\mathsf{SC}} \mathbb{K}_C\varphi \leftrightarrow \mathbb{K}_C\mathbb{K}_C\varphi$;
4. $\vdash_{\mathsf{SC}} \mathbb{K}_C\varphi \to \mathbb{B}_C\varphi$;
5. $\vdash_{\mathsf{SC}} \mathbb{K}_C\varphi \to \mathbb{B}_C\mathbb{K}_C\varphi$;

Proposition 3 presents key properties of modalities for common knowledge, belief and intention inherited from the behaviour of knowledge, belief, and intention operators. The first two items illustrate the positive introspection of common beliefs ($\mathbb{B}_C$) and intentions ($\mathbb{I}_C$). The third item deals with the idempotency of common knowledge ($\mathbb{K}_C$), which is due to the factivity of the knowledge operator K_a. The last two items establish a link between knowledge and common

---

[6] For example, if Alice and Bob are part of a group C of secret keepers, and Alice has the intention of preserving the "mission" of C, then Alice's intentions should include e.g. avoiding to threaten Bob's intention of secrecy by telling him he is no longer supposed to keep the information secret.

[7] A complete version of this paper including proofs of main results is available at the CIFMA-2024 workshop's website https://cifma.github.io/ .

belief, indicating that a group's knowledge implies that the proposition is commonly believed and that there is a common belief about the group's knowledge. These properties are crucial for modelling group coordination and transparency, especially in contexts like security, cooperation, and information management. Customary semantic arguments can easily prove the next propositions.

Proposition 4. *Let* $\varphi \in \mathrm{Fm_{SC}}$, $C, D \subseteq Ag$, $a, b \in C$, $d \in D$. *The following hold:*

1. $\vdash_{SC} \neg \mathbb{S}_{C,C} \varphi$;
2. $\vdash_{SC} \neg \mathbb{S}_{C,D} \top \wedge \neg \mathbb{S}_{C,D} \bot \wedge (\mathbb{S}_{C,D} \varphi \to \varphi)$;
3. $\vdash_{SC} \mathbb{S}_{C,D} \varphi \to B_a \mathbb{S}_{C,D} \varphi$;
4. $\vdash_{SC} \mathbb{S}_{C,D} \varphi \wedge \mathbb{B}_C \mathbb{I}_C \mathbb{S}_{C,D} \varphi \to \mathbb{B}_C \mathbb{S}_{C,D} \varphi$;
5. $\vdash_{SC} \mathbb{S}_{C,D}(\mathbb{S}_{C,D} \varphi) \to \mathbb{S}_{C,D} \varphi$;
6. $\vdash_{SC} \neg K_d \varphi \to \neg K_d \mathbb{S}_{C,D} \varphi$;
7. $\vdash_{SC} \neg \mathbb{S}_{C,D} K_d \varphi$;
8. $\vdash_{SC} \mathbb{S}_{C,D} \varphi \to \neg \mathbb{S}_{C,D} \neg \varphi$;
9. $\vdash_{SC} \neg \mathbb{S}_{C,D} \mathbb{K}_D \varphi$;
10. $\vdash_{SC} \mathbb{S}_{C,D} \varphi \to \neg (S_{a,b} \varphi \vee S_{b,a} \varphi)$;
11. $\vdash_{SC} B_a(K_b \varphi \to K_d \varphi) \to \neg \mathbb{S}_{C,D} \varphi$.

Proposition 4 establishes some basic features of group secrets that generalize results obtained in [1, Proposition 2]. The first item is clear: no group C of secret keepers may ever intend to keep a piece of information secret to itself. Item (2) introduces limits on secrecy by establishing that secrets must be *contingent*, meaning they cannot apply to universally true ($\top$) or false ($\bot$) statements as tautologies are known to everyone (this is a side effect of logical omniscience determined by using a normal box operator for knowledge). In contrast, contradictions cannot be known by anyone (after all, we are dealing with known secrets!). Moreover, group secrets are factive. Item (3) shows that $\mathbb{S}_{C,D}$ allows us to overcome (in a specific sense) the drawback highlighted in (B). Item (4) expresses a weak form of positive introspection of secrecy concerning common belief. If φ is a group secret of C w.r.t. D and it is a common belief that there is a joint commitment in guaranteeing that all the members of C have the intention of keeping φ secret, then there is a common belief that φ is a group secret. Items (5) to (9) highlight that, at least in a weak form, many properties of secrecy involving pairs of agents rather than groups still hold (cf. [1]). Item (10) resolves the drawback in (A) by showing that no member of a group of secret-keepers can have the intention of keeping the information they are supposed to conceal a secret from each other. Finally, item (11) expresses the idea that a necessary condition for the existence of a group secret φ is that no agent in the group C of secret keepers believes that there is a member of C (him/herself included) whose knowledge of φ entails that φ is revealed to at least one nescient in D. This rules out situations in which e.g. one includes in C agents which may hinder (intentionally or not) the group secret.

Of course, one might ask if some conditions from Proposition 4 might be somehow strengthened. The next proposition shows that this is not the case.

Proposition 5. *Let $\varphi \in \mathrm{Fm_{SC}}$, $C, D \subseteq Ag$. The following hold:*

1. $\nvdash_{\mathsf{SC}} \mathbb{S}_{C,D}\varphi \to \mathbb{B}_C \mathbb{S}_{C,D}\varphi$;
2. $\nvdash_{\mathsf{SC}} \mathbb{S}_{C,D}\varphi \to \mathbb{S}_{C,D}(\mathbb{S}_{C,D}\varphi)$
3. $\nvdash_{\mathsf{SC}} \mathbb{S}_{C,D}\varphi \to B_a \mathbb{S}_{C,D}\varphi$, *for any $a \in C$;*
4. $\nvdash_{\mathsf{SC}} \mathbb{S}_{C,D}\varphi \to \mathbb{I}_C \mathbb{B}_C \mathbb{S}_{C,D}\varphi$;
5. $\nvdash_{\mathsf{SC}} \mathbb{S}_{C,D}\varphi \to \mathbb{I}_C \mathbb{S}_{C,D}\varphi$;
6. $\nvdash_{\mathsf{SC}} \neg \mathbb{S}_{C,D} \mathbb{I}_D \varphi$;
7. $\nvdash_{\mathsf{SC}} \neg \mathbb{S}_{C,D} \mathbb{B}_D \varphi$.

Proposition 5 highlights the limitations and fragility of group secrets. Unlike individual secrets, group secrets do not necessarily propagate through common beliefs or intentions. The first items show that the existence of a group secret φ ($\mathbb{S}_{C,D}\varphi$) among agents from C does not imply that it is a common belief within C that φ is actually a group secret ($\mathbb{B}_C \mathbb{S}_{C,D}\varphi$). Moreover, unlike the operator $S_{a,b}$ (see [1, Proposition 2]), $\mathbb{S}_{C,D}$ is not idempotent. This reflects the complexity of maintaining secrecy in groups, where agreement might be limited to the content of the secret ("first-order secrecy") but not to the intention of keeping the secret itself ("second-order secrecy"). This is coherent with items (3)–(5), where it is shown that $\mathbb{S}_{C,D}\varphi$ fails to entail that any secret keeper recognizes φ as a group secret or that there is common intention to bring about a state of affairs in which (it is common belief that) φ is a group secret. Finally, (6) and (7) outline a kind of weakness of groups, i.e., group members D need not be aware there is a common commitment or belief about a proposition φ among them. Nevertheless, important properties of secrecy are still valid once group secrets come into play.

Proposition 6. *Let $\varphi \in \mathrm{Fm_{SC}}$ and $C, D \subseteq Ag$. The following hold:*

1. *If $\vdash_{\mathsf{SC}} \varphi \to \psi$ and $\vdash_{\mathsf{SC}} \psi \to \chi$, one has $\vdash_{\mathsf{SC}} (\mathbb{S}_{C,D}\varphi \wedge \mathbb{S}_{C,D}\chi) \to \mathbb{S}_{C,D}\psi$;*
2. *For any $n \geq 2$, $\vdash_{\mathsf{SC}} \varphi_i \to \varphi_{i+1}$ $(1 \leq i < n)$ implies $\vdash_{\mathsf{SC}} (\mathbb{S}_{C,D}\varphi_1 \wedge \mathbb{S}_{C,D}\varphi_n) \to \bigwedge_{i=1}^{n} \mathbb{S}_{C,D}\varphi_i$.*

This proposition shows that group secrets (modelled by $\mathbb{S}_{C,D}$) still satisfy the interpolation rule. Specifically, if the group C knows φ and χ, then they can infer ψ when $\varphi \to \psi$ and $\psi \to \chi$. This result is crucial in the phenomenon of group secrets, as it ensures that the collective knowledge of C and D evolves coherently through logical reasoning, maintaining secrecy while allowing for distributed inference.

Remark 1. It is reasonable to wonder if Proposition 6(1) could be strengthened to the effect that the formula

$$\mathbb{K}_C \mathbb{K}_D((\varphi \to \psi) \wedge (\psi \to \chi)) \to (\mathbb{S}_{C,D}\varphi \wedge \mathbb{S}_{C,D}\chi \to \mathbb{S}_{C,D}\psi) \tag{3}$$

is still a theorem of SC. Unfortunately, the answer is negative, as a counterexample can be already provided upon assuming $C = \{a\}$ and $D = \{b\}$. Indeed, in order to derive $S_{a,b}\psi$ from $S_{a,b}\varphi$ and $S_{a,b}\chi$, one has to make heavy use of $\vdash_{\mathsf{SC}} \varphi \to \psi$ and $\vdash_{\mathsf{SC}} \psi \to \chi$ since the former entails that $\vdash_{\mathsf{SC}} I_a \varphi \to I_a \psi$ which in turn, upon assuming $S_{a,b}\varphi$, and so also $I_a\varphi$, entails $I_a\psi$. This latter condition is no longer ensured if one assumes the antecedent of (3) which does not guarantee that $I_a(\varphi \to \psi)$ must hold as well.

Since Proposition 6(2) implies (1), and the latter does not hold, the former does not as well.

The next proposition extends to group secrets some results already proved in [1] concerning the behaviour of secrecy operators w.r.t. the main logical connectives.

Proposition 7. *Let* $\varphi, \psi \in \text{Fm}_{SC}$, $C, D \subseteq Ag$ *with* $C \cap D \neq \emptyset$, *and* $b \in D$. *The following hold:*

1. $\vdash_{SC} (\mathbb{B}_C K_b \psi \vee \mathbb{I}_C K_b \psi) \to \neg \mathbb{S}_{C,D}(\varphi \to \psi)$;
2. $\vdash_{SC} (\mathbb{B}_C K_b \neg \varphi \vee \mathbb{I}_C K_b \neg \varphi) \to \neg \mathbb{S}_{C,D}(\varphi \to \psi)$.
3. $\vdash_{SC} (\mathbb{S}_{C,D}\varphi \wedge \mathbb{S}_{C,D}\psi) \to \mathbb{S}_{C,D}(\varphi \wedge \psi)$;
4. $\vdash_{SC} (\mathbb{S}_{C,D}(\varphi \wedge \psi) \wedge \mathbb{S}_{C,D}(\varphi \vee \psi)) \to (\mathbb{S}_{C,D}\varphi \wedge \mathbb{S}_{C,D}\psi)$;
5. $\vdash_{SC} (\mathbb{S}_{C,D}\varphi \wedge E_C^K \psi \wedge \mathbb{B}_C E_C^K \psi \wedge \mathbb{I}_C E_C^K \psi \wedge \mathbb{B}_C E_C^I \psi) \to \mathbb{S}_{C,D}(\varphi \wedge \psi)$;
6. $\nvdash_{SC} (\mathbb{S}_{C,D}\varphi \wedge \mathbb{K}_C \psi \wedge \mathbb{I}_C \psi) \to \mathbb{S}_{C,D}(\varphi \wedge \psi)$.

Proposition 7 explores the interaction between group secrets and logical connectives. The first two items connect the truth-conditional properties of material implication and group secrecy. Indeed, (1) and (2) establish that it is impossible for a group C to intend to keep $\varphi \to \psi$ secret from members of D, if there is common belief or common intention among Cs that some member of D knows that ψ ($\neg\varphi$) Items (3) and (4) show that group secrets behave in a conjunctive manner: the secret of both φ and ψ leads to the secret of their conjunction, and the secret of their conjunction implies their individual secrets. This is strengthened by item (5) as it states the need for detailed coordination of knowledge, belief, and intention among secret keepers to hold the secret of a conjunction. Item (6) expresses the failure of a kind of "expandability" of group secrets. Namely, it is not the case that if C intends to keep φ secret from D, then adding a piece of information ψ to φ obliges C to have $\varphi \wedge \psi$ as a group secret w.r.t. D. Again, this suggests that common intention and belief included in group secrecy are limited to the content of the original secret and cannot be extended without further conditions on intentions and epistemic coordination between secret keepers.

We close this section with a proposition that makes explicit conditions under which one can derive the group secrecy of a given statement φ from the secrecy of the disjunction $\varphi \vee \psi$.

Proposition 8. *Let* $\varphi, \psi \in \text{Fm}_{SC}$, $C, D \subseteq Ag$. *Then:*

1. $\vdash_{SC} \mathbb{S}_{C,D}(\varphi \vee \psi) \to ((E_C^K \varphi \wedge \mathbb{I}_C E_C^K \varphi \wedge \mathbb{B}_C(E_C^I \varphi \wedge E_C^K \varphi)) \leftrightarrow \mathbb{S}_{C,D}\varphi)$;
2. $\nvdash_{SC} (\mathbb{S}_{C,D}(\varphi \vee \psi) \wedge \mathbb{K}_C \varphi \wedge \mathbb{I}_C \varphi) \to \mathbb{S}_{C,D}\varphi$.

This proposition addresses the interplay between group secret ($\mathbb{S}_{C,D}$) and some specific conditions (E_C^K, E_C^I, and $\mathbb{B}_C$) in group dynamics, particularly when a disjunction of secrets is involved. Part (1) demonstrates that if $\varphi \vee \psi$ is a group secret, then certain conditions holding on φ alone lead to equivalence with φ being a group secret alone. This result highlights the robustness of group secrecy when the group possesses detailed information. Part (2) introduces a limitation, showing that certain combinations of group conditions ($\mathbb{K}_C\varphi$ and $\mathbb{I}_C\varphi$) do not necessarily imply the group's ability to entirely derive the intention of keeping φ secret. This counterexample reflects the nuanced behaviour of group secrecy under incomplete or conflicting information and the possible lack of transparency in beliefs/intentions among secret keepers.

3   Metacommunicative Aspects of Revealing a Secret

While in the previous section we focused on the properties of group secrets, in this section we investigate those metacommunicative aspects that underlie the formation of a group keeping a secret.

In [2], the metacommunicative dimension of telling a secret is investigated. As B.L. Bellman writes:

> Secrecy is metacommunicative because when one hears the telling of a secret, several implicit instructions accompany it and constitute its key. That includes not only how the talk is to be understood but also that the information is not to be repeated and that the source where the knowledge was obtained is to be protected [2, p. 9].

In the sequel, we aim to elaborate on Bellman's perspective by addressing the problem of formalizing the statement:

(TS) "a intends to tell c a fact φ that a keeps secret from b"

where "to tell a secret" should be interpreted according to Bellman's interpretation. First, we argue that (TS) conveys at least three different contents: (i) that a is actually keeping φ secret from b; (ii) that a intends to let c believe that φ is indeed unknown to b, i.e., that b is factively ignorant about φ; and (iii) that a intends to let c know that a keeps φ secret from b. Now, a natural *desideratum* of our system would be that, if (TS) is true, then it should also be true that (iv) "a intends to let c keeping φ secret from b" since we are assuming that a intends to bring about a state of affairs in which b does not know that φ. While apparently modeling (i)-(iii) as $S_{a,b}\varphi$, $I_aB_cT_b\varphi$, and $I_aK_cS_{a,b}\varphi$ is quite obvious, actually the formalization of "a intends to let c knowing that $-$" simply as I_aK_c- is not satisfactory, because of the following

$$\nvdash_{\mathsf{SC}} (S_{a,b}\varphi \wedge I_aB_cT_b\varphi \wedge I_aK_cS_{a,b}\varphi) \to I_aS_{c,b}\varphi. \tag{4}$$

One can prove the stronger

Proposition 9. *Let* $\varphi \in \mathrm{Fm}_{\mathsf{SC}}$. *Then:*

$$\nvdash_{\mathsf{SC}} (S_{a,b}\varphi \wedge I_aK_cT_b\varphi \wedge I_aK_cS_{a,b}\varphi) \to I_aS_{c,b}\varphi. \tag{5}$$

Therefore, since it is easily seen that the formula in (4) entails the one in (5), a counterexample for the latter results in a counterexample for the former. However, such an inconvenience might be avoided by formalizing the kind of "letting know that" occurring in the telling of a secret in such a way as to include an element of "persuasion" w.r.t. intentions and beliefs. More precisely, we argue (and it is intuitively plausible) that the kind of communication involved in the telling of a secret includes that if a intends to act to bring about a state of affairs in which b does not know that φ and a intends to let c knowing the secret φ, then a intends to act in such a way that c has the same belief concerning the actual knowledge of b that φ and she intends to behave accordingly. These conditions can be formalized as instances of the following formulas:

$$P^B_{a,c}\varphi := (B_a\varphi \wedge I_a K_c B_a\varphi) \rightarrow I_a B_c\varphi, \quad P^I_{a,c}\varphi := (I_a\varphi \wedge I_a K_c I_a\varphi) \rightarrow I_a I_c\varphi. \quad (6)$$

Given the above discourse, we argue that (at least when the telling of a secret is considered) a slightly more precise formalization of "a intends to *tell* c that φ" could be the following:

$$C_{a,c}\varphi := P^I_{a,c}\varphi \wedge P^B_{a,c}\varphi \wedge I_a K_c\varphi.$$

Note that $C_{a,c}\varphi$ has been designed in such a way to *encode* but not to *entail* an element of persuasion about intentions. It is not difficult to see that:

$$\nvdash_{\mathsf{SC}} C_{a,c}\varphi \rightarrow (I_a I_c\varphi \vee I_a B_c\varphi).$$

Consequently, this operator is still general enough to cope with a range of situations wider than the one considered in this venue.

With the above definitions, we state and prove the following proposition.

Proposition 10. *The following holds:*

$$\vdash_{\mathsf{SC}} (S_{a,b}\varphi \wedge C_{a,c} T_b\varphi \wedge C_{a,c} S_{a,b}\varphi) \rightarrow (I_a S_{c,b}\varphi \wedge I_a S_{c,b} S_{a,b}\varphi).$$

However, the following final remark is in order.

Proposition 11. *For any $\varphi \in \mathrm{Fm}_{\mathsf{SC}}$, $C, D \subseteq Ag$:*

1. $\nvdash_{\mathsf{SC}} (S_{a,b}\varphi \wedge C_{a,c} T_b\varphi \wedge C_{a,c} S_{a,b}\varphi) \rightarrow I_a \mathbb{I}_{\{a,c\}} S_{\{a,c\},\{b\}}\varphi$;
2. $\nvdash_{\mathsf{SC}} (S_{a,b}\varphi \wedge C_{a,c} T_b\varphi \wedge C_{a,c} S_{a,b}\varphi) \rightarrow I_a \mathbb{S}_{\{a,c\},\{b\}}\varphi$.

The overall moral of Proposition 11 is that the intention of communicating a secret with the aim it remains so for a targeted nescient does not guarantee *per se* an intention of creating joint commitment in preserving confidentiality. Therefore, sharing a secret with the aim of becoming a group secret needs further conditions whose investigation is left to future work.

4   Conclusion

In this paper, we have investigated the logical properties of group secrets, focusing on how they can be defined. We provided a formal framework to model and analyze the conditions under which group secrets are preserved and how different types of knowledge/belief/commitment—including individual and common knowledge, belief, and intention—interact with them. In particular, our results demonstrate how logical implication and disjunction influence the persistence of secrets within groups and reveal subtle limitations in the derivation of certain types of knowledge from others. A key takeaway from our analysis is the weakness of group secrets under logical operations determined by the possible lack of mutual transparency of secret keepers w.r.t. intentions and beliefs and the necessary conditions for agents to keep confidential information. A further insight provided by the present work concerns the concept of secret disclosure and sufficient conditions on communication under which confidentiality persists.

There are several further promising directions for future research that the present framework hints at:

1. **Temporal Evolution of Secrets and Groups:** Future work could extend the current static framework to account for the temporal evolution of secrets and group membership to understand how secrets are maintained or lost over time, primarily as agents communicate and update their knowledge.
2. **Refinement of Group Secret Management:** Investigating additional logical constraints or different agent capabilities (e.g., partial observability, the presence of contradictions, and non-monotonic reasoning) could shed some light on complex multi-agent systems in concrete scenarios.
3. **Applications to Cryptographic Protocols for Multi-Agent Systems:** The aim is to adapt and apply the current results to the modelling of real-world cryptographic protocols that involve distributed group secrets, as in the case of multi-signature protocols and secure multi-party computations [3].
4. **Incorporation of Trust and Distrust among Agents:** Another interesting direction would be to study how trust or distrust between agents affects the preservation and distribution of secrets.

References

1. Aldini, A., Fazio, D., Graziani, P., Mascella, R., Tagliaferri, M.: The logical art of keeping a true secret (2024). https://arxiv.org/abs/2405.11654
2. Bellman, B.L.: The paradox of secrecy. Hum. Stud. **4**(1), 1–24 (1981)
3. Evans, D., Kolesnikov, V., Rosulek, M.: A pragmatic introduction to secure multi-party computation. Found. Trends Priv. Secur. **2**(2–3), 70–246 (2018)
4. Fedorenko, I., Berthon, P., Edelman, L.: Top secret: integrating 20 years of research on secrecy. Technovation **123**, 102691 (2023)
5. Halpern, J.Y., Moses, Y.: A guide to completeness and complexity for modal logics of knowledge and belief. Artif. Intell. **54**(3), 319–379 (1992)

6. Halpern, J.Y., O'Neill, K.R.: Secrecy in multiagent systems. ACM Trans. Inf. Syst. Secur. **12**(1), 5:1–5:47 (2008)
7. Hughes, G.E., Cresswell, M.J.: A Companion to Modal Logic. Methuen, New York (1984)
8. Ismail, H.O., Shafie, M.: A commonsense theory of secrets. In: Brodaric, B., Neuhaus, F. (eds.) Formal Ontology in Information Systems - Proceedings of the 11th International Conference, FOIS 2020, Cancelled, Bozen-Bolzano, Italy, 14–17 September 2020. Frontiers in Artificial Intelligence and Applications, vol. 330, pp. 77–91. IOS Press (2020)
9. Kelly, A.E.: The Psychology of Secrets. Springer, New York (2002)
10. Robertson, K.M., Hannah, D.R., Lautsch, B.A.: The secret to protecting trade secrets: how to create positive secrecy climates in organizations. Bus. Horizons **58**(6), 669–677 (2015). Special issue: The Magic of Secrets
11. Slepian, M.: The Secret Life of Secrets: How Our Inner Worlds Shape Well-Being, Relationships, and Who We Are. Crown (2022)
12. Slepian, M.L.: A process model of having and keeping secrets. Psychol. Rev. **129**(3), 542–563 (2022)
13. Slepian, M.L., Chun, J.S., Mason, M.F.: The experience of secrecy. J. Pers. Soc. Psychol. **113**(1), 1–33 (2017)
14. Volli, U.: Figure della reticenza. riservatezza, segreto, pudore, privacy, silenzio, sacro, storytelling. Versus quaderni di studi semiotici **130**(1), 19–32 (2020)
15. Xiong, Z., Ågotnes, T.: The logic of secrets and the interpolation rule. Ann. Math. Artif. Intell. **91**(4), 375–407 (2023)

Explicit Legg-Hutter Intelligence Calculations Which Suggest Non-Archimedean Intelligence

Samuel Allen Alexander[1]([⊠]) [iD] and Arthur Paul Pedersen[2] [iD]

[1] The U.S. Securities and Exchange Commission, New York, USA
samuelallenalexander@gmail.com
[2] The City University of New York, New York, USA

Abstract. Are the real numbers rich enough to measure intelligence? We generalize a result of Alexander and Hutter about the so-called Legg-Hutter intelligence measures of reinforcement learning agents. Using the generalized result, we exhibit a paradox: in one particular version of the Legg-Hutter intelligence measure, certain agents all have intelligence 0, even though in a certain sense some of them outperform others. We show that this paradox disappears if we vary the Legg-Hutter intelligence measure to be hyperreal-valued rather than real-valued.

1 Introduction

Legg and Hutter proposed [7] a theoretical measure of the intelligence of reinforcement learning (RL) agents—agents who interact with environments so as to maximize a reward signal. They proposed that the intelligence of an agent π be measured as $\Upsilon(\pi) = \sum_\mu 2^{-K(\mu)} V_\mu^\pi$, where μ ranges over the set of all suitably well-behaved computable RL environments, $K(\mu)$ is the Kolmogorov complexity of μ, and V_μ^π is the expected total reward π achieves in μ.

Because Kolmogorov complexity depends on the choice of a background universal Turing machine (UTM), the Legg-Hutter intelligence measure also implicitly depends on same. Alexander and Hutter showed [4] that if the UTM is symmetric in a certain sense, then agents satisfying a self-duality property have Legg-Hutter intelligence 0. In the present paper we generalize that result. We show that the Legg-Hutter intelligence of a self-dual agent π is $\sum_\nu 2^{-K(\nu)} V_\nu^\pi$ where ν is restricted to only range over those suitably well-behaved computable environments where the UTM is non-symmetric.

Armed with the above result, we will argue that for a certain choice of UTM, there are agents π_1 and π_2 such that $\Upsilon(\pi_1) = \Upsilon(\pi_2) = 0$ even though in some sense π_1 strictly outperforms π_2. We opine that this paradox is due to the inadequacy of the real numbers, $\mathbb{R}$, for measuring intelligence. Assuming a technical condition on the environments in the definition of Υ, we exhibit a variation Υ^* taking values in the hyperreal numbers (we do not assume prior familiarity with the hyperreals, so we gently introduce them using intuition about elections). The

J. Proença et al. (Eds.): SEFM 2024, LNCS 15551, pp. 148–164, 2026.
https://doi.org/10.1007/978-3-031-94748-3_13

hyperreal-valued Legg-Hutter intelligence measure avoids the above-mentioned paradox.

The structure of the paper is as follows:

- In Sect. 2 we will informally describe our results.
- In Sect. 3 we will develop preliminaries.
- In Sect. 4 we will generalize a result of Alexander and Hutter.
- In Sect. 5 we will discuss what we call almost-symmetric universal Turing machines.
- In Sect. 6 we introduce what we call the Garden-of-Eden paradox.
- In Sect. 7 we introduce a variation of the Legg-Hutter intelligence measure which is hyperreal-number-valued instead of real-number-valued, and show that it solves the Garden-of-Eden paradox.
- In Sect. 8 we respond to anticipated objections.
- In Sect. 9 we summarize and make concluding remarks.

2   Informal Description of Results

Consider a "Garden of Eden" reinforcement learning environment in which one action is "forbidden" and all others are "allowed". If an agent takes the forbidden action even one time, then the agent's total reward from the environment becomes 0 (there is no way for the agent to recover from its sin). But if the agent never takes the forbidden action, then its total reward from the environment is 1.

Consider two different agents. Agent $A_{1\%}$ is an agent who, every turn, takes the forbidden action with 1% probability, or takes an allowed action with 99% probability. Agent $A_{99\%}$ is an agent who, every turn, takes the forbidden action with 99% probability, or takes an allowed action with 1% probability. Using standard real-valued probability theory, both agents have the same expected total reward in the Garden of Eden environment, namely, 0. This perhaps counter-intuitive result is because, over infinitely many turns, the expected probability of $A_{1\%}$ eventually taking the forbidden action is 100%. There are non-standard variations of probability theory where $A_{1\%}$ has greater total expected reward than $A_{99\%}$ (but both these total expected rewards are infinitesimal—hence the necessity for the number system to be non-Archimedean, i.e., to fail to satisfy the Archimedean property of $\mathbb{R}$).

We show that by choosing the background universal Turing machine extremely carefully, we can arrange that for certain agents (including $A_{1\%}$ and $A_{99\%}$), the Legg-Hutter intelligence measure is entirely determined by performance in the Garden of Eden: because of said choice of universal Turing machine, the contributions from all other environments all perfectly cancel each other out. Thus, the above scandal is elevated from a paradox about probability theory to a paradox about intelligence measurement. Namely: $A_{1\%}$ and $A_{99\%}$ both have Legg-Hutter intelligence 0, even though in an intuitive sense $A_{1\%}$ is clearly the better agent if only the Garden of Eden environment matters. We present a variation of the Legg-Hutter intelligence measure, taking values in the hyperreal numbers (a non-Archimedean number system), where the paradox disappears.

3   Preliminaries

Fix a finite nonempty set $\mathcal{A}$ of *actions*, a finite nonempty set $\mathcal{O}$ of *observations*, and a finite nonempty set $\mathcal{R} \subseteq \mathbb{Q} \cap [-1, 1]$ of *rewards*. We assume that $\mathcal{R}$ is symmetric, in the sense that $\mathcal{R}$ contains $-r$ whenever $\mathcal{R}$ contains r. We also assume $0 \in \mathcal{R}$. We assume $\mathcal{A} \cap \mathcal{O} = \mathcal{A} \cap \mathcal{R} = \mathcal{O} \cap \mathcal{R} = \emptyset$. Let $\langle \rangle$ be the empty sequence. For any finite sequences s and t, let $s \frown t$ be the result of concatenating t to the end of s.

In the following definitions, we follow [4] except where otherwise indicated.

Definition 1. *(Reinforcement learning agents and environments)*

1. *Let* $(\mathcal{ORA})^*$ *be the set of finite sequences of the form* $o_0, r_0, a_0, \ldots, o_k, r_k, a_k$ *with each* $o_i \in \mathcal{O}$, $r_i \in \mathcal{R}$, *and* $a_i \in \mathcal{A}$; *we also include* $\langle \rangle$ *in* $(\mathcal{ORA})^*$.
2. *Let* $(\mathcal{ORA})^* \mathcal{OR}$ *be the set of all sequences of the form* $s \frown \langle o, r \rangle$ *where* $s \in (\mathcal{ORA})^*$, $o \in \mathcal{O}$, $r \in \mathcal{R}$.
3. *An* agent *is a function* π, *with domain* $(\mathcal{ORA})^* \mathcal{OR}$, *and with range the set of* $\mathbb{Q}$-*valued probability distributions on* $\mathcal{A}$. *For each* $s \in (\mathcal{ORA})^* \mathcal{OR}$, *we write* $\pi(\bullet|s)$ *for the value of* π *at* s *(so* $\pi(\bullet|s)$ *is a* $\mathbb{Q}$-*valued probability distribution on* $\mathcal{A}$*), and for each* $a \in \mathcal{A}$, *we write* $\pi(a|s)$ *for* $(\pi(\bullet|s))(a)$; *we think of* $\pi(a|s)$ *as the probability that the agent will take action* a *in response to stimulus* s.
4. *An* environment *is a function* μ, *with domain* $(\mathcal{ORA})^*$ *and with range the set of* $\mathbb{Q}$-*valued probability distributions on* $\mathcal{O} \times \mathcal{R}$. *For each* $s \in (\mathcal{ORA})^*$, *we write* $\mu(\bullet|s)$ *for the value of* μ *at* s *(so* $\mu(\bullet|s)$ *is a* $\mathbb{Q}$-*valued probability distribution on* $\mathcal{O} \times \mathcal{R}$*), and for each* $(o, r) \in \mathcal{O} \times \mathcal{R}$, *we write* $\mu(o, r|s)$ *for* $(\mu(\bullet|s))(o, r)$; *we think of* $\mu(o, r|s)$ *as the probability that the environment will issue observation* o *and reward* r *in response to stimulus* s.

Definition 2. *(Agent-environment interaction) Let* π *be any agent. Let* μ *be any environment.*

1. *For every* $n \in \mathbb{N}$, *let* $V_{\mu,n}^{\pi}$ *be the expected value of the sum of the rewards in the sequence* $(o_0, r_0, a_0, \ldots, o_n, r_n, a_n)$ *randomly generated as follows:*
   - *Choose* $(o_0, r_0) \in \mathcal{O} \times \mathcal{R}$ *randomly based on the probability distribution* $\mu(\bullet|\langle \rangle)$.
   - *Choose* $a_0 \in \mathcal{A}$ *randomly based on the probability distribution* $\pi(\bullet|o_0, r_0)$.
   - *For each* $0 < k \leq n$, *choose* $(o_k, r_k) \in \mathcal{O} \times \mathcal{R}$ *randomly based on the probability distribution* $\mu(\bullet|o_0, r_0, a_0, \ldots, o_{k-1}, r_{k-1}, a_{k-1})$.
   - *For each* $0 < k \leq n$, *choose* $a_k \in \mathcal{A}$ *randomly based on the probability distribution* $\pi(\bullet|o_0, r_0, a_0, \ldots, o_{k-1}, r_{k-1}, a_{k-1}, o_k, r_k)$.
2. *Let* $V_{\mu}^{\pi} = \lim_{n \to \infty} V_{\mu,n}^{\pi}$ *(if the limit converges to a real number; otherwise* V_{μ}^{π} *is undefined).*

Definition 3. *An environment* μ *is* well-behaved *if:*

- μ *is computable, and*
- *For every agent* π, V_{μ}^{π} *is defined and* $-1 \leq V_{\mu}^{\pi} \leq 1$.

Let W be the set of all well-behaved environments.

Definition 4. *(Duality)*

1. *For every sequence s, let $\overline{s}$ be the result of multiplying every reward in s by -1.*
2. *For every agent π, let $\overline{\pi}$, the dual of π, be the agent defined by $\overline{\pi}(a|s) = \pi(a|\overline{s})$ for all $a \in \mathcal{A}$, $s \in (\mathcal{ORA})^*\mathcal{OR}$.*
3. *For every environment μ, let $\overline{\mu}$, the dual of μ, be the environment defined by $\overline{\mu}(o, r|s) = \mu(o, -r|\overline{s})$ for all $o \in \mathcal{O}$, $r \in \mathcal{R}$, $s \in (\mathcal{ORA})^*$.*
4. *An agent π is self-dual if $\pi = \overline{\pi}$.*
5. *An environment μ is self-dual if $\mu = \overline{\mu}$.*

Lemma 1. *Let π be an agent, μ an environment, $n \in \mathbb{N}$.*

1. *$\overline{\overline{\pi}} = \pi$ and $\overline{\overline{\mu}} = \mu$.*
2. *$V^{\overline{\pi}}_{\overline{\mu},n} = -V^{\pi}_{\mu,n}$.*
3. *$V^{\overline{\pi}}_{\overline{\mu}} = -V^{\pi}_{\mu}$ (and the left-hand side is defined iff the right-hand side is).*
4. *$V^{\pi}_{\overline{\mu},n} = -V^{\overline{\pi}}_{\mu,n}$.*
5. *$V^{\pi}_{\overline{\mu}} = -V^{\overline{\pi}}_{\mu}$ (and the left-hand side is defined iff the right-hand side is).*
6. *μ is well-behaved iff $\overline{\mu}$ is well-behaved.*

Proof. Parts 1, 3, 5 and 6 are proved in [4]. The proofs of 3 and 5 in [4] work by proving 2 and 4. $\qquad\square$

For any sets X and Y, we write $f : \subseteq X \to Y$ to indicate that f is a function with codomain Y and with domain some subset of X.

Definition 5. *(Prefix-free universal Turing machines) Let 2^* be the set of finite binary strings.*

1. *A function $f : \subseteq 2^* \to 2^*$ is prefix-free if f is computable and for all $p, p' \in 2^*$, if $f(p)$ and $f(p')$ are defined, then p is not a strict initial segment of p'.*
2. *A prefix-free universal Turing machine (or PFUTM) is a prefix-free function $U : \subseteq 2^* \to 2^*$ such that for every prefix-free $f : \subseteq 2^* \to 2^*$, $\exists y \in 2^*$ such that $\forall x \in 2^*$, $f(x) = U(y \frown x)$ (we call such a y a computer program for f in programming language U).*

We fix a computable Gödel numbering $\ulcorner \bullet \urcorner : (\mathcal{ORA})^* \to 2^*$ assigning to each $s \in (\mathcal{ORA})^*$ a code $\ulcorner s \urcorner \in 2^*$. Likewise, if M is the set of $\mathbb{Q}$-valued probability distributions on $\mathcal{O} \times \mathcal{R}$, we fix a computable Gödel numbering[1] $\ulcorner \bullet \urcorner : M \to 2^*$ assigning to each $p \in M$ a code $\ulcorner p \urcorner \in 2^*$. We assume that for all $x, y \in (\mathcal{ORA})^* \cup M$ with $x \neq y$, $\ulcorner x \urcorner$ is not an initial segment of $\ulcorner y \urcorner$ and $\ulcorner x \urcorner$ is not a terminal segment of $\ulcorner y \urcorner$. In other words, we assume $\ulcorner \bullet \urcorner$ is both prefix-free and suffix-free. By fixing $\ulcorner \bullet \urcorner$ we differ from [4], where the dependence of concepts such as Kolmogorov complexity (in the following definition) on $\ulcorner \bullet \urcorner$ was emphasized.

---

[1] This makes sense because $\mathcal{O} \times \mathcal{R}$ is finite.

Definition 6. *(Kolmogorov complexity)*

- *If μ is an environment and U is a PFUTM, we say that a function $f :$ $\subseteq 2^* \to 2^*$ encodes μ if the following condition holds: For every $s \in (\mathcal{ORA})^*$, $f(\ulcorner s \urcorner) = \ulcorner \mu(\bullet|s) \urcorner$.*
- *For every computable environment μ and PFUTM U, let $K_U(\mu)$ be the Kolmogorov complexity of μ given by U, by which we mean the least $n \in \mathbb{N}$ such that there exists a computer program of length n in programming language U for some $f : \subseteq 2^* \to 2^*$ which encodes μ.*

Definition 7. *A PFUTM U is* symmetric *if the following condition holds: for every computable environment μ, $K_U(\mu) = K_U(\overline{\mu})$.*

In [4] it is shown that symmetric PFUTMs exist. In fact, the proof there shows more: there is a mechanical procedure for transforming any given PFUTM into a symmetric PFUTM.

In the following definition, we generalize the definition from [4] by introducing a new parameter W_0, for reasons which will become clear in Sect. 7.2. In [4], implicitly $W_0 = W$.

Definition 8. *(Legg-Hutter intelligence) Let U be a PFUTM and $W_0 \subseteq W$ a set of well-behaved environments. For every agent π, the* Legg-Hutter intelligence *of π according to U, W_0 is defined to be*

$$\Upsilon_{U,W_0}(\pi) = \sum_{\mu \in W_0} 2^{-K_U(\mu)} V_\mu^\pi$$

(the infinite sum is absolutely convergent by comparison with the sum defining Chaitin's constant, thus the sum does not depend on the order in which W_0 is enumerated).

The Legg-Hutter intelligence $\Upsilon_{U,W_0}(\pi)$ of an agent π (according to U, W_0) is intended to measure π's performance by averaging π's expected performance over the environments in W_0, using Kolmogorov complexity to assign lower weight to more contrived environments.

Theorem 1. *Let U be a symmetric PFUTM and let π be an agent.*

1. *$\Upsilon_{U,W}(\overline{\pi}) = -\Upsilon_{U,W}(\pi)$.*
2. *If π is self-dual then $\Upsilon_{U,W}(\pi) = 0$.*

Proof. See [4]. □

4   A Generalization of Theorem 1 Part 2

Definition 9. *A set W_0 of well-behaved environments is* symmetric *if the following condition holds: for every $\mu \in W_0$, $\overline{\mu} \in W_0$.*

Note that W itself is symmetric by Lemma 1 part 6.

Lemma 2. *If environment μ and agent π are both self-dual, then $V_\mu^\pi = 0$.*
Proof. To show $V_\mu^\pi = 0$, it suffices to show $V_\mu^\pi = -V_\mu^\pi$. Compute:

$$
\begin{aligned}
V_\mu^\pi &= V_{\overline{\overline{\mu}}}^{\overline{\overline{\pi}}} && \text{(Lemma 1 part 1)} \\
&= -V_{\overline{\mu}}^{\overline{\pi}} && \text{(Lemma 1 part 3)} \\
&= -V_\mu^\pi. && \text{(Self-duality)}
\end{aligned}
$$

$\square$

The following theorem is a generalization of Theorem 1 part 2.

Theorem 2. *Let U be any PFUTM. Let $W_0 \subseteq W$ be symmetric. Let $Z = \{\mu \in W_0 : K_U(\mu) \neq K_U(\overline{\mu})\}$ be the set of asymmetries of K_U. For any self-dual agent π, $\Upsilon_{U,W_0}(\pi) = \sum_{\mu \in Z} 2^{-K_U(\mu)} V_\mu^\pi$.*

Proof. Since $\sum_{\mu \in W_0} 2^{-K_U(\mu)} V_\mu^\pi = \sum_{\mu \in Z} 2^{-K_U(\mu)} V_\mu^\pi + \sum_{\mu \in W_0 \setminus Z} 2^{-K_U(\mu)} V_\mu^\pi$, it suffices to show $\sum_{\mu \in W_0 \setminus Z} 2^{-K_U(\mu)} V_\mu^\pi = 0$. Let $W_1 = \{\mu \in W_0 \setminus Z : \mu$ is self-dual$\}$. Let $W_2 \subseteq W_0 \setminus (Z \cup W_1)$ be a maximal set such that for every $\mu \in W_2$, $\overline{\mu} \notin W_2$. Let $W_3 = \{\overline{\mu} : \mu \in W_2\}$. It follows that $W_0 \setminus Z$ is the disjoint union of W_1, W_2, W_3. Thus:

$$
\begin{aligned}
&\sum_{\mu \in W_0 \setminus Z} 2^{-K_U(\mu)} V_\mu^\pi \\
&= \sum_{\mu \in W_1} 2^{-K_U(\mu)} V_\mu^\pi + \sum_{\mu \in W_2 \cup W_3} 2^{-K_U(\mu)} V_\mu^\pi && (W_1 \cap (W_2 \cup W_3) = \emptyset) \\
&= \sum_{\mu \in W_1} 0 + \sum_{\mu \in W_2 \cup W_3} 2^{-K_U(\mu)} V_\mu^\pi && \text{(Lemma 2)} \\
&= \sum_{\mu \in W_2} (2^{-K_U(\mu)} V_\mu^\pi + 2^{-K_U(\overline{\mu})} V_{\overline{\mu}}^\pi) && \text{(Definition of } W_3) \\
&= \sum_{\mu \in W_2} (2^{-K_U(\mu)} V_\mu^\pi + 2^{-K_U(\mu)} V_{\overline{\mu}}^\pi) && (K_U(\mu) = K_U(\overline{\mu}) \text{ by def. of } Z) \\
&= \sum_{\mu \in W_2} (2^{-K_U(\mu)} V_\mu^\pi - 2^{-K_U(\mu)} V_\mu^{\overline{\pi}}) && \text{(Lemma 1 part 5)} \\
&= \sum_{\mu \in W_2} (2^{-K_U(\mu)} V_\mu^\pi - 2^{-K_U(\mu)} V_\mu^\pi) && (\pi \text{ is self-dual}) \\
&= \sum_{\mu \in W_2} 0 = 0.
\end{aligned}
$$

$\square$

5   Almost-Symmetric PFUTMs

The infinite sum defining Legg-Hutter intelligence seems inherently intractable at first glance (if W_0 is nontrivial). Theorem 1 (part 2) was (in [4]) the first explicit computation of Legg-Hutter intelligence for a computable agent. In this section, we will develop machinery which will allow explicit computation of some non-integer Legg-Hutter intelligences.

Definition 10. *Let U be a PFUTM and let μ be a computable environment. We say U is* almost symmetric except at μ *if the following requirements are satisfied:*

1. $K_U(\mu) \neq K_U(\overline{\mu})$.
2. $K_U(\nu) = K_U(\overline{\nu})$ *for every computable environment $\nu \notin \{\mu, \overline{\mu}\}$.*

Proposition 1. *For every computable environment μ such that μ is not self-dual, there exists a PFUTM which is almost symmetric except at μ. In fact, for all positive integers $m \neq n$, there exists a PFUTM U such that $K_U(\mu) = m$, $K_U(\overline{\mu}) = n$, and $K_U(\nu) = K_U(\overline{\nu})$ for every computable environment $\nu \notin \{\mu, \overline{\mu}\}$.*

Proof. Let U_0 be any symmetric PFUTM. Let y_μ (resp. $y_{\overline{\mu}}$) be a computer program for μ (resp. $\overline{\mu}$) in programming language U_0. Let $t_1 = \langle 1 \rangle$, $t_2 = \langle 0, 1 \rangle$, $t_3 = \langle 0, 0, 1 \rangle$, and so on. Let $U : \subseteq 2^* \to 2^*$ be defined by

$$
U(s) = \begin{cases}
U_0(y_\mu \frown x) & \text{if } s = t_m \frown x; \\
U_0(y_{\overline{\mu}} \frown x) & \text{if } s = t_n \frown x; \\
U_0(x) & \text{if } s = t_{m+n} \frown x; \\
\text{undefined} & \text{in any other case.}
\end{cases}
$$

It is easy to see: U is a PFUTM; t_m is a computer program for μ in programming language U (and no shorter computer program for μ in programming language U exists); t_n is a computer program for $\overline{\mu}$ in programming language U (and no shorter computer program for $\overline{\mu}$ in programming language U exists); and that for every computable environment $\nu \notin \{\mu, \overline{\mu}\}$, the computer programs for ν in programming language U are exactly those strings $t_{m+n} \frown y$ such that y is a computer program for ν in programming language U_0. It follows that U witnesses the proposition. $\square$

Theorem 3. *If μ is a well-behaved environment, U is a PFUTM which is almost-symmetric except at μ, $W_0 \subseteq W$ is symmetric, $\mu \in W_0$, and π is a self-dual agent, then*

$$
\Upsilon_{U,W_0}(\pi) = (2^{-K_U(\mu)} - 2^{-K_U(\overline{\mu})})V_\mu^\pi.
$$

Proof. Compute:

$$
\begin{aligned}
\Upsilon_{U,W_0}(\pi) &= 2^{-K_U(\mu)}V_\mu^\pi + 2^{-K_U(\overline{\mu})}V_{\overline{\mu}}^\pi && \text{(Theorem 2)} \\
&= 2^{-K_U(\mu)}V_\mu^\pi - 2^{-K_U(\overline{\mu})}V_\mu^{\overline{\pi}} && \text{(Lemma 1 part 5)} \\
&= 2^{-K_U(\mu)}V_\mu^\pi - 2^{-K_U(\overline{\mu})}V_\mu^\pi. && \text{(Self-duality of } \pi\text{)}
\end{aligned}
$$

$\square$

By carefully choosing μ and π, one can use Theorem 3 to obtain explicit nonzero Legg-Hutter intelligences. For example, for any nonzero $\alpha \in \mathcal{R}$, let μ be a computable environment which ignores the agent's actions and always gives initial reward α and reward 0 forever thereafter, regardless of anything the agent does. So $V_\mu^\pi = \alpha$ for every agent π. Since $\alpha \neq 0$, μ is not self-dual. By Proposition 1, there is, for example, a PFUTM U which is almost-symmetric except at μ, such that $K_U(\mu) = 1$, $K_U(\overline{\mu}) = 2$. By Theorem 3, $\Upsilon_{U,W}(\pi) = (2^{-1} - 2^{-2})V_\mu^\pi = \alpha/4$ for every self-dual agent π.

6   A Garden-of-Eden Paradox

For the rest of the paper, we assume there are at least two distinct actions in the action-set $\mathcal{A}$. We also assume that the reward-set $\mathcal{R}$ contains 1 and -1.

Definition 11. *Let $X \in \mathcal{A}$. An X-forbidding Garden of Eden is an environment μ such that the following conditions hold:*

1. *("μ gives initial reward 1 with probability 100%") For all $o \in \mathcal{O}$ and $r \in \mathcal{R}$, if $\mu(o, r|\langle\rangle) > 0$ then $r = 1$.*
2. *("μ gives reward -1 after the first X action, if ever, and reward 0 in all other situations") For every sequence $s \frown \langle a, o, r \rangle \in (\mathcal{ORA})^*\mathcal{OR}$ such that $\mu(o, r|s \frown \langle a \rangle) > 0$,*
   (a) *If $a = X$ and X does not occur in s, then $r = -1$.*
   (b) *Otherwise, $r = 0$.*

Thus, when an agent π interacts with an X-forbidding Garden of Eden μ, initially π gets a reward of 1. As long as π does not take action X, π maintains that reward of 1. But if π ever takes action X, then π immediately loses that full reward, and π's total cumulative reward is always 0 forever thereafter.

Definition 12. *For all $X, Y \in \mathcal{A}$ (with $X \neq Y$) and all $q \in [0,1] \cap \mathbb{Q}$, let $\pi_{q,X,Y}$ be the agent which always takes action X with probability q or takes action Y with probability $1 - q$. So for every $c \in \mathcal{A}$ and every $s \in (\mathcal{ORA})^*\mathcal{OR}$,*

$$\pi_{q,X,Y}(c|s) = \begin{cases} q & \text{if } c = X \\ 1 - q & \text{if } c = Y \\ 0 & \text{otherwise.} \end{cases}$$

Lemma 3. *For all q, X, Y as in Definition 12, $\pi_{q,X,Y}$ is self-dual.*

Proof. Clearly $\pi_{q,X,Y}(c|s)$ does not depend on the rewards in s, so $\pi_{q,X,Y}(c|s) = \pi_{q,X,Y}(c|\overline{s})$. By arbitrariness of s, $\overline{\pi_{q,X,Y}} = \pi_{q,X,Y}$.   □

Lemma 4. *For each $X \in \mathcal{A}$, if μ is an X-forbidding Garden of Eden, then μ is not self-dual.*

Proof. Clearly $\overline{\mu}$ gives initial reward -1, whereas μ gives initial reward 1. Thus $\overline{\mu} \neq \mu$. □

Corollary 1. *For every $X \in \mathcal{A}$, there exists an X-forbidding Garden of Eden μ and a PFUTM U such that U is almost symmetric except at μ, and such that $K_U(\mu) = 1$ and $K_U(\overline{\mu}) = 2$.*

Proof. Clearly there exists some X-forbidding Garden of Eden μ. By Lemma 4, μ is not self-dual. The corollary now follows by Proposition 1. □

Theorem 4. *Let $X, Y \in \mathcal{A}$, with $X \neq Y$. Let μ be an X-forbidding Garden of Eden. Let U be a PFUTM which is almost symmetric except at μ, such that $K_U(\mu) = 1$ and $K_U(\overline{\mu}) = 2$. Let $W_0 \subseteq W$ be symmetric with $\mu \in W_0$. For every $q \in (0, 1] \cap \mathbb{Q}$, $\Upsilon_{U, W_0}(\pi_{q, X, Y}) = 0$.*

Proof. By Theorem 3, $\Upsilon_{U, W_0}(\pi_{q, X, Y}) = (2^{-1} - 2^{-2})V_\mu^{\pi_{q, X, Y}} = \frac{1}{4}V_\mu^{\pi_{q, X, Y}}$. For every $n \in \mathbb{N}$, if $(o_0, r_0, a_0, \ldots, o_n, r_n, a_n)$ are chosen randomly as in the definition of $V_{\mu, n}^{\pi_{q, X, Y}}$ (Definition 2), then, since $\pi_{q, X, Y}$ always takes action X with probability q, the probability that every $a_i \neq X$ (for $i = 0, \ldots, n-1$) is $(1-q)^n$. If so, then by Definition 11 it follows that $r_0 + \cdots + r_n = 1 + 0 + \cdots + 0 = 1$. Otherwise, by Definition 11 it follows that $r_0 + \cdots + r_n = 0$. Thus

$$V_{\mu, n}^{\pi_{q, X, Y}} = 1 \cdot (1-q)^n + 0 \cdot (1 - (1-q)^n).$$

Since $q \in (0, 1]$, it follows that $V_\mu^{\pi_{q, X, Y}} = \lim_{n \to \infty} V_{\mu, n}^{\pi_{q, X, Y}} = 0$. □

Theorem 4 is paradoxical because if $0 < q_1 < q_2 < 1$ then $\pi_{q_1, X, Y}$ ought to be strictly more performant than $\pi_{q_2, X, Y}$ in the X-forbidding Garden of Eden μ. If U, W_0 are as in Theorem 4 then Υ_{U, W_0} measures self-dual agent intelligence purely based on performance in μ. Thus, Υ_{U, W_0} measures intelligence entirely based on an agent's tendency to avoid taking the forbidden action X. Since $\pi_{q_1, X, Y}$ is less likely to take action X than $\pi_{q_2, X, Y}$ at each particular moment, the former agent ought to be considered more intelligent if intelligence is measured purely in terms of performance in this μ.

Theorem 4 shows that Legg-Hutter intelligence can be misleading even in a practical sense. Suppose we need an agent to perform in an X-forbidding Garden of Eden not for eternity, but for some unspecified positive number of steps. If our only options are $\pi_{q_1, X, Y}$ and $\pi_{q_2, X, Y}$, where $0 < q_1 < q_2 < 1$, then $\pi_{q_1, X, Y}$ is objectively the better choice, but $\Upsilon_{U, W}(\pi_{q_1, X, Y}) = \Upsilon_{U, W}(\pi_{q_2, X, Y}) = 0$ suggests that either option is just as good as the other.

This paradox is, of course, not surprising to the reader familiar with probability or measure theory. It falls under the same umbrella as the fact that if S and T are two countable subsets of $\mathbb{R}$ and m is, e.g., Lebesgue measure, then $m(S) = m(T) = 0$ even if S is a strict subset of T. In the Lebesgue measure case, what the paradox really shows is that m does not perfectly capture the notion of the size of a set. If it did, then $S \subsetneq T$ would imply $m(S) < m(T)$. In the same way, Theorem 4 shows that, at least for the contrived PFUTM in question,

Legg-Hutter intelligence does not perfectly capture environmental performance of an agent.

This is not a condemnation of Legg-Hutter intelligence any more than it is a condemnation of Lebesgue measure. If the so-called *regularity* property, i.e. that $S \subsetneq T$ implies $m(S) < m(T)$, is desired, one can attain it via measures taking their values from other number systems than the reals, such as the hyperreal number system; see [5]. In the next section, we will resolve the above Garden of Eden paradox, by introducing a hyperreal-valued variation of Legg-Hutter intelligence.

7   Legg-Hutter Intelligence Using Nonstandard Analysis

We will propose a hyperreal-valued variation of Legg-Hutter intelligence where the paradox in the previous section disappears. We do not assume the reader is familiar with the hyperreals, so we will briefly review (one construction of) the hyperreals.

7.1   Free Ultrafilters and the Hyperreal Numbers

To intuitively motivate ultrafilters[2], it is instructive to imagine that the natural numbers are *voters* who cast ballots in order to decide true-or-false questions about functions $f : \mathbb{N} \to \mathbb{R}$. For example, if the question is whether or not $f : \mathbb{N} \to \mathbb{R}$ is larger on average than $g : \mathbb{N} \to \mathbb{R}$, we could consider each $n \in \mathbb{N}$ to vote as follows:

- If $f(n) > g(n)$, then n votes that f is larger than g on average.
- If $f(n) \leq g(n)$, then n votes that f is not larger than g on average.

One way to decide the outcome of such elections would be to decide in advance which sets of voters are *majorities*. Having suitably decided this, the winning candidate would be whichever candidate has a majority of voters vote for it. What properties should a choice of majorities satisfy? Three axioms immediately come to mind:

Definition 13. *Let $p \subseteq \mathscr{P}(\mathbb{N})$ be a set of subsets of $\mathbb{N}$, thought of as* majorities.

- *(Properness) p satisfies the* Properness *axiom if $\emptyset \notin p$. (If no-one votes for you, you lose.)*
- *(Monotonicity) p satisfies the* Monotonicity *axiom if the following requirement holds. For every $X \in p$, for every $Y \subseteq \mathbb{N}$, if $Y \supseteq X$ then $Y \in p$. (More votes can't hurt.)*

---

[2] For a humorous presentation of this intuition in the form of a Socratic dialog, see [1]. This electoral motivation of ultrafilters was first made explicit in [2], though the theoretical underpinnings appeared in [6]. For a more direct application of the same idea to RL intelligence measurement, without any reference to Kolmogorov complexity or computability, see [3].

- (Maximality) p satisfies the Maximality axiom if the following requirement holds. For every $X \subseteq \mathbb{N}$, either $X \in p$ or $X^c = \{n \in \mathbb{N} : n \notin X\} \in p$. (The election must have a winner.)

A fourth axiom is counter-intuitive when one thinks of elections, but intuitive when one considers that the answers to questions about transitive properties should be transitive. For example: if the voters decide that f is larger on average than g, and also that g is larger on average than h, then the voters ought to decide that f is larger on average than h. If $X_{fg} = \{n \in \mathbb{N} : f(n) > g(n)\}$, $X_{gh} = \{n \in \mathbb{N} : g(n) > h(n)\}$, and $X_{fh} = \{n \in \mathbb{N} : f(n) > h(n)\}$, then by linearity of $<$, we have $X_{fh} \supseteq X_{fg} \cap X_{gh}$. Thus, given Monotonicity, a simple way to force our election decision to be so consistent is to impose the following axiom.

Definition 14. Let $p \subseteq \mathscr{P}(\mathbb{N})$ be a set of subsets of $\mathbb{N}$, thought of as majorities.

- ($\cap$-Closure) p satisfies the $\cap$-Closure axiom if the following requirement holds. For all $X, Y \in p$, $X \cap Y \in p$.

One trivial way to realize all four of the above axioms is as follows: choose some $n_0 \in \mathbb{N}$ as a *dictator* and declare that whoever n_0 votes for, automatically wins. For example, this would amount to declaring that f is larger on average than g iff $f(n_0) > g(n_0)$. This is clearly a poor way to decide elections. Therefore, we propose the following axiom.

Definition 15. Let $p \subseteq \mathscr{P}(\mathbb{N})$ be a set of subsets of $\mathbb{N}$, thought of as majorities.

- (Non-Dictatorship) p satisfies the Non-Dictatorship axiom if the following requirement holds. For every $n_0 \in \mathbb{N}$, $\{n_0\} \notin p$.

Although the above five axioms seem concrete, by combining them together we actually arrive at a mathematical concept which, without the above motivation, would seem quite abstract.

Definition 16. A set $p \subseteq \mathscr{P}(\mathbb{N})$ of subsets of $\mathbb{N}$ is an ultrafilter on $\mathbb{N}$ (or simply an ultrafilter) if p satisfies the Properness, Monotonicity, Maximality, and $\cap$-closure axioms. An ultrafilter is free if it also satisfies the Non-Dictatorship axiom.

The following lemma is well-known and we state it without proof. We mention, however, that logicians have proven that this lemma cannot be proved constructively; all of its proofs are necessarily non-constructive.

Lemma 5. There exists a free ultrafilter on $\mathbb{N}$.

Lemma 5 allows us to decide elections. Namely: fix a free ultrafilter p on $\mathbb{N}$, and declare that whenever the naturals vote in an election between candidates c_1 and c_2, then candidate c_i wins the election iff $\{n \in \mathbb{N} : n$ votes for $c_i\} \in p$. Such an i exists by Maximality; the Properness and $\cap$-Closure axioms ensure i is unique.

For the rest of the paper, fix a free ultrafilter p on $\mathbb{N}$.

Definition 17. *If $f, g : \mathbb{N} \to \mathbb{R}$, declare $f \sim g$ iff f and g are equally large on average, as voted by $\mathbb{N}$, using p to decide the election. That is, $f \sim g$ iff $\{n \in \mathbb{N} : f(n) = g(n)\} \in p$. Clearly $\sim$ is an equivalence relation.*

- *For every $f : \mathbb{N} \to \mathbb{R}$, let $[f]$ be the $\sim$-equivalence class which contains f. Let $^*\mathbb{R} = \{[f] : f : \mathbb{N} \to \mathbb{R}\}$; we call $^*\mathbb{R}$ the set of hyperreal numbers.*
- *For all $f, g : \mathbb{N} \to \mathbb{R}$, we define $[f] + [g] = [f + g]$ and $[f] \cdot [g] = [f \cdot g]$.*
- *For all $f, g : \mathbb{N} \to \mathbb{R}$, we declare $[f] < [g]$ iff g is larger on average than f, as voted by $\mathbb{N}$, using p to decide the election. That is, $[f] < [g]$ iff $\{n \in \mathbb{N} : f(n) < g(n)\} \in p$.*

The following lemma is well-known and we state it without proof.

Lemma 6. *The operations in Definition 17 parts 2 and 3 are well-defined. The resulting structure $(^*\mathbb{R}, +, \cdot, <)$ is an ordered field extension of $\mathbb{R}$ (we consider $\mathbb{R}$ to be embedded in $^*\mathbb{R}$ by identifying every $r \in \mathbb{R}$ with the equivalence class $[n \mapsto r]$ of the corresponding constant function).*

In the following lemma, we collect a few well-known facts which we state without proof. These are straightforward to prove and we invite the reader to try to prove them.

Lemma 7. *1. If $X \subseteq \mathbb{N}$ is finite, then $X \notin p$.*
2. Suppose $f, g : \mathbb{N} \to \mathbb{R}$. If $f(n) > g(n)$ for all $n \in \mathbb{N}$, then $[f] > [g]$.
3. Suppose $f : \mathbb{N} \to \mathbb{R}$. If $\lim_{n \to \infty} f(n)$ exists, then for every real $\epsilon > 0$, the difference $|[f] - \lim_{n \to \infty} f(n)| < \epsilon$. In other words, the distance between $[f]$ and $\lim_{n \to \infty} f(n)$ is zero or infinitesimal.

7.2 Hyperreal-Valued Legg-Hutter Intelligence

In Definition 8, the infinite sum $\sum_{\mu \in W_0} 2^{-K_U(\mu)} V_\mu^\pi$ does not depend on the order in which W_0 is enumerated, because the sum is absolutely convergent. Said absolute convergence is a consequence of the requirement $-1 \leq V_\mu^\pi \leq 1$ in the definition of well-behaved environments (Definition 3). In order to define a hyperreal-valued Legg-Hutter intelligence, we would like to instead consider sums $\sum_{\mu \in W_0} 2^{-K_U(\mu)} V_{\mu,n}^\pi$ for various $n \in \mathbb{N}$. Unfortunately, such sums are not necessarily convergent, much less absolutely convergent. This is because even though $-1 \leq V_\mu^\pi \leq 1$, there is, a priori, no bound at all on $V_{\mu,n}^\pi$. For this reason, we must restrict attention to even better-behaved environments (this is the reason why we generalized Legg-Hutter intelligence by introducing the additional parameter W_0).

Definition 18. *An environment μ is* strongly well-behaved *if the following requirements hold.*

1. *μ is well-behaved.*
2. *For every agent π and $n \in \mathbb{N}$, $-1 \le V_{\mu,n}^{\pi} \le 1$.*

Lemma 8. *The set of strongly well-behaved environments is symmetric.*

Proof. Follows by Lemma 1 part 4. □

The following variation of Legg-Hutter intelligence is hyperreal-valued instead of real-valued. This increased granularity will allow the measure to distinguish between the agents which the real-valued measure failed to distinguish in Sect. 6.

Definition 19. *(Hyperreal-valued Legg-Hutter intelligence) Let U be a PFUTM and let $W_0 \subseteq W$ be a set of strongly well-behaved environments. For every agent π, the* hyperreal-valued Legg-Hutter intelligence *of π according to U, W_0 (and, implicitly, p) is defined to be*

$$\Upsilon_{U,W_0}^*(\pi) = \left[n \in \mathbb{N} \mapsto \sum_{\mu \in W_0} 2^{-K_U(\mu)} V_{\mu,n}^{\pi} \right] \in {}^*\mathbb{R}$$

(the infinite sums in question are defined, and are independent of the order in which W_0 is enumerated, because they are absolutely convergent by comparison with Chaitin's constant).

We want to show that Υ_{U,W_0}^* does not differ much from Υ_{U,W_0}. In order to do this, we will need a theorem from real analysis called Tannery's Theorem. This theorem is standard, so we state it without proof.

Lemma 9. *(Tannery's Theorem) Assume $\{a_i : \mathbb{N} \to \mathbb{R}\}_{i=0}^{\infty}$ is a sequence of sequences such that each $\lim_{n \to \infty} a_i(n)$ converges. Assume $w_0, w_1, \ldots \in \mathbb{R}$ satisfy $\sum_{i=0}^{\infty} w_i < \infty$ and for all $i, n \in \mathbb{N}$, $|a_i(n)| \le w_i$. Then*

$$\lim_{n \to \infty} \sum_{i=0}^{\infty} a_i(n) = \sum_{i=0}^{\infty} \lim_{n \to \infty} a_i(n).$$

The following theorem shows that $\Upsilon_{U,W_0}^*(\pi)$ is infinitely close to $\Upsilon_{U,W_0}(\pi)$.

Theorem 5. *For any U, W_0, π as in Definition 19, $\Upsilon_{U,W_0}(\pi)$ and $\Upsilon_{U,W_0}^*(\pi)$ differ by an amount smaller than any positive real number.*

Proof. We assume W_0 is infinite (the other case is similar and easier). Let $\mu_0, \mu_1, \ldots$ enumerate W_0 (this is possible because the environments in W_0 are well-behaved, thus computable, thus countable). By Tannery's Theorem (Lemma 9) with $a_i(n) = 2^{-K_U(\mu_i)} V_{\mu_i,n}^{\pi}$ and $w_i = 2^{-K_U(\mu_i)}$,

$$\lim_{n \to \infty} \sum_{i=0}^{\infty} 2^{-K_U(\mu_i)} V_{\mu_i,n}^{\pi} = \sum_{i=0}^{\infty} \lim_{n \to \infty} 2^{-K_U(\mu_i)} V_{\mu_i,n}^{\pi}.$$

Since all the $\mu \in W_0$ are strongly well-behaved, it follows that all the infinite sums in question are absolutely convergent and so do not depend on the order of summation, so we can conclude $(*)$

$$\lim_{n \to \infty} \sum_{\mu \in W_0} 2^{-K_U(\mu)} V_{\mu,n}^{\pi} = \sum_{\mu \in W_0} \lim_{n \to \infty} 2^{-K_U(\mu)} V_{\mu,n}^{\pi}.$$

Thus:

$$\Upsilon_{U,W_0}(\pi) = \sum_{\mu \in W_0} 2^{-K_U(\mu)} V_{\mu}^{\pi} \qquad \text{(Definition 8)}$$

$$= \sum_{\mu \in W_0} 2^{-K_U(\mu)} \lim_{n \to \infty} V_{\mu,n}^{\pi} \qquad \text{(Definition 2 part 2)}$$

$$= \sum_{\mu \in W_0} \lim_{n \to \infty} 2^{-K_U(\mu)} V_{\mu,n}^{\pi} \qquad \text{(Algebra)}$$

$$= \lim_{n \to \infty} \sum_{\mu \in W_0} 2^{-K_U(\mu)} V_{\mu,n}^{\pi}. \qquad \text{(By } *)$$

The theorem now follows by Lemma 7 part 3.   □

To show that Υ_{U,W_0}^* avoids the Garden of Eden paradox, we will need to restate some of our above results for finite values of n instead of $n = \infty$.

Lemma 10. *Let $n \in \mathbb{N}$.*

1. *(Compare Lemma 2) If π is a self-dual agent and μ is a self-dual environment, then $V_{\mu,n}^{\pi} = 0$.*
2. *(Compare Theorem 2) For any PFUTM U, for any symmetric $W_0 \subseteq W$, if $Z = \{\mu \in W_0 : K_U(\mu) \neq K_U(\overline{\mu})\}$ is the set of asymmetries of K_U, then for any self-dual agent π,*

$$\sum_{\mu \in W_0} 2^{-K_U(\mu)} V_{\mu,n}^{\pi} = \sum_{\mu \in Z} 2^{-K_U(\mu)} V_{\mu,n}^{\pi}.$$

3. *(Compare Theorem 3) For any strongly well-behaved environment μ, for any PFUTM U which is almost-symmetric except at μ, for any symmetric $W_0 \subseteq W$ with $\mu \in W_0$, for any self-dual agent π,*

$$\sum_{\nu \in W_0} 2^{-K_U(\nu)} V_{\nu,n}^{\pi} = (2^{-K_U(\mu)} - 2^{-K_U(\overline{\mu})}) V_{\mu,n}^{\pi}.$$

Proof. (1) Similar to the proof of Lemma 2, but use Lemma 1 part 2 instead of Lemma 1 part 3.

(2) Similar to the proof of Theorem 2, but use (1) instead of Lemma 2 and use Lemma 1 part 4 instead of Lemma 1 part 5.

(3) Similar to the proof of Theorem 3, but use (2) instead of Theorem 2 and use Lemma 1 part 4 instead of Lemma 1 part 5.

Finally, we show that the hyperreal Legg-Hutter intelligence measure is free of the pathological behavior from Sect. 6.

Theorem 6. *(Contrast Theorem 4) Let $X, Y \in \mathcal{A}$, with $X \neq Y$. Let μ be a well-behaved X-forbidding Garden of Eden. Let U be a PFUTM which is almost symmetric except at μ, such that $K_U(\mu) = 1$ and $K_U(\overline{\mu}) = 2$. Let W_0 be a symmetric set of strongly well-behaved environments, with $\mu \in W_0$. For all $q_1, q_2 \in (0, 1] \cap \mathbb{Q}$ with $q_1 < q_2$, we have $\Upsilon^*_{U, W_0}(\pi_{q_1, X, Y}) > \Upsilon^*_{U, W_0}(\pi_{q_2, X, Y})$.*

Proof. By Definition 11, clearly μ is strongly well-behaved. By Lemma 10 part 3, for every $n \in \mathbb{N}$, for each $i \in \{1, 2\}$, $\sum_{\nu \in W_0} 2^{-K_U(\nu)} V^{\pi_{q_i}, X, Y}_{\nu, n} = \frac{1}{4} V^{\pi_{q_i}, X, Y}_{\mu, n}$. As in the proof of Theorem 4, for every $n \in \mathbb{N}$, for each $i \in \{1, 2\}$,

$$V^{\pi_{q_i}, X, Y}_{\mu, n} = 1 \cdot (1 - q_i)^n + 0 \cdot (1 - (1 - q_i)^n).$$

The theorem now follows by Lemma 7 part 2.   □

There might be other approaches to Legg-Hutter intelligence avoiding the Garden of Eden paradox. For example, in [8], Pedersen builds alternate foundations of nonstandard probability theory along similar lines to de Finetti's foundations of standard probability, without certain limitations of the latter. It might be possible to apply these nonstandard probability theory foundations to the problem.

8   Anticipated Objections

8.1   What Does It Really Matter If the Agent Takes the Forbidden Action only 1% of the Time or 99% of the Time? In an Infinite Garden of Eden Interaction, Either Agent Will Eventually Take the Forbidden Action with Probability 100%

In standard probability theory, an event having probability 100% does not necessarily mean that it is certain. In order to resolve the probability distribution output by the agent on the nth turn into an actual action, we might imagine that a random number $x_n \in [0, 1)$ is generated. For the 1% agent, the nth action is the forbidden action iff $x_n < 0.01$. For the 99% agent, the nth action is the forbidden action iff $x_n < 0.99$. If $S_{1\%} = \{(x_1, x_2, \ldots) \in [0, 1)^\infty : \forall n, x_n \geq 0.01\}$ (the event of the 1% agent going for all eternity without taking the forbidden action), and $S_{99\%} = \{(x_1, x_2, \ldots) \in [0, 1)^\infty : \forall n, x_n \geq 0.99\}$ (the event of the 99% agent going all eternity without taking the forbidden action), then $S_{1\%} \subsetneq S_{99\%}$.

Furthermore, in actual practice, we never run an RL agent for all eternity. At most, we run the agent for some indeterminate finite number of steps. Clearly the 1% forbidden action agent beats the 99% forbidden action agent in this case.

8.2   The PFUTM in Theorem 4 Is Too Contrived for Us to Draw Conclusions About Intelligence Measurement in More Realistic Contexts

We conjecture that similar paradoxes are embedded in Legg-Hutter intelligence measures based on more familiar PFUTMs, but it is difficult to explicitly exhibit them because of the intractible nature of the infinite sum defining Legg-Hutter intelligence.

8.3   The Non-Constructive Nature of Lemma 5 Renders Υ^*_{U,W_0} Impractical to Calculate

It is already impossible to compute Υ_{U,W_0}. In fact, the Kolmogorov complexity function itself is already non-computable, so we cannot generally even compute individual summands in the infinite sum defining $\Upsilon_{U,W_0}(\pi)$. One could actually argue that in a sense, Υ^*_{U,W_0} is *easier* to approximate than Υ_{U,W_0}. Here is what we mean by this. If one were to approximate the Legg-Hutter intelligence of $\pi_{q_1,X,Y}$ and $\pi_{q_2,X,Y}$ (in the context of Theorem 4) by running large amounts of finite agent-environment interactions (Monte Carlo style), one would see $\pi_{q_1,X,Y}$ outperforming $\pi_{q_2,X,Y}$ if $q_1 \ll q_2$, which is consistent with Theorem 6 and inconsistent with Theorem 4.

8.4   A Better Way to Resolve the Paradox Would Be to Use Discount Factors

The Garden-of-Eden paradox in Theorem 4 would disappear if one applied a discount factor in the definition of V^π_μ, say, weighing each nth reward by γ^n for some fixed discount factor $\gamma \in (0,1)$. And indeed, one could treat the paradox as evidence in favor of applying such discount factors. But Legg and Hutter specifically elected, in [7], not to use discount factors, and gave good reasons for their decision.

9   Summary and Conclusion

In Theorem 2 we generalized a result of Alexander and Hutter [4]. In Theorem 4 we used this to show that if the background universal Turing machine is carefully chosen, so that Legg-Hutter intelligence measures performance in one particular "Garden of Eden" environment, then, paradoxically, certain agents all have Legg-Hutter intelligence 0 despite the fact that in some sense some of them outperform others in said environment. We opine that this Garden-of-Eden paradox results from the coarseness of the real numbers. In Theorems 5 and 6 we show that the paradox can be resolved by allowing the Legg-Hutter intelligence measure to take its values from the hyperreal number system, a more granular number system than $\mathbb{R}$.

Acknowledgments. We gratefully acknowledge Aram Ebtakar and Cole Wyeth for comments and feedback.

References

1. Alexander, S., Dawson, B.: Big-oh notations, elections, and hyperreal numbers: a Socratic dialogue. Proc. ACMS **23**, 15–22 (2022)
2. Alexander, S., Hibbard, B.: Measuring intelligence and growth rate: variations on Hibbard's intelligence measure. J. Artif. Gen. Intell. **12**(1), 1–25 (2021)
3. Samuel Allen Alexander: Intelligence via ultrafilters: structural properties of some intelligence comparators of deterministic Legg-Hutter agents. J. Artif. Gen. Intell. **10**(1), 24–45 (2019)
4. Alexander, S.A., Hutter, M.: Reward-punishment symmetric universal intelligence. In: Artificial General Intelligence: 14th International Conference, pp. 1–10. Springer, 2022
5. Hofweber, T., Schindler, R.: Hyperreal-valued probability measures approximating a real-valued measure. Notre Dame J. Form. Log. **57** (2016)
6. Kirman, A.P., Sondermann, D.: Arrow's theorem, many agents, and invisible dictators. J. Econ. Theory **5**(2), 267–277 (1972)
7. Legg, S., Hutter, M.: Universal intelligence: a definition of machine intelligence. Mind. Mach. **17**, 391–444 (2007)
8. Arthur Paul Pedersen: Comparative expectations. Stud. Log. **102**, 811–848 (2014)

Cognitive Aspects in the Formal Modelling of Multi-party Human-Computer Interaction

Antonio Cerone$^{(\boxtimes)}$ and Olzhas Zhalgendinov

Department of Computer Science, School of Engineering and Digital Sciences,
Nazarbayev University, Astana, Kazakhstan
{antonio.cerone,olzhas.zhalgendinov}@nu.edu.kz

Abstract. The unpredictability of human behaviour makes formal analysis of human-computer interaction (HCI) already difficult when one single user is interacting with one computer system. However, nowadays interaction normally involves several users, i.e., human components, interacting simultaneously with separate interfaces which communicate with and/or act upon the same computer resources. Independently of whether human components aim at using computer resources to commu-·nicate with each other ór to concurrently act upon and modify stored information, interfaces should be designed in order to protect users from the potential negative effects caused by the behaviour of other users.

In this research paper, we define a framework that combines the formal modelling of cognitive aspects of human components and the modelling of the actual computer system into an overall model that can be formally analysed using model-checking. We use the Behaviour and Reasoning Description Language (BRDL) to model human cognition and implement our framework using Real-time Maude, whose model-checker is then used to carry out formal verification.

Keywords: Human-computer Interaction · Human Cognition · Behaviour and Reasoning Description Language · LTSs · Formal Analysis

1 Introduction

Although attempts to conceptualise human-computer interaction (HCI) and multi-party interaction date back to the late 1980s and early 1990s [6,10,15,16], most of HCI research still focuses nowadays on interactions between a single user and a single system [7] and we are still far from a unified theory of HCI. This in spite of the fact that current interactive systems involve a large variety of interaction modalities for dialog integration, from web forms to spoken dialogs up to sophisticated multimodal systems, to support access to shared data and

---

Work partly supported by CIDMA (Research Center of Mathematics and Applications) and the University of Aveiro through the SEFM local organization.

J. Proença et al. (Eds.): SEFM 2024, LNCS 15551, pp. 165–181, 2026.
https://doi.org/10.1007/978-3-031-94748-3_14

their manipulation and modification, to carry out computer-supported collaborative work (CSCW), to share own resources and even to just interact socially. Thus multiple users interact with the same system and, through a single system or a number of interconnected systems, with each other. The resultant forms of interaction involve simultaneous actions and reactions, which have to be consistent and should not negatively affect each other [17]. This makes it difficult to conceptualise multi-party HCI and even more difficult to tackle it using formal approaches. As a result, most formal approaches to HCI also tend to consider a single user and a single system [18] and neglect the verification of those properties that emerge from the possibly implicit user-to-user interaction mediated by an interconnected computer system.

In this paper, we propose an approach to the formal modelling of interactive systems in which multiple users interact with an interconnected system of servers and clients. We model computer systems using an extension of labelled transition systems (LTS) that supports communication via asynchronous messaging between system components and interaction with users. We model human tasks using the Behaviour and Reasoning Description Language (BRDL) [4,5], which characterises human memory and memory processes and the way they determine human behaviour in terms of cognitive rules that are enabled by the user's goal, mental state and perception. Rule execution determines actions on the system and evolution of the user's mental state. The labels of LTS transitions play the double role of receiving a message from another system component and reacting to a user's action. A further extension of both LTSs and BRDL is the use of time in the form of a timing interval that determines the minimum and maximum delay for the rule execution.

The rest of the paper is organised as follows. Section 2 introduces the LTS extension and Sect. 2.1 illustrates it on a course registration system example. Section 3 introduces the BRDL notation and Sect. 3.1 illustrates it on the example. Section 4 describes the communication between the extended LTSs and the interaction between systems and human components, while Sect. 4.1 illustrates them on the example. Section 4.2 shows the use of model-checking to formally verify two properties of the course registration system example. Section 5 concludes the paper and discusses possible future work.

2   Computer System Model

In order to model interconnected computer systems with asynchronous communication between each other and time constraints, we extend labelled transition systems by introducing messages that can be received and consumed through the transition labels. Message content production is modelled by adding it together with the recipient identifier to a component of the current state that we assume to instantaneously deliver the pair recipient-content to the network while keeping track of the set of sent messages and their recipients. Moreover, in order to support interaction with users, the system state is partitioned into an invisible part, which is used internally, and a visible part, which is used as output in the interaction, while transition labels can also assume the role of input in the interaction.

This approach allow us to uniformly model interaction, whether between two system components or between a human component and a system components. In fact, the transition label models the system component's reception of either another system component's message or a human action.

Definition 1 (CLTS). *A Communicating Labelled Transition Systems (CLTS) is an tuple* $\mathcal{S}_n = \langle \mathbb{I}, n, V_n, I_n, \mathbb{T}, A_n, M_n, T_n, \mathcal{V}_n, \mathcal{I}_n \rangle$ *where*

- $\mathbb{I}$ *is an identifier domain;*
- $n \in \mathbb{I}$ *is the CLTS identifier;*
- V_n *is a set of visible atomic states;*
- I_n *is a set of invisible atomic states;*
- $\mathbb{T}$ *is a time domain;*
- A_n *is a set of actions;*
- M_n *is a set of messages;*
- $T_n \subseteq 2^{V_n} \times 2^{I_n} \times (A_n \cup M_n) \times \mathbb{T}^2 \times 2^{V_n} \times 2^{I_n} \times 2^S$, *with*

$$S = \{sent(i, m) \mid i \in \mathbb{I}\backslash\{n\} \wedge m \in M_n\}$$

being a set of sent messages together with their recipients, is a set of transition rules whose elements are represented with the following syntax

$$visible_1 \; [invisible_1] \; \xrightarrow[{[a,b]}]{lab} \; visible_2 \; [invisible_2] \; msgSent$$

where $a, b, \in \mathbb{T}$*, sets* $visible_1, visible_2 \in 2^{V_n}$ *and* $invisible_1, invisible_2 \in 2^{I_n}$ *are denoted by elements separated by commas,* $lab \in A_n \cup M_n$*, and* $msgSent \in 2^S$*;*
- $\mathcal{V}_n \subseteq V_n$ *is the current set of visible atomic states;*
- $\mathcal{I}_n \subseteq I_n$ *is the current set of invisible atomic states;*

such that $A_n \cap M_n = \emptyset$ *and* V_n, I_n, A_n *are pairwise disjoint.*

Note that messages can also be elements of V_n or I_n.

A CLTS is statically identified by the unique identifier $n \in \mathbb{I}$ and evolves starting from the initial state consisting of a set of initial visible atomic states and a set of initial invisible atomic states and, as explained in Sect. 4. also depending on the set of sent messages and respective recipients available in the environment.

The execution of the transition rule is triggered by the label *lab* and the inclusion of $visible_1$ in the set of initial visible atomic states and $invisible_1$ in the set of initial invisible atomic states. The label *lab* may be either a message received from another CLTS or an action performed by a user.

A delay between a minimum a and a maximum b must occur before the transition is executed. When $a = b$, the time interval $[a, a]$ is shortened as a.

2.1   Example: A Course Registration System

We model a course registration system consisting of a central server that stores the information about user registrations and instances of client websites running locally for various students. Students interact with the system through the interface provided by the website. We model our system using separate CLTS, S_0 for the central server and S_i, with $i \in \mathbb{N} \setminus \{0\}$, for the i-th website instance. For sake of simplicity, we only consider two students using two separate client websites, modelled by S_1 and S_2, and just one course with a cap of one student, that is, only one student can register for the course. In this way, when one of the two students successfully registers for the course, the system should prevent the other student from registering for that same course. For each of our CLTSs we use a distinct natural number $n \in \mathbb{N}$ as an identifier and a time domain $\mathbb{T} = \mathbb{N}$, with a time unit of 1 millisecond (ms).

Central Server. When students intend to register for a course, they first check the availability of the course. The server waits for such a request in the form of a message and returns a new message depending on the availability of the course. Then the server waits for a student's message that requests to register for the course. When the registration message is received, the server makes the course unavailable, so that other students cannot register.

The initial configuration $S_0 = \langle \mathbb{N}, 0, V_0, I_0, \mathbb{N}, A_0, M_0, T_0, \mathcal{V}_0, \mathcal{I}_0 \rangle$ of the server CLTS is defined as follows:

- $V_0 = \emptyset$,
- $I_0 = \{available, unavailable, registered_i, labRegistered_i\}$,
- $A_0 = \emptyset$,
- $M_0 = \{check_i, register_i, checkLabs_i, labChosen_i, labInfo_i, labFailed_i\} \cup I_0$,
- $\mathcal{V}_0 = \emptyset$;
- $\mathcal{I}_0 = \{available\}$;
- T_0 consists of the following transition rules:

$$[available] \xrightarrow[{[10,1000]}]{check_i} [available] \; sent(i, available) \tag{1}$$

$$[unavailable] \xrightarrow[{[10,1000]}]{check_i} [unavailable] \; sent(i, unavailable) \tag{2}$$

$$[available] \xrightarrow[{[10,1000]}]{register_i} [unavailable, registered_i] \tag{3}$$

$$[unavailable] \xrightarrow[{[10,1000]}]{register_i} [unavailable] \tag{4}$$

$$[] \xrightarrow[{[10,1000]}]{checkLabs_i} [] \; sent(i, labInfo) \tag{5}$$

$$[] \xrightarrow[{[10,1000]}]{checkLabs_i} [] \; sent(i, labFailed) \tag{6}$$

$$[] \xrightarrow[{[10,1000]}]{labChosen_i} [labRegistered_i] \tag{7}$$

Each of these transitions may take between 10 and 1000 ms, as modelled by the $[10, 1000]$ time interval. This delay reflects both the server processing time and the network transmission time. Moreover, S_0 does not have visible states, since user's visibility only occurs at the level of the client websites. Instead, all transitions are labelled with messages received from the clients. In fact, the user cannot interact directly with the server and, as a result, the set of actions of the CLTS that models the server is empty.

Transition rules 1 and 2 model the response of the server to the student's check on course availability, which was sent through the website whose identifier is i. The received $check_i$ message triggers transition rule 1 or 2, depending on whether the invisible state of S_0 contains $available$ or $unavailable$, respectively. When executed, the transition rules send the course availability invisible atomic state to the website i that has sent the check request.

Transition rules 3 and 4 model the response of the server to the student's request for course registration. The received $register$ message triggers transition rule 3 or 4, depending on whether the invisible state of S_0 contains $available$ or $unavailable$, respectively. When executed, transition rule 3 replaces the $available$ invisible atomic state with $unavailable$ and adds the invisible atomic state $registered_i$, whereas transition rule 4 consume the messages without modifying the state.

Transition rules 5 and 6 model the response of the server to the student's request for lab information by sending either the information or a failure message to the website i that has sent the check request.

Transition rule 7 models the response of the server to the student's choice to enrol in the lab by adding $labRegistered_i$ to the invisible state.

Note that only transition rules 1 and 3 may be enabled in the initial configuration ($\mathcal{I}_0 = \{available\}$) provided that the appropriate message is received ($check_i$ and $register_i$, respectively).

Client Website. The client website waits for the page to be refreshed in order to get relevant course information. When the student clicks on the *refresh button*, the client sends a request to the server for checking the course availability. Then the client waits for the response and visualises the course availability according to the server response. If the course is available, the student can click the *enrol button* to send the registration message to the server and feedback on the successful enrolment is visualised. At this point, the student needs to click the *proceed button* and wait for the next page to load. This may take some time and it can fail due to external reasons such as too much internet traffic or temporary unavailability of the server. In case of failure, the student needs to click the *proceed button* again. Finally, the student must choose whether to also register for a lab. Clicking the *register lab button* allows the student to register for a lab whereas clicking the *proceed button* once again allows the student to skips this step. This choice ends the registration process.

The initial configuration $S_i = \langle \mathbb{N}, i, V_i, I_i, \mathbb{N}, A_i, M_i, T_i, \mathcal{V}_i, \mathcal{I}_i \rangle$, with $i \in \mathbb{N}\backslash\{0\}$, of the i-th client website CLTS is defined as follows where

- $V_i = \{emptyPage, waiting, available, unavailable, enrolled, chooseLab,$
  $noLab, labRegistered\}$,
- $I_i = \{labs, loadingLabs\}$,
- $A_i = \{refresh, enrol, proceed, registerLab\}$,
- $M_i = \{check_i, available, unavailable, register_i, checkLabs_i, labInfo_i,$
  $labFailed_i, labChosen_i\}$,
- $\mathcal{V}_i = \{emptyPage\}$;
- $\mathcal{I}_i = \emptyset$;
- T_i consists of the following transition rules:

$$emptyPage \; [] \; \xrightarrow[0]{refresh} \; waiting \; [] \; sent(0, check_i) \tag{8}$$

$$waiting \; [] \; \xrightarrow[0]{available} \; available \; [] \tag{9}$$

$$waiting \; [] \; \xrightarrow[0]{unavailable} \; unavailable \; [] \tag{10}$$

$$available \; [] \; \xrightarrow[0]{enrol} \; enrolled \; [labs] \; sent(0, register_i) \tag{11}$$

$$enrolled \; [labs] \; \xrightarrow[0]{proceed} \; enrolled \; [loadingLabs] \; sent(0, checkLabs_i) \tag{12}$$

$$enrolled \; [loadingLabs] \; \xrightarrow[0]{labInfo_i} \; chooseLab \; [] \tag{13}$$

$$enrolled \; [loadingLabs] \; \xrightarrow[0]{labFailed_i} \; enrolled \; [labs] \tag{14}$$

$$chooseLab \; [] \; \xrightarrow[0]{proceed} \; noLab \; [] \tag{15}$$

$$chooseLab \; [] \; \xrightarrow[0]{registerLab} \; labRegistered \; [] \; sent(0, labChosen_i) \tag{16}$$

All these transitions are instantaneous, as modelled by the $[0, 0]$ time interval represented by the shortening 0 in the notation. In fact, the delay experienced by the user is actually the delay in the response from the server, which we have considered in the model $\mathcal{S}_0$ of the server.

Transition rule 8 models the website waiting for the *refresh* user's action. Then the visible state is instantaneously changed by removing the *emptyPage* atomic state and adding the *waiting* atomic state, which provides feedback to the user that the client website is waiting for an answer from the server. In fact, message $check_i$ is sent to the $\mathcal{S}_0$ server to request information about course availability.

Transition rules 9 and 10 model the arrival of the response from the server as the message that labels the transition (*available* or *unavailable*) and instantaneously change the visible state by removing the *waiting* atomic state and adding the received message.

Transition rule 11 models the *enrol* user's action, which is enabled when the visible state contains *available*. It instantaneously removes such a visible atomic state, adds the *enrolled* visible atomic state, as a feedback to the user, and sends a registration message to the $\mathcal{S}_0$ server. Moreover, it adds the *labs* invisible atomic state to enable transition rule 12, which starts the optional lab registration process.

Transition rule 12 models the *proceed* user's action enabled after the course registration has succeeded. A message $checkLabs_i$ is sent to the $\mathcal{S}_0$ server to request information about labs and the *labs* invisible atomic state is instantaneously replaced by *loadingLabs*, to enable the reception of the response from the server.

Transition rules 13 and 14 model the successful reception of a response from the server and a failure in receiving the response, respectively. If the information is received successfully (label $labInfo_i$ in rule 13) the *enrolled* visible atomic state and the *loadingLabs* invisible atomic state are instantaneously replaced by the *chooseLab* visible atomic state to enable the lab choice. If there is a failure due to external reasons (label $labFailed_i$ in rule 14) the *loadingLabs* invisible atomic state is instantaneously replaced by the *chooseLab* invisible atomic state to enable a new request through rule 12.

Transition rule 15 models the *proceed* user's action that is enabled when the visible state is *chooseLab*. The effect of the action is to skip the lab choice and instantaneously replace the *chooseLab* visible atomic by *noLab*.

Transition rule 16 models the *registerLab* user's action, which is enabled when the visible state is *chooseLab*. The effect of the action is to register for a lab by instantaneously sending the $labChosen_i$ message to the $\mathcal{S}_0$ server and replacing the *chooseLab* visible atomic state by *labRegistered*.

Note that only transition rule 8 may be enabled in the initial configuration ($\mathcal{V}_i = \{refresh\}$) provided that the appropriate action (*refresh*) is performed by the user.

3   User Cognitive Model

The user's behaviour is modelled in terms of the way cognition affects the actions performed in response to visible states (*interface*) of the computer system. In this section, we recall the *Behaviour and Reasoning Description Language (BRDL)* [4,5], a notation for modelling user's knowledge. BRDL is based on the *information processing theory*, which was developed in cognitive psychology in the 1950s, and describes human thinking as a computational process with at least two levels of information storage: *long-term memory (LTM)* that stores knowledge and *short-term memory (STM)* that temporarily stores information used for processing [1]. This approach has originated a number of conceptual models of human memory in cognitive psychology, from the basic distinction between LTM and STM [1], to the most complex versions of the Multistore Working Memory Model [2].

The semantics of BRDL is based on the basic model of human memory [1]. In this paper, we are interested in the user's knowledge of the interface. This is modelled in BRDL in terms of *cognitive rules* that are stored in LTM and drive the user's response to visible states of the interface, which we call *perceptions* from the user's perspective. That is, the user perceives the visible state of the interface and responds to it by performing an action, either automatically or according to the current mental states and a goal. BRDL provides a standard structure of cognitive rules, with full flexibility concerning the complexity of its components, which may vary from just mnemonic identifiers or phrases in natural language to complex data structures. This allows us, on the one hand, to keep the syntax of the language to a minimum, thus making it easy to learn and understand for practitioners, and, on the other hand, to use semantic variations that correspond to alternative theories of memory and cognition and to combine BRDL models of the user with any formal notation that models the computer components.

User's current mental states and goals are stored in STM. Mental states reflect thinking or, more specifically, reasoning and decision making. A goal is determined by what is intended to be achieved in terms of mental state or action performed. We represent a mental state as a set of pieces of information that may contain perceptions. A number of processing activities are carried out on the information stored in STM. Thus STM together with such processing activities makes up what is called human *working memory (WM)* [2]. Typical processing activities of WM are: *attention*, which stores perceptions in STM, *retrieval*, which copies information from LTM to STM, and *inference*, which applies rules stored in LTM to transform information in STM.

Definition 2 (Goal). *Let A be a set of actions, P a set of perceptions and H a set of pieces of information, with $P \subseteq H$ and A and H disjoint. The notation goal(G), with $G \in 2^{A \cup H}$, denotes the goal that is achieved when*

- *either one of the actions in $G \cap A$ is performed;*
- *or one of the pieces of information in $G \cap H$ is in STM;*

We call G set of achievements.

The set of goals on A and H is denoted by $\mathcal{G}_{A,H}$.

Definition 3 (STM Models). *Let $\mathbb{T}$ be a time domain, A a set of actions, P a set of perceptions and H a set of pieces of information, with $P \subseteq H$ and A and H disjoint. An STM model of capacity $n \in \mathbb{N}$ and decay time $d \in \mathbb{T}$ on $\mathbb{T}$, A and H, is a set $\mathcal{H} \subseteq (A \cup H \cup \mathcal{G}_{A,H}) \times \mathbb{T}$ of cardinality lower than or equal to n and such that for each $p \in A \cup H \cup \mathcal{G}_{A,H}$ and $t_1, t_2 \in \mathbb{T}$, if $(p, t_1), (p, t_2) \in \mathcal{H}$, then $t_1 = t_2$.*

The set of STM models of capacity $n \in \mathbb{N}$ and decay time $d \in \mathbb{T}$ on $\mathbb{T}$, A and H is denoted by $STM_{\mathbb{T},A,P,H}^{n,d}$.

The decay time d denotes how long the information persists in STM. The time associated with the piece of information is called *lifetime*. The lifetime equals d when the piece of information is stored in STM, then it decreases with the passing of time, and the piece of information disappears from STM when its lifetime becomes 0. The capacity of STM that is widely accepted in psychology is 7 ± 2 pieces of information, as determined by Miller's experiments in 1956 [9]. Such capacity limits are based on the numbers of chunks of information that can be held in STM and are also supported by modern experimental cognitive psychology [11].

In our models, in order to be safe, we normally set STM capacity to 5. As an example, we may consider $STM_{N,A,P,H}^{5,2700}$, where

- $A = \{refresh, enrol, proceed, registerLab\}$;
- $P = \{emptyPage, available, enrolled, chooseLab, labRegistered\}$;
- $H = P$.

The elements of A are the actions of the client websites $\mathcal{S}_i$, with $i \in \mathbb{N}\setminus\{0\}$, introduced in Sect. 2.1, which are actually instances of the same website. The elements of P are visible states of those $\mathcal{S}_i$, that is, perceptions from the user's viewpoint. The *enrolled* piece of information models the user's feeling of having enrolled in the course. We may consider two goals $goal(enrolled), goal(registerLab) \in \mathcal{G}_{A,H}$. The user feels to have achieved goal $goal(enrolled)$ when the feedback provided by the system determines an *enrolled* mental state ($enrolled \in P = H$) and to have achieved goal $goal(registerLab)$ when performing the action of registering for the lab ($registerLab \in A$).

Definition 4 (LTM Model). *An* LTM *model is a tuple* $\mathcal{L} = \langle H, P, \mathbb{T}, A, C \rangle$ *where*

- *H is a set of pieces of information;*
- *$P \subseteq H$ is a set of perceptions;*
- *$\mathbb{T}$ is a time domain;*
- *A is a set of actions;*
- *$C \subseteq \mathcal{G}_{A,H} \times 2^H \times 2^P \times \mathbb{T}^2 \times A \times 2^{(H \cup \mathcal{G}_{A,H})}$ is a set of cognitive rules whose elements are represented with the following syntax*

$$goal : \; info_1 \uparrow perc \underset{[a,b]}{\Longrightarrow} act \downarrow info_2$$

where $a, b, \in \mathbb{T}$, $goal \in \mathcal{G}_{A,H}$, $info_1 \in 2^H$, $perc \in P$, $act \in A$ and $info_2 \in 2^{H \cup \mathcal{G}_{A,H}}$,

with H and A disjoint.

In cognitive rules, the $\uparrow$ symbol suggests removal from STM whereas the $\downarrow$ symbol suggests storage in STM. We call *enabling* the part of the rule on the left of $\Longrightarrow$ and *performing* the part of the rule on the right of $\Longrightarrow$. The execution of a cognitive rule is enabled by the presence of goal *goal* and information $info_1$ in STM, and by the perception *perc* from the environment, and results in the removal of $info_1$ from STM, the performance of action *act* on the environment and the storage of new information $info_2$ in STM. Note that $info_1$ only contains pieces of information whereas $info_2$ may also contain goals. In fact, when the goal *goal* has a nonempty set of achievements, it is the only goal enabling the rule, while goals that may be in $info_2$ are actually produced in STM by performing the rule. A goal without achievements (empty set of achievements) denotes the absence of actual goal. In this case the syntax of a cognitive rule is shortened as

$$info_1 \uparrow perc \underset{[a,b]}{\Longrightarrow} act \downarrow info_2$$

Definition 5 (UCM). *Let* $\mathbb{T}$ *be a time domain,* A *a set of actions,* P *a set of perceptions and* H *a set of pieces of information, with* $P \subseteq H$ *and* A *and* H *disjoint. A* User Cognitive Model (UCM) *with STM capacity* $n \in \mathbb{N}$ *and STM decay time* $d \in \mathbb{T}$ *on* $\mathbb{T}$, A *and* H *is a tuple* $\mathcal{U} = \langle \mathbb{J}, n, \mathcal{L}_n, \mathcal{H}_n \rangle$ *such that*

- $\mathbb{J}$ *is an identifier domain;*
- $n \in \mathbb{J}$ *is the UCM identifier;*
- $\mathcal{L} = \langle H, P, \mathbb{T}, A, C \rangle$ *is an LTM model;*
- $\mathcal{H} \in STM_{\mathbb{T},A,P,H}^{n,d}$ *is the* initial STM model.

3.1   Example: A Registration Task

In the context of the course registration system, the user has a goal to register for the course and may also have an additional goal to register for a lab. In Sect. 3, we modelled these goals as $goal(enrolled), goal(registerLab) \in \mathcal{G}_{A,H}$, respectively.

The registration task of a student who intends to also register for a lab is modelled in BRDL as the UCM

$$\mathcal{U}_{withLab} = \langle \mathbb{N}, withLab, \langle H, P, \mathbb{N}, A, C \rangle, \mathcal{H}_{withLab} \rangle$$

where

- $P = \{emptyPage, available, enrolled, chooseLab, labRegistered\}$,
- $H = P$,
- $A = \{refresh, enrol, proceed, registerLab\}$,
- C consists of the following cognitive rules:

$$\uparrow emptyPage \underset{[100,300]}{\Longrightarrow} refresh \downarrow \tag{17}$$

$$goal(enrolled) : \uparrow available \underset{[100,300]}{\Longrightarrow} enrol \downarrow \tag{18}$$

$$goal(enrolled) : \uparrow enrolled \underset{[100,300]}{\Longrightarrow} \downarrow enrolled \tag{19}$$

$$goal(enrolled) : enrolled \uparrow \underset{[100,300]}{\Longrightarrow} proceed \downarrow enrolled \tag{20}$$

$$goal(noLab) : \uparrow chooseLab \underset{[100,300]}{\Longrightarrow} proceed \downarrow \tag{21}$$

$$goal(noLab) : \uparrow noLab \underset{[100,300]}{\Longrightarrow} \downarrow noLab \tag{22}$$

$$goal(registerLab) : \uparrow chooseLab \underset{[100,300]}{\Longrightarrow} registerLab \downarrow \tag{23}$$

and the initial STM model is

$$\mathcal{H}_{withLab} = \{(goal(enrolled), 2700), (goal(registerLab), 2700))\}$$

In terms of timing we assume that the access to LTM requires between 100 ms and 300 ms and that the decay time of the information in STM is 2700 ms.

This timing is suggested by the most recent experimental evidence in cognitive psychology [3].

Cognitive rule 17 does not have a goal part. It models that the user automatically reacts to the perception of an empty page ($emptyPage \in P$) by refreshing ($refresh \in A$).

Cognitive rules 18–20 are driven by the $goal(enrolled)$ goal. Rule 18 models the action of enrolling in the course ($enrol \in A$) triggered by the perception of course availability ($available \in P$). Rule 19 models the attention to the feedback of the system that shows successful enrolment ($enrolled \in P$): the perception is transferred to STM ($enrolled \in H$). Rule 20 models clicking the proceed button ($proceed \in A$) once becoming aware that the enrolment was successful ($enrolled \in H$) and preserves the content of STM ($enrolled$ appears as information removed from STM in the enabling part of the rule as well as information stored in STM in the performing part of the rule).

Cognitive rules 21 and 22 are driven by the $goal(noLab)$ goal. Rule 21 models the action of skipping the lab registration by clicking the proceed button ($proceed \in A$) again and is triggered by the perception of the alternative choice (which is not taken) of choosing lab registration ($chooseLab \in P$). Rule 22 models the attention to the feedback of the system that shows that registration to lab has been successfully skipped ($noLab \in P$): the perception is transferred to STM ($noLab \in H$). Note that $\mathcal{H}_{withLab}$ cannot evolve to an STM model that enables these two cognitive rules, since $goal(noLab)$ is not in $\mathcal{H}_{withLab}$ and is not generated by any cognitive rule in C.

Cognitive rule 23 is driven by the $goal(registerLab)$ goal. It models clicking the register lab button ($chooseLab \in A$) once becoming aware that the course enrolment was successful ($enrolled \in H$).

A student

$$\mathcal{U}_{withoutLab} = \langle \mathbb{N}, withoutLab, \langle H, P, \mathbb{N}, A, C \rangle, \mathcal{H}_{withoutLab} \rangle$$

who does not intend to choose a course has instead an initial STMmodel

$$\mathcal{H}_{withoutLab} = \{(goal(enrolled), 2700, (goal(noLab, 2700)))\}$$

which cannot evolve to an STM model that enables cognitive rule 23. Instead, $\mathcal{H}_{withoutLab}$ can evolve to an STM model that enables cognitive rules 21 and 22.

4   Overall System Model and Dynamics

An overall system model consists of computer components modelled as CLTSs and human components modelled as UCMs. Each UCM has to interact with one and only one CLTS, which models a system interface. Therefore, interaction can be modelled as an injective function between UCMs and CLTSs. To facilitate modelling we index CLTSs and UCMs on their identifiers as we did for the CLTSs of the course registration system example introduced in Sect. 2.1. Then we can define an injective function between the sets of identifiers to characterise the interaction.

Definition 6 (OSM). *Given two sets of identifiers* $\mathbb{I}$ *and* $\mathbb{J}$ *and a time domain* $\mathbb{T}$, *let*

- $\{\mathcal{S}_i\}_{i\in\mathbb{I}}$ *be a family of CLTSs on time domain* $\mathbb{T}$,
- $\{\mathcal{U}j\}_{j\in\mathbb{J}}$ *be a family of UCMs on time domain* $\mathbb{T}$,
- $\varphi : \mathbb{J} \longrightarrow \mathbb{I}$ *be an injective function, which we call* interaction function,
- μ *be a set of sent messages together with their recipients*

Then $\mathcal{M} = \langle\{\mathcal{S}_i\}_{i\in\mathbb{I}}, \{\mathcal{U}j\}_{j\in\mathbb{J}}, \varphi, \mu\rangle$ *is an* Overall System Model (OSM) *on time domain* $\mathbb{T}$.

Definition 7 (Interaction). *Let* $\mathcal{M} = \langle\{\mathcal{S}_i\}_{i\in\mathbb{I}}, \{\mathcal{U}j\}_{j\in\mathbb{J}}, \varphi, \mu\rangle$ *be an Overall System Model (OSM) on time domain* $\mathbb{T}$ *with*

- $\mathcal{S}_i = \langle\mathbb{I}, i, V_i, I_i, \mathbb{T}, A_i, M_i, T_i, \mathcal{V}_i, \mathcal{I}_i\rangle$, *for each* $i \in \mathbb{I}$
- $\mathcal{U}_j = \langle\mathbb{J}, j, \langle H_j, P_j, \mathbb{T}, A_j, C_j\rangle, \mathcal{H}_j\rangle$, *for each* $j \in \mathbb{J}$

If, there exists $j \in \mathbb{J}$ *such that*

$$(goal(info) : \; info_1 \uparrow perc \underset{[a,b]}{\Longrightarrow} act \downarrow info_2) \in C_j$$

and

$$(visible_1 \; [invisible_1] \xrightarrow[{[c,d]}]{act} visible_2 \; [invisible_2] \; msgSent) \in T_{\varphi(j)}$$

satisfy the following conditions

C.1 $(goal(info), t_0), (h_1, t_1), \ldots (h_n, t_n) \in \mathcal{H}_j$
   for all $h_i \in info_1$, $i = 1, \ldots, n$, *and for some* $t_0, t_1, \ldots t_n \in \mathbb{T}$;
C.2 $perc \in visible_1$
C.3 $visible_1 \subseteq \mathcal{V}_{\varphi(j)}$;
C.4 $invisible_1 \subseteq \mathcal{I}_{\varphi(j)}$;

then the cognitive rule and the transition rule may synchronise on action act *and, if the synchronisation occurs,* $\mathcal{M}$ *evolves to* $\mathcal{M}'$ *where*

E.1 $\mathcal{V}_{\varphi(j)}$ *is replaced with* $\mathcal{V}'_{\varphi(j)} = \mathcal{V}_{\varphi(j)}\setminus visible_1 \cup visible_2$.
E.2 $\mathcal{I}_{\varphi(j)}$ *is replaced with* $\mathcal{I}'_{\varphi(j)} = \mathcal{I}_{\varphi(j)}\setminus invisible_1 \cup invisible_2$.
E.3 *Let be* $\mathcal{H}'_j = \mathcal{H}_j\setminus\{(h_i, t_i) \,|\, h_i \in info_1\} \cup \{(h, \Delta) \,|\, h \in info\}$, *with* Δ *denoting the STM decay time,* $\mathcal{H}_j$ *is replaced with*
  E.3.1 $\mathcal{H}'_j$, *if* $act \notin info$ *and there is no* $(h_i, t_i) \in \mathcal{H}_j$ *such that* $h_i \in info$.
  E.3.2 $\tilde{\mathcal{H}}_j = \mathcal{H}'_j\setminus\{(goal(info), t_0)\}$, *otherwise.*
E.4 μ *is replaced with* $\mu' = \mu \cup msgSent$.

Synchronisation may occur if the cognitive rule and the transition rule share the same action *act*, which is performed by the user on the interface, *goal(info)* and all pieces of information h_i in $info_1$ are in STM, associated with their current lifetime t_i (condition **C.1**), the perception *perc* of the cognitive rule is in the visible source state $visible_1$ of the transition rule (condition **C.2**), the visible source state $visible_1$ of the transition rule is included in the visible component $\mathcal{V}_{\varphi(j)}$ of the current state of the CLTS (condition **C.3**) and the invisible source state $invisible_1$ of the transition rule is included in the invisible component $\mathcal{I}_{\varphi(j)}$ of the current state of the CLTS (condition **C.4**).

When the synchronisation occurs, the current state of the CLTS, the current content of the STMand the current set of sent messages and respective recipients evolves. The visible part $visible_2$ (evolution **E.1**) and the invisible part $invisible_2$ (evolution **E.2**) of the target state replace the visible part $visible_1$ and the invisible part $invisible_1$ of the source state in the $\mathcal{V}_{\varphi(j)}$ visible component and $\mathcal{I}_{\varphi(j)}$ invisible component, respectively, of the current state of the CLTS. The current content $\mathcal{H}_j$ of STM evolves by removing the timed version of the $info_1$ information of the enabling part of the cognitive rule and by adding the timed version of the $info_2$ information of the performing part of the cognitive rule (evolution **E.3.1**) and, if the shared action is in the goal achievements ($act \in info$) or one of the pieces of information in the $info$ goal achievements has a timed version in STM, by also removing the timed version of goal $goal(info)$ from STM, because it has been achieved and is no longer needed (evolution **E.3.1**). The current set of messages μ evolves by adding the messages $msgSent$ generated by the transition rule (evolution **E.4**). When more synchronisations are possible the choice is nondeterministic.

Definition 8 (Message reception). *Let* $\mathcal{M} = \langle\{\mathcal{S}_i\}_{i\in\mathbb{I}}, \{\mathcal{U}_j\}_{j\in\mathbb{J}}, \varphi, \mu\rangle$ *be an Overall System Model (OSM) on time domain* $\mathbb{T}$ *and*

$$\mathcal{S}_e = \langle\mathbb{I}, e, V_e, I_e, \mathbb{T}, A_e, M_e, T_e, \mathcal{V}_e, \mathcal{I}_e\rangle$$

with $e \in \mathbb{I}$, *be an CLTS model in* $\mathcal{M}$. *If*

$$(visible_1 \ [invisible_1] \xrightarrow[[c,d]]{rec} visible_2 \ [invisible_2] \ msgSent) \in T_e)$$

satisfies the following conditions

C.3 $visible_1 \subseteq \mathcal{V}_e$;
C.4 $invisible_1 \subseteq \mathcal{I}_e$;
C.R $sent(e, rec) \in \mu$;

then the transition rule is enabled and, if it is executed, $\mathcal{M}$ *evolves to* $\mathcal{M}'$ *where*

E.1 $\mathcal{V}_{\varphi(j)}$ *is replaced with* $\mathcal{V}'_{\varphi(j)} = \mathcal{V}_{\varphi(j)}\backslash visible_1 \cup visible_2$.
E.2 $\mathcal{I}_{\varphi(j)}$ *is replaced with* $\mathcal{I}'_{\varphi(j)} = \mathcal{I}_{\varphi(j)}\backslash invisible_1 \cup invisible_2$.
E.R μ *is replaced with* $\mu' = \mu\backslash\{sent(e, rec)\}$.

4.1   Example: User's Interaction with Its Registration Website

The overall registration systems initial configuration is modelled by the OSM

$$\mathcal{M} = \langle\{\mathcal{S}_0, \mathcal{S}_1, \mathcal{S}_2\}, \{\mathcal{U}_1, \mathcal{U}_2\}, \varphi, \emptyset\rangle$$

where $\mathcal{S}_0$, $\mathcal{S}_1$ and $\mathcal{S}_2$ are defined as in Sect 2.1, $\mathcal{U}_1 = \mathcal{U}_2$ as $\mathcal{U}_{withLab}$ introduced in Sect. 3.1 and $\varphi : \{1,2\} \longrightarrow \{0,1,2\}$ is defined by $\varphi(1) = 1$ and $\varphi(2) = 2$.

As an example of interaction, both user $\mathcal{U}_1$ and user $\mathcal{U}_2$ are initially enabled to interact with the corresponding interface, $\mathcal{S}_1$ or $\mathcal{S}_2$, respectively, as characterised by the interaction function φ. Thus we can say generically that $\mathcal{U}_i$ performs cognitive rule 17 and interacts with $\mathcal{S}_i$, which concurrently performs transition rule 8. Cognitive rule 17 has neither a goal nor an enabling information to be removed from STM, thus the initial visible state $\mathcal{V}_i = \{emptyPage\}$ of $\mathcal{S}_1$ provides the $emptyPage$ perception that is sufficient to enable it. The performance of rule 17 determines the synchronisation on action $refresh$ with transition rule 8, which is also enabled by the $emptyPage$ visible atomic state. As a result of the synchronisation, there is no evolution of the user STM $\mathcal{H}_i$, since the performing part of the cognitive rule has no information to store in STM. Instead, the $waiting$ visible atomic state replaces $emptyPage$ in $\mathcal{V}_i$, resulting in $\mathcal{V}_i' = \{waiting\}$, and message $sent(0, check_i)$ is produced, changing $\mu = \emptyset$ to $\mu' = \{sent(0, check_i)\}$. This interaction requires a time between 100 and 300 ms, since $[100,300]$ is the time interval associated with rule 17 while rule 8 is instantaneous.

As an example of message reception, transition rule 1 is enabled on the invisible state $\mathcal{I}_0 = \{available\}$ of $\mathcal{S}_0$ and on the evolved set $\mu' = \{sent(0, check_i)\}$ of sent messages and respective recipients. The performance of the rule results in no change of the invisible state but in the consumption of message $sent(0, check_i)$ and the production of message $sent(i, available)$, that is, in the evolution of μ' to $\mu'' = \{sent(i, available)\}$. This message reception requires a time between 10 and 1000 ms, since $[10,1000]$ is the time interval associated with rule 1 that models the network delay.

4.2   Formal Analysis

Our approach is implemented using the Maude rewrite system [8,13] and its real-time extension Real-Time Maude [12,14]. Real-Time Maude model checker features a timed search command that traverses the reachable states using breadth first search and checks for each state whether it satisfies the search pattern and condition. We use the search command to formally verify two properties:

1. Only one student believes to have registered for the one place course;
2. A student cannot unintentionally skip the lab registration.

A reasonable time bound for the timed search command is $[0, 10000]$. It takes at most 1800 ms for the $UCM_{withLab}$ task to be completed by performing six out of seven cognitive rules. In absence of network failures, it takes at most 5000 ms for the task to be served by the $\mathcal{S}_0$ central server by performing five out of seven transition rules.

According to cognitive rule 19 the STM model stores the $enrolled$ piece of information when the student achieves the goal of registering for the course. Therefore, for property 1 we can use

search pattern: $\langle S, \{\langle \mathbb{N}, 1, \mathcal{L}_1, \mathcal{H}'\rangle, \langle \mathbb{N}, 2, \mathcal{L}_2, \mathcal{H}''\rangle\}, \varphi, M\rangle$

seach condition: $(enrolled, T') \in \mathcal{H}' \wedge (enrolled, T'') \in \mathcal{H}''$

where S is a placeholder for any set of CLTS, M is a placeholder for any set of sent messages, $T', T'' \in \mathbb{N}$ are placeholders for a time value, and $\mathcal{H}', \mathcal{H}''$ are placeholders for any STM. The search pattern looks for an OSM that contains two UCM models. The search condition specifies that both UCM models must contain the *enrolled* STM item. The search provides as a result an OSM evolution that satisfies the search condition thus showing that property 1 is not satisfied. The OSM evolution shows that the error occurs because in transition rule 4 the server does not provide the website client with the information about the registration failure. The erroneous belief could be prevented if transition rule 4 sends a failure message to the client website and this, upon reception, changes the visible state to provide the user with appropriate feedback.

In order to analyse property 2, we need to check whether the user may click the *proceed* button in rule 15 with intention of clicking it in rule 12. Therefore, for property 2 we can use

search pattern: $\langle \{\langle \mathbb{I}, N, V_N, I_N, \mathbb{N}, A_N, M_N, T_N, \mathcal{V}_N, \mathcal{I}_N \rangle\} \cup S, U, \varphi, M \rangle$
seach condition: $noLab \in \mathcal{V}_N$

where $N \in \{1, 2\}$ is a placeholder for the CLTS identifier, S is a placeholder for any set of CLTSs, U is a placeholder for any set of UCMs, and M is a placeholder for any set of sent messages and respective recipients. The search should result in an OSM with one website containing the *noLab* information

In a correct system behavior, this search would result in an OSM with one website containing the *noLab* visible atomic state only if the user's STM contains $goal(noLab)$ in the initial configuration. Instead, this also occurs when the user's STM contains $goal(registerLab)$ in the initial configuration, that is, also when the user intends to register for a lab. The OSM evolution shows that the error is due to the fact that the *proceed* action occurs both in transition rule 12 and transition rule 15. As a consequence, the user may keep clicking the *proceed* button to perform the interaction modelled by transition rule 12, whereas the performed *proceed* results in the execution of rule 15. The error could be prevented by using two distinct actions, that is, two distinct buttons, to enable the two rules.

5   Conclusion and Future Work

In this paper, we have defined a framework for the formal modelling and analysis of interactive systems in which multiple users interact with an interconnected system of servers and clients. To model such an interconnected system we have defined CLTSs, an extension of LTSs with asynchronous communication and time constraints. Our approach combines BRDL-based cognitive models of human components and the CLTS-based models of the computer system components into an overall system model (OSM). We have implemented our framework with Real-Time Maude and exploited its model-checking capabilities to formally verify two interaction properties of a course registration system example. The Maude code of the example presented in this paper can be downloaded from GitHub[1].

In our framework users are statically assigned to interfaces, as modelled by the interaction function φ. However, in the real world, users frequently need to switch attention between different interfaces. This is actually common in safety-critical systems, in which operators are requested to multitask by monitoring several interfaces at the same time, and is becoming more and more common in daily life, with multitasking emerging as a trendy life style. Therefore, in our future work, we are planning to extend our framework to dynamically assign users to interface.

Finally, for sake of simplicity, we have only considered two users using two separate client websites. In general, our model could virtually be used for an arbitrary number of users, servers and clients. However, the current Real-Time Maude implementation is not scalable and, when the number of components increases, formal analysis is limited by state space explosion. As part of our future work, we are also working at the optimisation of the Real-Time Maude code to overcome state space explosion problem.

Acknowledgments. Antonio would like to thank Alessandro Aldini, Pierluigi Graziani, Graham Pluck and Mirko Tagliaferri for insightful discussions. Special thanks to Pierluigi for his hospitality and support during Antonio's stay in Urbino and to Mirko for carefully reading a previous version of this paper and providing important feedback. Antonio is also grateful to Alexandre Madeira for his hospitality and support while staying in Aveiro.

Both authors would like to thank the anonymous referees for their helpful comments, the CIFMA 2024 audience for questions and suggestions, and Peter Csaba Ölveczky for extensive discussions on the intricacies and use of Real-Time Maude.

References

1. Atkinson, R.C., Shiffrin, R.M.: Human memory: a proposed system and its control processes. In: Spense, K.W. (ed.) The Psychology of Learning and Motivation: Advances in Research and Theory II, pp. 89–195. Academic Press (1968)
2. Baddeley, A.: The episodic buffer: a new component of working memory? Trends Cogn. Sci. **4**(11), 417–423 (2000). https://doi.org/10.1016/s1364-6613(00)01538-2, https://www.ncbi.nlm.nih.gov/pubmed/11058819
3. Campoy, G.: Evidence for decay in verbal short-term memory: a commentary on Berman, Jonides, and Lewis (2009). J. Exp. Psychol. Learn. Mem. Cogn. **38**(4), 1129–1136 (2012)
4. Cerone, A.: Behaviour and reasoning description language (BRDL). In: SEFM 2019 Collocated Workshops (CIFMA), LNCS, vol. 12226, pp. 137–153. Springer (2020)
5. Cerone, A.: Modelling and analysing cognition and interaction. In: Formal Methods for an Informal World, LNCS, vol. 13490, pp. 30–72. Springer (2023)
6. Dowell, J., Long, J.: Towards a conception for an engineering discipline of human factors. Ergonomics **32**, 1513–1535 (1989)

---

[1] https://antoniocerone.github.io/Publications/2024/CIFMA/.

7. Kirchhoff, K., Ostendorf, M.: Directions for multi-party human-computer interaction research. In: Proceedings of the HLT-NAACL 2003, pp. 7–9. Association for Computational Linguistics (2003)
8. Martí-Oliet, N., Meseguer, J.: Rewriting logic: roadmap and bibliography. Theor. Comput. Sci. **285**(2), 121–154 (2002)
9. Miller, G.A.: The magical number seven, plus or minus two: some limits on our capacity to process information. Psychol. Rev. **63**(2), 81–97 (1956)
10. Norman, D.A.: Cognitive engineering. In: User-Centred System Design: New Perspectives on Human-Computer Interaction, pp. 31–65. Lawrence Erlbaum Associates (1986)
11. Oberauer, K., Jarrold, C., Farrell, S., Lewandowsky, S.: What limits working memory capacity? Psychol. Bull. **142**(7), 758–799 (2016)
12. Ölveczky, P.C.: Real-Time Maude and its applications. In: Escobar, S. (ed.) WRLA 2014. LNCS, vol. 8663, pp. 42–79. Springer, Cham (2014). https://doi.org/10.1007/978-3-319-12904-4_3
13. Ölveczky, P.C.: Designing Reliable Distributed Systems. Undergraduate Topics in Computer Science, Springer (2017)
14. Ölveczky, P.C., Meseguer, J.: Semantics and pragmatics of Real-Time-Maude. High.-Order Symb. Comput. **20**(1–2), 161–196 (2007)
15. Storrs, G.: A conceptual model of human-computer interaction? Behav. Inf. Technol. **8**(5), 323–334 (1989)
16. Storrs, G.: A conceptualization of rnultiparty interaction. Interact. Comput. **6**(2), 173–189 (1994)
17. Tung, T., Gomez, R., Kawahara, T., Matsuyama, T.: Multi-party human-machine interaction using a smart multimodal digital signage. In: Proceedings of the CII 2013, LNCS, vol. 8007, pp. 408–415. Springer (2013)
18. Weyers, B., Bowen, J., Dix, A., Palanque, P. (eds.): The Handbook of Formal Methods in Human-Computer Interaction. Human–Computer Interaction Series, Springer, Cham (2017)

On the Morphic Problem in Artificial Neural Networks

Giovanni Galli[✉][iD]

University of Teramo, Teramo, Italy
ggalli@unite.it

Abstract. The paper focuses on the convergence between artificial neural networks and biological neural systems, addressing the challenges of establishing a "morphic relation" between the two. The central problem lies in replicating biological neural networks' dynamic, adaptive, and self-organising properties within artificial constructs. Neuromorphic engineering (NE), an interdisciplinary field at the intersection of neuroscience and computer science, seeks to design artificial neural networks that emulate the structure, function, and temporal dynamics of biological systems. Although artificial neural networks have succeeded in areas like pattern recognition and natural language processing, they often need more fluid adaptability and robustness of biological systems. The paper explores recent advances in deep learning models, in particular deep neural networks, and their ability to capture structure-sensitive cognitive properties. Challenges remain despite promising findings, such as meta-learning techniques and systematic generalization. Deep neural networks, though efficient, often exhibit opaque and fragile learning mechanisms. The paper advocates further exploring the criteria to establish a genuine morphic relation between artificial neural networks and biological neural systems, focusing on structural, functional, and dynamic correspondences to advance the field of neuromorphic engineering.

Keywords: Artificial Neural Networks · Vector Grounding Problem · Morphic Problem · Neuromorphic Engineering

1 Introduction

The development of the connectionist paradigm, especially through modern deep neural networks (DNNs), has profoundly impacted long-standing debates in cognitive science and the philosophy of mind. Historically, connectionism faced sharp critiques from proponents of the language of thought hypothesis. Critics argued that connectionist models either failed to represent cognition adequately or merely implemented classical symbol manipulation without offering a genuine alternative (Fodor and McLaughlin 1990; Fodor and Pylyshyn 1988; Pinker and Prince 1988). They contended that connectionist models could not capture essential structure-sensitive properties of cognition, such as systematicity (the capacity to understand and produce an infinite number of sentences) and productivity (the ability to generate and comprehend novel sentences), largely due to the

J. Proença et al. (Eds.): SEFM 2024, LNCS 15551, pp. 182–201, 2026.
https://doi.org/10.1007/978-3-031-94748-3_15

absence of compositional representations in these models. In fact, they fostered a long-standing debate explored in detail by Buckner (2024). In the current era of deep learning, this debate has resurfaced with renewed vigour (Buckner 2019). Critics argue that if DNNs can match human-level performance across a range of cognitive tasks, they must possess features central to language-of-thought architectures (Marcus 2018; Quilty-Dunn et al. 2023). However, proponents of connectionism suggest that human cognition may not be as strictly rule-governed as classicists claim. They argue that connectionist models can account for structure-sensitive cognitive properties without fully replicating the architecture of symbolic models (Johnson 2004; Smolensky 2022; Elman and McRae 2019). Recent advancements in DNNs, mainly through studies on systematic compositional generalization, offer promising evidence that connectionist models can bridge the gap with classical theories of cognition. For instance, Lake and Baroni (2023) demonstrated that a transformer-based network, trained via meta-learning on various tasks, achieved systematic generalization akin to human-like learning in few-shot tasks. This meta-learning network involved training on a stream of artificial tasks with an underlying "interpretation grammar", achieving high accuracy and human-like error patterns without explicit compositional rules. Similarly, Murty et al. (2023) found that training a network beyond optimal accuracy on training data could lead to better generalising hierarchical rules. These findings suggest that modern DNNs may approximate the structure-sensitive properties of cognition without relying on explicit symbolic manipulation. However, this interpretation depends on assumptions about implementing cognitive properties in DNNs and their relevance to broader cognitive theories (McGrath et al. 2023; Pavlick 2023). Moreover, mechanistic interpretability research reveals that while DNNs can acquire variable binding mechanisms, these remain "fuzzy" and are not functionally equivalent to the discrete symbol manipulation found in classical systems (Olsson et al. 2022). Consequently, while DNNs can compute over compositional representations with constituent structure, this structure is non-classical and exhibits degrees of role-filler independence, challenging classical notions of cognition.

Now, the paradigm seems to shift again toward Neuromorphic Engineering (NE), an interdisciplinary field at the intersection of neuroscience, computer science, and electrical engineering dedicated to designing artificial systems that emulate the architecture and dynamics of biological neural networks (Tsur 2022). The origins of NE can be found in Carver Mead's work in the late 1980s on an artificial model of visual processing (Mead and Mahowald 1988). Originating from the desire to overcome the limitations of traditional computing paradigms, neuromorphic engineering seeks to create hardware and algorithms inspired by the nervous system's efficiency, adaptability, and robustness. By replicating neural structures and processes, this field aims to develop artificial neural networks (ANNs) that perform complex computations more efficiently and capture biological cognition's fundamental features. The focus on neuron morphology is at the core of NE because its "complicated morphology is closely related to its functions and, therefore, capturing accurate morphologically and physiologically details are essential to link behaviour to its underlying biological mechanisms" (Tsur 2022: 99). A fundamental aspect of neuromorphic engineering is understanding how the morphological structure of individual neurons, circuits, applications, and overall architectures contributes to effective computations. This understanding influences how information is represented, enhances resilience to damage, incorporates learning and development, adapts to local changes (plasticity), and supports evolutionary change. The morphic relation between ANNs and biological neural systems is central to neuromorphic engineering. This relation involves establishing structure, function, and dynamics correspondences between artificial and natural neural networks. The goal is not merely to mimic superficial aspects of the brain but to embody the fundamental principles that underlie neural computation and learning. Neuromorphic systems aspire to replicate features such as synaptic plasticity, spike-timing-dependent processing, and energy-efficient information transmission; these properties give biological neural networks remarkable capabilities. Neuromorphic engineering also confronts the morphic problem: the difficulty of fully capturing the adaptive, context-dependent, and self-organizing properties of biological neural networks within artificial constructs. While ANNs have achieved impressive feats in pattern recognition, language processing, and game playing, they often lack the fluid adaptability and resilience of their biological counterparts. Biological neurons operate within a rich milieu of biochemical signals, structural plasticity, and environmental interactions that are challenging to replicate artificially. The pursuit of a morphic relation necessitates satisfying specific criteria, including structural correspondence (mirroring neural architectures), functional equivalence (replicating neural operations), dynamic coherence (aligning temporal behaviours), contextual integration (embedding within larger systems), and robustness (maintaining functionality under stress). Neuromorphic engineering endeavours to meet these criteria, pushing the boundaries of how closely artificial systems can approximate biological ones. So, this paper aims to foster the analysis of the conceptual challenges posed by the morphic relation between artificial neural networks and biological neural systems. Specifically, it focuses on identifying and articulating the features to be fulfilled to establish a robust morphic relation and its limits.

2   Deep Learning Models and Cognition

Deep learning models have emerged as a significant focus in cognitive science, sparking optimism and scepticism about their potential to serve as cognitive models (Kelleher 2019). These models, notably deep neural networks (DNNs), offer a new lens through which to examine cognitive processes, primarily due to their ability to learn and generalise across vast amounts of data, sometimes in ways that parallel human cognition (Milliére 2024). However, this promise is met with considerable debate as the capabilities and limitations of DNNs in truly capturing cognitive phenomena are scrutinised. Understanding the strengths and weaknesses of deep learning models as cognitive models requires a deep detour into their underlying mechanisms, their performance in cognitive tasks, and the philosophical implications of their use in modelling cognition. One of the primary advantages of deep learning models as cognitive models is their ability to handle vast amounts of data and learn complex patterns without requiring explicit programming of rules or symbolic structures. This characteristic is particularly significant in cognitive science, where human cognition involves processing and integrating vast amounts of sensory and experiential data. For instance, DNNs have shown remarkable success in visual recognition, natural language processing[1]., and game playing, often achieving or surpassing human-level performance. These successes suggest that DNNs can, in some respects, model human cognition's flexible, adaptive, and non-linear nature. Unlike classical symbolic models, which often rely on pre-defined rules and structures, DNNs learn representations and associations directly from data, which more closely mirrors the learning processes observed in humans. This ability to model complex, non-linear relationships makes DNNs powerful tools for simulating cognitive processes such as perception, language understanding, and decision-making. Moreover, DNNs have demonstrated an ability to generalise from limited data, capturing human-like reasoning and learning aspects. For example, research has shown that with appropriate training regimes, such as meta-learning, DNNs can achieve systematic generalisation—an ability previously thought to be a hallmark of symbolic cognitive architectures. The work of Lake and Baroni (2023) is particularly relevant in this regard, as they demonstrated that transformer-based networks could achieve human-like generalisation in few-shot learning tasks. It suggests that, under certain conditions, DNNs can mimic human cognition's compositional and systematic properties, challenging the long-held belief that such properties are exclusive to symbolic models. The potential for DNNs to model cognitive tasks without relying on pre-defined rules opens new avenues for understanding how cognitive processes might be implemented in the brain, offering a more biologically plausible alternative to classical models. However, the advantages of DNNs as cognitive models come with significant caveats. One of the primary criticisms is that while DNNs can achieve human-like performance on specific tasks, the mechanisms by which they do so are often opaque and difficult to interpret. This "black box" nature of deep learning models contrasts sharply with the transparency of classical symbolic models, where the rules and operations are explicitly defined and easily understood. The lack of interpretability in DNNs raises concerns about their utility as cognitive models, as it becomes challenging to map the learned representations and processes in DNNs onto known cognitive and neural mechanisms. If cognitive modelling aims to replicate human behaviour and explain the underlying processes, then the opacity of DNNs presents a significant obstacle. Understanding how DNNs process information, make decisions and generalise requires complex techniques from mechanistic interpretability, which is still in its infancy and far from providing a comprehensive understanding of these models. Another significant limitation of

---

[1] For an examination of some limits of deep learning models for natural language processing and a critic of using them for modelling Wittgenstein's private language argument, see Galli (2024).

DNNs as cognitive models is their reliance on vast amounts of data and computational resources, which may not reflect how human cognition operates. Human learners often generalise from a few examples, demonstrating a remarkable ability to learn efficiently and robustly in environments where data is scarce or noisy. In contrast, DNNs typically require large datasets to achieve high performance, and their generalisation abilities can be fragile, especially when faced with out-of-distribution examples or adversarial attacks. This discrepancy raises questions about the ecological validity of DNNs as models of human cognition. If human cognition is characterised by its efficiency and robustness in learning from limited data, then models that require extensive data and careful tuning may not accurately capture the essence of human cognitive processes. Additionally, while DNNs have shown promise in modelling specific cognitive tasks, they may fall short in capturing higher-order cognitive processes such as abstract reasoning, theory of mind, and complex decision-making. These processes often involve symbolic manipulation, logical reasoning, and the ability to understand and generate explanations—capacities that are traditionally associated with classical cognitive architectures. While there have been advances in integrating symbolic reasoning with deep learning (e.g., neural-symbolic systems), these approaches are still in their early stages and have yet to fully demonstrate that DNNs can model the full range of human cognitive abilities. The challenge lies in bridging the gap between the associative, pattern-based learning that DNNs excel at and the more structured, rule-based reasoning that characterises much of human cognition.

Thus, using DNNs as cognitive models raises essential questions about the nature of representation and computation in cognitive systems. Critics argue that DNNs, even when they achieve human-like performance, may do so in fundamentally different ways from how the human brain operates. For instance, while DNNs can learn compositional representations, these representations are often "fuzzy" and lack the discrete, rule-governed structure that characterises classical symbolic representations. This fuzziness challenges the classical notion of cognitive architectures based on clear, well-defined symbols and rules, leading to debates about whether DNNs can be considered cognitive models or represent a fundamentally different kind of computation. Whether DNNs implement a form of the "language of thought" or offer a new paradigm for understanding cognition remains an open and contentious issue in cognitive science. Deep learning models, particularly DNNs, offer exciting possibilities and significant challenges as cognitive models. Their ability to learn from data and generalise across tasks aligns them with crucial aspects of human cognition, making them valuable tools for exploring cognitive processes. However, their opacity, data requirements, and potential misalignment with higher-order cognitive functions highlight the limitations of these models. As research advances, DNNs will play an increasingly important role in cognitive science, but whether they can fully capture the complexities of human cognition or need to be integrated with other approaches remains a critical question. The ongoing dialogue between proponents of connectionist and symbolic models will likely shape the future of cognitive science as researchers strive to develop models that not only replicate human behaviour but also provide insights into the underlying mechanisms of the mind.

3   The Neuromorphic Engineering Project

Neuromorphic Engineering (NE) is an interdisciplinary field that aims to bridge the gap between artificial neural networks (ANNs) and biological neural networks by capturing and replicating the underlying morphic relations. These are the structural, functional, and dynamic relationships that define how biological neural systems operate. The morphic relationships encompass the intricate interactions of neurons and synapses in the brain to process information, adapt to new stimuli, and enable complex behaviours. The goal of neuromorphic engineering is to design artificial systems that not only mimic the architecture of the brain but also replicate its operational principles. It aims to create more efficient, adaptable, and powerful computing systems closely resembling human cognition. According to Tsur (2022), at the heart of NE lies the comparison between biological neural networks and artificial spiking neural networks (SNNs). NNNs operate on the principles of real-time adaptive learning, energy efficiency, and decentralised processing. Tsur emphasises that while these biological systems are optimised for sparse communication and energy efficiency, ANNs, particularly the spiking variety, are striving to replicate this in artificial hardware. However, the challenge is more than replicating the neural architecture: it is about understanding how the mechanisms underlying NNNs can inspire innovations in ANNs. At the core of the morphic relations that neuromorphic engineering seeks to capture is the fundamental structure of neural networks in the brain. Biological neural networks consist of neurons interconnected by synapses, forming complex circuits that transmit and process information. These neurons exhibit a wide range of behaviors depending on the strength and timing of synaptic inputs, the properties of the neuronal membrane, and the broader network context. Neuromorphic engineering attempts to emulate this complexity by designing ANNs that are deeply rooted in the biological principles governing neural activity. This includes developing artificial neurons that replicate the nonlinear dynamics of real neurons and creating synapses that mimic plasticity—the ability to strengthen or weaken over time—which is essential for learning and memory in the brain. Plasticity is one of the most critical aspects of morphic relations—the brain's ability to adapt its structure and function in response to experience. In biological systems, synaptic plasticity allows the strength of connections between neurons to change based on activity, which is crucial for learning and memory formation. Neuromorphic engineering seeks to incorporate similar mechanisms into ANNs, enabling them to learn and adapt in a manner more akin to human cognition. This involves developing learning algorithms inspired by synaptic plasticity processes observed in the brain. For example, spike-timing-dependent plasticity (STDP), where the timing of neuronal spikes influences synaptic strength, has been a critical focus in neuromorphic research. By implementing STDP in artificial systems, engineers aim to create networks that can learn and adapt in real time, just as the human brain does. Another essential morphic relation that neuromorphic engineering aims to capture is the energy efficiency of the brain. Despite its incredible computational power, the human brain operates on only about 20 W of power, a fraction of what traditional computers consume. This efficiency arises from several factors, including sparse coding of information (where only a small subset of neurons is active at any given time), parallel processing across multiple neural circuits, and the ability to perform complex computations with low-precision signals. Neuromorphic systems seek to emulate these energy-efficient strategies by developing hardware that performs computations in a manner more similar to the brain. For instance, neuromorphic chips are often designed to use event-driven processing, where computations are performed only when certain conditions are met, much like how neurons fire only when they receive sufficient input. This approach can significantly reduce power consumption, making neuromorphic systems more viable for applications where energy efficiency is crucial. The temporal dynamics of neural activity are another critical aspect of the morphic relations that neuromorphic engineering seeks to replicate. In the brain, neurons communicate through spikes—brief, all-or-nothing electrical impulses—that convey information through their rate and precise timing. The brain's ability to process information rapidly and in real-time is mainly due to these temporal dynamics, where the timing of spikes can encode complex patterns and relationships. Neuromorphic engineering captures this aspect by designing ANNs that operate on similar temporal principles. Spiking neural networks (SNNs), for example, are a type of ANN where information is encoded in the timing of spikes rather than continuous values, allowing for more biologically realistic models of information processing. By capturing the temporal dynamics of the brain, neuromorphic systems can potentially achieve faster and more efficient processing, particularly in tasks that require real-time responses. Moreover, the connectivity patterns within the brain represent another crucial morphic relation that neuromorphic engineering aims to emulate. The human brain is characterized by a highly complex and non-uniform network of connections, with different regions specialized for various functions and connected in intricate ways that allow for both localized and distributed processing. This connectivity reflects the brain's evolutionary optimization for specific cognitive tasks like vision, language, and motor control. Neuromorphic engineering seeks to replicate these specialized connectivity patterns in ANNs by designing hierarchically organized networks capable of dynamic reconfiguration based on the task at hand. This might involve developing modular networks where different subsets of artificial neurons are dedicated to different tasks or creating networks that can rewire themselves in response to new information, much like how the brain's connectivity can change over time. In addition to these structural and functional aspects, the robustness of biological neural networks is another key morphic relation that neuromorphic engineering aims to capture. The brain is remarkably resilient and capable of functioning effectively despite noise, damage, or variability in its components. This robustness arises from factors like redundancy in neural connections, the ability of neurons to compensate for damaged areas, and the brain's capacity to filter out irrelevant noise. Neuromorphic systems aim to replicate this robustness by designing ANNs that can continue functioning even when parts of the network fail or when faced with noisy input. This might involve developing fault-tolerant architectures with multiple pathways for information flow or creating networks that can adapt to changes in their environment without extensive retraining. One of the broader goals of capturing these morphic relations is to move beyond the limitations of current ANNs, which, despite their success in many applications, are still far from replicating the full range of capabilities exhibited by the human brain. While traditional ANNs can be powerful tools for pattern recognition and prediction, they often struggle with tasks requiring real-time processing, adaptability, or understanding of complex, dynamic environments. Biological neural networks evolved over millions of years, optimising survival, adaptability, and energy efficiency. By contrast, ANNs are designed by humans for human purposes—typically to maximise performance on specific computational tasks. In attempting to bridge this gap, Tsur notes that while artificial networks like SNNs can mimic certain aspects of their biological counterparts (such as spike-timing-dependent plasticity), they do so in fundamentally different contexts. The context of biological intelligence is survival and adaptability in a dynamic world; the context of artificial intelligence is task optimisation within a designed framework. One concern Tsur (2022) raises is whether the biological and artificial systems are converging towards the same end. If artificial networks continue to improve, will they one day exhibit the same kind of intelligence that biological systems possess? Or is the difference between them irreconcilable? Tsur does not provide a definitive answer but leaves the question open, inviting readers to reflect on the nature of intelligence and the future of neuromorphic engineering. The technological side of the debate focuses on practical implementations. Tsur delves into how SNNs are constructed using principles of neuromorphic hardware, including projects like IBM's TrueNorth chip or Intel's Loihi chip. These systems use spiking neurons to mimic biological neurons' asynchronous, event-driven nature. However, the efficiency of such systems is still far from matching biological systems, particularly in terms of power consumption and adaptability. Tsur points out that while systems like Loihi have shown promise, they are still in the early stages of development compared to the complexity of biological neural systems (Tsur, 2022). He also explores the limitations of neuromorphic computing, particularly regarding energy efficiency and scalability. He acknowledges that while SNNs offer advantages for certain types of computation—such as real-time pattern recognition and low-power operations— they are unsuitable for all computational tasks. The morphing relation between NNNs and ANNs, then, is not one of seamless integration but one of careful balancing, where the strengths of each system are leveraged for specific tasks. Biological systems may never be fully replicable in artificial hardware, but their inspiration is invaluable for advancing both fields (Tsur, 2022).

4   From the Vector Grounding Problem to the Morphic Problem

This section discusses a problem similar to the Symbol Grounding Problem in AI (Harnad 1990) but in the context of connectionist systems like Large Language Models (LLMs) that use vectors instead of symbols and the connection to the morphic problem. This issue is called the Vector Grounding Problem (Coehlo Mollo and Millière, 2023). The Symbol Grounding Problem questions how abstract symbols in computational systems can acquire intrinsic meaning rather than relying solely on syntactic relationships. Harnad (1990) argued that symbols are meaningful only if grounded in sensory or experiential data, as humans understand words like "apple" through direct experience, not abstract associations. He proposed hybrid systems combining symbolic reasoning with a subsymbolic grounding in perception and action. This problem has profound implications for AI, linguistics, and the philosophy of mind, emphasizing the need for systems that connect abstract representations to the real world for genuine understanding. Moreover, the Vector Grounding Problem refers to the challenge faced by LLMs, which use vectors as numerical representations of text tokens based on statistical relationships. Despite their advanced capabilities, these models manipulate these vectors without any intrinsic connection to real-world entities or meanings, leading to outputs that appear meaningful to humans but are inherently ungrounded in reality. The problem highlights that LLMs, much like symbolic AI systems, struggle to connect their internal representations (vectors) to the external world, rendering their outputs devoid of intrinsic meaning. As artificial neural networks (ANNs), LLMs like GPT-3 operate by processing vectors. Yet, questions arise regarding whether these systems can produce genuinely meaningful outputs despite lacking direct interaction with the real world. This problem mirrors the earlier "Symbol Grounding Problem", which questioned the capacity of classical AI systems to ground symbols in real-world referents. Coehlo Mollo and Millière differentiate five distinct types of grounding discussed in the literature: referential, sensorimotor, relational, communicative, and epistemic grounding. While these terms are often used interchangeably, the paper argues that referential grounding, i.e. the capacity of internal representations to refer to actual entities in the world, is central to the Vector Grounding Problem. The authors suggest that some LLMs, especially those fine-tuned with Reinforcement Learning from Human Feedback (RLHF), possess the necessary features to overcome this challenge. Despite not being embodied or directly multimodal, these models maintain causal-historical relationships with the world through their training data, which enables them to generate outputs that bear intrinsic meaning. This claim challenges the assumption that multimodality (using inputs beyond text) or embodiment is required for an AI system to ground its representations meaningfully. Ultimately, the paper argues that current advancements in LLMs show promise in addressing the Vector Grounding Problem. This implies that artificial systems can potentially develop meaningful representations of the world despite their disembodied nature.

The morphic problem generalizes the symbol grounding problem and the vector grounding problem by addressing the grounding of representations at the morphological level of neurons in artificial neural networks (ANNs). The symbol grounding problem, as articulated by Harnad (1990), highlights the challenge of enabling abstract symbols in AI systems to acquire intrinsic meaning through sensory or experiential data rather than mere syntactic relationships. Extending this, the vector grounding problem critiques how connectionist systems like large language models (LLMs) use vectors that lack intrinsic links to real-world entities, resulting in syntactically coherent but semantically ungrounded outputs. The morphic problem deepens this inquiry by asking whether the morphology of neurons—both biological and artificial—can inherently establish such grounding. Like the human brain, biological neural systems develop their structure and functions through continuous interaction with the environment, enabling them to ground representations in sensory experiences and evolutionary pressures. In contrast, ANNs, inspired by biological morphology but trained on disembodied datasets, lack this direct connection to the real world. Consequently, while their architecture may resemble biological systems, their internal representations remain ungrounded. This disconnection raises a fundamental challenge for the morphic program, which seeks to optimize ANNs by mimicking the structure and functionality of biological systems. Grounding in biological brains is not solely a product of their morphology but also of their integration with sensory and experiential contexts. For ANNs to approach the adaptability and meaningful representation capabilities of biological systems, some strategies are necessary, such as embodied cognition, where ANNs are embedded in environments for real-world interaction, or multimodal learning, which simulates sensory richness. Ultimately, the morphic problem emphasizes that meaningful grounding requires more than structural mimicry; it demands embedding systems in contexts that enable genuine interaction with and understanding of the real world. This perspective unifies and extends the challenges of symbol and vector grounding, focusing on the intrinsic connection between morphology and meaningful representation. Biological neural networks, such as the human brain, are deeply embedded in and influenced by their environment. They develop and refine their connections through continuous interactions with the real world, gaining meaning and understanding through sensory experiences, embodied action, and evolutionary processes. The brain's ability to ground its representations in the real world is not just a byproduct of its complex structure but also a result of millions of years of evolution, during which neural architectures were honed to solve specific survival-related problems in dynamic environments. This grounding is what enables humans to perceive, understand, and respond to their surroundings in a meaningful way. Thus, the brain's architecture is not merely a computational tool but a deeply integrated system that connects abstract representations to concrete experiences. In contrast, ANNs are artificial constructs that, while inspired by the brain's architecture, operate within fundamentally different contexts. Unlike biological systems, ANNs are trained on data sets that are often divorced from the sensory-rich and dynamic environments that shape human cognition. These networks learn to recognise patterns and make predictions based on vast amounts of data. However, they do so mainly in statistical and syntactic ways, lacking the semantic grounding that biological neural networks possess. The ANNs' vectors, representing data points or features, are mathematical abstractions that may correspond to patterns in the training data but do not inherently link to real-world entities or experiences. As a result, the outputs generated by ANNs, while sometimes impressively accurate or human-like, are ultimately ungrounded like biological neural responses. Therefore, the morphic program, which aims to optimise ANNs by mimicking the structure and functionality of biological brains, must grapple with this fundamental disconnection. If the goal is to create ANNs that approach the versatility and adaptability of biological neural networks, merely copying the brain's structure may not suffice. The brain's power lies not only in its architecture but also in its deep integration with the sensory and experiential world—a connection that ANNs currently lack. This raises a crucial question: Can the morphic program succeed in optimising ANNs without somehow embedding them in a world that allows for meaningful interactions and grounding of representations? One potential approach to resolving this issue is to focus on developing ANNs that incorporate embodied cognition elements. This would involve designing systems where artificial neural networks are modelled after the brain's architecture and embedded in environments that allow real-world interaction. For instance, integrating ANNs with robotics or other forms of embodied agents could provide a platform for these networks to develop more grounded and contextually relevant representations[2]. By engaging with the physical world, these networks could begin to form associations between their internal vectors and the external entities they represent, much like how a child learns about the world through sensory experiences and interaction. Moreover, the morphic program could explore the incorporation of multimodal learning, where ANNs are trained on diverse data types that simulate the sensory inputs received by biological organisms. This could involve integrating visual, auditory, tactile, and proprioceptive data, allowing ANNs to develop more prosperous and interconnected representations. Such an approach might help bridge the gap between the statistical patterns recognised by ANNs and the meaningful, grounded representations seen in biological systems. However, even with these strategies, the question remains whether ANNs can genuinely achieve the kind of grounding that biological neural networks possess. The human brain is a product of evolution, with its structures and functions finely tuned for survival in a complex and dynamic world. ANNs, on the other hand, are designed and trained by humans, often for specific tasks that do not require the broad adaptability and understanding that biological systems have. While the morphic program can undoubtedly lead to improvements in ANN performance—making them more efficient, flexible, or capable of generalisation—the extent to which

---

[2] It is clear that in this area, the inquiry into relevance logic has become increasingly fundamental to developing a system capable of navigating the uncertainty of real-world scenarios. To deepen the understanding of the statistical approach to relevance logic, see Fazio and Mascella (2023).

these improvements can replicate the true grounding of biological systems is uncertain. The morphic problem also touches on more crucial questions about the nature of meaning and understanding in artificial systems. Even if ANNs could be designed to mimic the brain's structure and trained in environments that provide rich sensory data, would this lead to genuine understanding or merely the appearance of understanding? This echoes debates in AI regarding whether machines can ever truly "understand" or whether they simulate understanding through sophisticated pattern recognition. The grounding problem, whether in the context of symbols or vectors, suggests that without a connection to the real-world entities they are meant to represent, any "understanding" in ANNs may be superficial at best. The morphic problem of artificial neural networks highlights a critical challenge in optimising AI through biological inspiration[3]. At the same time, the brain's architecture provides a powerful model for ANN design; its strength lies in its deep connection to the real world—a connection that current ANNs lack. To address this, the morphic program must go beyond structural mimicry and seek ways to embed ANNs in environments that allow for meaningful interactions and grounding. Whether through embodied cognition, multimodal learning, or other innovative approaches, the goal should be to create systems that not merely simulate understanding but achieve a form that is as close as possible to that seen in biological systems.

5 Types of Morphism and the Morphic Relationship in NE

Morphism is not a new notion in the philosophy of science. In structuralist accounts of scientific representation, developed in what is sometimes called the "semantic view" of theories (Suppes 1960 [1969]; van Fraassen 1980, 1997, 2008), scientific models represent their target systems in virtue of a structure-preserving mapping or morphism between the two (Resnik 1997; Shapiro 2000; Frigg and Nguyen 2021). Various types of morphisms have been proposed. Isomorphisms require a one-to-one correspondence that preserves all relations (Bartels 2006; Mundy 1986), while isomorphic embeddings focus on embedding a model into a larger structure (van Fraassen 1980, 1997, 2008; Redhead 2001). Homomorphisms relax certain strictures of isomorphism and still allow meaningful correspondences (Lloyd 1984; Bartels 2006). Proponents of the partial structures

---

[3] The vector grounding problem in the morphic framework, akin to the symbol grounding problem, indeed points to a fundamental limitation: artificial systems lack intrinsic links between their internal representations and real-world referents. As one anonymous reviewer suggests, progress on this issue likely requires significant advances in neuroscience to elucidate how biological systems ground their symbols through embodied interaction, sensory experiences, and neural plasticity. Without a deeper understanding of how the human brain achieves symbol grounding, attempts to replicate this in artificial systems remain speculative. This reinforces the importance of interdisciplinary collaboration between AI researchers and neuroscientists to bridge these conceptual gaps.

approach (Da Costa and French 1990, 2003; Bueno 1997; Bueno and French 2011; French 2003; French and Ladyman 1999) introduce partial isomorphisms, acknowledging that scientific models often represent their targets incompletely or with idealizations. All these proposals are collectively seen as identifying some kind of mapping—be it whole or partial—underpinning how surrogative reasoning and the transfer of insights from a model to its real-world target become possible.

Against this backdrop, as we have seen, neuromorphic engineering can be understood as an endeavour to establish similarly robust morphic relations between artificial neural networks and biological neural systems in the human brain. By capturing these structure-preserving correspondences—what we may broadly call "morphic relations"—neuromorphic engineering aims to create systems that are more efficient, more adaptable, and capable of performing a broad range of cognitive tasks in ways reminiscent of human intelligence. Yet, achieving such a morphism is no trivial matter. It calls for a nuanced understanding of how the brain's structural, functional, and dynamic properties map onto computational models. Much remains unknown about large-scale brain networks, so researchers refine their models as new insights emerge—making neuromorphic engineering both a process of discovery and design (Tsur 2022: 100). Ultimately, the morphic relations that neuromorphic engineering pursues attempt to encapsulate the intricate interplay among structure, function, and dynamics in biological neural networks. By emulating these relations, neuromorphic systems aim to mirror the brain's architecture and operational principles, thereby advancing AI toward the flexibility, resilience, and power of human cognition. A morphic relation in this context involves deeper correspondences than mere surface similarities: it requires that an ANN emulate key structural (neurons and synapses), functional (learning rules, plasticity mechanisms), and dynamic (temporal evolution, responses to stimuli) features of biological neural systems. To meet this standard, the artificial network must exhibit what can be called structural correspondence by adopting an architecture of interconnected "neurons" and "synapses" that faithfully reflects the brain's components while preserving the integrity and functionality of its network. At the same time, it must demonstrate functional equivalence by performing cognitive tasks and adapting to inputs in a way that parallels key processes in the brain, such as learning through synaptic plasticity or spike-timing mechanisms. It should also manifest dynamic coherence, evolving over time in patterns that echo the temporal rhythms and stimulus responses found in natural neural circuits. Furthermore, the ANN needs to be situated in a manner that parallels the larger environment of the biological network, a requirement that can be termed contextual integration, whereby the artificial system's role in its computational or ecological setting aligns with the brain's own place within broader cognitive architectures. Just as biological networks maintain their activity despite disruptions like noise or damage, a robust and resilient ANN preserves its functionality when exposed to comparable perturbations. When a network satisfies these structural, functional, dynamic, contextual, and resilient demands, it achieves a robust morphic relation in which the artificial and biological systems are mutually intelligible through a deep, structure-preserving mapping. By capturing the core principles that guide neural processing, neuromorphic engineering moves beyond superficial resemblances to offer AI systems endowed with adaptability, efficiency, and cognitive sophistication more similar to the human mind. Moreover, this gap between artificial and biological neural networks encourages the strategy of focusing on smaller, specific portions of neural activity, such as isolated circuits or modular functionalities, rather than attempting to replicate the entirety of a human brain. Neuromorphic engineering already follows this approach to some extent by modelling particular aspects like synaptic plasticity or spike-timing-dependent processing. However, such a reductionist strategy has inherent limitations in achieving the broader target of creating systems with general intelligence and adaptability akin to biological systems. These limitations arise because biological cognition emerges not just from localized processing but also from the intricate interplay of distributed, interconnected systems. Circumventing this challenge entirely may be difficult because it hinges on understanding and replicating emergent properties of large-scale neural interactions, which current technology and theoretical frameworks struggle to address. A more achievable short-term target may involve integrating multiple small-scale models into larger, functionally coherent systems while recognizing that full equivalence with biological neural systems remains a long-term goal dependent on breakthroughs in computational power and neuroscience.

6   Conceptual and Methodological Challenges

The morphic problem discussed in the paper explores the challenge of replicating the structural, functional, and dynamic properties of biological neural systems in ANNs. Central to this issue is the difficulty of bridging the gap between the adaptive, self-organizing nature of biological neurons and the rigid, context-limited operations of ANNs. This bears an analogy to Searle's Chinese Room argument, which critiques the notion that syntactic manipulation of symbols equates to genuine understanding or semantic comprehension (Searle 1980). Similarly, the morphic problem reveals that ANNs may achieve task-specific outputs but lack the "grounding" that ties those outputs to a real-world, meaningful context. Despite its complexity, the neural architecture of ANNs struggles to replicate the inherent embodiment and environmental integration of biological systems. This issue mirrors Searle's assertion that symbol manipulation alone does not constitute complete cognition or understanding. Furthermore, the morphic problem aligns with Jackson's knowledge argument, wherein Mary—a neuroscientist with full knowledge of the physical properties of colour vision—lacks the experiential understanding of seeing red until she steps out of her monochrome room (Jackson 1982). The morphic challenge highlights a similar dichotomy in ANNs. Despite their capacity to mimic neural architectures and process data, they operate in a detached, disembodied framework devoid of the experiential and sensory richness that characterizes biological cognition. Just as Mary's new qualitative experience adds a dimension to her knowledge that could not be achieved through theoretical understanding alone, the paper suggests that ANNs require integration with environments that facilitate grounding and embodiment to achieve capabilities closer to human-like cognition.

Both philosophical arguments emphasize the limitations of purely mechanistic or computational approaches in capturing the qualitative essence of human understanding and cognition. While the morphic problem seeks to overcome these limitations through neuromorphic engineering—introducing features like synaptic plasticity, spike-timing-dependent processing, and energy-efficient architectures—it also acknowledges the fundamental gap between artificial constructs and the biologically evolved systems they seek to emulate. The Chinese Room and Mary's scenario collectively highlight that without addressing the grounding of representations and the context of their operation, the morphic relation between biological and artificial systems remains superficial and incomplete. Thus, the morphic problem in ANNs resonates deeply with the epistemic gaps underscored by Searle and Jackson, underscoring the necessity of bridging not just structural and functional similarities but also the experiential and grounding dimensions of cognition for meaningful progress in artificial intelligence. The relationship between psychology and neuroscience complicates the explanatory frameworks for neuromorphic computation. Psychology often deals with abstract, high-level constructs like cognition, emotion, and behaviour, while neuroscience focuses on low-level neural mechanisms. Bridging these domains to explain how neuromorphic systems function or emulate human cognition involves significant epistemological challenges. The paper implicitly highlights these tensions by noting the difficulty of translating biological processes into computational models. Neuromorphic systems that aim to emulate neural mechanisms often do so without an accompanying theoretical framework that aligns with psychological constructs. This explanatory gap limits our ability to interpret the outputs of neuromorphic systems in terms of human-like cognition or behaviour. Addressing this issue may require a new theoretical synthesis that integrates insights from neuroscience and psychology with computational modelling.

Comparing deep neural networks (DNNs) to human cognition presents significant methodological challenges, particularly when considering the concept of morphic relations. The "morphic problem" underscores the difficulty of optimizing artificial neural networks by merely mimicking the biological structures of the human brain. Meaningful comparisons between DNNs and humans are complex; they require meticulously matched conditions and rigorous experimental designs that account for the profound differences in how artificial and biological systems process information and interact with the world. One primary methodological challenge is the fundamentally different ways these systems are trained and operate. Human cognition develops through a lifetime of sensory experiences, embodied interactions, and social learning within a dynamic environment. In contrast, DNNs are typically trained on static datasets, often consisting of labelled examples that lack the rich, multimodal experiences shaping human understanding. This disparity leads to significant differences in how DNNs and humans represent and process information. To compare these systems meaning-fully, researchers must ensure that the conditions under which DNNs are tested closely mirror those under which humans perform similar tasks. Achieving such parity is challenging. The data used to train and test DNNs often lacks the com-plexity and contextual richness of stimuli humans encounter. For instance, while a DNN might be trained to recognize objects in images based on pixel patterns and statistical correlations, it does so without the broader contextual under-standing humans possess. A human recognizes a chair not just by its appearance but also by its function, its relationship to other objects, and its cultural signif-icance. Experimental designs must account for these contextual factors, which are often difficult to quantify and incorporate into the data used for training DNNs. Additionally, DNNs and humans often operate under different constraints and objectives. Humans balance a wide range of cognitive functions—including memory and attention—while interacting with a complex environment. DNNs are typically optimized for a single task or a narrow set of tasks, often with-out consideration for the broader cognitive processes involved in the human performance of the same task. This focused optimization can lead DNNs to achieve high performance under controlled conditions, but it does not necessar-ily mean that their underlying cognitive processes are comparable to those of humans[4]. To address these challenges, experimental designs must carefully con-trol for differences in how DNNs and humans approach tasks. This might involve creating testing environments for DNNs that better simulate human experiences. For example, instead of training a DNN on a static dataset, researchers could use dynamic, interactive environments requiring the DNN to engage with the world more like humans do. Such environments could provide feedback based on the DNNs' actions, encouraging the development of representations grounded in real-world interactions. While this approach requires significant advancements in how DNNs are trained and tested, it could lead to more meaningful compar-isons with human cognition. Interdisciplinary collaboration is crucial in designing experiments that compare DNNs to humans. Insights from psychology, neuro-science, and cognitive science are essential for capturing the nuances of human thought processes. Similarly, expertise in machine learning and artificial intel-ligence is vital for understanding the capabilities and limitations of DNNs. By combining these fields, researchers can design experiments that more accurately

---

[4] The use of performance-based metrics to evaluate imitation or similarity between bio-logical and artificial systems has inherent limitations. As the paper suggests, the mor-phic problem unfolds across multiple dimensions: structural, functional, dynamic, and contextual. Performance comparisons focus on functional outcomes but may neglect deeper correspondences in these other dimensions. Effective similarity can-not be guaranteed by performance alone, as artificial systems may achieve similar outcomes through fundamentally different processes. For example, an ANN might classify images accurately but use statistical correlations rather than the contextual and experiential understanding employed by humans. To address this limitation, the evaluation of artificial systems should include multi-dimensional analyses that assess structural and dynamic alignment with biological systems, not just functional performance.

reflect the conditions under which both DNNs and humans operate, leading to more valid and reliable comparisons. Interpreting results from such comparisons poses its own challenges. Even when DNNs and humans perform similarly on a given task, it does not necessarily mean they use the same underlying processes. A DNN might classify objects based on statistical regularities, while a human relies on visual features, contextual information, and prior knowledge. Without understanding the mechanisms underlying each system's performance, drawing parallels can be misleading. This underscores the importance of not only comparing performance outcomes but also investigating the processes leading to those outcomes. Techniques like neuroimaging in humans and feature visualization in DNNs can provide insights into internal representations and processes, but interpreting these results requires careful consideration of the differences between artificial and biological systems. Another methodological challenge arises from the inherent differences in scale and complexity between human brains and DNNs. The human brain is vastly more complex, with approximately 86 billion neurons interconnected in intricate networks supporting a wide range of cognitive functions. DNNs, while inspired by the brain, are simplified models with far fewer neurons (or units) and connections. This difference in scale means that even if a DNN replicates a specific human behaviour, it might do so in a way that is not scalable to the broader, more complex tasks humans perform. Experimental designs must, therefore, be cautious in extrapolating findings from specific tasks to broader claims about human-like cognition in DNNs. The issue of interpretability also plays a crucial role. Human cognition, though not fully understood, is generally interpretable to some extent through introspection, behavioural analysis, and neuroscience. DNNs often function as "black boxes", where the internal processes leading to a particular output are difficult to decipher. This opacity makes it challenging to determine whether a DNN's behaviour truly mirrors human cognition or is simply a coincidental outcome of its architecture and training data. Developing methods to improve the interpretability of DNNs, such as analyzing activation patterns or using techniques like saliency mapping, is essential for making more meaningful comparisons. In conclusion, comparing DNNs to humans presents significant methodological challenges stemming from differences in training, information processing, and environmental interactions. The morphic problem highlights the limitations of optimizing DNNs solely by mimicking biological structures, and these limitations extend to experimental designs used in comparisons. To make these comparisons meaningful, researchers must carefully match conditions between the two systems, considering contextual richness, cognitive complexity, and results from interpretability. This requires sophisticated experimental designs and collaborative efforts across disciplines to ensure that comparisons between DNNs and human cognition are valid and insightful. By addressing these methodological challenges, we can advance our understanding of both artificial and human intelligence, moving closer to creating AI systems that reflect the human mind's capabilities.

7   Conclusion

This paper on the assumption of the NE project examines the convergence between natural neural networks (NNNs) and artificial neuromorphic systems (ANNs), presenting an exploration of the "morphic problem" This issue, central to NE, underscores the challenge of translating the flexible, adaptive nature of biological neurons into artificial systems, which often rely on static, rigid architectures. Neuromorphic systems, inspired by the brain's neural architecture, aim to replicate its efficiency, adaptability, and energy usage while addressing the philosophical and technical complexities that arise from this convergence. One core aspect of the morphic problem involves the difficulty in mapping biological neural networks' dynamic plasticity and continuous learning abilities onto artificial networks. Natural neural networks possess dynamic synapses, non-linear interactions, and the ability to reorganise themselves in response to stimuli, creating a level of flexibility that artificial systems struggle to mirror. Artificial networks, especially early ANNs, often rely on pre-defined architectures and rules, limiting their adaptability. This fundamental gap represents a critical element of the morphic problem: the tension between the static nature of artificial systems and the fluid, evolving properties of natural neurons. In addressing the morphic problem, the paper explores the role of spiking neural networks, which attempt to bridge this gap by emulating biological neurons' time-dependent, spike-based communication system. SNNs represent a significant advancement in neuromorphic computing by mimicking the asynchronous, event-driven processing found in the brain, such as how neurons fire in response to stimuli or how the brain processes sensory information. However, despite these innovations, challenges persist. SNNs, while capable of performing specific tasks such as pattern recognition and cognitive functions, still fall short of the biological system's scalability, adaptability, and efficiency. The computational power of biological neurons, honed through millions of years of evolution, surpasses what current artificial systems can replicate. In conclusion, the morphic problem in neuromorphic engineering is both a technical and conceptual challenge, highlighting the difficulties inherent in replicating the adaptability and plasticity of natural neural networks within artificial systems. By addressing this problem, neuromorphic engineering has the potential to revolutionise computing, paving the way for breakthroughs in fields such as artificial intelligence, robotics, and bioinformatics. For instance, solving the morphic problem could lead to developing more adaptive and efficient learning algorithms. In robotics, it could enable the creation of more human-like and adaptable robots. In bioinformatics, it could enhance our understanding of biological systems and their computational principles. The paper also underscores that while technology can approximate the workings of the brain, achieving proper neural-like computation may require a fundamental shift in our understanding of biology and computation.

References

Bartels, A.: Defending the structural concept of representation. Theoria **21**(1), 7–19 (2006)

Buckner, C.J.: Deep learning: a philosophical introduction. Philosophy Compass **14**(10), e12625, 1–19 (2019)

Buckner, C. J.: From Deep Learning to Rational Machines. What the History of Philosophy Can Teach Us about the Future of Artificial Intelligence. Oxford University Press, New York (2024)

Bueno, O.: Empirical adequacy: a partial structure approach. Stud. Hist. Philos. Sci. **28**(4), 585–610 (1997)

Bueno, O., French, S.: How theories represent. Br. J. Philos. Sci. **62**(4), 857–894 (2011)

Da Costa, N., French, S.: The model-theoretic approach to the philosophy of science. Philos. Sci. **57**(2), 248–265 (1990)

Da Costa, N., French, S.: Science and Partial Truth: A Unitary Approach to Models and Scientific Reasoning. Oxford University Press, Oxford (2003)

Elman, J.L., McRae, K.: A model of event knowledge. Psychol. Rev. **126**(2), 252–291 (2019)

Fazio, D., Mascella, R.: Some remarks on the logic of probabilistic relevance. Log. Log. Philos. **33** (1), 101–144 (2023)

Fodor, J.A., McLaughlin, B.P.: Connectionism and the problem of systematicity: why smolesnky's solution doesn't work. Cognition **35**, 183–204 (1990)

Fodor, J.A., Pylyshyn, Z.W.: Connectionism and cognitive architecture: a critical analysis. Cognition **28**(1–2), 3–71 (1988)

French, S.: A model-theoretic account of representation (or, I Don't Know Much About Art...But I Know It Involves Isomorphism). Philos. Sci. **70**(5), 1472–1483 (2003)

French, S., Ladyman, J.: Reinflating the Semantic Approach. Int. Stud. Philos. Sci. **13**(2), 103–121 (1999)

Frigg, R., Nguyen, J.: Seven myths about the fiction view of models, in models and idealizations in science. In: Casini A., Redmond J. (eds.), Artifactual and Fictional Approaches, pp. 133–157. Springer, Cham (2021)

Galli, G.: Language Models and the Private Language Argument: A Wittgensteinian Guide to Machine Learning, in Wittgenstein and Artificial Intelligence, Volume 1: Mind and Language, Helliwell, A., Rossi, A. and Bell, B. (eds.), Anthem Press, London (2024)

Harnad, S.: The symbol grounding problem. Physica D **42**(1–3), 335–346 (1990)

Jackson, F.: Epiphenomenal qualia. Philos. Q. **32**, 127–136 (1982)

Johnson, K.: On the systematicity of language and thought. J. Philos. **101**, 111–139 (2004)

Kelleher, J.D.: Deep Learning. The MIT Press, Massachusetts (2019)

Lake, B.M., Baroni, M.: Human-like systematic generalization through a meta-learning neural network. Nature **623**, 115–121 (2023)

Lloyd, E.: A semantic approach to the structure of population genetics. Philos. Sci. **51**(2), 242–264 (1984)

Mandelbaum, E., et al.: Problems and mysteries of the many languages of thought. Cogn. Sci. **46**, 1–6 (2022)

Marcus, G.: The Algebraic Mind. MIT Press, Cambridge (2001)

Marcus, G.: Deep learning: a critical appraisal, arXiv:1801.00631v1 (2018)

McGrath, S.W., Russin, J., Pavlick, E., Feiman, R.: Properties of LoTs: the footprints or the bear itself? Behav. Brain Sci. **46**, e284 (2023)

Mead, C.A., Mahowald, M.A.: A silicon model of early visual processing. Neural Netw. **1**(1), 91–97 (1988)

Milliére, R.: Philosophy of cognitive science in the age of deep learning. WIREs Cogn. Sci. **15**(e1684), 1–9 (2024)

Mollo, D.C., Millière, R.: The Vector Grounding Problem, arXiv:2304.01481 (2023)

Mundy, B.: On the general theory of meaningful representation. Synthese **67**(3), 391–437 (1986)

Murty, S., Sharma, P., Andreas, J., Manning, C.: Grokking of hierarchical structure in vanilla transformers. In: Proceedings of the 61st Annual Meeting of the Association for Computational Linguistics. (Volume 2: Short Papers), pp. 439–448 (2023)

Olsson, C., Elhage, N., Nanda, et al.: In-context learning and induction heads. Transf. Circuits Thread. (2022)

Pavlick, E.: Symbols and grounding in large language models. Phil. Trans. R. Soc. A **381**, 1–19 (2023)

Pinker, S., Prince, A.: On language and connectionism: analysis of a parallel distributed processing model of language acquisition. Cognition **28**(1–2), 73–193 (1988)

Quilty-Dunn, J., Porot, N., Mandelbaum, E.: The best game in town: the reemergence of the language-of-thought hypothesis across the cognitive sciences. Behav. Brain Sci. **46**, e261 (2023)

Redhead, M.: The intelligibility of the universe. In: O'Hear, A. (ed.), Philosophy at the New Millennium, pp. 73–90. Cambridge University Press, Cambridge (2001)

Resnik, M.D.: Mathematics as a Science of Patterns. Oxford University Press, Oxford (1997)

Searle, J.: Minds, brains and programs. Behav. Brain Sci. **3**, 417–457 (1980)

Shapiro, S.: Philosophy of Mathematics: Structure and Ontology. Oxford University Press, Oxford (1997)

Smolensky, P., McCoy, R.T., Fernandez, R., Goldrick, M., Gao, J.: Neurocompositional computing: from the central paradox of cognition to a new generation of AI systems. AI Mag. **43**, 308–322 (2022)

Suppes, P.: A Comparison of the Meaning and Uses of Models in Mathematics and the Empirical Sciences, reprinted in Suppes 1969, Studies in the Methodology and Foundations of Science: Selected Papers from 1951 to 1969. Dordrecht Reidel. 10–23 (1960)

Tsur, E.E.: Neuromorphic Engineering. The Scientist's, Algorithms Designer's and Computer Architect's Perspectives on Brain-Inspired Computing. CRC Press, Abingdon (2022)

van Fraassen, B.C.: The Scientific Image. Oxford University Press, Oxford (1980)

van Fraassen, B.C.: Structure and perspective: philosophical perplexity and paradox. In: Dalla Chiara, M.L. (ed.), Logic and Scientific Methods, pp. 511–530. Kluwer, Dordrecht (1997)

van Fraassen, B.C.: Scientific Representation: Paradoxes of Perspective. Oxford University Press, Oxford (2008)

Time Factor in Neural Learning Processes

Fabrizia Giulia Garavaglia$^{(\boxtimes)}$ ⓘ, Marco Giunti ⓘ, and Giuseppe Sergioli ⓘ

University of Cagliari, Cagliari, Italy
giuliafabrizia@gmail.com, giunti@unica.it, giuseppe.sergioli@gmail.com

Abstract. This paper explores the role of neural plasticity and environmental influences in cognitive development and learning processes in humans. The brain's ability to reorganize its synaptic connections is examined both during embryonic development and throughout the lifespan. The first part focuses on the impact of the environment on neural plasticity, from cellular influences to epigenetic ones. The analysis also includes the effects of epigenetics on cognition and the implications of environmental stress on brain function, with particular attention to changes in dendritic spines. The second part investigates how the environment continues to affect neuronal changes through learning, emphasizing the importance of timing and the synchronization of external stimuli and synaptic modifications at certain stages of development This study suggests that understanding the timing and coherence of synaptic activations is crucial for optimizing learning and improving cognitive rehabilitation strategies. A timing approach to neural plasticity, which is influenced by temporal and environmental factors, could also have significant implications for education, mental health, and therapeutic practices.

Keywords: Neural plasticity · learning processes · timing signals · synchronization

1 Introduction

Understanding the mechanisms by which the brain adapts to new experiences is one of the most challenging and fascinating areas of neuroscience. The ability of the brain to remodel itself, known as neural plasticity, is fundamental to the processes of learning and memory. This paper explores how neural plasticity functions across the lifespan, focusing on the key role that environmental factors play in shaping synaptic configurations and how these changes contribute to cognitive development and learning. Specifically, we will examine the concept of neural plasticity from a neurophysiological perspective, investigating its relationship with synaptic modifications and how these are influenced by timing and external stimuli.

In Sect. 2, we discuss the mechanisms of neural plasticity during brain development, exploring how neurons migrate, differentiate, and establish synaptic

J. Proença et al. (Eds.): SEFM 2024, LNCS 15551, pp. 202–218, 2026.
https://doi.org/10.1007/978-3-031-94748-3_16

connections. This section highlights the critical role of the environment at different levels, from cellular interactions to epigenetic influences. Subsection 2.1 focuses on the early stages of brain development, particularly the role of glial cells and the importance of environmental stimuli in shaping neural architecture through processes like synaptic pruning. The discussion also delves into the impact of epigenetic factors, such as parental behavior during pregnancy, and their long-term effects on brain development. In Subsect. 2.2, we extend the analysis to neural plasticity throughout life, focusing on how experience and environmental changes continue to shape synaptic connections, particularly in learning and memory processes.

Section 3 focuses on the relevance of timing in neural plasticity. We analyze how the synchronization of neural activations, often referred to as synaptic timing, is essential for effective learning and memory consolidation. This section introduces the paradigm of spike-timing-dependent plasticity (STDP), exploring how precise timing between stimuli and neural responses enhances or weakens synaptic connections. Subsection 3.1 investigates how learning is related to timing of neural information processing and proposes that neural plasticity is not just a matter of structural changes but also of temporal coordination across neural networks. Subsection 3.2 examines the relationship between timing, conscious agency, and the perception of voluntary versus conditioned learning. The section concludes by proposing that the sense of agency in learning is modulated by the temporal architecture of external stimuli.

Throughout the paper, we aim to demonstrate how the intricate interplay between genetic, environmental, and temporal factors contributes to the brain's capacity for learning and adaptation. By understanding these mechanisms about functioning of the human brain we could also explore potential applications in education, cognitive rehabilitation, and mental health interventions.

2   Neural Plasticity Features and the Role of the Environment

The basic concept of new neuroscience is that over time the brain is always willing to reform and change. The brain, like life, is not a static system, but a process of self-creation known as *autopoiesis*. It was the great Polish neuroscientist Jerzy Konorski [11] who used the term *plasticity* in 1948 to describe brain changes, which are due to the strength of connection between neurons expressed by the influence of experience. In the same years, Donald Hebb devoted several deep researches to the brain's ability to change morphology and connectivity, which converge in a very rich book [9]. Previously, Ramòn y Cajal [2] had argued that the ability of neurons to mature and their power to create new connections can explain learning. In the early 1950s, several studies had also shown that "repeated administrations of an electrical stimulus to a nerve pathway were able to alter the synaptic transmission in that way generating a neural plasticity, that could be associated to learning improvement and emotional subjective responses" [13][1].

We cite this sentence that exposes a strong claim of the author, because it contains the most relevant elements that we are going to deal with. The possible connections between neural processes, learning and conscious perception is one the most complicated themes debated in the philosophy of mind. We will expose, in the following many different researches and theories that explore the problems involved in this connection, and we will try to explore it through a new situated and timing-based paradigm.

The work of Larrabee and Bronk [12] and the one by Lloyd [14] were also relevant in shedding light on neural plasticity. Thompson and Spencer [22] showed evidence that synaptic modifications could explain learning. John Eccles studied changes in the synaptic activation to motivate an interactionist dualism neurobiological perspective, which he developed together with Karl Popper in *The Self and Its Brain* [5][2].

2.1 Plasticity During Brain Development

During development, after a period of intense proliferation, nerve cells emit extensions, the axons, which navigate under the action of recognition molecules, heading to a certain region and coming into contact with other cells. Through the process of *migration* neurons develop and reach their final position in the different levels in the neural tissue assuming their morphology and function. Morphological neural differentiation occurs during the development of the axon migration process (stretching and reconnaissance) to target neural cells that have receptors (NMDA) on their synaptic membrane that "approve" such a link. This differentiation is conditioned by position of the cells within the brain's stratification and the presence of neighbouring cells [13]. The brain configurations that originate in this way are only partly genetic, since we do not have enough genes to codify for all the synaptic junctions we possess (this argument already provides a solid basis for a counterargument of a rigid materialistic innatism).

There is an active role of glia cells in structuring channels for neural migration. This is a very important discovery because the protagonists of neural functions used to be associated only with neural structures. But now a more relevant role is attributed to the glial cells, and this demonstrates another relevant role of the environment, in this case of the neural cell and its surroundings. These

---

[1] Le Doux offers a fertile account based on an accurate analysis of neurophysiological processes in order to explain the construction of the self and the main features that we can ascribe to subjectivity. But his assumptions are limited to a descriptive level, so that they cannot have the causal powers that they are supposed to have in his account.

[2] This interesting perspective is carried out through a dialogue between the two authors, who argue for the existence of three different worlds, each one irreducible to the others. Eccles then describes the existence of functional modules, some closed and some open. The latter ones are able to share contents with other modules. This claim is the base of global workspace theory.

types of glial cells are important for the nutrition and support of all neural structures, but they are also truly relevant in structuring channels and pathways during the development of the brain that neural cells go through in the process of migration. Also, at a broader level we can consider the active role of the environment because the context, the situation in which the subject is, impacts on the activity of glial cells and neurons through epigenetics processes (as we will see in next section), by modulating their gene expressions. At this point electrical activity, partly intrinsic and partly driven by stimuli of the environment, becomes essential to strengthen some connections at the expense of others and thus build that fine architecture that allows our brains the most sophisticated performance. Functional and morphological adaptation driven by electrical activity is crucial in learning processes. This extreme ability to grow and shape the connections typical of development persists for the rest of life, albeit to a more limited extent. It consists of structural changes that underlie the processes of learning and memory, both motor and cognitive, and the processes of adaptation of the organism to changing environmental conditions: activity-dependent mechanisms that govern the formation and elimination of synapses.

One of the most important processes of change in the spacetime architecture is *pruning*. This process cuts the overabundant neural structure to sculpt the neural architecture. Many major mental illnesses start to emerge in adolescence and may be caused by aberrant synaptic pruning. Although we are only beginning to unravel the ramifications of synaptic pruning in the human brain, this process clearly has significant consequences for normal human brain function and may provide key insights into the causes of some devastating and mysterious neuropsychiatric diseases.

Modifications of this process seem to be involved in some cognitive diseases that concern learning and social abilities, like autism and schizophrenia [1]. Disordered synaptic pruning could, in fact, explain the age of onset of schizophrenia; a group of researchers [21] published genetic and experimental evidence supporting this association. While schizophrenia seems to be characterized by over-effective pruning, autism disorders seem to be connected to a lack of effective pruning.

Coinciding with specific patterns of pre-synaptic and post-synaptic activity, functional changes in the efficiency of synaptic transmission, known as Long Term Potentiation (LTP) or long-term depression (LTD), are induced. These phenomena are associated with changes in gene expression in the neurons involved, followed by structural remodeling of connections: the number of contacts between neural cells increases as a result of LTP, decreases as a result of LTD. Neural plasticity is believed to initiate initial changes in the efficiency of synaptic transmission, induced by precise patterns of nerve activity. These functional modifications are followed by structural remodeling processes that lead to the new training or elimination of connections. According to a theory put forward by Donald Hebb [9][3] synchronous activation of pre-post synaptic neurons induces a strengthening of connections, while the activity that is mismatched over time tends to reduce their efficiency.

Epigenetic Factors

Environment and experience in neural networks are very relevant during development of the brain, particularly because configurations that originate during the process of migration are only partly genetic, because we do not have enough genes that encode for all the synaptic junctions we possess.

The environment can modify function, more precisely it can amplify the activity of a gene or reduce it through biochemical mechanisms. Epigenetic processes encompass heritable alterations in gene expression that do not entail modifications to the DNA nucleotide sequence. The central mechanisms that regulate gene expression through epigenetic processes encompass DNA methylation. Additionally, histone modification constitutes a pivotal component, as do functionally significant biochemical changes in chromatin that affect the accessibility of specific genomic loci to transcription enzymes. Ultimately, the regulation of gene expression at varying levels of genetic information is facilitated by the involvement of regulatory non-coding RNAs. Phenotypic aspects could be derived from previous cells without changes in genetic sequences [19].

Epigenetics is the research field that focuses on these processes and lots of recent studies investigate the deep meaning of this. This in fact implies a revolutionary perspective that has a strong impact on the models and methodology of neural investigation. One of the main claims of epigenetics is that there is a sort of footprint, or more precisely an epigenetic mark, which changes the activity of either a gene or a group of them, and this comes from the experiences of the subject. The molecular response to a specific situation could be responsible for the degree and way of activation of a specific gene. This means that, through epigenetic mechanisms it is possible to modify the activity of genes, giving them the input to generate one or more of those fragments that we mentioned before, the epigenetic marks, the genes can therefore be regulated in this way.

Even if the complexity of the molecular processes that let this happen is the root of a strong debate on this kind of explanation, the epigenetic impact is evident in many situations. In our opinion it is also a very interesting topic for the purpose of the present analysis, because phenotypic aspects, under this perspective, are one side of the environment, as they derive in some way from it and reflect some aspects of it. Therefore, a comprehensive understanding of subjective faculties must include an adequate analysis of this deep connection.

An important factor of the environment that is crucial in the development of the brain is the parents' behavior, as lots of epigenetic studies demonstrate [23]. In particular, the mother's behavior during pregnancy plays a relevant role in structuring the development of the children's brain. The first nine months of life are very relevant to determine the fate of our entire lives. The fetus receives

---

[3] This work is very important, not only for the study of neural plasticity, but also because it opens the possibility of a treatment of timing windows of activations of neural units.

everything that the mother transmits, positive and negative, from food to substances that she can take, to the degree of work stress, for example through levels of glucocorticoids. We speak of glucocorticoids because they have been marked better, but there are definitely other molecules that pass the placental barrier and reach the fetus going to genes.

The fetus develops many cells of great variability, complexity and behavior, and the psychophysical state of the mother, for instance a depression or some other pathology, can cause alterations in these delicate codes.

Thus, during the development of the brain, experience and environment are allied with genetics to originate effective synaptic junctions and to determine learning.

2.2   Neural Plasticity During Life

During life neural plasticity occurs thanks to the environment too. In the adult, neural plasticity is mainly related to synapses. Here, as a result of experience there is a strengthening or weakening of the effectiveness of the transmission of the nervous impulse from one cell to another. These changes can range in duration from milliseconds to months. From a structural point of view, synapses, especially those that form on dendritic spines, increase or decrease their surface area or vary in number. Additionally, there may be variations in the number of synaptic receptors and the molecules released into the synaptic space, such as neurotransmitters.

Dendritic spines are small neural membranous protrusions on a dendrite surface that typically receive input from a single axon [4]. Dendritic spines contain neuro-transmitters and receptors. Signaling systems essential for synaptic function and plasticity have different sizes and shapes. In this scheme we see the mainly relevant shapes. They appear in those circuits that are more used, so they are useful markers for learning effects.

Within a neurophysiological analysis we talk about neural circuits and systems. A circuit is defined as a group of neurons that connect through synaptic connections (observed from the outside to investigate certain functions). Instead, a system is defined as a set of circuits that perform a given function. Neurophysiological investigations describe sequences of impulses and try to ascribe a functional meaning to them, indirectly connecting a class of activations to previous stimuli, occuring in a specific time window that allows for this causal explanation. Here, we wish to point out that these methodologies have a problematic epistemological aspect. In fact, when we talk about a function, in neurophysiological analysis, we refer to a relation between some neural activations. This functional attribution is based on a perspective cut, which means to isolate activations (that we choose as relevant in the process that we are examining) and to consider some of them as origins or inputs and the others as responses or outputs.

In order to better understand this aspect of the enquiry in neural functions, we need to remember that any neural system is always active and works in synergy with many other systems. Therefore, the level of neural circuitry that undergoes certain functions depends on a functional and finalized delimitation of the observer. To explore a function and a target, the observer operates a cut, selecting a portion of the dynamical structure, the part that seems to be mostly involved in the process he is interested in. *Involved*, under this perspective, means that a group of neural cells is active in a time interval that can be considered causally determined by the stimulus that hit the network in the previous moment. This could be considered a coherent activation in a stream of activations that come after a specific stimulus (and in an experimental condition, stimulus structure is controlled, as the features of the output related to it). The intrinsic dynamicity of the neural system (*i.e.*, the constant activity that depends on the morphology of the neural network and the shape and type of function that each neural cell exhibits), as well as its extrinsic dynamicity (that depends on the correspondence between the structure and timing of stimuli), imposes an epistemological relativization.

The differentiated structure and morphology of neural cells does not depend on a perspectival choice of the type just exposed. We can observe and describe a lot of shapes of neural cells and their relative positions, and we can also observe the level and typology of neural tissue in which that group of cells is located. These descriptions of the features of neural cells, material connections, and neural tissue are based on static observations. They don't depend on a perspective cut, like in the case of functional circuits, but they are objective descriptions of static components. So, we can see that the epistemological problem seems to be connected with the functional description of dynamical processes.

Thus, at this level of explanation, the diatribe concerns the weights that we can associate to the different functional units in the network that we are considering. This distribution implies a stance regarding the weight and the role of the different inputs from the environment that influence the individual network in a specific way. We could say that different neuro-computational approaches differ from each other with respect to how this distribution is construed. Computational explanations presuppose a distribution of weights on which the system computes, and these weights represent, in some way, the relevance of environment features for the individual system, in a specific context. This implies a stance about the boundaries of the subject and his identity. Neural Darwinism is a large-scale selectionist theory of brain development and function that has been hypothesised to relate to consciousness. According to this approach reentrant interactions among neuronal populations in the thalamocortical system permit high-order discriminations among possible core states, confer selective advantages on organisms possessing them by linking current perceptual events to a past history of value-dependent learning. There are two basic neurophysiological theses in this regard, that we would like to briefly summarize here.

The first one is Neural Darwinism, the second one is strong neural Darwinism, which will be discussed later. In this model the self is not built from simple elements to form a complex. Rather, it is selected from a complex structure by the possibilities in the environment. This interesting theory of brain development during life was formulated by Gerald Edelman, in a book called *The Mindful*

Brain (1978)[4] [7]. It was then revised and extended in a subsequent famous work (1987) by the same author. The name Darwinism alludes to the fact that this theory is presented by the author as an extension of Darwin's natural selection theory. More specifically, it is an extension with respect to the process of neural development in the human system. The analogy is played on different levels and it starts from the previous studies of the author in the field of immunology [8].

Even if it is necessary that different levels of explanation contribute to research on brain workings, neither is there a spiritual claim, nor a reification of language contents. Edelman refuses the linguists' explanation for the genesis of mental faculties. He argues that the integration of functions and responses, to be valid and correct, must also respond, without the involvement of language, to evolutionary requirements, as demonstrated by advanced neurophysiology. There must be some signs of the evolutionary process in the development of the brain, and some of them can be investigated.

Before approaching his perspective in more detail, we need to anticipate one of its crucial notions: the neural map. We will briefly introduce this concept in order to better understand Neural Darwinism: a neural map consists of an organized topological structure, and the activity of groups of neurons and fibers in the brain of an organism. The neural map is the functional unit of a neural network that corresponds to a function that manifests perceptual or motor output. We can talk of two hierarchical levels of neural maps. The first level, the most basic one, is the local neural map and it corresponds to an interconnection of smaller spatial and numerical portions of neurons that perform more specific and limited functions. The global neural map, more plastic, corresponds to an interconnection of different local maps.

We could think of the global map as the road network of a city that interconnects the local neighborhood networks (local maps). The closure of a street in a neighborhood involves the redefinition of the whole traffic at the city level.

In a nutshell, the groups neuronal selection theory is based on three main evolutionary principles:

1. The first principle refers to the fact that there is a neural selection in fetal development; on this basis, a primary repertoire of functional maps is constructed during development of the fetus, thanks to genetic and epigenetic factors.
2. The second principle refers to neural selection that depends on the animal's experiences during its existence; this provides for the construction of a secondary repertoire of functional configurations of maps and circuits.
3. The third principle, the most debated one, refers to the existence of the *re-entry mechanism*. This means that the experience generates some individual perceptions in presence of some specific conditions of the external world.

---

[4] The theory exposed by Edelman here retraces the immunology functions of the body and applies a concept of selection and adaptation, taken from an evolutionary paradigm, to the neurophysiological functions. But this analogy especially in its extension to psychological function is nowadays very debated.

These perceptions correspond to the formation of specific signals about individual conditions that are sent back into the maps of neuronal networks and continuously contribute to update them, producing their continuous change at the level of synaptic connections.

If we consider all these principles together, we get a synthetic view of neural Darwinism theory. The entire process is based on selection and involves populations of neurons engaged in topobiological competition. A variable population of groups of neurons in a specific area of the brain is defined as the primary repertoire, which includes networks of neurons that emerge through somatic selection processes. The genetic code does not provide a precise and detailed pattern for the formation of these repertoires, but rather imposes a set of constraints on the selection process. [6].

In order to explore more deeply the process of neural selection in the brain cells, we can refer to three fundamental assumptions of the theory: 1) Redundancy: there is in every individual an overabundance of synaptic endowments. 2) Reinforcement: there are reinforcement processes of the synapses most commonly used. 3) Subtraction or degeneration: there is a removal process of unused synapses.

From this point of view the baby has an overabundance of synaptic connections; in this "synaptic cloud" every experience and learning process contributes to cut ineffective or useless ones and to reinforce the useful ones. Then, experience in the environment sculpts the subject, by selecting, among the many synaptic possibilities, only some of them and reinforcing the most used.

There is also a more rigid version of the neural Darwinism model, called *Strong Neural New-Darwinism,* which maintains that neural activity contributes to avoid neural death, which is to result in the death of those cells that do not receive input. Neural activity, therefore, in this model, preserves existing patterns from death. The focus is on the role of neural death in the structuring complexity of synaptic ramification and its contribution to the demarcation between cortical areas, and not on the reinforcement and re-entrant processes.

Neural plasticity, the changing in synaptic connections through dendritic spines, on a molecular level of explanation, occurs by simultaneous input and by the presence of neurotrophies (NGF, BNDF, N3, N4) or function stimulants and growth factors. However, they act in an anterograde path, that means they contribute to the reinforcement of those junctions (which make up observable circuits) that have proven to have effective outputs. So, the process develops according to the following steps: at first a stimulus occurs, an evaluation of the effectiveness of a useful output is required, the reiteration of some output in concomitance with a situation generates the reinforcement and production of neurotrophy. The result of this process is precisely what in neurophysiology is called *learning.*

More briefly, neural plasticity develops by virtue of neurotrophies, growth factors, which act in an anterograde sense: they contribute to the reinforcement of those junctions that had proven to have effective outputs. This means that there must be an integrated evaluation that judges whether an output related to a particular stimulus is better than another one with respect to the best functionality of the whole system.

Features of Environment and Complementary Systems

The evaluation of efficacy appears to be a crucial aspect to have a satisfactory output in a specific context. What it means to be effective and what it means to evaluate the relevant parameters of a situation in order to perform an action is very debated, and we will take up this problem in the following sections, not only from a neurophysiological point of view, but also from a psychological point of view.

The role of hormones is another important aspect, which heavily influences neural changings, since intrauterine life and during the whole subsequent life. These molecules work in synergy with some neurotransmitters to modulate the activity of neurons. For example, the brain hemispheres of a healthy woman vary in volume during the menstrual cycle depending on hormone levels. It has been observed that hormones, both progesterone and estrogen, play an important role in regulating trophism: in women these neurons are going through cycles of hypertrophy.

There is another relevant system which is a complementary element to the work of the neural system. This is less studied, and it has a lot to do with pleasure and satisfaction. It is known as the endocannabinoid *system* and it refers to the trade of endocannabinoids and molecules. Endogenous cannabinoids work in synergy with many other molecules, and especially with hormones. Endocannabinoids are lipid-based retrograde neurotransmitters that bind to cannabinoid receptors (CBRs) and cannabinoid receptor proteins that are expressed throughout the vertebrate brain and peripheral nervous system. The endocannabinoid system appears to be involved in regulating physiological and cognitive processes, including fertility, pregnancy, pre- and postnatal development, various immune system activities, appetite, pain sensation, mood, and memory [15]. But here we just want to highlight that there is a strong impact of the environment on the individual neural system, and this occurs by the modulation of parallel and complementary other systems. How this modulation is possible will be the topic of Sect. 3.

Hippocampal Trophism: Neurobiology of Aging and Environmental Factors

The hippocampus and its connections are a crucial neural structure for the topic of this work. In fact, talking about learning means also talking about memory. The hippocampus is involved in memory, location in space and time and the initial phase of action performance, so it is a truly relevant structure for the learning process. During life, as we saw earlier, our brain constantly changes its structure. Studying the neural features of age range allows us to highlight and reinforce the strong connection between synaptic changings and efficacy in learning performance. Many features characterized a lot of old subjects: decreasing of white and grey matter, hyper-activity of glial cells, changes in vascularization, decreasing of trophism of some brain areas, especially hippocampus. Alzheimer disease exhibits a dramatic volume loss in this area that is one of the most relevant roots of the symptoms.

The decrease in dimension of the brain in old age is due to three main factors: loss of neural cells, decrease of dendritic arborizations and reduction of dendritic spines. While changes in brain trophism are physiologically normal in the later stages of life, other factors can cause a decrease in hippocampal volume even earlier in life. We talked before about the role that some kind of hormones play during our life in brain activity.

Stress is one of the most relevant environmental factors in hormones balance. Under stressful conditions the structural problem that occurs in the hippocampus could be seen as similar to what happens in the age range case. Even though the primary cause is different, the process that leads to a decrease in synaptic arborization is more or less the same. In the hippocampus there are a huge number of glucocorticoid receptors. Under stressful conditions the number of these receptors sharply decreases, and so the hippocampus becomes unable to metabolize cortisol [17]. A considerable increase of cortisol levels, that is evident also in elderly people, determines problems in the synaptic arborization and, on the behavioral level, an evident worsening of learning abilities and memory performance. All these aspects of the change in neural plasticity are well studied in post-traumatic stress disease (PTSD), and to shed light on these processes becomes relevant for treating patients successfully.

3   Neural Plasticity and Synchronicity

The importance of timing, particularly the study of synchronicity and coherence between neural activation sequences, appears to be crucial in advancing our understanding of brain function and subjective perception. In this context, we aim to explore the significance of synchronicity within neurophysiological research at the synaptic level. The first aspect of synchronicity relates to the timing of external stimuli, suggesting a strong connection between simultaneous environmental stimuli and the subsequent organization of neural activations in the brain. This concept is well illustrated by the Hebbian model.

Hebbian plasticity emphasizes the strengthening of synaptic connections through synchronized activity. The central principle of a Hebbian synapse is that neurons that fire together form stronger connections. The idea that synaptic changes driven by experience underlie associative learning dates back to the early development of the synapse concept itself [2]. Hebb's formulation of this hypothesis states that when a presynaptic neuron consistently contributes to the firing of a postsynaptic neuron, there is a lasting alteration that enhances both the quality and timing of the postsynaptic response. Here, when we talk about quality, we mean the coherence of the postsynaptic activation with the context and, when we talk about timing, we mean that there is a stronger sensibility in firing after a repeated signal under specific context conditions. In Hebbian synaptic structure, the activity in the presynaptic neuron becomes more likely to excite activity in the postsynaptic neuron, under specific conditions.

Martin provides a comprehensive review of evidence supporting this hypothesis, which is widely endorsed by psychologists, cognitive scientists, and neuroscientists alike [16]. The neurobiological process most commonly associated with Hebbian synapses is long-term potentiation (LTP). Recently, attention has shifted towards a variant of LTP known as spike-timing dependent plasticity (STDP) [3]. In various neural networks, long-lasting changes in synaptic transmission occur by adjusting the timing between strong and weak synaptic inputs within a span of several milliseconds. The nature of this change critically depends on the relative strength of the inputs and their timing. Under certain conditions, transmission is enhanced, meaning that a presynaptic spike results in a "potentiated" postsynaptic response, characterized by increased amplitude or reduced latency. In other cases, transmission weakens, leading to a diminished postsynaptic response. Much of the research on LTP has focused on its cellular and molecular mechanisms. The relevance of this research to the neuroscience of learning lies in the hypothesis that connects LTP with associative learning and memory. Behavioral studies on the formation of associations based on interstimulus and intertrial intervals are heavily influenced by these timing parameters.

It is essential to understand what is meant by synchrony. From an external observer's perspective, stimuli may seem to occur at different speeds. However, perception is a highly complex and contentious issue. Some theories suggest that perception is a reconstructive process, where the mind gathers various environmental inputs and reassembles them into a coherent, meaningful reality. We will attempt to clarify the aspects of this issue that are pertinent to the goals of this work in the following section.

3.1 Plasticity Through Timing

In Sect. 2 we explored a neurophysiological approach to learning, explaining it through the concept of neural plasticity. The focus was on morphological changes in the spatial structure of neurons, particularly through dendritic spines and synapse formation. This perspective emphasized the production, exchange, and metabolism of neurotransmitters, receptors, and the numerous molecules involved in modulating these processes. Thus, this explanation centers on the material alterations in neural connections at the cellular or molecular level. What we aim to focus on in this section is that informational changes determine the expression, retraction, and activity of dendritic spines. These structures modulate synapses, network plasticity, and the outcome of the learned output. The most decisive morphological aspect in learning processes seems to be related to synapses or, more precisely, to dendritic spines. In this section, we also suggest that the morphological structure of dendritic spines and their connectivity depend on informational variation, which is largely encoded at the level of the temporal architecture of signaling.

In this section, we present a new approach to understanding neural learning processes by focusing on information and its temporal structure. The core idea is that morphology of dendritic architectures is influenced by information encoded in neural spikes. In other words, learning occurs due to prior changes in the way information is coded and decoded by neural cells. The key shift is in how these cells process and transmit information to their connected counterparts. Recent studies in predictive coding framework suggest also a dendritic relevant role in processing prediction error signals. To address this, the authors connect the predictive coding aspect of prediction error signaling to previous research on efficient coding in balanced networks with lateral inhibition and predictive computation in apical dendrites. Their work suggests an efficient implementation to the theory using spiking neurons, where prediction errors are computed locally within dendritic compartments rather than in separate units [18].

A crucial factor in producing a learned response is a specific harmony between different neural regions or groups of neurons. Even the synchrony between a few neurons can be significant in interpreting how information is encoded. Here, the emphasis is not on spatial connections but on the patterns of neural activations and their temporal coherence. From this perspective, learning is best explained as a change in neural activity patterns. Therefore, to understand learning processes more thoroughly, we must examine the timing of neural pulses, either from individual neurons or groups of neurons. While we can observe neural activations using neurophysiological techniques, it is essential not only to identify which brain regions are active but also to study the rhythm of neural communication, its informational units, or, metaphorically, the "alphabet" of neural coding.

To comprehend learning, we must pay close attention to these changes in activation patterns. We will explore some key findings in this field to highlight the importance of timing, reframe learning processes from this perspective, and offer suggestions on how these processes can be enhanced. While we have previously discussed learning from a material, morphological, and informational standpoint, this section focuses primarily on the role of time and timing in learning processes. A particularly relevant aspect of neural plasticity in this context is Spike Timing-Dependent Plasticity (STDP) and its influence on learning. In Sect. 2, we discussed Hebbian reinforcement, which refers to the strengthening of synaptic connections, but we did not address the time window in which this occurs. STDP ensures a causal interpretation of neural activations by considering the sequence in which neurons activate within a synaptic connection (a recurrent synapse).

For example, if two connected neurons activate and one is activated by an earlier stimulus, the synapse is strengthened in the direction starting from the neuron that responded to the first stimulus. This strengthening only occurs in one direction, not the reverse. This has been demonstrated in various studies and provides insight into how the brain interprets causality as a sequence of temporal activations. This explanation aligns with a different level of causality interpretation, such as the psychological perspective proposed by Hume [10], in his opinion in fact, causality experience is only the experience of repeated connections in the time.

Another important point to consider is the short time window required for these synaptic connections to form, which is measured in milliseconds. If the interval exceeds a second, the connection loses its effectiveness. This observation leads us to another key issue, which is crucial for attributing identity and possibly for the sense of agency: the problem of size-distance invariance. Humans learn to identify objects despite changes in distance, size, or perspective. We propose that temporal contiguity plays a fundamental role in recognizing identity. Timing enables the subject to distinguish between different elements in the environment. When certain neural activation patterns consistently occur in close temporal proximity, the mind associates them into a meaningful whole. This proposal can be seen as an extension of the argument regarding the role of the body in perception. The synchronization factor thus appears to be fundamental for the conscious association between elements and events, which is crucial in learning processes, while also playing a key role in the morphological modification of synapses, particularly at the level of dendritic spines.

3.2   Plasticity and Agency

Timing sequences might also explain the different perceptions of agency in various motor learning processes, whether voluntary (active) or afferent (passive), even though the neural changes are largely similar in both cases. When we examine the process of learning a motor action, neural changes occur due to neural plasticity, which can be explained by Hebbian learning and Spike-Timing-Dependent Plasticity (STDP).

In voluntary learning processes, individuals experience a strong sense of agency, while neural plasticity simultaneously modifies the brain, likely as a result of action repetition. However, significant changes in neural pathways can also occur during passive motor action reproduction, such as through the use of prosthetics, orthoses, or other devices. Some of these tools restrict the range of motion, thereby reinforcing neural networks associated with specific, effective movements [20] Other devices aim to facilitate learning by providing passive stimulation to specific body parts. It's important to note that, in both these cases, the subjective sense of agency is not as pronounced as it is in active learning.

Based on the neurophysiological, morphological, and temporal data reviewed in this study, we propose a timing-based explanation for the differing senses of agency associated with these two types of learning.

In voluntary learning, the underlying causal mechanisms seem to align with the principles of Spike-Timing-Dependent Plasticity (STDP). This model explains how the speed and efficiency of neural configurations associated with a particular motor task improve progressively with repeated practice. Through each repetition, the brain refines the timing of neuronal firing, making the neural circuits more adept at executing the task. The increase in efficiency is a direct consequence of this precise temporal coordination, which strengthens the connection between neurons involved in the motor action.

On the other hand, conditioned learning follows a different path. Although the end goal is still the production of a learned outcome, the subjective experience of control, or the sense of agency, may be diminished. This weakening of agency does not stem from alterations in the motor system itself, nor from spatial changes in neural connections. Instead, it appears to arise from differences in timing. More specifically, it may relate to how the internal timing mechanisms of the brain synchronize with one another. In conditioned learning, these variations in timing, particularly the coordination between distinct internal timing architectures, play a crucial role in shaping the learning process.

We aim to highlight the crucial role that timing dynamics play in the regulation specifically of dendritic spine behavior, including their expression, retraction, and overall activity. This timing dynamic could also help to understand the differences between various learning processes and the levels of agency perception connected to them. Dendritic spines are key mediators of synaptic transmission and plasticity determining the flexibility and adaptability of neural networks. These structures are not static; rather, they continuously respond to changes in informational flow, dynamically adjusting to optimize synaptic connections. This modulation of dendritic spines directly impacts network plasticity and shapes the output of learned behaviors, making them central to the mechanisms underlying learning. As said before, among the various morphological components involved in learning, dendritic spines emerge as particularly pivotal. While synapses in general are fundamental to neural communication, it is the morphological and functional properties of dendritic spines specifically that appear to exert the most significant influence on how learning is encoded and maintained at the cellular level. Their structural plasticity allows for the fine-tuning of synaptic strength, and this, in turn, contributes to the overall adaptability of the neural network.

Additionally, we propose that the morphology and connectivity of dendritic spines are closely tied to variations in information processing. These changes in spine structure and connectivity are not random but are highly dependent on informational signals. This informational modulation is largely governed by the temporal architecture of neural signaling, how signals are temporally coordinated and sequenced across the network. Temporal patterns in signaling play a key role in encoding information, and it is through this temporal framework that dendritic spines adapt, reorganizing themselves to support more efficient and precise synaptic transmission. In this context, the temporal organization of information serves as a driving force behind both the physical structure of dendritic spines and their functional integration within the neural circuitry.

4   Conclusions

The complexity of learning and cognitive development clearly emerges from the analysis of neural plasticity, a dynamic process that reflects the brain's ability to reorganize its synaptic connections in response to environmental stimuli. This study highlights how neural changes, from neuronal migration during embryonic development to learning processes in adulthood, are strongly influenced by genetic, epigenetic, and environmental factors. In particular, temporal factor and the synchronization of synaptic activations are critical for optimizing learning and memory formation. The concept of neural plasticity cannot be reduced to a mere structural remodeling; instead, it encompasses a wide range of functional processes that allow the brain to adapt to environmental changes.

The ability of the environment to influence the genome and, consequently, brain function, clearly demonstrates that learning is not solely a genetic process but rather the product of a complex interaction between heredity and lived experience. This is particularly evident in synaptic plasticity processes, where the temporal synchronization of activations plays a decisive role. The effectiveness of learning appears to depend not only on the intensity of the stimuli received but also on the temporal coherence between these stimuli and the corresponding neural responses. This research also highlights how adverse environmental factors, such as chronic stress, can impair brain function, particularly by negatively affecting hippocampal trophism and synaptic integrity. This underscores the importance of a favorable environmental context not only for facilitating learning and memory consolidation but also for preventing cognitive decline.

Moreover, the crucial role of temporal synchronization extends to our understanding of conscious perceptions of action and intentionality. The distinction between voluntary and conditioned learning can be explained not only by structural or functional differences in neural circuits but also by the distinct temporal patterns of synaptic activations. In this sense, the concept of temporal plasticity provides a new framework for interpreting the sense of agency that accompanies voluntary learning, suggesting that temporal coherence between external stimuli and internal neural responses is fundamental to the conscious perception of action.

Finally, the practical implications of these findings are numerous. Understanding the mechanisms of neural plasticity, particularly the role of time and synchronization, can offer new perspectives for education and cognitive rehabilitation. Interventions aimed at improving the temporal synchronization between environmental stimuli and synaptic modifications could enhance learning processes, especially in individuals with cognitive deficits or in rehabilitation contexts. Additionally, managing stress and creating favorable learning environments can reduce the risk of cognitive decline and improve psychological well-being.

In summary, this study demonstrates how neural plasticity is profoundly influenced by a combination of temporal, genetic, and environmental factors. Understanding the complex interaction between these elements not only broadens our knowledge of learning and memory processes but also opens new avenues for developing innovative therapeutic strategies in educational and clinical settings, with the aim of optimizing cognitive abilities and improving quality of life.

References

1. Cardozo, P.L., de Lima, I.B., Maciel, E.M., Silva, N.C., Dobransky, T., Ribeiro, F.M.: Synaptic elimination in neurological disorders. Curr. Neuropharmacol. **17**(11), 1071–1095 (2019)

2. Cajal, R.: The Neuron and the Glia Cell. Charles C Thomas Pub Ltd. (1984)
3. Caporale, N., Dan, Y.: Spike timing-dependent plasticity: a hebbian learning rule. Ann. Rev. Neurosci. **31**, 25–46 (2008)
4. Chidambaram, S.B., et al.: Dendritic spines: revisiting the physiological role. Prog. Neuropsychopharmacol. Biol. Psychiatry **92**, 161–193 (2019)
5. Eccles, C.J.: How the Self Controls Its Brain. Springer, Cham (1994)
6. Edelman, G.: Neurobiology: An Introduction to Molecular Embriology. Basic Books, New York (1988)
7. Edelman, G., Mountcastle, V.B.: The Mindful Brain: Cortical Organization and the Group-Selective Theory of Higher Brain Function. MIT Press (1978)
8. Edelman, G.: Neural Darwinism: The Theory of Neuronal Group Selection. Basic Books, New York (1987)
9. Hebb, D.: The Organization of Behavior: A Neuropsychological Theory. Wiley, New York (1949)
10. Hume, D.: An Enquiry Concerning Human Understanding (1748)
11. Konorski, J.: Conditioned Reflexes and Neuron Organization. Cambridge University Press, Cambridge (1948)
12. Larrabe, M.G., Bronk, D.J.: Prolonged facilitation of synaptic excitation in sympathetic ganglia. Neurophysiology **10**, 139–154 (1947)
13. LeDoux, J.: Synaptic Self: How Our Brains Become Who We Are. Penguin Putnam (2002)
14. Lloyd, D.P.: Post-tetanic potentiation of responses of monosynaptic reflex pathways of the spinal cord. Physiology **33**, 147–170 (1949)
15. Lowe, H., Toyang, N., Steele, B., Bryant, J., Ngwa, W.: The endocannabinoid system: a potential target for the treatment of various diseases. Int. J. Mol. Sci. **22**(17), 9472 (2021)
16. Martin, S.J., Morris, R.: New life in an old idea: the synaptic plasticity and memory hypothesis revisited. Hippocampus **12**, 609–636 (2002)
17. McEwen, B.S.: Stress and hippocampal plasticity. Annu. Rev. Neurosci. **22**(1), 105–122 (1999)
18. Mikulasch, F.A., Rudelt, L., Wibral, M., Priesemann, V.: Dendritic predictive coding: a theory of cortical computation with spiking neurons. arXiv preprint arXiv:2205.05303 (2022)
19. Petronis, A.: Epigenetics as a unifying principle in the aetiology of complex traits and diseases. Nature **465**(7299), 721–727 (2010)
20. Pittaccio, S., et al.: Passive ankle dorsiflexion by an automated device and the reactivity of the motor cortical network. In: 5th Annual International Conference of the IEEE Engineering in Medicine and Biology Society (EMBC) (2017)
21. Rose, S.A., Handsaker, R.E., Daly, M.J., Carroll, M.C.: Schizophrenia risk from complex variation of complement component 4. Nature **530**, 177–183 (2016)
22. Thompson, R.F., Spencer, W.A.: Habituation: a model phenomenon for the study of neuronal substrates of behaviour. Psychol. Rev. **73**, 16–43 (1966)
23. Weaver, I., et al.: Epigenetic programming by maternal behavior. Nat. Neurosci. **7**(8), 847–854 (2004)

A Non-geographical Approach to the Study of Culture-Mediated Acceptance of Social Robots

Leonardo Lapomarda[1]([⊠]) [iD], Alex Barco[2] [iD], and Edoardo Datteri[1] [iD]

[1] University of Milano Bicocca, 20150 Milan, Italy
l.lapomarda@campus.unimib.it
[2] Deusto University, 20012 San Sebastian, Spain

Abstract. Culture plays a fundamental role in shaping how individuals perceive and accept technology, influencing their willingness to adopt it. Social robots, as interactive agents, are subject to cultural variations in acceptance, yet existing Human-Robot Interaction (HRI) literature predominantly equates culture with nationality, overlooking more nuanced frameworks. This paper advocates for a non-geographical approach to culture, grounded in Hofstede's model, specifically focusing on Uncertainty Avoidance (UA). The proposed model posits that UA exerts a moderating influence on the relationship between Perceived Control (PC) and social robot acceptance, such that the positive effect of PC is more pronounced for low-UA individuals and less so for high-UA individuals. This speculative analysis introduces novel perspectives for future empirical research, challenging conventional methodologies in the domain of cultural HRI studies.

Keywords: Human Robot interaction · Social Robot Acceptance · Uncertainty Avoidance · Cultural Dimension · Perceived Control · Hofstede

1 Introduction

It has been suggested that culture plays a fundamental role in shaping how individuals perceive and interact with technology, impacting their willingness to adopt and integrate it into daily life (Gong et al., 2007; Dwyer et al., 2005; Kumar & Krishnan, 2002). Cultural differences have been shown to make an important difference in the way people perceive, accept, and interact with technological innovations. Contrary to the assumption that technology adoption follows a universal trajectory, research indicates that perceptions of usefulness, ease of use, and trust in technology vary widely across cultural contexts (McCoy, Galletta & King, 2005).

There are reasons to believe the same regarding social robots. Social robots are not "simple" technological tools, but agents with which people interact in a dynamic way. It is reasonable to hypothesize that people with different cultural profiles and backgrounds may "differently" accept social robots - in a sense of 'acceptance' to be discussed. This hypothesis has been made and corroborated in several theoretical and empirical studies carried out in the field of social robotics (Bartneck et al., 2009; de Graaf

© The Author(s), under exclusive license to Springer Nature Switzerland AG 2026
J. Proença et al. (Eds.): SEFM 2024, LNCS 15551, pp. 219–236, 2026.
https://doi.org/10.1007/978-3-031-94748-3_17

et al., 2017; Złotowski et al., 2018). However, the existing literature on Human-Robot Interaction (HRI) has traditionally examined culture through a purely geographical lens, often equating it with nationality (Mansouri et al., 2024; Bajones et al., 2017; Belpaeme et al., 2013). Within this framework, differences in the acceptance of social robots have been primarily attributed to national origin, neglecting the nuanced cultural dynamics that exist within social groups (Kamide & Arai, 2017; Lee & Šabanović, 2014; Li, Rau & Li, 2010). This approach risks oversimplifying the role of culture by treating it as a static, homogeneous factor rather than a complex and evolving phenomenon that directly influences the acceptance of technology.

The aim of the present paper is to provide a reflection on how culture shapes the acceptance of social robots under a non-geographical conception of 'culture' that is substantially based on the model proposed and developed by Geert Hofstede (1980, 2001, 2010). We will focus on one of Hofstede's dimensions that we believe is particularly relevant to understanding the relationship between culture and the acceptance of social robots, namely Uncertainty Avoidance (UA) (Hofstede 1980; Minkov et al. 2012). A few hypotheses will be formulated about how UA relates to the acceptance of social robots, and how other less cultural, more psychological factors interact with this relationship. We will propose that UA moderates the relationship between (a) people's level of perceived control of the robot and (b) their acceptance of social robots, such that the positive effect of perceived control on acceptance is weaker for high-UA individuals and stronger for low-UA individuals. This hypothesis, whose plausibility will be discussed later in the paper, is based on previous research on technology acceptance. It is worth noting that this is a purely speculative paper, whose ultimate purpose is to suggest novel ways of investigating (through quantitative or qualitative research methods) how culture affects the dynamics of human-robot interaction (HRI). The novelty of this analysis, as suggested above, lies in the adoption of a conception of 'culture' that is more nuanced and articulated than that adopted in the existing empirical literature on social robotics.

The structure of the paper is as follows. Section 2 provides a theoretical background, which emphasizes the predominant geographical conception of culture in contemporary research on social robot acceptance and discusses its limitations. Previous studies on cultural influences in Human-Robot Interaction (HRI) will be analyzed, and the need for a more nuanced approach that moves beyond national categorization will be proposed. Section 3 describes Hofstede's model and discusses how it has been used in the HRI literature. Section 4 focuses on Uncertainty Avoidance and Perceived Control and proposes a hypothesis on how these two factors might together influence the acceptance of social robots. Finally, Sect. 5 presents concluding remarks, emphasizing the theoretical contributions of the study and outlining directions for future empirical research.

2   Theoretical Background

2.1   The Concept of 'Acceptance'

The concept of 'acceptance' (of a technological artifact or a technology in general) is interpreted in many ways in the literature. Some authors (Davis, 1986; Heerink et al., 2010 in De Jong et al., 2019) identify acceptance with the conscious decision to adopt and repeatedly use a technology, manifesting itself in a behavior of continuous use over time. Quite differently, Nielsen (1993) defines acceptance as the awareness that a system "is good enough to satisfy all the needs and requirements of the users and other potential stakeholders" (Nielsen, 1993). This is a rather broad view and would imply that a technology must meet all the user's needs to be accepted - a requirement that sounds little realistic, as people often accept 'imperfect' technologies, such as driver assistance systems in automobiles, even though they fall short of satisfying *all* the needs and requirements of the users and other potential stakeholders.

Other authors have proposed finer-grained definitions that focus on distinct elements of the acceptance process. Chismar and Wiley-Patton (2002) define acceptance as 'the intention to adopt an application', thus emphasizing the intentional aspect. Ausserer and Risser (2005) offer a related perspective, characterizing it as a phenomenon reflecting the extent to which potential users are willing to adopt a system. Both definitions primarily address the predisposition to adopt rather than actual usage behavior. However, this does not inherently undermine their validity as conceptual definitions. While it is true that, in the absence of observable behavior, the impact of a technology, such as its influence on operational safety or efficiency, cannot be measured with certainty, this issue pertains to the methodological challenges of assessing acceptance rather than to its theoretical definition.

Simon (2001, p. 87) has proposed a slightly different analysis. He sees acceptance as the opposite of rejection. From this perspective, accepting a technology means making a rational decision to integrate it into one's daily practices, evaluating its benefits and implications, which may be of a practical, social, emotional or economic nature. Rejection, on the other hand, can result from a rational and conscious choice or from an emotional, intuitive or automatic reaction influenced by psychological, cultural or experiential factors. In some cases, rejection is determined by fear of change, lack of familiarity with the system or pre-existing prejudices, irrespective of an objective assessment of its potential.

Other authors have proposed more elaborated models - chiefly including the Theory of Reasoned Action (TRA) (Fishbein et al. 1975), the Theory of Planned Behaviors -TPB- (Ajzen, 1991), the Technology Acceptance Model (TAM) (Davis, 1989), and the Unified Theory of Acceptance and Use of Technology (UTAUT) (Venkatesh et al. 2003), which analyze the concept of acceptance along different dimensions and identify key factors affecting (technology) acceptance.

The Technology Acceptance Model (TAM) is a widely utilized paradigm within the field of acceptance models, which seeks to elucidate the mechanisms through which individuals adopt and utilize novel technologies. The model operates under the assumption that behavioral intention directly precipitates actual behavior, with this intention being contingent upon two pivotal factors: perceived ease of use (PEU), defined as the extent to which a user believes that a technology is effortless to use, and perceived usefulness (PU), defined as the belief that using the technology will enhance job performance (Davis et al., 1989). Following the initial development of TAM, several extensions have been proposed to overcome its limitations. These include an exclusive focus on the functional aspects of technology and a neglect of users' psychological and cognitive conditions. (Venkatesh & Davis, 2000). TAM2 introduced additional variables such as social norms, voluntariness of use, job relevance, and output quality to account for external influences on technology acceptance (Venkatesh & Davis, 2000). Subsequently, TAM3, a more comprehensive extension, incorporated factors related to human decision-making processes, including computer self-efficacy, computer anxiety, and perceived enjoyment (Venkatesh & Bala, 2008).

Despite the enhancements made to TAM, the theory has been criticized for being overly simplistic (Benbasat & Barki, 2007). More precise critics claim that TAM assumes too much about how external variables influence acceptance Beaudry and Pinsonneault (2005). These critics argue that such variables may have direct effects on behavioral intention and actual use. In this regard, scholars have posited that other key factors, including expected outcomes and habitual use (LaRose & Eastin, 1994), motives to use technology (Katz, Blumler, & Gurevitch, 1973), and environmental constraints (Bandura, 1977), may also play a significant role in shaping acceptance behavior.

To address these concerns, the Unified Theory of Acceptance and Use of Technology (UTAUT) was developed as a more holistic framework. This model consolidates constructs from eight prior theories, including TAM and TPB, to provide a more comprehensive explanation of technology adoption (Venkatesh et al., 2003). It identifies four key determinants of technology acceptance: performance expectancy (similar to PU in TAM); effort expectancy (similar to PEU in TAM), social influence (the impact of norms and external expectations); facilitating conditions (availability of resources and support). Additionally, UTAUT incorporates moderating variables such as age, gender, experience, and voluntariness of use, making it more adaptable to diverse contexts (Venkatesh et al., 2003). However, despite its high explanatory power, it has been criticized for its complexity and lack of parsimony, as it requires numerous variables to account for variance in technology acceptance (Straub & Burton-Jones, 2007).

Moreover, UTAUT closely resembles the Theory of Planned Behavior (TPB) in that its constructs of social influence and facilitating conditions significantly overlap with subjective norm and perceived behavioral control from TPB (Ajzen, 1991). While both TAM and UTAUT were developed for utilitarian systems in workplace settings, their applicability to hedonic or pleasure-oriented systems is limited (van der Heijden, 2004). However, social robots in domestic environments introduce a new layer of interaction that extends beyond mere utility, as they tend to evoke social responses from users (Kahn et al. 2006; Lee et al. 2005; Reeves et al. 1996). The fact that TAM and UTAUT were primarily validated in work environments further questions their suitability for explaining social robot acceptance in domestic contexts. This highlights the need for alternative models that better capture the social and emotional dynamics of human-robot interaction (HRI) in home settings.

To sum up, the concept of acceptance (of technology) has been defined in several ways in the literature, though often without a clear or consistent definition. The goal of this paper is to reflect on the cultural (and psychological) factors that may affect the acceptance of social robots. Even though the general conclusions that will be reached here do not strictly speaking depend on the adoption of one or the other model of acceptance, in the rest of the paper the concept of acceptance will be provisionally interpreted as "the intention to integrate a social robot into one's daily life over time, rather than merely engaging with it on a single occasion" (De Jong et al. 2020; De Graaf et al. 2018). While many studies on robot acceptance focus on short-term engagement, intentional acceptance reflects a more sustained adoption, capturing the willingness to repeatedly use and integrate a social robot. This distinction is crucial, as initial enthusiasm often declines over time (Baxter et al., 2017; Kanda et al., 2004). In HRI, several scales measuring social robot acceptance have been validated (Eyssel et al., 2011; Shin et al. 2011). However, they focus on utilitarian aspects overlooking the social, emotional, and psychological factors crucial in non-workplace adoption (van der Heijden, 2004). In this study, we aim to consider these broader dimensions of acceptance, recognizing their importance in shaping long-term engagement with social robots. Models like TAM and UTAUT, designed for task-oriented workplace technologies, may not fully capture social robot acceptance, which involves hedonic, emotional, and social factors (De Jong et al., 2019). Following De Jong et al. 2020 and De Graaf et al. (2018); De Graaf et al., 2019 definition of intentional acceptance we want to incorporate both utilitarian and socioemotional aspects, shifting the focus from initial interaction to sustained engagement. Accordingly, this study examines the cultural and psychological factors shaping intentional acceptance, offering a more comprehensive view of why and how individuals adopt social robots.

2.2 The Concept of 'Culture'

Culture is a complex and multidimensional concept, whose meaning varies depending on the disciplinary context in which it is analyzed. In fields such as anthropology, for example, culture is often understood as a set of practices, beliefs and traditions shared by a social group and transmitted through learning and socialization processes (Smith, 2013). In psychology, on the other hand, it is regarded as a set of cognitive and value patterns that influence the perception and behavior of individuals (Jones, 2017; Gallagher, 2000). In the social sciences, such as sociology, linguistics and political science, culture is conceptualized as a social structure, a system of communication, or a set of norms and institutions that regulate collective life. These diverse definitions share a common characteristic: human culture is understood as a system of meanings and information shared by a group and transmitted through generations (Matsumoto et al. 2006).

This variety of perspectives has resulted in the formulation of numerous definitions over time, thereby complicating the identification of a universally accepted concept. Attempts to define culture date back more than a hundred years (e.g., Baumeister, 2005; Berry, Poortinga et al. 1992; Jahoda, 1984; Kroeber & Kluckhohn, 1952/1963; Pelto & Pelto, 1975; Rohner, 1984; Tylor, 1865). Even today, no universally accepted definition exists. According to Baldwin and colleagues (2006), there are at least 313 definitions of culture, each of which reflects a particular disciplinary or theoretical perspective. Such conceptual fragmentation complicates not only its theoretical understanding, but also the possibility of operationalizing culture in a clear and replicable way in empirical studies (Matsumoto et al. 2006).

The absence of a shared definition has thus resulted in researchers developing divergent approaches to measuring culture, frequently adopting objective indirect indicators such as language, laws, traditions, or even subjective ones such as values, beliefs and social norms (Triandis, 1972). These are produced and reproduced by individuals and then emerge in the resolution of complex social problems (Matsumoto et al. 2006; Kashima, 2000; Triandis, 1994).

While this approach allows researchers to quantify and compare different cultures by identifying specific indicators, thereby facilitating cross-cultural studies and highlighting differences between groups (e.g., nations, ethnicities), it has a significant limitation: it reduces culture to the presence or absence of these indicators, thereby limiting both the dynamic and stratified nature (Baldwin et al. 2006; Kroeber et al. 1952; Berry et al. 1997) and the internal variability of culture itself (generational, regional, socio-economic and individual differences). The notion that observed variations between groups are inherently cultural in nature is referred to as the cultural attribution fallacy: the mistaken assumption that differences observed between groups—such as variations in attitudes, behaviors, or preferences—are necessarily due to cultural factors, without considering alternative explanations such as socio-economic status, education, individual psychological traits, historical context, or institutional structures (Matsumoto et al., 2006). This intuitive yet unsubstantiated hypothesis lacks empirical support.

Treating culture as synonymous with nationality risks oversimplifying the relationship between cultural values and technology acceptance by assuming homogeneity within national groups (Arnett, 2002). A key limitation of this approach is that it does not reflect the reality of globalized societies, where individuals are shaped by multiple cultural influences beyond their country of origin. Contemporary social structures are increasingly characterized by cultural hybridity, where exposure to different cultural values, migration and digital connectivity challenge rigid, nation-based classifications of culture (Smith, 2013; Kashima, 2000; Matsumoto et al., 2006). For example, individuals within a single country may have different attitudes towards technology due to generational, socio-economic or educational differences that are not adequately captured by nationality-based models of culture (Baldwin et al., 2006; Berry et al., 1997). Furthermore, cross-cultural research in psychology and sociology has shown that cultural identity is often fluid and multidimensional, meaning that individuals may identify with different cultural values depending on the context (Triandis, 1994; Kashima, 2000).

2.3 Empirical Studies on Culture-Mediated Acceptance of Social Robots

Empirical research on the acceptance of social robots has predominantly framed culture through a geographical lens, equating it with nationality. Several studies have explored how these cultural dimensions influence individuals' attitudes and behaviors toward robots, often comparing participants from different countries to identify variations in acceptance and perception.

For example, Bartneck et al. (2006) investigated attitudes toward robots among participants from Japan, China, and Germany, finding that Japanese respondents generally exhibited more positive attitudes and lower levels of anxiety about robots compared to their German counterparts. This aligns with cultural narratives in Japan, where robots are frequently portrayed as helpful and socially integrated entities, in contrast to the more skeptical or dystopian views prevalent in Western media (Kaplan, 2004). Similarly, Li, Rau, and Li (2010) compared attitudes between Chinese and German participants and found that cultural differences influenced perceptions of robot sociability and acceptability, with Chinese participants reporting greater openness to robot integration in everyday life.

Expanding on this perspective, Nomura et al. (2008) examined cross-cultural differences in robot anxiety, comparing participants from Japan, Korea, and the United States. Their findings indicated that Western participants, particularly from the U.S., expressed higher levels of anxiety regarding robots, which was attributed to lower exposure to robotics and a stronger emphasis on human-robot differentiation in Western societies. Broadbent et al. (2009) further reinforced this trend by demonstrating that prior exposure to robots through media or personal experiences significantly influenced attitudes toward them, with Japanese participants being more comfortable with humanoid robots than those from Western countries.

More recent studies have sought to refine the geographical approach by examining cultural differences within specific technological and social contexts. Mansouri et al. (2024) compared robot acceptance in Germany and three Arab countries (Egypt, Jordan, and Saudi Arabia), revealing that while broad cultural similarities exist, significant variations in robot perception and acceptance were present even within nations with shared traditions. These results challenge the assumption that nationality alone can fully explain cultural attitudes toward robots, highlighting the importance of factors such as technological exposure, societal norms, and religious beliefs in shaping robot acceptance.

Further insights come from studies analyzing how culture interacts with specific robot attributes and task types. Lee and Šabanović (2014) found that Korean and Chinese participants perceived social robots as more trustworthy, likable, and satisfactory than German participants, who viewed them more as tools rather than companions. The study suggested that cultural dimensions such as masculinity, individualism, and exposure to industrial robots contributed to these differences, with highly individualistic and masculine cultures (such as Germany) showing a preference for robots in functional roles rather than social interactions. Similarly, Kamide and Arai (2017) explored the impact of high-context vs. low-context communication cultures on engagement with robots, concluding that individuals from high-context cultures (e.g., East Asian countries) responded more to non-verbal cues and body language in robot interaction, while those from low-context cultures (e.g., Germany) were more influenced by verbal communication and explicit task instructions.

Finally, experimental research has also investigated how robot design and functionality interact with cultural preferences. Libin and Libin (2004) demonstrated that participants from different cultural backgrounds rated robots differently on anthropomorphism and perceived sociability, with zoomorphic robots generally being preferred for entertainment tasks, while machine-like robots were deemed more appropriate for security roles. Additionally, Nomura et al. (2008) found that cultural background influenced engagement levels with robots, particularly when the robot's appearance and task were mismatched. For example, German participants exhibited lower engagement in low-sociability tasks, such as security monitoring, whereas Korean and Chinese participants maintained higher engagement across various robot roles.

The findings of empirical research demonstrate an overwhelming tendency in robotics research to equate culture with nationality, and to treat it as the primary valid conceptualisation (Bajones et al., 2017; Belpaeme et al., 2013; Kamide & Arai, 2017; Lee & Šabanović, 2014; Li et al., 2010; Ros et al., 2011; Rosenthal-von der Putten & Kramer, 2015; Shiomi & Hagita, 2017; Mansouri & Taylor, 2023; Shiomi, 2023). This nation-based perspective facilitates cross-national comparisons of robot acceptance by assuming that users' responses are shaped predominantly by their national cultural background (Baker et al., 2018; Nomura, 2017, Wang 2020). The prevalence of this interpretation is so strong that a survey on cultural robotics identified at least 50 studies that define culture exclusively in geographical terms (Lim 2010; Lim et al., 2021). While this approach has contributed to broad cross-cultural analyses, it fundamentally reduces culture to nationality, overlooking the internal diversity and contextual nature of cultural influences. By assuming culture is a static and homogeneous entity tied to national identity, this perspective neglects any internal variations, as well as individual experiences that significantly shape robot acceptance and behavior. This national approach remains incomplete and restrictive to understanding human-robot interaction. To achieve a more complete understanding of how cultural factors influence robot acceptance, it is necessary to adopt a more refined, non-geographical model.

3   A Refined Conception of 'Culture'

Many studies have treated culture as synonymous with nationality, without exploring alternative conceptions. However, a notable exception is Hofstede's Cultural Dimensions Model (1980), which defines culture not in terms of nationality but as a system of shared values and norms that shape individual and group behavior (Hofstede, 1980). According to Hofstede, culture can be defined as 'collective programming of the mind', which influences the way in which individuals perceive reality, make decisions and interact with others (Hofstede, 1980, p. 25). For this reason, in the analysis of national cultures, the main challenge is to identify comparable parameters between different societies without excessively reducing cultural complexity. To this end, he developed a model based on six fundamental dimensions that reflect variations in collective values and behaviors (Hofstede, 2001; Hofstede et al., 2010). The dimensional approach enables researchers to measure cultural differences by comparing them on a standardized scale, rather than treating them as fixed or absolute traits, thereby providing a structured framework for understanding how cultural values influence economic, social and organizational phenomena. The six dimensions are: 1) Power Distance Index (PDI), that measures the extent to which power inequalities are accepted and legitimized in a society; 2) the Uncertainty Avoidance index (UA) which is a measure of a culture's level of tolerance for ambiguity and uncertainty; 3) the Individualism vs. Collectivism (IDV) dimension, which differentiates societies according to the degree of integration of the individual in social groups; 4) the Masculinity vs. Femininity dimension (MAS), which represents the distribution of values associated with gender roles and the degree of emphasis on competition and material success versus quality of life and cooperation; 5) the Long-Term vs. Short-Term Orientation dimension (LTO), which measures the degree of pragmatism and adaptability of a culture; 6) the Indulgence vs. Restraint dimension (IVR), which describes the level of social control exercised over the satisfaction of individual needs and desires.

Hofstede's dimensions - at least in principle - allow for a systematic and structured analysis of how specific cultural traits - rather than nationality itself - influence technology acceptance (Hofstede, 2001; Gong, 2011). They break down culture into quantifiable dimensions that can be empirically tested across different populations. This is one powerful reason to adopt Hofstede's model as a framework for obtaining a more nuanced understanding of how culture shapes acceptance of social robots. Rather than assuming that nationality itself, as a 'black box', determines attitudes toward technology, Hofstede's model identifies underlying value orientations—such as uncertainty avoidance, power distance, and individualism vs. collectivism—that may be connected to how people perceive and interact with technological innovations.

Another reason for choosing Hofstede's model is its widespread use in technology acceptance research. A considerable body of research has been dedicated to investigating the correlation between the dimensions of culture on the one hand, and technology-related behavior, on the other (Yeniyurt & Townsend, 2003; Van Everdingen & Waarts, 2003; Dwyer et al., 2005; Ganesh et al., 1997; Alshare et al. 2011; Kumar and Krishnan, 2002; La Ferle et al., 2008; Tellis et al., 2003; Van Everdingen and Waarts, 2003; Yeniyurt and Townsend, 2003). For instance, La Ferle et al. (2008) examined Internet adoption in Japan and the United States and found that the variation in Internet penetration and adoption patterns could be explained by cultural dimensions, such as uncertainty avoidance and individualism-collectivism (Gong, 2007). Yeniyurt and Townsend (2003) suggest a strong association between cultural dimensions and penetration rates of new high-technology products (Internet, mobile phones and PCs), pointing out that this relationship is influenced by socio-economic variables. Straub and colleagues (1997) suggest that uncertainty avoidance (UAI) and collectivism (low IDV) in Japan may impede technology adoption. Huang and colleagues (2003) show that Spanish and Chinese teachers exhibited divergent intentions to utilize technology, with a substantial impact of collectivism (low IDV) and long-term orientation (high LTO). Teo and Huang (2017) also found that perceived ease of use, a key variable of technology acceptance model, was not significant among Chinese participants. This finding suggests that in a highly collectivist culture, individuals may prioritize group expectations and social norms over their personal evaluation of a technology's usability. Srite (2006) found that subjective norms, reflecting the influence of social expectations, significantly shaped the behavioral intention of Chinese respondents, but not Americans. This aligns with the role of collectivism (low IDV), where individuals tend to conform to group norms when making decisions. Conversely, perceived usefulness and ease of use were strong predictors only for the American sample, highlighting the influence of individualism (high IDV), were personal evaluation and autonomy drive technology adoption. Sun and colleagues (2019) demonstrated that long-term benefits positively influence technology acceptance, and that cultures with low masculinity (low MAS) are more likely to adopt new technologies in the hospitality industry than those with high masculinity (high MAS). Furthermore, a meta-analytic study by Sarkar and colleagues (2020) demonstrated that culture is a significant moderator in the acceptance of technology in mobile commerce.

These examples suggest that Hofstede's model has been often used to study the acceptance of technology in general, or of non-robotic technology. Interestingly, they have rarely, if ever, been applied to the study of acceptance of social robots, leaving a significant gap in the literature on how cultural values affect dynamic human-robot interaction. Even in one of the few studies that have explicitly considered cultural values in the context of human-robot interaction, Hofstede's dimensions have not been analyzed as independent variables that directly influence specific outcomes (Spatola et al., 2022).

4 How Do Uncertainty Avoidance and Perceived Control Shape Acceptance of Social Robots?

Hofstede's model is very broad. It includes several cultural dimensions that may interact in complex ways. While it would in principle be interesting to explore the relationships between people's cultural profiles along all of Hofstede's dimensions and their acceptance of social robots, it may be methodologically sensible to start from one of them. While dimensions such as individualism-collectivism or power distance may play a role in shaping attitudes towards robots, Uncertainty Avoidance (UA) stands out as particularly relevant due to its direct link with how individuals and societies respond to unpredictability, risk, and innovation.

The concept of UA has been defined as the extent to which individuals experience feelings of comfort when confronted with uncertain or ambiguous situations (Hofstede, 1980). As pointed out before, the Uncertainty Avoidance index (UAI) represents the degree to which societies can tolerate uncertainty and ambiguity. Cultures exhibiting low levels of uncertainty avoidance have been shown to demonstrate higher risk tolerance, and their populations tend to exhibit greater innovation and entrepreneurial spirit, along with a greater willingness to experiment with new ideas (Gong, 2011). In contrast, cultures with high levels of uncertainty avoidance place a significant value on security, the adoption of clear rules, and a formal structure of life management that does not tolerate changes from established patterns (Gong, 2011). Consequently, these countries exhibit a less favorable cultural environment for innovation. This can be further explained also through the Uncertainty Orientation Theory (Sorrentino & Roney, 2000), which distinguishes between uncertainty-oriented (UO) and certainty-oriented (CO) individuals. UOs actively seek information and approach ambiguity with curiosity, whereas COs prefer structured environments and strategies that minimize unpredictability. Individuals with high UA, who align more closely with COs, may exhibit greater reluctance toward new technologies, while those with low UA, akin to UOs, are more inclined to experiment despite uncertainty. Therefore, while cultural norms shape the general tendency toward uncertainty avoidance, the way individuals interact with technology is also influenced by personal cognitive styles and the extent to which they feel in control of uncertain situations.

UA is not merely about regulatory strictness; it also reflects underlying societal anxieties and perceptions of uncertainty, rather than objective institutional structures. Studies show that UA can be replicated using nationally representative data, and its predictive properties remain consistent with Hofstede's original formulation (ESS 2010; Hofstede, 2009). Yet, contrary to the assumption that high-UA societies enforce stronger rules and order, people in such societies tend to perceive their environment as disorganized and lacking structure (McCrae et al., 2008). This paradox suggests that UA may not measure actual societal rigidity, but rather the extent to which individuals experience anxiety and hold self-stereotypes about disorder. This is further supported by evidence that high-UA individuals advocate for strict rules but do not necessarily adhere to them personally

(Peterson & Smith, 2008). Rather than a universal psychological trait, UA may be an ideological construct shaped by managerial and societal perceptions (Minkov, 2006; Smith, 2006). Indeed, middle managers in high-UA cultures describe their societies as less structured than those in low-UA cultures, contradicting the expectation of stronger rule enforcement (Hofstede, 2009; Minkov, 2013).

Furthermore, a growing body of research, including a meta-analysis (Jan, 2024), has identified UA as a key moderating factor in technology acceptance models, influencing relationships between TAM factors as perceived ease of use, perceived usefulness, and behavioral intention (La Ferle et al., 2008; Lynn & Gelb, 1996; Yeniyurt & Townsend, 2003). These considerations justify the hypothesis that UA may be tightly connected with acceptance of social robots. As pointed out before, social robots are, by their very nature, dynamical, interactive and relatively unpredictable. Unlike conventional digital tools, social robots are autonomous agents whose behaviors cannot always be fully anticipated, potentially triggering anxiety and resistance in cultures with a high UA, where stability and control are highly valued (McSweeney, 2002). Conversely, societies with low UA display a greater openness to new technologies, even when these technologies introduce elements of uncertainty and lack full controllability.

Despite its considerable influence, one may object that UA alone cannot be the only factor affecting acceptance of social robots. Other more psychological factors may be relevant too, possibly connected to objective features of the robot. Here we surmise that another critical factor to be considered is the Perceived Control (PC)—the degree to which individuals feel they can predict their interactions with technology. Perceived control is a well-established psychological construct that refers to an individual's belief in their ability to influence events and outcomes in their environment (Ajzen, 2002; Heckhausen & Schulz, 1995). In the context of technology adoption, PC has been linked to higher self-efficacy, lower anxiety, and increased willingness to engage with new tools and systems (Bandura, 1997; Venkatesh et al., 2016). More specifically, the hypothesis proposed here can be stated as follows:

Uncertainty avoidance (UA) moderates the relationship between perceived control (PC) and the acceptance of social robots, such that the positive effect of PC on acceptance is weaker for high-UA individuals and stronger for low-UA individuals.

Our hypothesis suggests that UA interacts with PC, shaping attitudes toward social robots which function dynamically and interactively, often introducing elements of unpredictability. This unpredictability may trigger concerns about control. Understanding how these two factors interact can clarify the psychological and cultural mechanisms underlying technology acceptance. Specifically, we propose that UA moderates the relationship between PC and the acceptance of social robots. Individuals with high UA tend to be more resistant when they perceive robots as unpredictable or difficult to control, whereas those with low UA or a high sense of control over the robot's behavior are more likely to accept it.

This relationship can be further understood by considering how high-UA individuals experience greater anxiety in uncertain situations and tend to avoid sources of unpredictability. Prior research has shown that when robots behave unpredictably, users feel less capable of managing their interactions, increasing anxiety and negative attitudes toward them (Bartneck & Forlizzi, 2004; Złotowski et al., 2018). Conversely, low-UA individuals are generally more tolerant of uncertainty and more willing to engage with a social robot even when they cannot fully predict its behavior (Złotowski et al., 2018). Accordingly, perceived control plays a pivotal role in shaping attitudes toward social robots: individuals who feel they can manage and anticipate a robot's actions are more likely to accept it. This suggests that PC may, in some cases, override cultural differences, making it a key factor in cross-cultural research. However, further investigation is needed to determine whether PC operates independently of cultural background or interacts with specific cultural dimensions.

To better understand the mechanisms underlying this moderation effect, it is essential to examine whether UA operates primarily as a cultural dimension or as an individual psychological trait. If UA is considered a key cultural dimension, then it stands to reason that differences in UA levels across various contexts should correspond to differences in how individuals perceive and respond to uncertainty. Conversely, if UA is primarily considered to be a stable psychological trait, its effect, particularly its moderating role in the relationship between perceived control and robot acceptance, should remain consistent across different contexts, rather than varying with cultural background. The relevance of UA in this framework is twofold: first, as a measure of a shared cultural dimension, i.e. the collective management of uncertainty by societies; and second, as an indicator of individual cognitive tendencies, i.e. how people personally respond to uncertain situations. The definition of cultural background in terms of UA rather than nationality enables the analysis of its role in moderating the effect of perceived control on robot acceptance. This, in turn, allows for the determination of whether UA levels, rather than nationality, influence attitudes towards technology. Should UA significantly alter this relationship, it would suggest that uncertainty management is shaped by cultural values. Conversely, an absence of a significant moderating effect may indicate that uncertainty management functions more as an individual psychological trait than a cultural construct.

The present study puts forward the hypothesis that the relationship between Perceived Control (PC) and Acceptance (A) of social robots is shaped by different levels of Uncertainty Avoidance (UA). Specifically, it is proposed that in cultures with low UA, there is a stable and predictable relationship between these two factors: as individuals feel more in control of a social robot, their willingness to accept it increases proportionally. This suggests that in low UA contexts, Perceived Control acts as a consistent and reliable driver of Acceptance. In high UA cultures, however, this relationship appears to be more complex. At lower levels of Perceived Control, individuals who are high in UA tend to exhibit significantly lower Acceptance, indicating a greater initial reluctance to engage with social robots. This suggests that uncertainty-averse individuals are hesitant to adopt technology unless they feel a strong sense of control over it. However, as perceived control increases, so too does acceptance, albeit at a more gradual and circumspect rate in comparison to low UA contexts. That is to say, individuals operating within high UA environments necessitate a higher degree of confidence in their capacity to predict and regulate the robot's conduct prior to its acceptance.

In high-UA contexts, the relationship between Perceived Control (PC) and Acceptance (A) may not be straightforward but rather more complex and reactive. At lower levels of PC, individuals tend to exhibit significantly lower Acceptance, showing an initial reluctance to adopt social robots unless they feel a strong sense of control. As PC increases, individuals in high UA settings require stronger assurances before meaningfully engaging with and accepting social robots. This means that as PC increases, individuals in high-UA settings require stronger assurances before meaningfully engaging with and accepting social robots. Compared to those in low UA contexts, individuals with high UA demonstrate a more cautious and gradual increase in Acceptance as their sense of control improves. Moreover, Acceptance in high-UA contexts appears to be more sensitive to fluctuations in PC: small decreases in perceived control may lead to a decline in Acceptance, whereas individuals with low UA are less affected by such variations. As a result, fostering long-term engagement with social robots in high-UA settings depends on maintaining stable perceptions of control.

To test this hypothesis, validated scales can be employed to measure UA, PC, and Acceptance. UA is commonly assessed using Hofstede's Uncertainty Avoidance Index (Hofstede, 2001) or the CVSCALE by Yoo et al. (2011), which capture cultural variations in uncertainty management. PC is frequently measured using scales from the Technology Acceptance Model (TAM; Venkatesh & Davis, 2000) or perceived behavioral control items from the Theory of Planned Behavior (Ajzen, 1991). Acceptance of social robots can be evaluated using adapted versions of the Unified Theory of Acceptance and Use of Technology (UTAUT; Venkatesh et al., 2003) or scales such as the Almere Model (Heerink et al., 2010). Experimental studies could manipulate robot predictability and control conditions, assessing whether high-UA individuals exhibit stronger avoidance responses when perceived control is low. Survey-based and cross-cultural studies would help clarify whether UA functions primarily as a cultural construct or an individual psychological trait.

5 Conclusions

This paper has examined the role of culture in shaping the acceptance of social robots, moving beyond the conventional nation-based perspective that has historically dominated Human-Robot Interaction (HRI) research. While empirical studies have demonstrated significant cultural variations in robot acceptance, they have predominantly equated culture with nationality, thereby overlooking the complex nature of cultural influences. To address this limitation, an alternative approach is proposed, based on Hofstede's cultural framework, with a focus on one dimension of the model: Uncertainty Avoidance (UA). We argue that UA moderates the relationship between Perceived Control (PC) and social robot Acceptance. Specifically, individuals with high UA require stronger assurances of control before they meaningfully engage with social robots, whereas individuals with low UA are more open to interaction even when control is not fully established. This theoretical proposition highlights the need for empirical studies to examine UA as an independent cultural factor influencing technology acceptance, rather than relying solely on nationality-based comparisons. The present study proposes a shift in focus from nationality to measurable cultural dimensions, with the aim of refining the cultural analysis of robot acceptance. Future research should empirically test the proposed moderation effect of UA and explore whether enhancing Perceived Control can mitigate resistance to social robots. The integration of cultural dimensions into HRI research provides a more precise and structured understanding of how individuals across different cultural backgrounds engage with robotic technologies.

References

1. Ajzen, I.: The theory of planned behavior. Organ. Behav. Hum. Decis. Process. **50**(2), 179–211 (1991)
2. Ajzen, I.: Perceived behavioral control, self-efficacy, locus of control, and the theory of planned behavior. J. Appl. Soc. Psychol. **32**(4), 665–683 (2002)
3. Alshare, A., Mesak, H., Grandon, E., Badri, M.: Examining the moderating role of national culture on an extended technology acceptance model. J. Glob. Inf. Technol. Manag. **14**(3), 27–53 (2011)
4. Arnett, J.J.: The psychology of globalization. Am. Psychol. **57**(10), 774–783 (2002)
5. Ausserer, J., Risser, R.: Acceptance of driver assistance systems: a question of timing? In: Proceedings of the 3rd European Congress on Intelligent Transport Systems, pp. 1–8 (2005)
6. Bajones, M., Weiss, A., Vincze, M.: Investigating the influence of culture on helping behavior towards service robots. In: HRI 2017: Proceedings of the Companion of the 2017 ACM/IEEE International Conference on Human-Robot Interaction, pp. 75–76. ACM (2017)
7. Baker, A.L., Phillips, E.K., Ullman, D., Keebler, J.R.: Toward an understanding of trust repair in human-robot interaction: current research and future directions. ACM Trans. Interact. Intell. Syst. **8**(4), 1–30 (2018)
8. Baldwin, J.R., Faulkner, S.L., Hecht, M.L., Lindsley, S.L.: Redefining Culture: Perspectives Across the Disciplines. Routledge, New York (2006)
9. Bandura, A.: Self-efficacy: toward a unifying theory of behavioral change. Psychol. Rev. **84**(2), 191–215 (1977)
10. Bandura, A.: Self-efficacy: The Exercise of Control. W. H. Freeman, New York (1997)
11. Bartneck, C., Forlizzi, J.: A design-centred framework for social human-robot interaction. In: CHI Conference on Human Factors in Computing Systems, pp. 591–594 (2004)
12. Bartneck, C., Kulić, D., Croft, E., Zoghbi, S.: Measurement instruments for the anthropomorphism, animacy, likeability, perceived intelligence, and perceived safety of robots. Int. J. Soc. Robot. **1**(1), 71–81 (2009)
13. Baumeister, R.F.: The cultural animal: human nature, meaning, and social life. Oxford University Press, Oxford (2005)
14. Baxter, P., Kennedy, J., Read, R., Looije, R., Leite, I., Belpaeme, T.: From characterizing three years of HRI to methodology and reporting recommendations. In: Proceedings of the 2016 ACM/IEEE International Conference on Human-Robot Interaction, pp. 391–398 (2017)
15. Beaudry, A., Pinsonneault, A.: Understanding user responses to information technology: a coping model of user adaptation. MIS Q. **29**(3), 493–524 (2005)
16. Belpaeme, T., Baxter, P., de Greeff, J., Kennedy, J., Read, R., Looije, R., et al.: Child-robot interaction: perspectives and challenges. In: Herrmann, G., Pearson, M., Lenz, A., Bremner, P., Spiers, A., Leonards, U. (eds.) Social Robotics, vol. 8239, pp. 452–459. Springer, New York (2013)
17. Benbasat, I., Barki, H.: Quo vadis, TAM? J. Assoc. Inf. Syst. **8**(4), 211–218 (2007)
18. Berry, J.W.: Immigration, acculturation, and adaptation. Appl. Psychol. **46**(1), 5–34 (1997)
19. Berry, J.W., Poortinga, Y.H., Segall, M.H., Dasen, P.R.: Cross-cultural psychology: research and applications, 2nd edn. Cambridge University Press, Cambridge (1992)
20. Broadbent, E., Stafford, R., MacDonald, B.: Acceptance of healthcare robots for the older population: review and future directions. Int. J. Soc. Robot. **1**(4), 319–330 (2009)

21. Chismar, W.G., Wiley-Patton, S.: Does the extended technology acceptance model apply to physicians. In: Proceedings of the 36th Hawaii International Conference on System Sciences, pp. 1–8. IEEE (2002)
22. Davis, F.D.: A technology acceptance model for empirically testing new end-user information systems: theory and results. Doctoral dissertation, MIT (1986)
23. Davis, F.D.: Perceived usefulness, perceived ease of use, and user acceptance of information technology. MIS Q. 13(3), 319–340 (1989)
24. De Graaf, M.M.A., Allouch, S.B., van Dijk, J.A.G.M.: Why would I use this in my home? A model of domestic social robot acceptance. Hum.-Comput. Interact. 34(2), 115–173 (2019)
25. de Graaf, M.M.A., Ben Allouch, S., van Dijk, J.A.G.M.: Long-term evaluation of a social robot in real homes. Interact. Stud. 18(2), 190–224 (2017)
26. De Jong, C., Kühne, R., Peter, J., van Straten, C.L., Barco, A.: Intentional acceptance of social robots: development and validation of a self-report measure for children. Int. J. Hum. Comput. Stud. 139, 102426 (2020)
27. Dwyer, F.R., Schurr, P.H., Oh, S.: Developing buyer-seller relationships. J. Mark. 51(2), 11–27 (2005)
28. European Social Survey (ESS): ESS Round 5: Uncertainty Avoidance Indicators. https://www.europeansocialsurvey.org (2010)
29. Eyssel, F., Kuchenbrandt, D., Bobinger, S., de Ruiter, L., Hegel, F.: 'If you sound like me, you must be more human': on the interplay of robot and user features on human–robot acceptance and anthropomorphism. In: Proceedings of the 6th ACM/IEEE International Conference on Human-Robot Interaction, pp. 125–126 (2011)
30. Fishbein, M., Ajzen, I.: Belief, Attitude, Intention, and Behavior: An Introduction to Theory and Research. Addison-Wesley, Boston (1975)
31. Gallagher, S.: Philosophical conceptions of the self: implications for cognitive science. Trends Cogn. Sci. 4(1), 14–21 (2000)
32. Ganesh, J., Arnold, M.J., Reynolds, K.E.: Understanding the customer base of service providers: an examination of the differences between switchers and stayers. J. Mark. 61(2), 65–87 (1997)
33. Gong, W.: The impact of uncertainty avoidance on e-commerce adoption: a cross-national study. Asia Pac. J. Mark. Logist. 23(1), 56–72 (2011)
34. Gong, W., Li, Z.G., Stump, R.L.: Global internet use and access: cultural considerations. Asia Pac. J. Mark. Logist. 19(1), 57–74 (2007)
35. Heckhausen, J., Schulz, R.: A life-span theory of control. Psychol. Rev. 102(2), 284–304 (1995)
36. Heerink, M., Kröse, B., Evers, V., Wielinga, B.: Assessing acceptance of assistive social agent technology by older adults: the Almere Model. Int. J. Soc. Robot. 2(4), 361–375 (2010)
37. Hofstede, G.: Culture's Consequences: International Differences in Work-Related Values. Sage Publications, Beverly Hills (1980)
38. Hofstede, G.: Culture's Consequences: Comparing Values, Behaviors, Institutions, and Organizations Across Nations, 2nd edn. Sage Publications, Beverly Hills (2001)
39. Hofstede, G.: Cultures and organizations: software of the mind. McGraw-Hill, New York (2009)
40. Hofstede, G., Hofstede, G.J., Minkov, M.: Cultures and Organizations: Software of the Mind: Intercultural Cooperation and its Importance for Survival, 3rd edn. McGraw-Hill, New York (2010)
41. Huang, L., Lu, M., Wong, B.: The impact of power distance on email acceptance: Evidence from the PRC. J. Comput. Inf. Syst. 44(1), 93–101 (2003)
42. Jahoda, G.: A cross-cultural perspective in social psychology. Academic Press, London (1984)
43. Jan, J., Alshare, K.A., Lane, P.L.: Hofstede's cultural dimensions in technology acceptance models: a meta-analysis. Univ. Access Inf. Soc. 23, 717–741 (2024)

44. Jones, T.: Cultural psychology and its implications for human–robot interaction. Cult. Psychol. 23(3), 414–430 (2017)
45. Kahn, P.H., Friedman, B., Pérez-Granados, D.R., Freier, N.G.: Robotic pets in the lives of preschool children. Interact. Stud. 7(3), 405–436 (2006)
46. Kamide, H., Arai, T.: Perceived comfortableness of anthropomorphized robots in U.S. and Japan. Int. J. Soc. Robot. 9, 1–7 (2017)
47. Kanda, T., Ishiguro, H., Imai, M., Ono, T.: Development and evaluation of interactive humanoid robots. Proc. IEEE 92, 1839–1850 (2004)
48. Kaplan, F.: Who is afraid of the humanoid? Investigating cultural differences in the acceptance of robots. Int. J. Humanoid Rob. 1(3), 465–480 (2004)
49. Katz, E., Blumler, J.G., Gurevitch, M.: Uses and gratifications research. Public Opin. Q. 37(4), 509–523 (1973)
50. Kumar, N., Krishnan, R.: Multinational diffusion models: an alternative framework. Mark. Sci. 21(3), 318–330 (2002)
51. Kroeber, A.L., Kluckhohn, C.: Culture: A Critical Review of Concepts and Definitions. Peabody Museum, Cambridge (1952)
52. La Ferle, C.L., Edwards, S.M., Lee, W.N.: Culture, attitudes, and media patterns in China, Taiwan, and the U.S.: balancing standardization and localization decisions. J. Glob. Mark. 21(3), 191–205 (2008)
53. LaRose, R., Eastin, M.S.: A social cognitive theory of internet uses and gratifications: toward a new model of media attendance. J. Broadcast. Electron. Media 48(3), 358–377 (1994)
54. Lee, H.R., Šabanović, S.: Culturally variable preferences for robot design and use in South Korea, Turkey, and the United States. In: HRI 2014: Proceedings of the 2014 ACM/IEEE International Conference on Human-Robot Interaction, pp. 17–24. ACM, New York (2014)
55. Lee, K.M., Jung, Y., Kim, J., Kim, S.R.: Are physically embodied social agents better than disembodied social agents? Int. J. Hum. Comput. Stud. 64(10), 962–973 (2005)
56. Li, D., Rau, P., Li, Y.: A cross-cultural study: effect of robot appearance and task. Int. J. Soc. Robot. 2, 175–186 (2010)
57. Libin, A., Libin, E.: Person–robot interactions from the robopsychologists' point of view: the robotic psychology and robotherapy approach. In: Proceedings of the IEEE, pp. 1789–1803 (2004)
58. Lim, V.: Attitudes towards robots: a cross-cultural perspective. Int. J. Soc. Robot. 2(3), 235–247 (2010)
59. Lim, V., Rooksby, M., Cross, E.S.: Social robots on a global stage: establishing a role for culture during human-robot interaction. Int. J. Soc. Robot. 13, 1307–1333 (2021)
60. Lynn, M., Gelb, B.D.: Identifying innovative national markets for technical consumer goods. Int. Mark. Rev. 13(6), 43–57 (1996)
61. Mansouri, M., Taylor, H.: Does cultural robotics need culture? Conceptual fragmentation and the problems of merging culture with robot design. Int. J. Soc. Robot. 16, 385–401 (2024)
62. Matsumoto, D., Yoo, S.H.: Toward a new generation of cross-cultural research. Perspect. Psychol. Sci. 1, 234–250 (2006)
63. McCoy, S., Galletta, D., King, W.: Integrating national culture into is research: the need for current individual level measures. Commun. Assoc. Inf. Syst. 15 (2005)
64. McCrae, R.R., Terracciano, A., Realo, A., Allik, J.: Interpreting GLOBE societal practices scales. J. Cross Cult. Psychol. 39(6), 805–810 (2008)
65. McSweeney, B.: Hofstede's model of national cultural differences and their consequences: a triumph of faith—a failure of analysis. Hum. Relat. 55(1), 89–118 (2002)
66. Minkov, M.: Cultural differences in a globalizing world. Emerald Group, Bingley (2013)
67. Minkov, M.: What makes us different and similar: a new interpretation of the world values survey and other cross-cultural data. Klasika i Stil, Sofia (2006)

68. Minkov, M., Hofstede, G.: Hofstede's fifth dimension: new evidence from the world values survey. J. Cross Cult. Psychol. **43**(1), 3–14 (2012)
69. Nielsen, J.: Usability Engineering. Morgan Kaufmann, San Francisco (1993)
70. Nomura, T.: Cultural differences in social acceptance of robots. In: 2017 26th IEEE International Symposium on Robot and Human Interactive Communication (RO-MAN), pp. 533–538. IEEE, New York (2017)
71. Pelto, P.J., Pelto, G.H.: Intra-cultural diversity: some theoretical issues. Am. Ethnol. **2**(1), 1–18 (1975)
72. Peterson, M.F., Smith, P.B.: Social structures and processes in cross-cultural management. J. Int. Bus. Stud. **39**(6), 919–922 (2008)
73. Reeves, B., Nass, C.: The Media Equation: How People Treat Computers, Television, and New Media Like Real People and Places. Cambridge University Press, Cambridge (1996)
74. Rohner, R.P.: Toward a conception of culture for cross-cultural psychology. J. Cross Cult. Psychol. **15**(2), 111–138 (1984)
75. Ros, R., Baroni, I., Demiris, Y.: Adaptive human–robot interaction in a therapy context. Paladyn J. Behav. Robot. **2**(1), 1–13 (2011)
76. Rosenthal-von der Pütten, A.M., Krämer, N.C.: Individuals' evaluations of and attitudes towards potentially uncanny robots. Int. J. Soc. Robot. **7**(5), 799–824 (2015). https://doi.org/10.1007/s12369-015-0321-z
77. Sarkar, S., Chauhan, S., Khare, A.: A meta-analysis of antecedents and consequences of trust in mobile commerce. Int. J. Inf. Manag. **50**, 286–301 (2020)
78. Shin, D.H., Choo, H.: Modeling the acceptance of socially interactive robotics: social presence in human–robot interaction. Interact. Stud. **12**(2), 251–279 (2011)
79. Shiomi, M.: A systematic survey of multiple social robots as a passive- and interactive-social medium. Adv. Robot. **38**(7), 440–454 (2023)
80. Simon, H.A.: The Sciences of the Artificial, 3rd edn. MIT Press, Cambridge (2001)
81. Smith, P.: Acquiescent response bias as an aspect of cultural communication style. J. Cross Cult. Psychol. **34**, 50–61 (2013)
82. Smith, P.B.: When elephants fight, the grass suffers: cultural dimensions as moderators of organizational change. J. Cross Cult. Psychol. **37**(1), 50–61 (2006)
83. Sorrentino, R.M., Roney, C.J.R.: The Uncertain Mind: Individual Differences in Facing the Unknown. Psychology Press, New York (2000)
84. Spatola, N., Marchesi, S., Wykowska, A.: Different models of anthropomorphism across cultures and ontological limits in current frameworks: the integrative framework of anthropomorphism. Frontiers in Robotics and AI **9**, 863319 (2022)
85. Srite, M.: Culture as an explanation of technology acceptance differences: an empirical investigation of Chinese and U.S. users. MIS Q. **30**(3), 679–704 (2006)
86. Straub, D., Burton-Jones, A.: Veni, Vidi, Vici: breaking the TAM logjam. J. Assoc. Inf. Syst. **8** (2007)
87. Sun, H., Fang, Y., Lim, K.H., Straub, D.: User satisfaction with information technology services: a social capital perspective. Inf. Syst. Res. **27**(4), 862–880 (2019)
88. Tellis, G.J., Stremersch, S., Yin, E.: The international takeoff of new products: the role of economics, culture, and country innovativeness. Mark. Sci. **22**(2), 188–208 (2003)
89. Teo, T., Huang, F., Hoi, C.: Explicating the influences that explain intention to use technology among English teachers in China. Interact. Learn. Environ. **26**, 1–16 (2017)
90. Triandis, H.C.: The Analysis of Subjective Culture. Wiley Interscience, New York (1972)
91. Triandis, H.C.: Culture and Social Behavior. McGraw-Hill, New York (1994)
92. Tylor, E.B.: Researches into the early history of mankind and the development of civilization. Murray, London (1865)
93. Van der Heijden, H.: User acceptance of hedonic information systems. MIS Q. **28**(4), 695–704 (2004)

94. Van Everdingen, Y.M., Waarts, E.: The effect of national culture on the adoption of innovations. Mark. Lett. **14**(3), 217–232 (2003)

95. Venkatesh, V., Morris, M.G., Davis, G.B., Davis, F.D.: User acceptance of information technology: toward a unified view. MIS Q. **27**(3), 425–478 (2003)

96. Venkatesh, V., Thong, J.Y.L., Xu, X.: Unified theory of acceptance and use of technology: a synthesis and the road ahead. J. Assoc. Inf. Syst. **17**(5), 328–376 (2016)

97. Wang, W.: Cultural differences in the perception of robots: evidence from cross-cultural psychology. Int. J. Soc. Robot. **12**(6), 1433–1445 (2020)

98. Yoo, B., Donthu, N., Lenartowicz, T.: Measuring Hofstede's five dimensions of cultural values at the individual level: development and validation of CVSCALE. J. Int. Consum. Mark. **23**(3–4), 193–210 (2011)

99. Złotowski, J., Yogeeswaran, K., Bartneck, C.: Can we control it? Autonomous robots threaten human identity, uniqueness, safety, and resources. Int. J. Hum. Comput. Stud. **100**, 48–54 (2018)

Executive Cognitive Control of Free Choices

Graham Pluck⬤, Fei Gu⬤, Natasha Asawanuchit⬤,
and Suphasiree Chantavarin(✉)⬤

Faculty of Psychology, Chulalongkorn University, Bangkok, Thailand
{graham.ch,fei.g,Suphasiree.C}@chula.ac.th,6338022238@alumni.chula.ac.th

Abstract. Originating in computer science in the 1950's, executive function is now an important concept in behavioral sciences. This Tool paper examines the core definitions of executive function, and how that relates to free, willed choices in human behavior. We contrast this with cognitive assessment methods that tend to push test takers into convergent thinking. We show how a common form of cognitive test used in behavioral sciences to measure executive functioning, the Trail Making Test, can be altered so that it requires divergent thinking. To analyze and summarize performance of multiple, individual, free choices we apply statistical methods taken from computer science to test for randomness. The tool presented, the Choice Trails Test, and the proposed analysis method, allow for novel ways to investigate top-down, executive, cognitive control using a simple paper-and-pencil test. The benefit of this approach is that it produces indices of performance that are closely aligned with the essential meaning of executive functions. Additionally, this method provides a denser data set than traditional methods that examine total performance metrics. Denser data allows for analysis that is consistent with traditional approaches to examining task performance in cognitive science that stress continuous analysis of processes across tasks.

Keywords: Executive function · Divergent thinking · Action selection · Trail making test · Task switching · Willed action · Free choices

1 Executive Cognitive Control

The concept of executive controllers, programs that oversee other programs, originated in computer science in the 1950's, but was later adopted widely by neurological and cognitive sciences [34]. The modern concept of executive control in cognitive science has thus developed from two fields. Firstly, it has been used widely in neuropsychology to functionally describe disorganized behavior seen after damage to the frontal lobes of the primate brain [38]. Secondly, the concept of a supervisory attentional controller, or central executive, has been included in highly influential cognitive models developed in experimental psychology [3,27]. Despite the concept of executive control spreading to a range

© The Author(s), under exclusive license to Springer Nature Switzerland AG 2026
J. Proença et al. (Eds.): SEFM 2024, LNCS 15551, pp. 237–253, 2026.
https://doi.org/10.1007/978-3-031-94748-3_18

of other disciplines, the influence of neuropsychology and experimental cognitive psychology has defined how the executive functions are conceptualized and measured in quantitative cognitive research.

The vast majority of assessments of executive functions used in diverse fields including, education, linguistics, public health, human-resources management etc. have followed the experimental psychology influence in attempting to quantify executive control (essentially a latent variable) by measuring accuracy of performance on demanding, yet highly constrained tasks.

Take for example the various towers tasks, such as the Towers of Hanoi, which are widely used to measure planning as an executive function [44]. There are various Tower tasks which include Tower of London and Tower of Hanoi; however, they are quite similar in that they both require transforming an initial configuration into to a goal state, so for the purposes of this paper they will be considered as examples from the general class of Towers tasks. Towers tasks involve moving from a prespecified start state of different sized disks on any of three pegs, to a predefined finishing goal state configuration. It is cognitively demanding because there are strict rules concerning how the disks can be moved. To perform efficiently, the moves must be planned several steps in advance, with goal states decomposed into sub-goals. In fact, it is the highly constrained nature of such tasks, and limited search space, that has made them of substantial interest also to artificial intelligence [22,50].

But how well does the manifest performance on such tasks relate to the concept of an executive controller? Performance on towers tasks have, in fact, been interpreted as indicating a wide range of cognitive processes including planning [44,50], spatial working-memory [30], or resolution of sub-goal/goal conflicts [15], among others. Similar ambiguity of process issues affects other commonly used tests of executive function, such as the Stroop task and n-back tasks, raising problems of what is exactly being studied by these executive function tests [37]. At this stage it is necessary then, to consider in more detail the definition of executive control.

1.1 Defining Executive Control

Executive function is the term often used in cognitive psychology to describe the top-down processes underlying control of action. Specifically, it refers to processes underlying goal-directed action that is required to face non-routine challenges [34,45]. Furthermore, it has to be more than just goal-directed, it has to produce 'intelligent' outcomes, as some goal-directed mechanisms can nevertheless be incapable of adaption [24].

Within cognitive neuroscience, the term *cognitive control* is often preferred but refers to the same idea, defined as: "Cognitive, or executive, control refers to the ability to coordinate thought and action and direct it toward obtaining goals.... Executive control contrasts with automatic forms of brain processing." [25, p. 99]. As mentioned above, one of the historical reasons for the concept of executive controllers moving from computer sciences into cognitive neurosciences, was the application of the concept of executive cognitive control to understanding behavioral disorders seen after experimental damage to the frontal lobes in non-human primates [38].

As an extension of that, from a clinical perspective, cognitive control is used to explain deficits seen in human patients after damage to the frontal lobes [33,34]. As an example, take this clinical description: "one straightforward difficulty common after frontal lesions is defective control of behavior in the face of choice, complexity, or ambiguity" [1, p. 1515]. The same authors also offer a further conceptual definition: "Cognitive control is required when. . .a stimulus is ambiguous and potentially conflicting responses might be generated". Similarly, definitions of executive control from developmental psychology emphasize that they represent top-down control of cognition when the correct responses are 'ambiguous' [1,18,41]. In this sense, ambiguous means that appropriate behavior cannot be directly driven by sensation.

It is well known that definitions of executive function and cognitive control used in behavioral sciences are vague and variable [4]. Nevertheless, key aspects are their top-down coordination of intelligent goal-directed behavior, in non-routine situations, and in contexts in which the appropriateness of stimulus-response associations are ambiguous. Indeed, the behavioral outcome of such executive control processes are often referred to as being 'willed', as opposed to being automatic and stimuli-driven [14,20,25,27,42]. How well then does such an analysis describe the task goals of common laboratory and clinical assessments of executive functions used in clinical neuroscience and psychology?

If we stay with the towers tasks as an example, we can clearly see why performance of them is often considered a measure of executive cognitive control. They are certainly goal-directed, one of the key, defining features of executive control, in that the task is to move from a start state to a goal state, and there are many choices that need to be made. And at least on the first attempts, they are non-routine and cannot be completed through automatic routines triggered by stimuli.

However, on closer examination, we can see that participants in research studies, or clinical patients, do not just perform a single tower task that is novel to them. In order to obtain scores with a wide dispersion across individuals, usually multiple trials are performed, each with different start and end goal states. Typically, between 8 and 20 different trials are performed per person, involving potentially hundreds of separate moves. Total scores are calculated based on using the fewest number of moves possible to reach the goal states. There are in fact simple routines that can be applied to efficiently achieve the end goal states, and people do spontaneously apply them [46,50]. Furthermore, substantial learning occurs during task performance. Some of the learning is procedural, but also declarative discovery of rules, which means that people can effectively identify and apply schematic routines to achieve the goal state on each trial [48]. For this reason, towers tasks, as they are typically analyzed, tend to be actually quite unreliable measures of processes supposedly under executive cognitive control [32].

The problem may be that most quantitative measures of executive cognitive control have originated in laboratory-based experimental psychology. Within that field it is very common for test procedures to constrain the response space and to classify and score all responses as correct or incorrect. The measure of performance is then simply the total accuracy. Consequently, such lab-based tasks are inherently convergent, in the sense proposed by Guilford. He defined convergent cognitive processing in this way: "In convergent thinking, there is usually one conclusion or answer that is regarded as unique, and thinking is channeled or controlled in the direction of that answer" [16, p. 274]. Reasoning using deductive logic is a classic example of convergent thought. Most cognitive tests used in experimental psychological research or clinical practice channel performance in ways that meet the definition for convergent thinking given by Guildford. Responses are essentially scored as being right or wrong, according to predefined criteria. Even in tasks in which response time is taken as a variable of interest, it is still inevitably the time taken to produce the unique response that is considered correct by the experimenter.

1.2 Divergent Thinking and Executive Control

One of us has previously argued that the conceptual definitions of executive functions are often more consistent with tasks that involve divergent thinking [34]. Divergent thought, the antipode to convergent thought, was originally defined by Guilford in terms of task-related processing in which "...there is much searching or going off in various directions. This is most clearly seen when there is no unique conclusion." [16, p. 274].

Guilford gives the task of verbal fluency as an example of a divergent thinking task [16]. This is in fact one of only a few examples of tests used with the intention of measuring executive functions that clearly involves divergent thought. In verbal fluency tasks, people are asked to think of as many words as possible that meet a criterion, within a short period, usually one minute.

Phonemic fluency involves producing words beginning with pre-specified letters, in English often the letter 'F'. Similarly, category fluency involves producing words within a predefined semantic set, in English 'animals' is the most commonly used set. Another example of a test described by Guilford as an exemplar of divergent thinking is production of alternative uses for objects, most commonly a brick is the target, and the participant is required to produce as many possible uses as possible (e.g., a door stop, to crush cans for recycling...). Together the tests as described here, and others such as gestural fluency, are well-known to be sensitive to damage to the frontal lobes of the brain and are considered tests of executive cognitive control involving voluntary generation of responses [40].

It appears that the human cognitive system finds fluency tasks, such as verbal fluency, difficult because retrieval in that way is an unusual task requirement, and we thus lack routines to do so, necessitating top-down executive control. Evidence to support this interpretation comes from the observation that in verbal fluency tasks people spontaneously cluster items that they recall, and frequently switch cluster types. In comparison, patients with cognitive impairment caused by dementia produce fewer, and smaller clusters. This is interpreted as indicating a loss of volitional, spontaneous strategy application [5]. Furthermore, verbal fluency is impaired the most for sets with large numbers of items [11], suggesting that search strategies are the limiting factor, not availability of lexical items.

Another rare example of an executive function assessment method that invokes divergent thinking is the Hayling Sentence Completion Test [7]. The test consists of two sets of 15 sentences each having the last word missing. The second part requires participants to quickly complete the sentence with a word that does not make any sense within the sentence context. The free choice aspect of this task makes it difficult as there are so many possible words to choose from, even neurologically healthy people struggle and tend to make errors by reverting to routines, in that they give words that do in fact make sense. Mounting evidence suggests that performance on this test is much more closely associated with real-life performance in challenging environments than conventional, convergent cognitive tests [35,36], suggesting that whatever it measures conforms well to that expected from the concept of an executive controller.

We argue that tasks such as described here which promote voluntary, divergent thinking, where constraints are ambiguous because decisions can go in unforeseen directions, are better at eliciting measurable behavior that conforms to the conceptual definitions of 'executive cognitive control', at least, as opposed to the majority of tests used in cognitive research and clinical practice, which are decidedly convergent. This is because tasks that require divergent thinking generally do not allow for routine, automatic processing. In fact, they are highly executive because they measure free choices.

1.3   Free Choices in Experimental Tasks

The reason that quantitative cognitive research has generally avoided addressing free choices is that it is difficult to operationalize behavioral experiments to measure them. Modern cognitive psychology is extremely experiment based. Approximately 97% of all published cognitive psychology articles describe experiments [49]. In cognitive psychology, experimentation is viewed in terms of stimuli and response—the experimenter manipulates some variable (the stimulus) and observes the effect on behavior (the response).

But willed actions, the behaviors said to result from executive cognitive control [14,20,25,27,42], by definition are not stimuli-driven. In the cognitive psychology laboratory then, the standard stimulus-response experimental design is of little use. If an experimenter asks a research participant to make free choices, perhaps lift a finger whenever they want to, then the response cannot be readily categorized as correct or not, nor the response time from will to action calculated.

In cognitive neuroscience this is less of a problem, as physiological measures are taken as the response. This was demonstrated in one of the earliest functional brain imaging studies, in which it was shown that free choice finger movements activate the frontal lobes of the brain [14]. In fact, they activated the exact same subregion which had been identified, and is still recognized, as the neurological hub of executive cognitive control [29]. Furthermore, which willed action will be made can be predicted at the neurophysiological level before the decision is made by executive control [42]. This is because free choices appear to be influenced, at least partly, by random noise of neuronal firing—if one set of cells are randomly more active at a particular time point, then they are more likely to influence the outcome when a decision is called for. In this sense, free choices are difficult to maintain and require top-down control.

Free choices could potentially be used as a behavioral measure of top-down executive cognitive control if the convergent paradigm is not used. Instead of accuracy of responses, one could measure the ability to override decision making that is driven by factors such as routines, stimuli-response associations, and neuronal noise. In a free-choice paradigm a research participant could be asked to respond randomly and to not plan ahead, but still within a constrained task. However, deviation from routineness in task performance is more difficult to measure than accuracy, and it is an undeveloped field of cognitive research. In the following section we describe a novel task, and a mathematical method to quantify performance, which targets how well participants can avoid patterns in their free choices. This procedure also allows for the collection of 'dense' data [47], making it more amenable to a detailed cognitive analysis.

In the remainder of this paper, we describe a novel method for collecting data on free choices, as well as a suggested statistical approach for its analysis (Sect. 2). We then describe an example of the analysis using a sample of data we collected (Sect. 3). The paper finishes with a discussion on the wider context of the research reported, including applications and implications of this novel approach (Sect. 4).

2   A Method for Eliciting Free Choices as Behavioral Data

As previously described, the majority of laboratory tests of cognitive function promote convergent thinking, encouraging research participants to produce pre-defined correct responses. As another example of this we could examine the Trail Making Test [39]. This has been widely in use in clinical and educational cognitive assessment since the 1950's. It is a paper-and-pencil test that involves participants being presented with a page that has 25 circles marked on it. Each of the circles contains a number (from 1 to 13) or an English alphabetic letter (from A to L). The task is to draw lines as quickly as possible to join the circles consecutively, but alternating number and letter sequences (i.e., 1-A-2-B-3- etc.).

There are numerous versions of this test [10,39] and also task modifications, one of the most common modified forms is the Color Trails Test which dispenses with the alphabetic letters and instead requires participants to switch between joining pink and yellow circles [23]. This produces a more culture-fair test, in that knowledge of the English alphabet is not needed for task completion. But it necessitates that foils be provided- each number is shown twice, once in pink and once in yellow. Both the standard version [10,39] and Color version [23] require convergent processing, as only one of the circles is ever considered correct as the target of the line. We took this basic design but altered it to allow divergent, responding via free choices of color.

2.1 The Choice Trails Test

To allow free choices, A4 size pages were produced which contained the numbers 1 through 25. However, each number was shown four times, each time in a different color. The same pink and yellow as the original test were used, but additionally blue and violet circles were included. The four colors were selected to have different brightness levels, so that they would be distinguishable even for color-blind people. A sample task is shown in Fig. 1. The basic task requirement is that participants must join the circles in numerical sequence, starting from 1, finishing at 25, choosing a different color each time. This and other rules are described in more detail below.

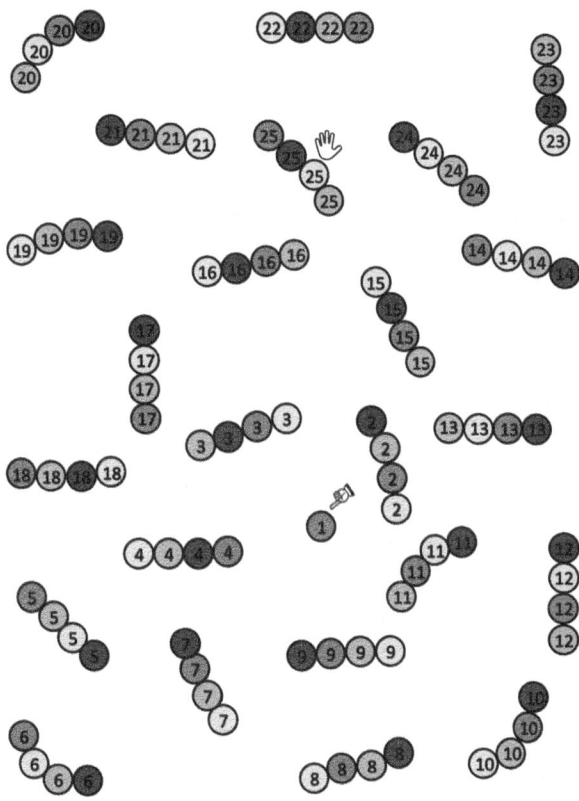

Fig. 1. The Choice Trails Test. (Color figure online)

When a participant performs the task correctly the lines that they draw will not transect each other. For this task the completion of each page (i.e., joining all numbers from 1–25) is considered a single trial. Within each trial 24 free choices are made. We refer to each of these as 24 movements as steps. As the starting point is a pink circle, the first step made within a trial is to choose whether to select a yellow, blue, or violet circle 2. This continues until the participant completes the 24th step (connecting circle 24 to circle 25) with their pencil. To allow for multiple trials by the same participants, multiple versions were made with the circles in different configurations on each page. All were very similar, containing the same 4 colors, and each requiring 24 steps to complete. The minimum line length to make all 24 steps was within 5% of the total distance on all versions. A set of materials for 8 trials are available to download from https://gpluck.co.uk/Tests/.

When completing a trial of the task, an individual sits at a table and the Choice Trails test is placed in front of them. The test is obscured by the experimenter's hand while the participant listens to the verbal instructions of the task. The participant is given a pencil and told that they must draw lines to connect all of the circles starting at circle 1. The specific rules used were:

1. They should join the numbers in sequence with the pencil.
2. They should perform as quickly as possible without making mistakes.
3. They should not choose the same color twice in succession.
4. They should try to choose all the colors equally often.
5. They should avoid using any plans or strategies.

On the experimenter's instruction to begin, a stopwatch is started. The experimenter watches performance and if the participant breaks a rule, such as missing out a number, they are stopped and told to continue from the last point before the error was made. The stopwatch is left running until the participant completes the final drawn line (completing step 24, terminating on circle 25). The completion time is recorded. To create the data set for the current study, three trials were completed by a sample of 30 participants. This sample size is sufficiently powered to detect large effect sizes, according to standardized criteria. The participants were all undergraduate students. In addition to task completion times all choices from all steps were tabulated in sequence. As there were 24 steps made on each trial, this totaled 72 choices per research participant, and 2,160 choices recorded in total from the sample. This is an ongoing study and the analyzed sample will be larger in future studies on this assessment tool.

2.2   A Method to Test the Randomness of Responses

In the task described above, the requirement faced by the research participants is to make choices that will use all colors equally often, without using any strategy. By this we mean the commonly understood meaning of strategy, being the application of a plan to achieve a goal. This rule was introduced as, from our experience in cognitive testing, research participants often do spontaneously apply simple strategies, such as repeating patterns. Although, from a philosophical perspective the concept of a strategy could be interpreted in many other ways, we expected participants to understand the instruction as to not apply explicit, conscious plans to meet the task requirements. Therefore, although not explicitly instructed, the task implicitly required them to try to produce random free choices.

From a data analysis perspective we have three trials of performance, each with sequences of 24 steps/free choices, totaling sequences of 72 separate responses. The question is then, how random are their responses? Logically, it is impossible to prove that a set of numbers are truly random, it is only possible to show that statistically speaking, they do not appear to be random [19]. Much of the research on detection of randomness stems from attempts to create random number generators for commercial computing purposes, for use in industries such as gaming and online gambling. However, the largest application is cryptography. These industries require computations acting as random number generators, producing information that is highly unpredictable, unbiased, and trustworthy. As computer programs in practice use pre-established, finite lists of numbers to produce seemingly random actions, their output over time will become predictable. Thus, research on testing the efficacy of computerized random number generators has developed methods to detect non-randomness (not randomness per se).

One approach widely used in cryptography and in many other fields is the chi-squared method [2]. This creates a p value for the analyzed string to indicate the probability that it comes from a set of numbers that are unpatterned (i.e., randomly assorted). Over multiple strings analyzed the resulting p values can then be used as a data set. Although behavioral scientists are more familiar with using p values to evaluate hypotheses for individual research studies, the p values generated from analyzing data sets can themselves comprise a data set, and can be analyzed with normal inferential statistics. The most notable example of this in recent years is the Open Science Collaboration which revealed that most psychology research studies fail to be replicated [28]. Part of their analysis involved examining the p values reported in published psychology articles, and using null-hypothesis testing to decide the extent to which the p values from replications of the same protocols showed the same score distributions.

Basically, p values are random variables, technically transformed test-statistics (in our case from chi-squared tests) which puts them into a standard form, allowing interpretation independent of the particular statistical test used [26]. They have the benefit of being potentially normally distributed when they are derived from hypothesis tests in which the null-hypothesis is incorrect. For this reason, the transformed scores (i.e., the p values) will usually produce distributions more amenable to further parametric statistical analysis, compared to the raw test statistics (i.e., the chi-squared test values). This is because, for example, the chi-squared statistic is calculated from the sum of squares of both positive and negative values, the accumulation of relatively higher values will produce positively skewed distributions.

Each chi-squared calculation is done at the level of the individual participant (not group data). For each analysis performed, at the individual level a high p value will indicate that the responses made by the participant appear to be more random. Therefore, relatively higher p values can be interpreted as showing relatively better top-down, executive control of behavior. The potential range of p values is between 0 and 1.

3   An Example of the Analysis Method Using Task Performance Data

From the data acquired from the 30 participants tested, our goal is to test whether each participant appears to have chosen the colors randomly. If a participant chooses colors in a purely random fashion, given 24 choices in a single trial, the expected counts of a single color is 6 ($=\frac{24}{4}$) in a single trial. Because each participant had three trials, the expected counts of a single color is 18 in three trials combined. Similarly, we can calculate the expected counts of two-color bigrams (e.g., how often yellow-blue occur) are chosen in a single trial and in three trials combined. Particularly, given 4 colors, there are 12 possible permutations of 2 different colors. Then, the 24 choices in a single trial produce 23 permutations of 2 different colors. Thus, the expected counts of 2 different color bigrams is ($=\frac{23}{12}$) (roughly 1.92) in a single trial, and that is ($=\frac{23}{4}$) (which is 5.75) in three trials combined.

Based on these calculations, we can apply the chi-squared goodness of fit test [8] to check if the observed counts follow the same distribution as the expected counts. We conduct this test five times to the data of each participant. The first three chi-squared tests each check the randomness of single-color choices in each of the three trials. The fourth chi-squared analysis checks the randomness of a single color over three trials combined (i.e. 72 choices). The fifth and final chi-squared checks the randomness of permutations of different color bigrams over all three trials. For all of these analyses the expected counts were greater than 5 (which is a precondition of analysis with chi-squared). The FREQ procedure in SAS 9.4 [43] was used to implement the chi-squared tests, and a SAS macro was written to automate the analysis procedure across the 30 participants.

Across the group of 30 participants who provided the test data, the mean p values for the randomness of individual choices (i.e., did they select all colors equally often) were all around 0.8, these p values were derived from single trials, as well as the calculation using performance across all three trials. As higher p values indicate greater appearance of randomness of responses, it appears that participants were quite good at this, and the measure may therefore not sufficiently challenge executive processes in this type of participant.

More challenging appears to be randomness of responding when measured by bigram frequencies (totals over three trials). The mean p value for this measure was 0.61 (range of scores = 0.02–0.99). The lower p value indicates that in general, the scores appeared to be less like a random set. For the proposed methods of response-by-response analysis with chi-squared to be useful as a method of quantifying executive control, certain qualities of the data distributions are desirable. One is that there should be a normal distribution of scores. This appears to be the case of the p values of bigram frequencies, as shown by a Shapiro-Wilk test: $W = 0.95$, $df = 30$, $p = 0.20$. In addition, skew values ($z = 1.12$) and kurtosis values ($z = 0.62$) were both within limits for assumption of normal distribution of data [21]. In contrast, equivalent analyses for the frequencies of single-color choices indicated that all had statistically non-normal distributions. Consequently, the p values of bigram frequencies appear to be more appropriate measures of the ability of participants to deliberately avoid patterned responding (i.e., give responses that appear random). For this reason, only the bigram frequencies were further analyzed.

The score distribution also has to be sufficiently broad that it can distinguish different levels of performance, that is, it contains sufficient variance. The coefficient of variance was found to be 0.45. This is somewhat higher than the coefficient of variance for the total task completion time (the conventionally used measure of performance on trail-making tasks), which was 0.21. As both the distributions for total time and the p values of bigram frequencies were normally distributed, we examined the Pearson zero-order correlation between the two measures of performance. That revealed a significant negative correlation, $r = -0.49$, $p = 0.006$. This suggests that, across participants, relatively poor task performance as measured by completion time is associated with relatively poor performance as measured by bigram frequencies.

These preliminary analyses therefore suggest that randomness of single choices is not a good way to measure top-down executive control in this novel task. However, bigram frequencies, represented as p values of how much the responses appear random, may function better as a summary measure of executive control. The potential implications and applications of this are described in the final section.

4   Discussion and Conclusions

4.1   Summary

In this preliminary report, we provided first details of a novel cognitive tool, that is nevertheless similar in many respects to other paper-and-pencil 'trails tasks' used widely in behavioral sciences to measure executive cognitive control [10,23, 39]. The principal difference being that this new task requires participants to make free choices, rather than to perform the task in a predefined way, which is the format of previous trails tasks. Moreover, we provide a method to analyze how well participants who perform the task can resist tendencies to pattern their responses.

The concept of free choice here is that the participants can, at each of 24 steps within each trial, choose between any of three colors without violating any rules. Admittedly, they are told to not choose the same color twice (hence limiting them from 4 to 3 options at each step), and they are instructed not to use any plans or strategies. So, they are constrained at the overall task level within a trial, but not at the individual choice level at each step. Although not told to respond randomly, to attempt to do so is the only remaining approach they have to guide their choices. This is why we consider them free choices. Nevertheless, following discussions from the workshop, additional studies are being run excluding Rule 4 (Try to choose all the colors equally often) as it may contradict the goal of randomness of single choices.

In addition, we provide a statistical method to describe how well individual participants were at avoiding patterned responding and effectively responding randomly. This approach uses p values derived from chi-squared analyses, calculated at the level of the individual.

However, the wider context is that we show how data collection methods in behavioral sciences can be approached differently, to allow measures that more closely align to the concept of executive cognitive control. We have previously argued that definitions of executive control, which emphasize processing in nonroutine or ambiguous situations to produce appropriate responses are best considered as divergent thinking [34]. Divergent and convergent thinking are concepts in the classification of cognitive processes that have been popular since the 1950's [16]. Despite this, the vast majority of tests used in experimental and clinical practice attempt to measure executive processes that are substantially convergent in their structure and analysis methods. Because divergent processes, as we have attempted to elicit in our Choice Trails Test via free choices, do not have unique right answers, novel ways of deriving a performance measure have to be explored, necessitating meditations on what exactly is meant by top-down executive cognitive control.

Consequently, our suggested method uses a procedure adopted from computer science, one that is frequently employed to test the abilities of random number generators [2,19]. Although this approach is a relatively novel application within cognitive sciences, similar approaches have been used to measure behavior in clinical neuroscience. For example, a statistical measure of randomness of responses was used to examine stereotypical responding in patients with schizophrenia when asked to guess the color of playing cards presented sequentially in a random order [13]. Similarly, patients with Alzheimer's disease have been shown to overproduce ascending counting patterns (e.g., 3-4-5) when asked to imagine repeatedly throwing a normal six-sided die and orally reporting the outcomes [6]. These and other similar divergent thinking studies of neuropsychiatric patients have mainly used the Random Number Generation Index of Evans (1978) [12]. However, that calculation appears to be very similar to chi-squared anyway. The benefits of using chi-squared-derived p values are that they are more easily computed in standard statistical software packages, and are well understood from their use in null-hypothesis testing.

4.2   Implications and Applications

The task described here may be useful as an alternative way to measure the ability of people to make free choices, in a nevertheless constrained task that allows for the individual to make choices that appear random, or which follow predictable, routine patterns. Much evidence from cognitive and brain sciences suggests that the human neurocognitive system tends to revert to routine patterns, as the alternative, top-down executive control, is resource demanding and subjectively effortful [34]. Moreover, the proposed methodology, of requesting that study participants avoid routine response biases and then estimating the randomness of their free choices, can potentially be applied to many other existing cognitive laboratory and clinical assessment methods.

In the specific task presented here, we found that that the analysis method produced results that overlapped with the traditional methods of measurement in similar tasks (i.e., time taken to task completion). Both measures were correlated, suggesting that both are measuring some aspect of executive control. One observation made was that our approach involving a response-by-response analysis produced greater between-individual variance in performance scores than the traditional overall time-based method. This may have some practical application. There has recently been concern within cognitive sciences involving behavioral studies that task measures are often statistically unreliable, producing many Type II statistical errors when used for hypothesis testing [9,17]. This is because cognitive tasks have generally been developed for laboratory-based experimental studies to elicit effects which are more apparent and easier to detect when between-individual variance is low. However, that reduces their reliability and makes them poor measures of how people differ in their abilities. That reliable variability is often needed when, for example, making brain-behavior associations by linking cognitive test scores to functional or structural neuroanatomy, genetic and biomarkers etc. The methods proposed here may therefore function better as indices of individual differences in executive processing than they will in tests of experimental manipulations on processing.

However, this need not be a limitation. We argue that the method of analysis described here, which focuses on a more microanalysis of response-by-response data, can be performed in tandem with traditional analyses which focus on overall task performance. This can be done whether the study paradigm is experimental or individual-differences based. This is a wise approach anyway in that the current methods which focus on overall task performance can obscure real differences in cognitive processes that underlie performance. It is known that multiple different processes can produce the same behavior. This is known as functional equivalence in traditional cognitive science [46] and degeneracy in clinical and cognitive neurosciences [31]. Multiple analyses of task performance can help to delineate those different underlying processes.

In fact, one of us has previously argued that there is a need for clinical assessments of cognitive abilities to learn from traditional cognitive sciences [33]. Paper-and-pencil based cognitive test methods, such as described in this paper, are widespread in clinical cognitive assessment, due to their simplicity and portability. That allows them to be used in bedside testing. This contrasts with often highly-technical methods used in experimental cognitive psychology that are difficult to transpose from the laboratory setting. However, even bedside-derived cognitive data can benefit from the process-based analyses used in cognitive sciences. Traditionally, cognitive science analyses on behavioral data have used methods to produce data with 'temporal density' that can be used to track processing over short-time periods [47]. Although this is now common in laboratory-based cognitive studies (e.g., eye tracking), clinical testing tends to rely on overall performance measures. In this paper we show how dense data can still be elicited using the traditional paper-and-pencil tests typical of clinical cognitive assessments.

4.3 Conclusions

Executive functions, by definition, deal with ambiguous stimulus-response associations and require that willed choices be made [14, 20, 25, 27, 42]. This conceptually aligns closely with the idea of divergent thinking—a broad definition that invokes cognitive processes that are creative and result in free choice of responses [16]. However, there has long been a disjunction between conceptualization of executive functions, and methods of measurement used in behavioral sciences. Here we show that common testing methods, such as the paper-and-pencil trails tests [10, 23, 39] can be altered to change them from evoking convergent, schematic action selections, to evoking divergent, free choices. This necessarily requires a different approach to how performance is quantified. We suggest a method using p values. We argue that this approach allows for new ways to operationalize and measure top-down cognitive control in human behavior. And these new ways may allow fresh insights into these high-level cognitive processes. Future research will ultimately support, or challenge, the utility of this approach.

Acknowledgments. This research was supported by a grant from Research Affairs at the Faculty of Psychology, Chulalongkorn University.

Disclosure of Interests. The authors have no competing interests to declare that are relevant to the content of this article.

References

1. Alexander, M.P., Stuss, D.T., Picton, T., Shallice, T., Gillingham, S.: Regional frontal injuries cause distinct impairments in cognitive control. Neurology **68**(18), 1515–23 (2007). https://doi.org/10.1212/01.wnl.0000261482.99569.fb
2. Almaraz Luengo, E., Alaña Olivares, B., García Villalba, L.J., Hernandez-Castro, J., Hurley-Smith, D.: Stringent test suite: Ent battery revisited for efficient p value computation. J. Cryptogr. Eng. **13**(2), 235–249 (2023). https://doi.org/10.1007/s13389-023-00313-5
3. Baddeley, A.: Is working memory working? The fifteenth Bartlett lecture. Q. J. Exp. Psychol. A Hum. Exp. Psychol. **44**(1), 1–31 (1992). https://doi.org/10.1080/14640749208401281

4. Baggetta, P., Alexander, P.A.: Conceptualization and operationalization of executive function. Mind Brain Educ. **10**(1), 10–33 (2016). https://doi.org/10.1111/mbe.12100

5. Beatty, W.W., Testa, J.A., English, S., Winn, P.: Influences of clustering and switching on the verbal fluency performance of patients with Alzheimer's disease. Neuropsychol. Dev. Cogn. B Aging Neuropsychol. Cogn. **4**(4), 273–279 (1997). https://doi.org/10.1080/13825589708256652

6. Brugger, P., Monsch, A.U., Salmon, D.P., Butters, N.: Random number generation in dementia of the Alzheimer type: a test of frontal executive functions. Neuropsychologia **34**(2), 97–103 (1996). https://doi.org/10.1016/0028-3932(95)00066-6

7. Burgess, P.W., Shallice, T.: Response suppression, initiation and strategy use following frontal lobe lesions. Neuropsychologia **34**(4), 263–72 (1996). https://doi.org/10.1016/0028-3932(95)00104-2

8. Cochran, W.G.: The x2 test of goodness of fit. Ann. Math. Stat. **23**, 315–345 (1952). https://doi.org/10.1214/aoms/1177729380

9. Dang, J., King, K.M., Inzlicht, M.: Why are self-report and behavioral measures weakly correlated? Trends Cogn. Sci. **24**(4), 267–269 (2020). https://doi.org/10.1016/j.tics.2020.01.007

10. Delis, D., Kaplan, E., Kramer, J.: Delis-Kaplan Executive Function System Technical Manual. The Psychological Corporation, San Antonio, TX (2001)

11. Diaz, M., Sailor, K., Cheung, D., Kuslansky, G.: Category size effects in semantic and letter fluency in Alzheimer's patients. Brain Lang. **89**(1), 108–14 (2004). https://doi.org/10.1016/S0093-934X(03)00307-9

12. Evans, F.J.: Monitoring attention deployment by random number generation: an index to measure subjective randomness. Bull. Psychon. Soc. **12**(1), 35–38 (1978). https://doi.org/10.3758/BF03329617

13. Frith, C.D., Done, D.J.: Stereotyped responding by schizophrenic patients on a two-choice guessing task. Psychol. Med. **13**(4), 779–86 (1983). https://doi.org/10.1017/s0033291700051485

14. Frith, C.D., Friston, K., Liddle, P.F., Frackowiak, R.S.: Willed action and the prefrontal cortex in man: a study with pet. Proc. R. Soc. Lond. B Biol. Sci. **244**(1311), 241–246 (1991). https://doi.org/10.1098/rspb.1991.0077

15. Goel, V., Grafman, J.: Are the frontal lobes implicated in "planning" functions? Interpreting data from the tower of Hanoi. Neuropsychologia **33**(5), 623–42 (1995). https://doi.org/10.1016/0028-3932(95)90866-p

16. Guilford, J.: The structure of intellect. Psychol. Bull. **53**(4), 267–293 (1956). https://doi.org/10.1037/h0040755

17. Hedge, C., Powell, G., Sumner, P.: The reliability paradox: why robust cognitive tasks do not produce reliable individual differences. Behav. Res. Methods **50**(3), 1166–1186 (2017). https://doi.org/10.3758/s13428-017-0935-1

18. Hughes, C., Ensor, R.: Individual differences in growth in executive function across the transition to school predict externalizing and internalizing behaviors and self-perceived academic success at 6 years of age. J. Exp. Child Psychol. **108**(3), 663–76 (2011). https://doi.org/10.1016/j.jecp.2010.06.005

19. Hurley-Smith, D., Patsakis, C., Hernandez-Castro, J.: On the unbearable lightness of fips 140–2 randomness tests. IEEE Trans. Inf. Forensics Secur. **17**, 3946–3958 (2020). https://doi.org/10.1109/TIFS.2020.2988505

20. Jahanshahi, M.: Willed action and its impairments. Cogn. Neuropsychol. **15**(6–8), 483–533 (1998). https://doi.org/10.1080/026432998381005

21. Kim, H.Y.: Statistical notes for clinical researchers: assessing normal distribution (2) using skewness and kurtosis. Restor. Dent. Endod. **38**(1), 52–4 (2013). https://doi.org/10.5395/rde.2013.38.1.52

22. Knoblock, C.A.: Abstracting the tower of Hanoi. In: Working Notes of AAAI-90 Workshop on Automatic Generation of Approximations and Abstractions, Boston, MA, no. 4976, pp. 1–11 (1990)

23. Maj, M., et al.: Evaluation of two new neuropsychological tests designed to minimize cultural bias in the assessment of HIV-1 seropositive persons: a who study. Arch. Clin. Neuropsychol. **8**(2), 123–35 (1993). https://doi.org/10.1016/0887-6177(93)90030-5

24. McMillen, P., Levin, M.: Collective intelligence: a unifying concept for integrating biology across scales and substrates. Commun. Biol. **7**(1), 378 (2024). https://doi.org/10.1038/s42003-024-06037-4

25. Miller, E., Wallis, J.: Executive function and higher-order cognition: definition and neural substrates. In: Squire, L.R. (ed.) Encyclopedia of Neuroscience, vol. 4. Academic Press, Oxford (2009)

26. Murdoch, D.J., Tsai, Y.L., Adcock, J.: P-values are random variables. Amer. Statist. **62**(3), 242–245 (2008). https://doi.org/10.1198/000313008X332421

27. Norman, D.A., Shallice, T.: Attention to action: willed and automatic control of behavior. In: Davidson, R.J., Schwartz, G.E., Shapiro, D. (eds.) Consciousness and Self-regulation: Advances in Research and Theory, vol. 4, pp. 1–18. Plenum, New York (1986)

28. Open Science Collaboration: Estimating the reproducibility of psychological science. Science **349**(6251), aac4716 (2015). https://doi.org/10.1126/science.aac4716

29. Panikratova, Y.R., Vlasova, R.M., Akhutina, T.V., Korneev, A.A., Sinitsyn, V.E., Pechenkova, E.V.: Functional connectivity of the dorsolateral prefrontal cortex contributes to different components of executive functions. Int. J. Psychophysiol. **151**, 70–79 (2020). https://doi.org/10.1016/j.ijpsycho.2020.02.013

30. Phillips, L.H., Wynn, V., Gilhooly, K.J., Della Sala, S., Logie, R.H.: The role of memory in the tower of London task. Memory **7**(2), 209–31 (1999). https://doi.org/10.1080/741944066

31. Pluck, G.: The misguided veneration of averageness in clinical neuroscience: a call to value diversity over typicality. Brain Sci. **13**(6), 860 (2023). https://doi.org/10.3390/brainsci13060860

32. Pluck, G., Amraoui, D., Fornell-Villalobos, I.: Brief communication: Reliability of the D-KEFS tower test in samples of children and adolescents in Ecuador. Appl. Neuropsychol. Child **10**(2), 158–164 (2021). https://doi.org/10.1080/21622965.2019.1629922

33. Pluck, G., Ariyabuddhiphongs, K.: Clinical cognitive sciences. In: Aldini, A. (ed.) Software Engineering and Formal Methods. SEFM 2023 Collocated Workshops. SEFM 2023. Lecture Notes in Computer Science, vol. 14568. Springer, Cham (2024). https://doi.org/10.1007/978-3-031-66021-4_9

34. Pluck, G., Cerone, A., Villagomez-Pacheco, D.: Executive function and intelligent goal-directed behavior: perspectives from psychology, neurology, and computer science. In: Masci, P., Bernardeschi, C., Graziani, P., Koddenbrock, M., Palmieri, M. (eds.) Software Engineering and Formal Methods. SEFM 2022 Collocated Workshops. SEFM 2022. Lecture Notes in Computer Science, vol. 13765, pp. 324–350. Springer, Cham (2023). https://doi.org/10.1007/978-3-031-26236-4_27

35. Pluck, G., Crespo-Andrade, C., Parreño, P., Haro, K.I., Martínez, M.A., Pontón, S.C.: Executive functions and intelligent goal-directed behavior: a neuropsychologi-

cal approach to understanding success using professional sales as a real-life measure. Psychol. Neurosci. **13**(2), 158–175 (2020). https://doi.org/10.1037/pne0000195

36. Pluck, G., Villagomez-Pacheco, D., Karolys, M.I., Montano-Cordova, M.E., Almeida-Meza, P.: Response suppression, strategy application, and working memory in the prediction of academic performance and classroom misbehavior: a neuropsychological approach. Trends Neurosci. Educ. **17**, 100121 (2019). https://doi.org/10.1016/j.tine.2019.100121

37. Poldrack, R.A., et al.: The cognitive atlas: toward a knowledge foundation for cognitive neuroscience. Front. Neuroinform. **5**, 17 (2011). https://doi.org/10.3389/fninf.2011.00017

38. Pribram, K.: The primate frontal cortex– executive of the brain. In: Pribram, K., Luria, A. (eds.) Psychophysiology of the Frontal Lobes, pp. 293–314. Academic Press, New York (1973). https://doi.org/10.1016/B978-0-12-564340-5.50019-6

39. Reitan, R.M.: The relation of the trail making test to organic brain damage. J. Consult. Clin. Psychol. **19**(5), 393–394 (1955). https://doi.org/10.1037/h0044509

40. Robinson, G., Shallice, T., Bozzali, M., Cipolotti, L.: The differing roles of the frontal cortex in fluency tests. Brain **135**(7), 2202–14 (2012). https://doi.org/10.1093/brain/aws142

41. Roebers, C.M., Rothlisberger, M., Cimeli, P., Michel, E., Neuenschwander, R.: School enrollment and executive functioning: a longitudinal perspective on developmental changes, the influence of learning context, and the prediction of pre-academic skills. Eur. J. Dev. Psychol. **8**(5), 526–540 (2011). https://doi.org/10.1080/17405629.2011.571841

42. Rolls, E.T.: Willed action, free will, and the stochastic neurodynamics of decision-making. Front. Integr. Neurosci. **6**, 68 (2012). https://doi.org/10.3389/fnint.2012.00068

43. SAS Institute Inc: SAS/STAT® 15.3 user's guide. SAS Institute Inc., Cary, NC (2023)

44. Shallice, T.: Specific impairments of planning. Philos. Trans. R. Soc. Lond. B Biol. Sci. **298**(1089), 199–209 (1982). https://doi.org/10.1098/rstb.1982.0082

45. Shallice, T., Burgess, P.: The domain of supervisory processes and temporal organization of behaviour. Philos. Trans. R. Soc. Lond. B Biol. Sci. **351**(1346), 1405–1411 (1996). https://doi.org/10.1098/rstb.1996.0124

46. Simon, H.: The functional equivalence of problem solving skills. Cogn. Psychol. **7**(2), 268–288 (1975). https://doi.org/10.1016/0010-0285(75)90012-2

47. Simon, H.A.: Information processing models of cognition. Annu. Rev. Psychol. **30**(1), 363–396 (1979). https://doi.org/10.1146/annurev.ps.30.020179.002051

48. Winter, W.E., Broman, M., Rose, A.L., Reber, A.S.: The assessment of cognitive procedural learning in amnesia: why the tower of Hanoi has fallen down. Brain Cogn. **45**(1), 79–96 (2001). https://doi.org/10.1006/brcg.2000.1257

49. Youyou, W., Yang, Y., Uzzi, B.: A discipline-wide investigation of the replicability of psychology papers over the past two decades. Proc. Natl. Acad. Sci. U.S.A. **120**(6), e2208863120 (2023). https://doi.org/10.1073/pnas.2208863120

50. Zhang, C., Lipovetzky, N., Kemp, C.: Comparing AI planning algorithms with humans on the tower of London task. In: Goldwater, M., Anggoro, F.K., Hayes, B.K., Ong, D.C. (eds.) Proceedings of the Annual Meeting of the Cognitive Science Society, vol. 45 (2023). https://escholarship.org/uc/item/5164p0rz

Towards a Readability Criterion for Humans and Machines

Pedro Quaresma[1] and Pierluigi Graziani[2]

[1] University of Coimbra, Coimbra, Portugal
pedro@mat.uc.pt
[2] University of Urbino, Urbino, Italy
pierluigi.graziani@uniurb.it

Abstract. Previous research has explored criteria for evaluating the simplicity and readability of geometric proofs generated by theorem provers, primarily from a human perspective. In particular, Graziani and Quaresma examined the simplicity and readability of proofs produced by theorem provers implementing the area method, introducing geometrographic coefficients to quantify different aspects of proof complexity. Building on their work, this study extends their analysis by investigating the computational effort involved in the proof process, specifically by measuring CPU time. The objective is to determine whether, within the context of proof generation, the hypothesised human effort aligns with the machine's measured computational workload. Given the strong connection between human effort and proof readability, this comparison may offer valuable insights for improving the readability of machine-generated proofs by considering both human cognitive constraints and computational limitations.

1 Introduction

Automated Theorem Proving (ATP) is a well-established area of research in mathematics, boasting numerous methods and results alongside many open problems that highlight its vitality. Among the various domains within ATP, geometry stands out due to its history and the challenging problems it proposes.

Two prominent challenging problems in ATP are particularly noteworthy: the *simplicity of a proof* and the *readability of a proof*.

- The first problem seeks a criterion to quantify the simplicity of a proof.
- The second problem seeks a criterion to quantify the readability of a proof.

The first author was partially financed through national funds by FCT - Fundação para a Ciência e a Tecnologia, I.P., in the framework of the Project UIDB/00326/2025 and UIDP/00326/2025. The second author was supported by the Italian Ministry of Education, University, and Research through the PRIN 2022 project *Developing Kleene Logics and their Applications* (DeKLA), project code 2022SM4XC8.

J. Proença et al. (Eds.): SEFM 2024, LNCS 15551, pp. 254–270, 2026.
https://doi.org/10.1007/978-3-031-94748-3_19

Regarding the simplicity problem, historical contributions from scholars such as David Hilbert, who proposed a framework for identifying the simplest possible proofs [4,5,19], and Émile Lemoine [11], who introduced the notion of *Geometrography* to measure the simplicity of geometric constructions, underscore the enduring importance of this concept. Recent advancements in automated theorem proving have refined these studies on simplicity. For instance, Graziani and Quaresma's modernisation of Lemoine's Geometrography [16–18] exemplifies contemporary efforts to integrate historical methods with cutting-edge technology. Their modernisation leverages tools and automated proving methods, such as the *Geometry Constructions LaTeX Converter (GCLC)* and the *area method*[1].

Concerning the readability problem, it is a cornerstone of mathematical communication. Readability refers to the ease with which a reader can comprehend a written text, distinct from legibility, which pertains to recognising individual characters. To our knowledge, there are two precise proposals to measure the readability of a proof: the first by Shang-Ching Chou et al. [2], and the second by Freek Wiedijk [20], known as the *de Bruijn factor*. Also, in this case, recent advancements in automated theorem proving have refined these studies on readability. Graziani and Quaresma [16], dissatisfied with the previous criteria—one being too restrictive and the other too general—applied methodologies from the study of simplicity to explore the readability of geometric proofs, proposing not only their criterion but also a general methodology for analysing this characteristic in the context of proofs produced via the area method. Analysing the issue of proof readability, they aimed to bridge the gap between automated systems and human mathematicians. Making proofs easier to understand not only helps people grasp concepts more effectively but also improves how automated systems communicate their results.

The study of the simplicity and the readability issues led Graziani and Quaresma to analyse interesting elements in the geometric proofs. Given a mathematical proof as a sequence of steps, in addition to the coefficient of simplicity, CS_{proof}, giving the simplicity coefficient for the overall proof, it is possible to consider other coefficients, e.g.,

- CS_{gcl}, simplicity coefficient for the geometric construction (the conjecture);
- CT_{proof}, the total number of steps in the proof;
- $CS_{proofmax}$, the highest simplicity coefficient of the lemmas/definitions applications, it gives the simplicity coefficient for the most difficult step of the proof;

---

[1] The *area method* is a decision procedure for constructive theorems in euclidean plane geometry. It is a mix of algebraic and synthetic methods. The method express the theorem as a sequence of geometric constructions and proceeds by eliminating every occurrence of the constructed points in the goal, using a set of elimination lemmas. At the end, the conclusion expressed by an equality between polynomials in some geometric quantities (areas, ratios and pythagoras differences), collapses to an equality between two rational expressions involving only free points, if the expressions on the two sides are equal, the conjecture is a theorem, otherwise it is not.

- CD$_\text{typeproof}$, the number of different types of lemmas used in the proof;
- CD$_\text{highproof}$, the number of different steps of high difficulty in the proof;

and also

- The proof script (all the steps in the formal proof);
- The corresponding line chart or proof trace, given by the simplicity coefficient of each step.

Graziani and Quaresma called all these coefficients the *Geometrographic Coefficients*.

Let's consider, for example, the Ceva's theorem. In the rest of the paper, capital letters will denote points in the plane, ΔABC will denote the triangle with vertices A, B, and C, $\overline{AB}$ will denote the length of segment AB and $AB \cap CD$ will denote the intersection of lines AB and CD (Fig. 1).

Theorem 1 (Ceva's Theorem, [8]). *Let ΔABC be a triangle and P be any point in the plane. Let $D = AP \cap CB$, $E = BP \cap AC$, and $F = CP \cap AB$. Show that:* $\frac{\overline{AF}}{\overline{FB}} \times \frac{\overline{BD}}{\overline{DC}} \times \frac{\overline{CE}}{\overline{EA}} = 1$. *$P$ should not be in the lines parallels to AC, AB and BC and passing through B, C and A respectively.*

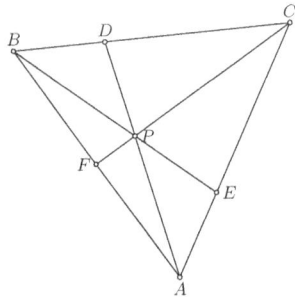

Fig. 1. Geometric Construction, Ceva's Theorem

The proof script of Ceva's theorem, produced by the *GCLC* prover based on the area method, has all the details explained, and it fills two pages, almost three pages if the notes about the non-degeneracy conditions and the proof itself are considered (see [16]).

The Geometrographic coefficients of Ceva's Theorem Proof are the following:

$$\textbf{Ceva's Theorem} \begin{cases} \text{CS}_\text{proof} = 220 \\ \text{CS}_\text{gcl} = 22 \\ \text{CT}_\text{proof} = 32 \\ \text{CS}_\text{proofmax} = 84 \\ \text{CD}_\text{typeproof} = 3 \\ \text{CD}_\text{highproof} = 0 \end{cases}$$

The line chart (or proof trace) is shown in Fig. 2. In it, the sequences of algebraic simplifications are condensed in only one step (for a more condensed view of the graph).

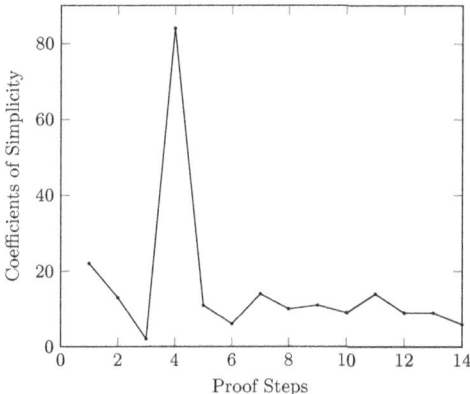

Fig. 2. Ceva's Theorem, Geometrography Proof Trace

This line chart graphically represents the progress of the proof with weights associated with the various steps, expressing their difficulty via their *simplicity coefficient*. It is based on assumptions about the weight (effort) of certain parameters related to the generation of geometric proofs (using a specific method) by humans.

This article focuses on the study of line charts in relation to geometric proofs, addressing a key question: do the assumptions and weights used to generate these charts reflect solely the reasoning of the human proving the theorem, or do they also take into account the computational effort of the machine in constructing the proof by forward reasoning? In other words, if the line chart resembles an electroencephalogram, as Graziani and Quaresma wrote [16], can it be considered also a kind of electroencephalogram of the machine during the theorem proving? Or is the encephalogram related to the human-proving activity and the machine-proving activity different from each other?

Therefore, building on the foundational concepts and issues analysed in [16], this paper introduces a new objective: comparing the complexity of line charts generated in geometric constructions with the computational effort required by processors in theorem proving. By examining the correlation between the hypothesised human effort and the measured machine computational effort during the proof process, we aim to determine whether the weights/efforts hypothesised for humans align with the actual computational workload of the machine. Furthermore, given that human effort is closely linked to proof readability, this comparison may also provide valuable insights into this aspect.

Overview of the Paper. The paper is organised as follows: Sect. 2 provides an introduction to *GCLC*; Sect. 3 summarises Graziani and Quaresma's research on simplicity and readability; Sect. 4 describes the methodology for analysing processor activity; Sect. 5 presents line charts that compare proof simplicity coefficients with the computational effort required for theorem proving; Sect. 6 presents the analysis of the results, conclusions and future work.

2   *GCLC* (from Geometry Constructions → LATEX Converter)

To better understand Graziani and Quaresma's approach to *Geometrography* and our approach to the problem analysed in the present paper, it is useful to briefly introduce the *GCLC* tool. *GCLC* (Geometry Constructions → LATEX Converter),[2] developed by Predrag Janičić [6], is a specialised software tool designed to facilitate the creation of geometric constructions and their seamless conversion into LATEX format. This tool bridges the gap between geometric visualisation and high-quality typesetting, making it invaluable for educational and research purposes in mathematics.

GCLC describes geometric constructions using a simple and intuitive language known as *gcl* [7]. This language allows users to define points, lines, circles, and other geometric objects and specify their relationships and constructions. The core idea is to use a sequence of primitive construction steps, such as drawing a line between two points, finding the intersection of two lines, or drawing a circle given its centre and a point on the circumference. These primitive steps can be combined to form more complex constructions.

To illustrate the capabilities of *GCLC*, consider the following example, which constructs a basic geometric figure, a triangle with a circumcircle. The *gcl* code for this example is as follows:

```
%%% Constructive steps
point A 50 65
point B 45 35
point C 90 35
med a C B
med b A C
intersec O a b
%%% Drawing steps
cmark_lt A
cmark_lb B
cmark_rb C
drawsegment A B
drawsegment B C
drawsegment C A
drawcircle O A
```

Listing 1.1. *gcl*—Specification—Triangle & circuncircle

---

[2] https://github.com/janicicpredrag/gclc.

The *gcl* language has commands to build the geometric construction and commands to draw the corresponding figure. This code (see Listing 1.1) defines three points, A, B, and C, with their respective coordinates, the segments CB and AC perpendicular bisectors (mediatrice), and the intersection of those two lines, the point O, the centre of the circuncentre. The geometric construction is independent of the coordinates, which are solely used to draw the figure. The cmark commands, marks these points on the figure. The drawsegment commands are used to draw the sides (segments) of the triangle ABC and the drawcircle command constructs the circumcircle passing through the three vertices of the triangle. As it can be seen by this example, the construction and the drawing are two separate parts of a *gcl* specification. A user cannot draw an non-existing element, but what to draw, or not, it is a user's decision. From the automated theorem provers, embedded in $GCLC$, point of view, the drawing section is superfluous.

Once the gcl file (e.g., triangle.gcl) is created, it can be processed by $GCLC$ to generate a LaTeX file.

This process integrates the geometric figure into the LaTeX document, ensuring the final output is mathematically precise and visually appealing (Fig. 3).

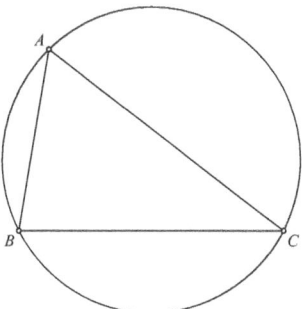

Fig. 3. *gcl*—Drawing—Triangle & circuncircle

$GCLC$ also supports more advanced geometric constructions and transformations see [6,7] and also the manual, distributed with the software.

$GCLC$ also contains a set of embedded automated theorem provers for geometry, e.g. the one based in the *Area Method* [8–10].

With GCLC introduced, we can now return to *Geometrography*.

3   *GCLC* and Geometrography

Geometrography, "alias the art of geometric constructions", aims at providing a tool: (i) to designate every geometric construction by a symbol that manifests its simplicity and exactitude; (ii) to teach the simplest way to execute an assigned construction; (iii) to discuss a known solution to a problem and eventually replacing it with a better solution; (iv) to compare different solutions for a problem, by deciding which is the most exact and the simplest solution from the point of view of *Geometrography*.

Émile Lemoine [11] in his *Geometrography* defined two coefficients to measure the relative difficulty of performing some geometric constructions. This approach is applied to ruler and compass geometry, i.e., geometric constructions made only with the help of a ruler and a compass. Considering the modifications proposed by John S. Mackay [12], the following **R**uler and **C**ompass constructions and the corresponding coefficients can be analysed.

To place the edge of the ruler in coincidence with one point . . . . R_1
To place the edge of the ruler in coincidence with two points . . . . $2R_1$
To draw a straight line . . . . R_2
To put one point of the compasses on a determinate point . . . . C_1
To put the points of the compasses on two determinate points . . . . $2C_1$
To describe a circle . . . . C_2

Then a given construction is measured against the number of uses of those elementary steps. For a given construction expressed by the equation:

$$l_1 R_1 + l_2 R_2 + m_1 C_1 + m_2 C_2$$

where l_i and m_j are coefficients denoting the number of times any particular operation is performed. The number $(l_1 + l_2 + m_1 + m_2)$ is called the *coefficient of simplicity* of the construction, and it denotes the total number of operations performed. The number $(l_1 + m_1)$ is called the *coefficient of exactitude* of the construction and it denotes the number of preparatory operations on which the exactitude of the construction (made with the help of physical, inaccurate, tools) depends [12,13].

Graziani and Quaresma proposed a modernisation and generalisation of classical[3] *Geometrography* in [16–18] using the tools of the dynamic geometry systems (DGS) and using *GCLC*.

Considering the operations: *define a point, anywhere in the plane*, D and *define a given object, using other objects*, C, the following values for the *GCLC* basic constructions are obtained:

point – fix a point in the plane . . . . D
line – uses two points . . . . $2C$
circle – uses two points . . . . $2C$
intersec – uses two lines . . . . $2C$
intersec – uses four points . . . . $4C$
intersec2 – uses a circle and a circle or line . . . . $2C$
midpoint – uses two points . . . . $2C$

---

[3] We will refer to the *Geometrography* of Lemoine or Mackay as *classical Geometrography*.

`med` – uses two points .... $2C$
`bis` – uses three points .... $3C$
`perp` – uses a point and a line .... $2C$
`foot` – uses a point and a line .... $2C$
`parallel` – uses a point and a line .... $2C$
`onsegment` – uses two points .... $2C$
`online` – uses two points .... $2C$
`oncircle` – uses two points .... $2C$

In the modernisation of the *Geometrography*, the *coefficient of exactitude* loses its meaning; the DGS executes the constructions, so they are accurate (exact). However, the *coefficient of simplicity* of the constructions can still be useful. It can be used to classify constructions by levels of simplicity. A new dimension can also be added, the *coefficient of freedom*, given by the degree of freedom a given geometric object has, e.g., "a point in a line" has one degree of freedom, a point in the plane has two degrees of freedom, etc. This new coefficient gives a value to the dynamism of the geometric construction. Graziani and Quaresma calculated these coefficients for all constructions in the *TGTP* repository [14].[4] In this article only the *coefficient of simplicity* will be considered. For the *GCLC* constructions contained in *TGTP* an average value of simplicity (CS_{gcl}) of 20.8 was obtained. Using the k-means clustering function implemented in the statistics package of *Octave*,[5] three classes of geometric constructions, describing an increasing level of complexity, were defined: simple constructions, $1 \leq CS_{gcl} \leq 18$; average complexity constructions, $18 < CS_{gcl} \leq 28$; complex constructions, $CS_{gcl} > 28$. *TGTP* contain 71 simple constructions; 81 average complexity constructions; 28 complex constructions.

For example (*TGTP* problem `GE00369`): "In triangle $\triangle ABC$, let F be the midpoint of the side BC, and D and E the feet of the altitudes on AB and AC, respectively. FG is perpendicular to DE at G. Show that G is the midpoint of DE", has a geometric construction with a coefficient of simplicity 19 (see Fig. 4), so an average complexity construction.

Graziani and Quaresma used the same approach to take into consideration of synthetic geometric proofs, i.e., proofs based on a geometric axiomatic theory, using geometric inference rules. Considering the proofs produced by the Geometric Automated Theorem Prover (GATP) *GCLC*, implementing the area method [6,8], they calculated a more general *coefficient of simplicity* for all the axioms and lemmas of the theory.

Apart from the geometric constructions in which the proof is based (with the coefficient of simplicity $n\mathbf{Cnst}$), other steps must be considered.

(Elementary) Algebraic Simplification.................................(**AS**)
(Elementary) Geometric Simplification.................................(**GS**)

---

[4] http://hilbert.mat.uc.pt/TGTP/.
[5] GNU Octave, version 6.1.1, package octave-statistics, function means https://octave.sourceforge.io/statistics/function/kmeans.html.

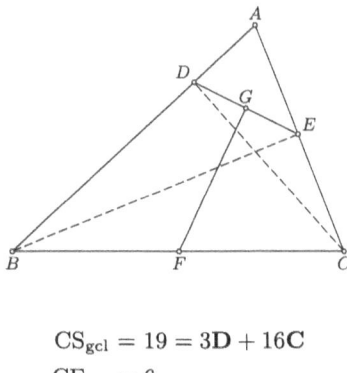

$$\text{CS}_{\text{gcl}} = 19 = 3\textbf{D} + 16\textbf{C}$$
$$\text{CF}_{\text{gcl}} = 6$$

Fig. 4. Geometric Construction, *TGTP* problem GEO0369

Application of the Area Method Lemma n .... $(\textbf{AML}_\textbf{n})$

A given proof can thus be measured against the number of those steps.[6] For a given proof expressed by the equation:

$$n_1\textbf{Cnst} + n_2\textbf{AS} + n_3\textbf{GS} + \sum_{j=l_1}^{l_k} \textbf{AML}_\textbf{j}$$

The coefficient of simplicity for the proof would be:

$$\text{CS}_{\text{proof}} = n_1 + n_2 + n_3 + \sum_{j=l_1}^{l_k} \text{CS}_{\text{proof}}(\textbf{AML}_\textbf{j})$$

Each lemma of the area method, $\textbf{AML}_\textbf{j}$, has a corresponding simplicity coefficient, the term, $\sum_{j=l_1}^{l_k} \text{CS}_{\text{proof}}(\textbf{AML}_\textbf{j})$, is the sum of all those values, for all the lemmas used in the proof. To achieve this for each area method lemma, the corresponding simplicity coefficients were calculated [15].

Given that a mathematical proof is a sequence of steps, in addition to the coefficient of simplicity, Graziani and Quaresma defined the other coefficients shown in the *Introduction*: e.g., the total number of steps in the proof; the value of the most difficult step in the proof; the number of different steps of high difficulty in the proof; the number of different types of steps (lemmas) in the proof; and finally a proof script, a numerical description of the proof, and a corresponding line chart or proof trace.

---

[6] By elementary algebraic simplification, it is understood the basic algebraic operations: addition, subtraction, multiplication, division, and their properties of commutativity, associativity, and distributivity. By elementary geometric simplification, the direct application of the definition of the area method quantities is understood. These steps are called *trivial steps*.

It is important to note that to obtain the coefficient $CD_{highproof}$ (hp) the area method lemmas implemented in the GATP $GCLC$ were analysed, and, using the k-means clustering function implemented in the statistics package of $Octave$, divided into three categories: low difficulty ($hp < 284$), medium difficulty ($284 \leq hp < 1848$) and high difficulty ($hp \geq 1848$).

The examined coefficients reveal key aspects of the proof framework used by Graziani and Quaresma [16] to analyse the issue of proof readability.

Applying the $Geometrography$ to the area method proofs contained in the repository $TGTP$, using the GATP $GCLC$ with the full level of detail, and using the geometrographic coefficients Graziani and Quaresma argued in favour of the following new readability coefficient [16] for geometric proofs:

Geometrographic Readability Coefficient of Proofs (GRCP)

$$GRCP = ((CS_{proof} - CT_{proof}) \times (CD_{highproof} + CD_{typeproof}))$$

This coefficient relates four quantities: the simplicity coefficient of the proof, the total number of steps in the proof, the number of different steps with high-difficulty in the proof, the number of different lemmas used in the proof.

The first factor approximates the simplicity coefficient of the non-trivial steps in the proof. Given that in CT_{proof} the construction is equal to 1 step, as well as every application of a lemma, every **AS** step and every **GS** step (i.e., the **AS** and **GS** steps weight is 1), if CT_{proof} is subtracted from CS_{proof} what will be removed are surely all the trivial steps and also 1 from CS_{gcl} and 1 for each application of the lemmas (but the weight of those steps is much grater then 1).

The second factor accounts for the difficult steps. Steps that potentiality make the proof much harder to follow, steps where the normal flow of the proof would be interrupted to jump to the proof of the lemma, resuming after completing the lemma's proof. Adding the number of high-difficulty steps with the number of different lemmas used in the proof gave a multiplying factor for the overall complexity of the proof. A final note about this second factor: a high-difficulty step is, for sure, a lemma application, nevertheless, it is felt that the high-difficulty nature of the lemma is a sufficient reason for this double counting.

Multiplying these factors, the approximation for the overall simplicity coefficient and the number of difficult steps—both elements that are believed to characterise the readability of a proof—the readability coefficient of a proof is obtained.

Therefore, considering 71 theorems and their area method proofs, from the $TGTP$ repository and using, again, the k-means clustering function from $Octave$, the proofs can be divided into the following classes of Geometrographic readability:[7]

---

[7] The actual values were rounded for better readability.

- readable ($high - readability$), $GRCP \leq 48000$;
- medium-readability $48000 < GRCP \leq 135000$;
- low-readability, $GRCP > 135000$.

For example the $GRCP$ for GEO0001, Ceva's proofs is: $GRCP_{GEO0001} = (220 - 32) \times (0 + 3) = 564 \leq 48000$, so a readable (high-readability) proof.

Each geometric proof can thus be analysed in terms of its simplicity and readability by examining its various coefficients. Finally, a line chart or proof trace can be associated with each proof, graphically representing its simplicity and readability.

Armed with these analyses, we can now proceed to tackle our problem: to examine, through the study of line charts or proof traces, the correlation between the hypothesised human effort and the measured machine computational effort during the proof process.

The next step in addressing the problem is methodological. We begin by examining how it can be approached technically, a possibility made feasible by the very nature of $GCLC$.

4   Methodological Interlude: Insights into Processor Computational Effort

As we have seen, $GCLC$ plays a fundamental role in defining a modernisation of $Geometrography$. Beyond this role, $GCLC$ can also be useful for studying the computational effort of the machine's processor when proving a given geometry theorem using the area method.

The $GCLC$ prover is a open source project.[8] For that reason it was possible to access the source code and modify it to include the "watch points". The chrono $C++$ library, for dealing with time, was used. To match the first step of the (human) proof, the comprehension of the geometric construction, the step of the prover's algorithm where the input is analysed and checked to be in conformity to the area method was measured in term of CPU clock. After this first step all the remain steps of the (computer) proof where measured. At the beginning of the proof cycle the CPU clock was kept in a variable start (see Listing 1.2) and at each step of the proof the CPU clock was kept in a variable stop, the duration is given by the difference stop-start and the process was re-initialised, taken again the CPU time and kept it in the variable start (see Listing 1.3).

```
start = std::chrono::high_resolution_clock::now();
```

Listing 1.2. start measuring the time taken by a computational proof step

---

[8] $GCLC$, GitHub repository, https://github.com/janicicpredrag/gclc.

```
std :: cout << "el" << elLema++ << " ; " << " El. Point " + it->arg[0];
stop = std :: chrono :: high_resolution_clock :: now();
duration = std :: chrono :: duration<double, std :: micro> (stop - start);
std :: cout << " ; "<< duration.count() << "\n" ;
start = std :: chrono :: high_resolution_clock :: now();
```

Listing 1.3. `stop` the time, at the end of computational proof step, take the `duration` and restart, for the next step

For simplicity the output was sent to the *standard output*, and, at running time, redirected to a file (see Listing 1.4).

```
gclc GEO0021 > GEO0021_CPU.txt
```

Listing 1.4. Calling *GCLC* and redirecting its output

The output file is in the CSV[9] format, for an easy treatment and the construction of the line graph (see Listing 1.3).

5 Proof Simplicity vs Computer Effort

Building on the method just introduced, this section presents line charts that illustrate the simplicity coefficients of the proof and the computational effort expended by processors during the theorem-proving process. In this section, we will consider only three paradigmatic examples taken from the *TGTP* repository: i.e., an example of a high-readability proof, a medium-readability proof, and a low-readability proof. The limitation to only three examples is due to space constraints, but all the analyses can, of course, be extended to all the theorems examined in [16].

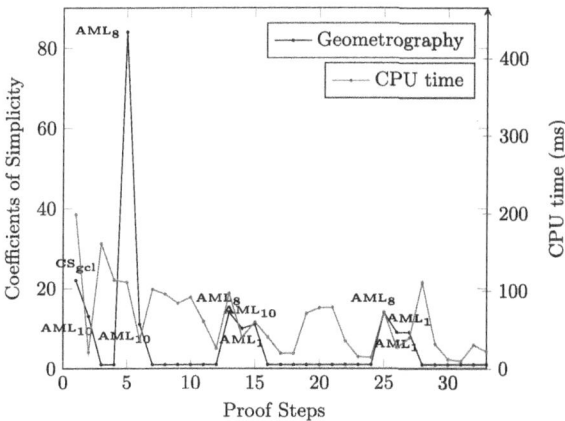

Fig. 5. Ceva's Theorem, Geometrography & CPU Proof Trace

---

[9] Comma Separated Values.

In the line charts 5–7 (Figs. 5–7) all the steps are counted, not like in the previous line chart (see Fig. 2) where the algebraic steps were condensed to one position only. In the study of the simplicity coefficients, the algebraic steps were considered trivial, so its weight is always 1. This is something that must be reformulated as shown by the computation effort (CPU time) line. We will return to this in more detail in the conclusions (see Sect. 6).

Example 1: Ceva's Theorem *TGTP* GE00001, (see Theorem 1).

The proof by *GCLC* area method takes 32 steps and 0.003 s. By the GRCP criteria it is a high-readability proof. The line chart (or proof trace) is shown in Fig. 5.

Example 2: Circumcentre of a Triangle *TGTP* GE00021.
Theorem 2 (Circumcentre of a Triangle). *The circumcentre of a triangle can be found as the intersection of the three perpendicular bisectors.*

The proof by *GCLC* area method takes 599 steps and 0.091 s. By the GRCP criteria it is a medium-readability proof. See Fig. 6 for the proof trace (the fist 72 steps of it), with the lines for the geometrography coefficients and CPU times.

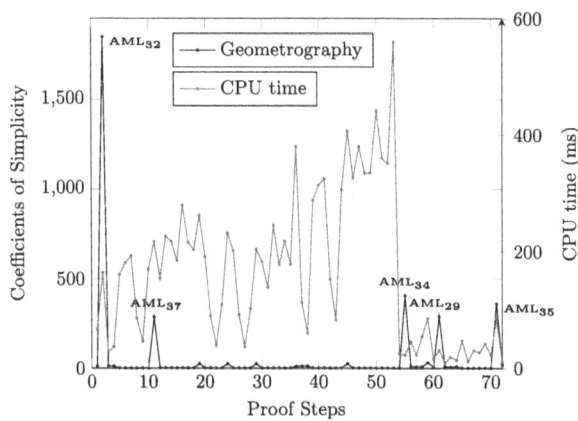

Fig. 6. GE00021—the first 72, out of 599, steps

Example 3: Distance of a line containing the centroid to the vertices *TGTP* GE00020.
Theorem 3 (Distance of a line containing the centroid to the vertices). *Given a triangle $\triangle ABC$ and a point X, the sum of the distances of the line XG, where G is the centroid of $\triangle ABC$, to the two vertices of the triangle situated on the same side of the line is equal to the distance of the line from the third vertex.*

The proof by *GCLC* area method takes 4149 steps and take 15.972 s. By the GRCP criteria it is a low-readability proof. See Fig. 7 for the proof trace (the fist 72 steps of it), with the lines for the geometrography coefficients and CPU times.

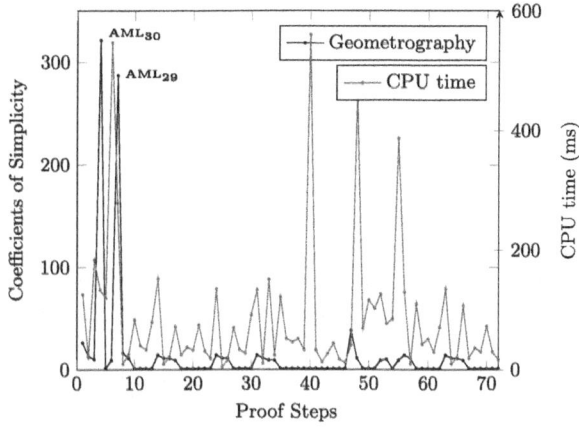

Fig. 7. GE00020—the first 72, out of 4149, steps

6   Analysis of the Results, Conclusions and Future Works

Analysing the previous examples, we can observe that there are two issues in the simplicity coefficients of the human proof trace that are quite different from their computational effort counterparts.

The first issue relates to the use of the same lemma several times. It was assumed [16] that the first time a lemma from the area method is applied in a proof, the effort to prove that lemma must be taken into consideration, to all the other times only the effort to check if this step is a correct instance of that lemma is needed. It is considered that, from the second application of a lemma onward, its proof is accepted, so, only its adaptation to the new configuration is needed, i.e., the pattern matching of the lemma configuration to a new setting. For that reason, in any second, third, etc. application of a lemma, only the **GS** coefficient values are considered. This led to a high spike for the first instance and a relative low spike for the next applications of the lemma. This is not the case for the computational effort. All the lemmas of the area method are part of the program, so apart from the effort of finding the correct pattern (an effort that can be compared to the human effort), every application of the lemmas has the same computational effort, there is no attempt to prove it, before applying it. It can be said that the prover would be the counterpart of an expert in the area method, someone that already have proved all the lemmas and use them, without any extra efforts in its application. On the other hand in Graziani and Quaresma initial view, exposed in [16], a mathematician, not necessary knowledgable of the area method, is considered.

The second issue relates to the treatment of algebraic steps. In previous work, algebraic steps were considered trivial in terms of effort. However, based on the computational effort line, it has become clear that this assumption is inaccurate. There is a need for a more detailed analysis of the algebraic steps, similar to what was done for geometric steps, to develop appropriate simplicity coefficients. This insight underscores the importance of reevaluating algebraic operations to reflect better their contribution to the overall effort.

This study reveals key differences in how humans and machines handle geometric proof. Humans can reuse previously proven lemmas with reduced effort in subsequent applications, while machines treat each lemma application independently, requiring the same computational resources each time. Additionally, humans tend to treat algebraic steps as trivial, whereas machines apply consistent computational effort regardless of the simplicity perceived by humans.

These findings suggest important directions for the future design of automatic proof systems. By recognising patterns in lemma reuse and adapting proofs to match human activity, developers can create systems that generate more user-friendly proofs. From a computational perspective, minimising redundant calculations and optimising the reuse of previously computed steps can significantly reduce the machine's workload.

For example, Fig. 8 shows as the proof trace of Ceva's Theorem using Geometrography (see Fig. 5) can be manually edited to reflect a human expert's perspective. Specifically, all algebraic steps have been assigned the same minimal CPU value. It is evident that the traces are very similar.

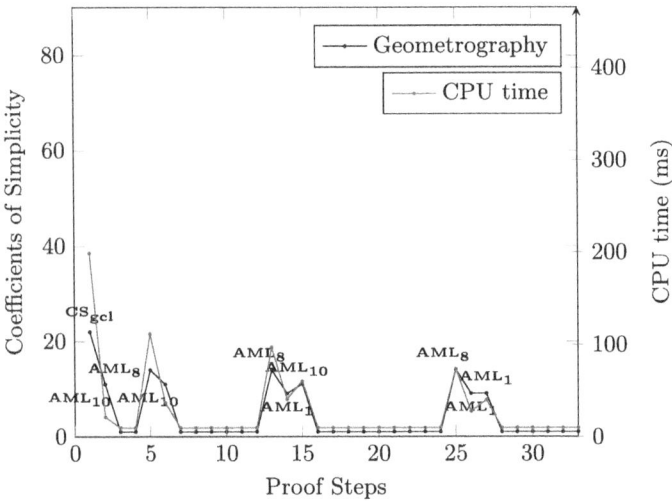

Fig. 8. Ceva's Theorem, Geometrography Proof Trace—edited

Considering the connection between the line chart or proof trace of a demonstration and its readability, this study also provides insights into the readability of proofs generated by automated theorem provers. Moreover, it offers guidance on how to improve readability of computer proof by taking into account not only our hypotheses but also the machine's processes, supporting research toward the development of a readability criterion for both humans and machines.

Moving in this direction, however, two methodological remarks seem necessary to us.

First, in this study the *area method* was used, given the fact that this is the last (for now) effort in a continuous project about simplicity and the readability of proofs, using the *area method* as a case study. Other synthetic methods, or more generally, axiomatic methods, could be used. Staying in the area of geometry, a similar study could be conducted using the geometry deductive database method [1,3], given the fact that it uses a set of axioms and rules of inference and its proofs can be tailored for different levels of readability.

Second, the two resources used by a computer, for a specific task, are CPU running time and the amount of RAM employed for the computation. It is our perception that the memory allocation is, in this context, less important, for a couple of reasons: first, if the program uses static structures, they are initialised at the beginning of the program and them seldom modified; second the large amount of RAM memory available and the speed of access to SSD[10] disks make this resource less demanding; lastly it is our impression that this would be more difficult to measure against any human measurement of the proof (e.g. the number of A4 pages used!?). Nevertheless this could be something to explore in the future.

In conclusion, looking ahead, this study serves as a foundational test case for research into hybrid proof systems that aim to balance human comprehension with computational efficiency. Future work could focus on exploring these concepts using different provers and/or methods different from GCLC area method, as well as developing algorithms that dynamically adjust the structure of proofs to accommodate both human-readable formats and machine-efficient processing. This dual approach has the potential to improve tools for teaching and learning mathematics, as well as enhance the efficiency of automated proof verification in advanced research contexts. Such advancements could make formal proofs more accessible, both by reducing the cognitive load on human users and optimising the computational resources required for their verification.

References

1. Baeta, N., Quaresma, P.: Towards a geometry deductive database prover. Ann. Math. Artif. Intell. **91**(6), 851–863 (2023)
2. Chou, S.-C., Gao, X.-S., Zhang, J.-Z.: Automated generation of readable proofs with geometric invariants, I. Multiple and shortest proof generation. J. Autom. Reason. **17**, 325–347 (1996)
3. Chou, S.-C., Gao, X.-S., Zhang, J.-Z.: A deductive database approach to automated geometry theorem proving and discovering. J. Autom. Reason. **25**(3), 219–246 (2000)
4. Hilbert, D.: Mathematical problems. Bull. Am. Math. Soc. **8**, 437–479 (1902)
5. Hipolito, I., Kahle, R.: Discussing Hilbert's 24th problem. Philos. Trans. R. Soc. A: Math. Phys. Eng. Sci. **377**(2140), 20180040 (2019)

---

[10] Solid State Drive.

6. Janičić, P.: GCLC — a tool for constructive Euclidean geometry and more than that. In: Iglesias, A., Takayama, N. (eds.) ICMS 2006. LNCS, vol. 4151, pp. 58–73. Springer, Heidelberg (2006). https://doi.org/10.1007/11832225_6

7. Janičić, P.: Geometry constructions language. J. Autom. Reason. **44**, 3–24 (2010)

8. Janičić, P., Narboux, J., Quaresma, P.: The area method: a recapitulation. J. Autom. Reason. **48**(4), 489–532 (2012)

9. Janičić, P., Quaresma, P.: System description: GCLCprover + GeoThms. In: Furbach, U., Shankar, N. (eds.) IJCAR 2006. LNCS (LNAI), vol. 4130, pp. 145–150. Springer, Heidelberg (2006). https://doi.org/10.1007/11814771_13

10. Janičić, P., Quaresma, P.: Automatic verification of regular constructions in dynamic geometry systems. In: Botana, F., Recio, T. (eds.) ADG 2006. LNCS (LNAI), vol. 4869, pp. 39–51. Springer, Heidelberg (2007). https://doi.org/10.1007/978-3-540-77356-6_3

11. Lemoine, É.: Géométrographie ou Art des constructions géométriques. Number 18 in Scientia, Série Physico-Mathématique. C. Naud, Éditeur, Paris, Février (1902)

12. John Sturgeon Mackay: The geometrography of Euclid's problems. Proc. Edinb. Math. Soc. **12**, 2–16 (1893)

13. Merikoski, J.K., Tossavainen, T.: Two approaches to geometrography. J. Geom. Graph. **13**(1), 15–28 (2010)

14. Quaresma, P.: Thousands of geometric problems for geometric theorem provers (TGTP). In: Schreck, P., Narboux, J., Richter-Gebert, J. (eds.) ADG 2010. LNCS (LNAI), vol. 6877, pp. 169–181. Springer, Heidelberg (2011). https://doi.org/10.1007/978-3-642-25070-5_10

15. Quaresma, P., Graziani, P.: The geometrography's simplicity coeficient for the axioms and lemma of the area method. Technical report TR 2021-001, Center for Informatics and Systems of the University of Coimbra (2021)

16. Quaresma, P., Graziani, P.: Measuring the readability of geometric proofs—the area method case. J. Autom. Reason. **67**(1) (2023). https://doi.org/10.1007/s10817-022-09652-0

17. Quaresma, P., Santos, V., Graziani, P., Baeta, N.: Taxonomy of geometric problems. J. Symb. Comput. **97**, 31–55 (2020)

18. Santos, V., Baeta, N., Quaresma, P.: Geometrography in dynamic geometry. Int. J. Technol. Math. Educ. **26**(2), 89–96 (2019)

19. Thiele, R.: Hilbert's twenty-fourth problem. Am. Math. Mon. **110**(1), 1–24 (2003)

20. Wiedijk, F.: The de Bruijn factor. In: Poster at International Conference on Theorem Proving in Higher Order Logics (TPHOL2000), 2000. Portland, Oregon, USA, 14–18 August 2000

From Birth to Loss of Representations in Artificial Neural Networks

Philipp Stecher(✉)

Eberhard-Karls-University Tübingen, Tübingen, Germany
philippmstecher@gmail.com

Abstract. "[In] unguarded moments I do think that everything is concepts", stated Murphy in his popular big book of concepts [1] emphasizing the pivotal role of concepts or "mental representations" in understanding the mind. Inspired by Murphy's unguarded moments, we propose a framework asserting that *in artificial neural networks (ANNs) everything is representations and mechanisms*. Specifically, based on an interdisciplinary literature review, we propose a framework called the representations' lifecycle. The framework consists of two main contributions: first, we propose a template that characterizes representational change in ANNs along compositional, hierarchical, and temporal dimensions. Second, the latter template allows for the characterization and demarcation of six representation-altering processes: abstract primitives' integration, perceptual primitives' integration, assembly, abstraction, differentiation and decay. Our framework provides the foundation for a more universal description of representational change in neural networks and thus, contributes to the broader efforts towards more transparent and explainable ANNs.

Keywords: Representational development · neural representation · artificial neural networks · neuro-representationalism

1 Introduction

Building upon neuro-representationalism and following Hubbard [2], we conceptualize "representation" as encompassing two interconnected worlds: the "represented world" and the "representing world" [2]. Thus, we define an *artificial* representation (hereinafter referred to interchangeably as "representation") as an element within a particular representing world – an artificial neural network (ANN). Thereby, the element "reflects, stands for, or signifies some aspect of the represented world" [2]. Specifically, representations in ANNs are the neural components that are "activated" during the prediction of an aspect presented to the input layer of an ANN. The represented world pertains to the domain with which the ANN interacts. For example, considering a vehicle detection neural network designed to support automous driving. In this context, the represented world can include various aspects such as vehicles, pedestrians, traffic signals, and environmental factors, as well as movements of the steering wheel.

Representations in ANNs are subject to change. We define representational change as the process by which neural components are modified through learning mechanisms

J. Proença et al. (Eds.): SEFM 2024, LNCS 15551, pp. 271–289, 2026.
https://doi.org/10.1007/978-3-031-94748-3_20

such as the integration of new data under the application of learning rules. These mechanisms reconfigure the network's elements, representing, if successful, novel or more refined aspects of the represented world. Notably, many core achievements in AI research are attributed to effective representational change: deep learning researchers often trace their models' successes back to processes such as generalization [3, 4], abstraction [5, 6], differentiation [7], or association [8, 9]. These processes, each playing a unique role, collectively contribute to nowadays sophistication of ANNs. Generalization, for example, broadens the applicability of learned representations. Abstraction and differentiation are instrumental to form representations through distilling and distinguishing complex inputs, respectively [5–7]. Association, on the other hand, creates representations by connecting existing representations, and integrating their informational content [8, 9].

Despite recognizing individual contributions, however, a cohesive framework that demarcates these processes and integrates them into a uniform model of representational change in ANNs is notably absent. Such a framework could, for example, offer a model-agnostic description of how neural structures evolve across various architectures to effectively represent entities of a given represented world. These insights, in turn, could, for example, inform more effective architecture designs and optimization strategies. To lay the groundwork for such uniform approach, we present a framework, we call the representations' lifecycle, consisting of six processes responsible for representational change in ANNs, namely abstract primitives' integration, perceptual primitives' integration, assembly, abstraction, differentiation and decay. Taking together these processes reflect a 'complete' set capable to describe the development of representations in ANNs 'from their birth to their loss'. With this framework, however, we do not offer a precise neurological account; rather, to provide a comprehensive overview, we focus on high-level descriptions of neurological input and output structures leaving precise neural correlates and causal mechanisms open for further inquiry.

Understanding representational change in the mind has longstanding tradition [10–12]. While the representations' lifecycle draws from research on representational development discussed in the context of (non-human) animals at conceptual levels [1, 13–18] or at neural levels [19–24], we primarily focus on and aim to describe representational development in ANNs. The process-integrative view taken in this paper is complementary to existing ideas that approach representational development in ANNs emphasizing the value of single processes [5, 6, 8], mathematical principles [7], or provide nonneural accounts of representational development [25, 26]. In addition, with its representation-centric perspective, our approach stands in contrast to other non-representational accounts such as computational phenomenology [27]. Furthermore, in contrast to other contributions [27–31], we do not question the nature of representations or discuss their epistemic usefulness for better understanding the inner dynamics of the mind respectively ANNs. Rather, following the neuro-representational approach [27], we axiomatically posit the existence and usefulness of representations in ANNs. Specifically, as we will elaborate in Sect. 2, we posit that representations are hierarchically-related compositions that change in a computational manner through mechanisms that operate on them [32]. Additionally, other than it has been suggested [33], tying in with other deep learning researchers [34, 35], we assume that it is useful to describe representations as entities that differ in their abstractness.

The paper is organized as follows. In Sect. 2, we first introduce the template used to characterize representational change. Latter template provides the basis to understand the in Sect. 3 presented representations' lifecycle consisting of the six representation-altering processes. We conclude with a conclusion, limitations and propositions for future research.

2 Dimensions of Representational Change in ANNs

Representations change during training. In the representations' lifecycle we model these changes through a template, called the representation-altering process. The template characterizes representational change in ANNs along three dimensions: the compositional dimension, the hierarchical dimension, and the temporal dimension. First, representations are composed of finer representational constituents [28, 34]. Second, these compositions differ depending on their degree of specificity/generality and are related to each other [28, 34–36]. Third, latter hierarchical compositions change during training. In the subsequent section, we will elaborate on each of these dimensions. The notations and illustrations provided in this section form the basis to understand the representations' lifecycle in Sect. 3.

2.1 Compositional Dimension

The possibility of localizable or modular 'subunits' in neural networks has been a long-standing point of debate [37], given that neural representations are commonly described as distributed [38]. However, recent interpretability research suggests that certain neuron populations can act as compositional sub-representations [39, 40], indicating that, in practice, these networks may indeed exhibit aspects of the compositionality. In addition, conceptualizing representations as compositions is a widely applied practice. For example, explainable AI researchers, aiming at explaining the inner workings of ANNs mechanistically, regularly draw from such compositional understanding [41–43]. Following the compositional thought, we model compositions of representations by using conceptual graphs as illustrated in Fig. 1. For example, in the conceptual graph (A) the structure of a representation DOG including its constituents HEAD, BODY, and TAIL is shown. (B) illustrates how the conceptual graph maps to a picture of DOG, presented to an idealized image recognition ANN. Finally, (C) exemplifies how this structure could be represented in the neural elements within the imagine recognition ANN. As such the structure reflects the activated neural elements involved in a prediction. For example, assuming the task of identifying a DOG in a picture through an image recognition ANN, the composition of DOG is displayed by the activated neural elements, or in other words, by the neural correlates of the ANN causing the prediction of DOG in dependence of data presented to the input layer. The constituents, in turn, reflect excerpts of the totality of activated neural elements involved in the DOG prediction, and as such refer to differentiable subunits of the DOG representation such as HEAD, BODY, or TAIL.

2.2 Hierarchical Dimension

While Barsalou, et al. [33] caution that concrete and abstract representations are inherently intertwined and shaped by contextual factors, AI researchers (e.g., [7, 34–36, 44])

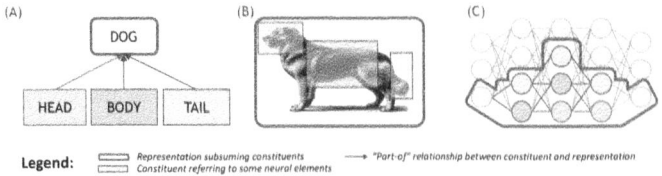

Fig. 1. Conceptual graph and its relation to neural elements in an ANN

routinely employ hierarchical explanation by emphasizing how progressively deeper layers of a network acquire increasingly abstract, modality-independent, and invariant representations, informed by shallower layers. Thus, abstract representations are hypothesized to form and develop in a reciprocal relationship with more perceptual representations [7, 34, 35]. Building on these observations, and drawing on Petkov and Petrova's [45] illustrations (see Fig. 2), we model representational capacities of ANNs' along two axes: composition and hierarchy (A). Particularly, we model the hierarchical relationship of representations in ANNs through (a difference in) shared constituents, whereby, abstract representations share constituents with related perceptual representations but possess less.

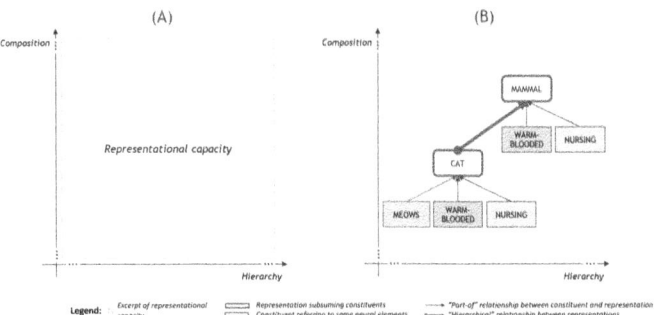

Fig. 2. Excerpt of a representational capacity

For example, in (B) the representation CAT is composed of the attributes MEOWS, WARM-BLOODED and NURSING. The CAT representation is hierarchically-related to the superordinate representation, MAMMAL. Both CAT and MAMMAL share attributes like WARM-BLOODED and NURSING. However, CAT has a differentiating attribute such as MEOWS that distinguishes it from MAMMAL and other, subordinate representations associated with MAMMAL. Thus, the abstractness of representations is modelled based on associated constituents, with fewer constituents, or in other words, fewer neural components involved, indicating a higher position in the hierarchy, making it more abstract compared to other representations in the same hierarchy.

2.3 Temporal Dimension

As shown in Fig. 3 (A), representation-altering processes describe the changes of representations from a neural state to another neural state or, in other words, "from [an input] structure to [an output] structure" [2] through a mechanism. The mechanism describes how an output structure was reached given an input structure. Specifically, the mechanism provides a causal explanation that demonstrates how and why an input structure produces an output structure given the application of a learning rule responding to (training) data presented to the input layer. As introduced before, the structure of a representation describes its hierarchically organized composition. Hence, ultimately representation-altering processes describe how hierarchically-related constituents of representations are modified, added, or deleted as a result of a mechanism. In (B) the input and output structures of the representation-altering process differentiation are illustrated. Differentiation is characterized by forming more specific representations based on more abstract representations given in the input structure. Accordingly, as illustrated in Fig. 3 (B), the DOG representation was formed integrating constituents of its hierarchical parent AGENT with additional, differentiating constituents such as BARKS.

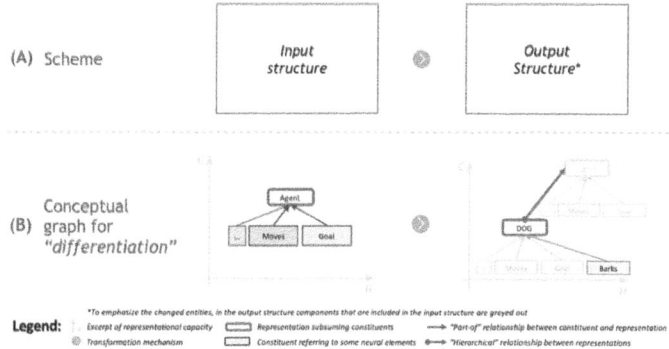

Fig. 3. Example of a representation-altering process: "differentiation"

3   From Birth to Loss: The Representations' Lifecycle

The representations' lifecycle is composed of six representation-altering processes that are being organized along three phases: innate, form & change, and decay. In the innate phase, the ANN is in a pre-training state, not yet influenced by external data. Processes in this phase concern the integration of primitives into an ANN through developers. Once the incorporation of data starts, the ANN enters the form & change phase. From this point, the system forms new representations or changes existing ones by doing both, incorporating training data, and leveraging already integrated representations. Finally, representations are being deleted. The latter refers to the removal of representations from the ANN's representational capacity.

In the following the representation-altering processes for each of three phases will be presented. Figure 4 introduces illustrative examples of the representation-altering processes. Shows a summary of characteristics of the representation-altering processes as described for (non-human) animals and ANNs, respectively. The representation-altering processes introduced in the Sects. 3.1 to 3.3 are about descriptions of the processes in terms of input and output structures. Each process presentation starts with a definition, followed by a characterization of the process derived from the cognitive science literature. Hereafter, analogous findings identified in AI literature are summarized.

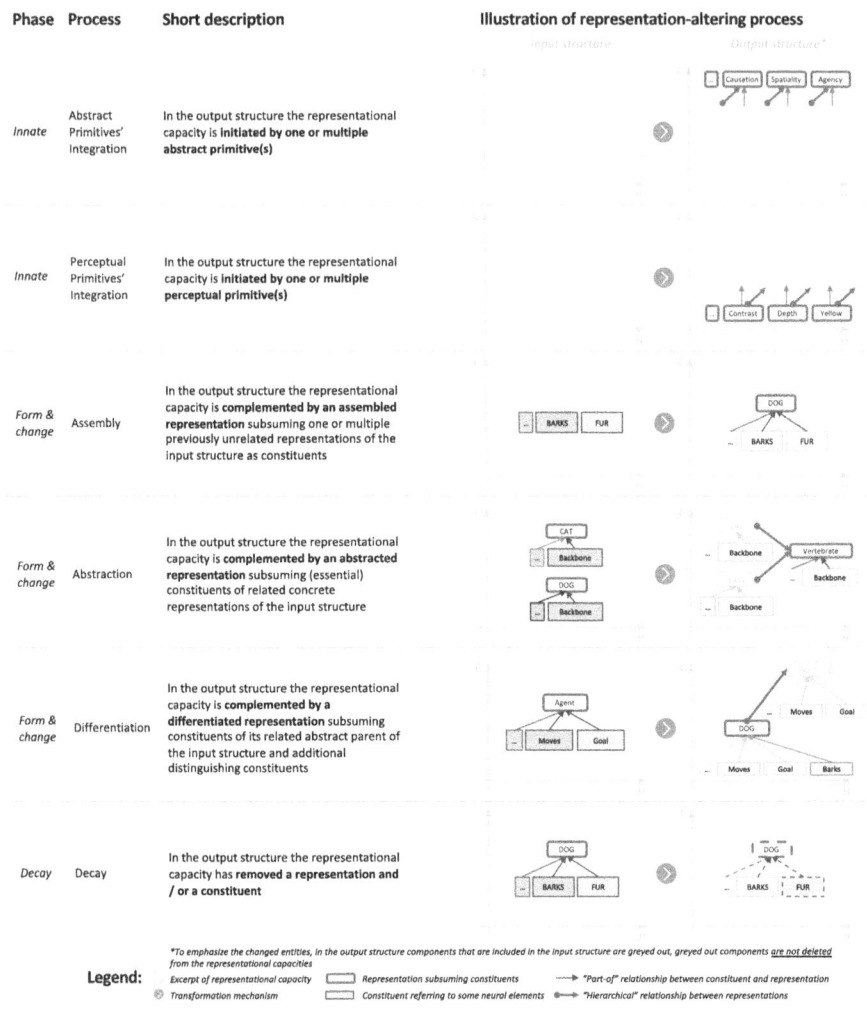

Fig. 4. Overview of representation-altering processes

3.1 Innate

The debate of how much of the mind is innate, and how much is formed by experience is stretching far back in history. Back then, primarily two schools of thought opposed each other [16]: nativism and empiricism. Proponents of the former argued that, to explain the complex behavior of biological cognitive systems right after birth, an innate machinery is required [16]. On the other hand, empiricists have argued that biological cognitive systems learn everything by observation respectively through their experiences, and possess little to no innate representational capacity [46, 47]. Nowadays, it seems to be widely acknowledged [46], however, that "genes and experience" work together. This interplay stance accepts that both components are important to model cognitive biological systems: innate machinery as well as experience [46]. Thereby, the innate machinery enables the system to learn, while learning, in the terminology of this paper, refers to the process of acquiring novel representations based on sensory data and in the system existing representations.

In AI, the above controverses seem to be mirrored. However, while cognitive scientists mostly aim to discover whether (non-human) animals have innated representational capacities, the AI debate rather revolves around whether and what innate representational structures are useful to develop more capable systems. Thus, empiricists argue that ANNs require little to no primitives to work effectively [7, 48]. On the other hand, scholars leaning toward the nativist viewpoint [16, 34, 49] argue that leveraging innate structures could help building more successful machines. The interplay stance proposes that ANNs should be modelled as a function over innate structures and experience, or in AI, acquired training data [46]. The stance emphasizes first, that innate structures and training data are relevant to describe the inner workings of ANNs and second, that ANNs differ in their richness of innate structures, but that their innate structure "cannot literally be zero" [46]. Following this stance, in this paper we assume that every ANN starts with an innate set of representational structures which in later stages of development is enriched by additional structures through training. Specifically, we conceptualize the initial representational capacity of an ANN, emerging from its initial architecture, objective function, and learning rule, as a set of primitives, or in other words, a set of innate representations, that both enables and restricts what the ANN can learn over the course of training.

Leaning toward the "nativist" side of the interplay stance, cognitive and computer scientists have tried to identify specific primitives that allow to explain the learning capabilities of biological cognitive systems, or that are useful to design capable AI, respectively. In the following, we systematize these primitives along two angles assuming that primitives can occur in abstract [14, 17, 18, 23, 46, 50, 51] and perceptual varieties [13, 14, 52]. Accordingly, it is assumed that the "life" of some abstract and perceptual representations starts with their integration into the ANN before the network is trained.

Abstract Primitives' Integration. Abstract primitives' integration refers to the insertion of abstract representations into an ANN, before training. As illustrated in Fig. 4, in the output structure abstract primitives are in the upper right section of a representational capacity. As such, they are considered the most abstract representations and thus, containing the fewest constituents compared to related perceptual representations. The input structure is empty since an ANN's representational capacity comes into existence with having them integrated. Abstract primitives contain constituents which, at later stages of representational development, are inherited by the more perceptual representations formed on their basis.

In (non-human) animals, abstract primitives are often characterized as innate representations on which basis more perceptual representations are formed [13, 14, 50, 52]. A primitive is considered as abstract if, unlike a perceptual one, it allows for subsuming a wide range of different aspects of the represented world [50, 52] and if it contains rather functional constituents than perceivable ones [13, 52, 53]. According to Mandler [13], contrarily to perceptual primitives, abstract ones include knowledge that is beyond the information provided by the senses and rather describe "what [an aspect] is" instead of "what [an aspect] looks like". For humans, various kinds of abstract primitives have been proposed such as AGENCY [14, 17, 18, 50], CAUSATION [14, 17, 50], NUMERICS [14, 18], SOCIALITY [17, 18] and SPATIALITY [14, 50, 51]. For latter stages of representational development, it is assumed that the initial set of abstract primitives is expanded through top-down processes (see Sect. 3.2) [13, 14, 50, 52]. For example, pointing to experiments with infants, Mandler [13, 50] concludes that "many early [representations] appear to be global, relatively crude, and lacking in detail" [13] and, at latter stages, are differentiated through leveraging perceptual primitives and sensory data [50]. The products of the differentiation are newly formed, more perceptual representations added to the representational capacity.

In AI, abstract primitives increasingly move to the center of current research efforts [5, 6, 46]. In this vein, Mitchell [6] emphasized their importance: "unless we create AI systems that can master [abstract primitives] we have little hope of creating anything like human-level AI". Although considered worthy endeavors [6, 16, 34, 46], efforts to equip modern AI with "[rich] priors, that orientate learning and improve acquisition speed" [16], or with "general priors about the world around us, i.e., priors that are not task-specific but [...] useful" [34], seem to remain in an early stage of development [6]. Nonetheless, scholars already suggested abstract primitives that may be worth considering for AI. While pointing to the work of developmentalists, Marcus [46] proposes a set of ten primitives such as SPATIOTEMPORAL CONTIGUITY, CAPACITY FOR COST-BENEFIT ANALYSIS or CAUSALITY. Bengio, et al. [34] proposed general primitives "about the world around us" such as A HIERACHICAL ORGANIZATION OF EXPLANATORY FACTORS, SMOOTHNESS and MANIFOLDS that enable "the learner to discover and disentangle some of the underlying (and a priori unknown) factors of variation that the data may reveal" and which are partially artificially implemented already [34]. However, it remains unknown "how long the list [of abstract primitives] really ought to be" [46]. Generally, identifying a comprehensive list of abstract primitives relevant to AI is significantly complicated by the lack of understanding of how useful abstract representational structures can be artificially generated [5, 6, 54].

Perceptual Primitives' Integration. Perceptual primitives' integration refers to the insertion of perceptual representations into an ANN, before training. As illustrated in Fig. 4, in the output structure perceptual primitives are in the lower left section of a representational capacity. The input structure is empty since an ANNs' representational capacity comes into existence with having them integrated. Perceptual primitives encompass constituents which, at later stages of representational development, are subsumed by assembled representations formed on their basis.

In (non-human) animals, perceptual primitives are often characterized by encompassing sensory, or sensorimotor representations [13, 14, 55] and are likely to be bounded to the senses respectively likely to be modality-specific [56]. For example, visual perceptual primitives allow the interpretation of accumulated bits of sensory data [14] and can result in perceptions such as EDGES, CONTRAST or DEPTH. Visual perceptual primitives are used for the interpretation of combinations of wavelengths of light that stimulated the visual detectors of a given cognitive system. The "most basic" primitives are likely to have in common that they allow a cognitive system to detect the presence of elements of pattern in sensory data [55]. At a neurological level, perceptual primitives are supposed to be represented as "hard-wired" neuronal networks that allow biological cognitive systems to recognize complex stimuli [56]. These kinds of neuronal networks have been reported across species (e.g., humans [57, 58], reptiles [56], insects [59]) and across different modalities (e.g., lexical [57, 58], visual [58], auditive [57, 59]). The perceptual primitives complement the innate set of abstract primitives and are supposed to be involved in the enrichment of the representational capacity through bottom-up processes (see Sect. 3.2). It is assumed that during the formation of representations, after the system came to life, both, abstract and perceptual primitives are involved simultaneously [13, 53]. For example, while humans learn new representations such as DOG or CAT, they differentiate their abstract primitives such as AGENCY and SPATIALITY and draw from perceptual primitives involved during the pre-interpretation of streams of sensory data which finally lead to an assembly of perceptions such as BROWN, FLUFFY, or BARKS as constituents, in this case, subsumed under the DOG representation.

In AI, artificial analogies that most closely match the scheme of perceptual primitives are representations that help to pre-process incoming raw data, i.e., the data collected by the virtual (e.g., program/data interfaces) or physical sensors (e.g., cameras, microphones) connected to a given ANN. Pre-processing of incoming raw data is supposed to facilitate the learning from or classification of data in AI [60, 61]. Artificial perceptual primitives are domain-specific and thus, help to process data that is coined by a specific modality (e.g., visual/pixels, auditive/tones) and often is collected within a specific application area (e.g., traffic, weather forecast). Same as their biological counterparts, they enable AI to interpret chunks of sensory data. For example, artificial feature detectors are dedicated to enable better predictions through the pre-interpretation of chunks of *visual* sensory data [60]. For the interpretation of images, feature detection methodologies are used that can detect shape-entities, such as edges, contours, corners, or blobs [60] based on e.g., trained representations of those shapes available in ANNs. The detected features can then be combined to assemble new representations that associate the interpreted shape features [60, 62]. We assume that both, abstract and perceptual primitives, are involved when novel representations are formed in ANNs. For example, while an image recognition ANN learns the visual representation of a DOG, it differentiates its abstract primitives and leverages its perceptual primitives, involved in the pre-processing of pixels delivered by the virtual or physical sensors, leading to detected edges, or corners. Latter edges, or corners, are then assembled as constituents of the visual representation of DOG.

3.2 Form and Change

During training an ANN forms new representations or changes existing ones by incorporating data and combining already integrated representations. In humans, the processes that form and change representations underpin higher-level cognitive abilities like decision-making, reasoning, language comprehension, and planning [22, 63–65]. In ANNs, given proper training data and effective execution, these processes provide the system with novel and/or refined representations resulting in enhanced predictions. As suggested by Gibson and Gibson [66], there are two theoretical stances to explain the formation of representations: the enrichment theory and the specificity theory. Recasting the two stances in the terminology of this paper, the enrichment theory assumes that an ANN's representational capacity is starting with a set of perceptual primitives and is then, through bottom-up processes, gradually expanded by further abstract representations; on the other hand, the specificity theory argues that a representational capacity starts with abstract primitives on which basis, through top-down processes, more perceptual representations are derived [66]. As emphasized in literature [13, 14, 52] and as described above, both types of processes are mutually dependent and deeply intertwined. Thus, we argue that starting with innate structures a representational capacity can be expanded through bottom-up processes such as assembly and abstraction as well as through top-down processes such as differentiation. Bottom-up processes either assemble representations through associating one or multiple representations, or produce abstract representations based on input structures which are composed of more perceptual representations. On the other hand, top-down processes either produce perceptual representations from abstract ones or specify existing representations.

Assembly. Assembly refers to the process of forming representations along the "Composition" dimension through the association of two or more representations/constituents. As illustrated in Fig. 4, in the output structure the newly assembled representation contains constituents that in the input structure were unrelated. Assembly can take as input representations of any kind, modality, or abstraction and can produce representations of any kind, modality, or abstraction.

In (non-human) animals, assembled representations are often characterized by containing relationships between "separate (i.e., formerly unrelated) [...] representations" [67]. In humans, these assembled representations can be multimodal and therefore, can consist of representations from different sensory modalities [68, 69]. Additionally, assembly is characterized as a process that produces representations which are supposed to contain information about the propositional and semantic quality of the relationship in addition to the information that representations are related [22, 70]. The example given in Fig. 4 illustrates how representations of a given input structure derived from sensorimotor and auditive data, i.e., FLUFFY and BARKS, get subsumed as constituents under the newly assembled representation of DOG in the output structure. In this case, the relationship "part of" may describe the shared semantic content of the two associated representations, i.e., FLUFFY and BARKS, with the assembled representation DOG. The latter type of assembly refers to the formation of simple associations, whereby objects or sensory impressions are classified as associatively related if they tend to spatially or temporally co-appear [22]. Besides the here given entity representation, it is assumed that assembly can result in relational representations that are primarily defined by their relations outside themselves. Consequently, assembly can result in representations such as HUNTING by associating multiple representations such as PREDATOR and BAIT [45, 71] through, for example, extracting the common essences of event representations in which the act of one animal chasing another was observed. Furthermore, assembly also includes the formation of more abstract relations between representations, which are not formed based on co-occurrences but are, nonetheless, "judged as related, or conveying a common concept" [22]. In this sense, it is assumed that the process of assembly can result in all kinds of complex representations such as schema representations. For example, assembly can result in representations that reflect temporal/causal events (e.g., AFTER PUSHING THE BUTTON THE TV TURNS ON) or functional relationships (e.g., A SPOON IS USED TO EAT SOUP) [22]. In summary, the term assembly used in this paper refers to a process in which pre-existing representations of any kind, modality, and abstraction are subsumed as constituents under a newly formed representation of any kind, modality, and abstraction along the "Composition"-dimension, while at the same time propositional respectively semantic content about their association is integrated.

In AI, assembly-like processes are often entitled to be essential to the operation of modern ANNs [9, 11, 35]. Indeed, just like the human variant of simple associations, modern AI algorithms recognize patterns in data by analyzing statistical co-occurrences. For example, Wang and Raj [11] argue that machine learning methods in general cluster "samples that are near to each other (under a defined distance) [...] in one group" and that they draw more attention to "explanatory variables that frequently occur with response variables". Associations have been created both within and between artificial representations of different modalities [9]. For example, deep learning computer vision algorithms [72–74] have established relationships between visual representations by analyzing their spatial and temporal co-occurrences, resulting in newly assembled modal-specific representations [9, 62]. Furthermore, modern deep learning algorithms have successfully assembled multimodal representations (for comprehensive review, see Guo, et al. [9]), whereby, e.g., representations with lexical and visual formats were combined. As reported by Guo, et al. [9], the resulting representations differed in efficacity depending on the modalities that are combined. For instance, while effective representations combining image and language modalities have been successfully assembled and applied, other representations such as, for example, the ones combining audio and video modalities are in a comparably early stage of development [9]. Furthermore, whereas first artificial associations between representations of different modalities have been established, the question of how to effectively assemble representations which integrate propositional content such as causality remains "largely open" [54].

Abstraction. Abstraction refers to the formation of representations along the "Hierarchy" dimension. As illustrated in Fig. 4, in the output structure the newly abstracted representation is characterized by a reduction in specificity and an expansion in scope. The reduction in specificity refers to a decrease in constituents of the more abstract representation relative to the related perceptual representation(s). The expansion in scope refers to an increase of subsumed perceptual representations that participate in constituents of the abstracted representations. Abstracted representations include essences distilled from more perceptual representations contained in the input structure.

In (non-human) animals, abstraction is often associated with a reduction in specificity and an expansion of scope [75] of the newly formed representations. The reduction of specificity is characterized by a decreasing number of associated constituents of the newly formed abstract representation in comparison to the original more perceptual representation(s) [75, 76]. The set of reduced constituents of an abstract representation encompasses a set of "invariant central characteristics" [77] of an aspect and thereby, represents "any properties that increase the likelihood of accurately identifying [the aspect] across various contexts". For example, in Fig. 4 the representations CAT and DOG have one or more common constituents such as BACKBONE. In the output structure, this set of common constituents is used to characterize the newly formed, more abstract representation VERTEBRATE. Latter set of constituents describing the abstract representation VERTEBRATE encompasses less associated constituents than CAT or DOG and therefore is less specific. The expansion of scope refers to an increase in the number of subordinate representations associated with the newly formed abstract representation compared to the perceptual representation(s) of the input structure [75, 76]. For example, the output representation VERTEBRATE is not characterized by constituents such as BARKS, or MEAT-EATER which, however, can be attributed to its subordinate DOG. In addition, VERTEBRATE subsumes representations of DOG and CAT and their underlying subordinates (e.g., SHEPHERD and POODLE) as well as other representations that are characterized by having a BACKBONE such as HUMAN or AMPHIBIAN. VERTEBRATE is associated with an expanded scope of subordinate representations and consequently, covers a wider range of aspects. Finally, an abstract representation can encompass constituents from different modalities. Accordingly, it has been argued [66, 78] that abstract representation likely involve perceptual and functional constituents; but in contrast to perceptual ones, abstract representations tend to have more functional constituents attached and are considered to be less associated with sensory impressions.

In AI, a popular explanation for why artificial networks tend to work so well is that they construct "more complex [...] representations from simpler and less abstract ones" [79]. In this vein, LeCun, et al. [35] pointed out that modern deep learning networks operate on the basis of abstraction, whereby higher-level layers of a network contain abstractions formed on the basis of representations from lower-level layers. Thereby, representations in lower-level layers are more likely to be changed by local variations of the input data. Those of higher-level layers are "generally invariant" [34] to most variations of the input. Furthermore, representations contained in higher-level layers re-use representations that were learned by lower-levels, which makes them particularly suited for learning across domains [36] indicating their capability of subsuming wider ranges of aspects. While abstract representations have been artificially produced, there remain major differences to the abstractions that humans can produce and apply. Indeed, unlike humans, who effectively can apply their abstractions to novel situations, modern AI systems require vast amounts of data to create less generalizable representations that tend to produce mediocre results when applied to new situations/domains [5, 80]. As emphasized by Shanahan and Mitchell [5], although modern AI systems are able to "achieve a certain degree of generalization", the abstract representations formed by modern AI often remain "tied to the domain in which they were acquired". The authors Shanahan and Mitchell [5] conclude that the "shortcomings of contemporary neural network methods such as low sample efficiency, limited transfer ability, and poor out of distribution generalization [...] result from an inability to form sufficiently general abstractions". In general, the quest to understand how abstract representations are formed and what qualities they ought to possess to be effectively applied is ongoing [6, 78].

Differentiation. Same as abstraction, differentiation refers to the formation of representations along the "Hierarchy" dimension. Contrarily to abstraction, differentiation results in perceptual representations with an increased specificity and a reduced scope. As illustrated in Fig. 4, the increase in specificity refers to an increase in constituents of the more differentiated representation relative to the related abstract representation; the additional constituents among others differentiate the newly formed representations from other representations participating in the same hierarchy. On the other hand, the decrease in scope refers to a decrease of subsumed perceptual representations relative to its associated more abstract parent.

In (non-human) animals, output structures resulting from differentiation are often characterized by an increased specificity and a reduced scope in comparison to the input structure. The increase in specificity refers to the differentiated representation containing more constituents than its parent [50, 66, 81]. These additional constituents distinguish the resulting representations from other representations related to the parent [81]. For example, as shown in Fig. 4, based on a given representation AGENT the more specified representation DOG is derived which encompasses besides the constituents which were inherited from the superordinate representation (GOAL and ACTS) additional constituents such as BARKS. Thereby, the additional constituents distinguish DOG from other representations that were also considered as AGENT such as CAT. The DOG representation represents a smaller range of aspects and therefore, possesses a reduced scope. Latter allows a cognitive system to separate stimuli that were once indistinguishable [82]. Furthermore, contrarily to their more abstract parents, it is assumed that differentiated representations are likely to have more perceptual and less functional constituents attached than their parent [66].

In AI, during learning, abstract primitives and representations get adjusted or refined to fit the presented data. The process of fitting the rather general primitives and representations to data suggests differentiation-like processes [7]. Hereby, the general-purpose primitives serve as a starting point from which a more specific purpose is derived. For example, in their nonlinear ANN, Saxe, et al. [7] observed "hierarchical, progressive differentiation of structure in its internal hidden representations, in which animals vs. plants are first distinguished, then birds vs. fish and trees vs. flower, and, finally, individual items". Moreover, they claim that "progressive differentiation of hierarchical structure [...] is an inevitable consequence of deep-learning dynamics" [7]. Broadly, to accelerate the AI's learning process, AI researchers regularly aim to apply the weights of higher layers (containing more abstract information) collected in a particular domain to other domains. However, as mentioned above, the transfer of gathered abstract representations attained in a specific domain remain often tied to the domain in which they were acquired [5].

3.3 Decay

Decay results in the removal of representations and/or constituents from the representational capacity. Decay is more than a mere biproduct of representation altering. Contrarily, it has been suggested that decay provides cognitive systems with several benefits [83–86] such as efficient storage management, attention direction, and better decision making. Both, the formation and decay respectively "forgetting" of representations, are considered as "complementary processes which construct and maintain useful representations" [87]. The decay of representations can be a product of deleting, overriding, suppressing, or sorting out outdated information [85].

In deep ANNs learned representations change depending on the data presented to the input layer; this change, in turn, can result in a decay of representations or constituents. For example, if a pretrained network is trained with novel data from a new domain, the network's representations change to reflect the contingencies of the new domain. If the new domain's data is significantly different from the original data, the network can "forget" [88]. When the AI is then confronted with input data similar to that of the original domain, it often cannot successfully classify the data because the corresponding representations have been overwritten [89]. While this may be acceptable for ANNs that only work and will work in the new domain, the performance of networks that are expected to switch between the domains suffer significantly. To encounter this issue of co-called "catastrophic forgetting" [88, 89] various strategies have been proposed [88–90] which have in common that they aim to segment the representations in a network and thereby, prioritize the learned representations and constituents that were useful in the original domain. Through this segmentation methods, constituents of representations become more disentangled which, in turn, allows to forget them more systematically respectively allows to forget unrequired parts independent from the required ones. Thus, neurologically forgetting is likely caused by a gradual change in weights to reflect contingencies of the input data. Thereby ANNs previously captured representations in ANNs may be altered to the extent that they are no longer useful for predictions.

4 Conclusions, Limitations and Further Research Avenues

This paper presents the representations' lifecycle framework, detailing representational change across compositional, hierarchical, and temporal dimensions. It consists of six processes: abstract primitives' integration, perceptual primitives' integration, abstraction, differentiation, assembly, and decay—serving as a basis to a more uniform description of representational change.

Several limitations exist. First, an implicit assumption of the framework is that there is a prototypical form of information that can be consistently represented across different ANN architectures. Representational structures, however, may vary between architectures due to differences in learning mechanisms, layer configurations, or data inputs. These variations cast doubt on the universality of the processes, as what constitutes a "representation" may differ significantly across networks. Future research should investigate whether such prototypical representations exist or if architecture-specific models are required to better capture the distinct characteristics of different networks.

Additionally, the current work focuses primarily on the input and output structures of representational changes, without describing the underlying mechanisms that drive these transitions. According to the definition provided in this paper, mechanisms describe the causal operations that explain how an input structure leads to a particular output structure. However, this paper's scope was limited to modelling structural changes in representations, leaving the mechanisms themselves largely unexplored.

The completeness of the framework, as illustrated in Fig. 5, derives from its ability to encompass all necessary processes that govern the evolution of representational capacities across compositional and hierarchical dimensions. The graph shows how movements along these axes—whether through abstraction, differentiation, assembly, or decay—can capture any possible state of a representational capacity. The framework assumes that any representational state can be reached starting from an initial set of primitives by applying these processes. While this is merely theoretical completeness, future work must investigate whether it holds across varying neural architectures, where differing mechanisms may affect the actual pathway of representational change.

Finally, another limitation of our framework concerns the challenge of linking the identified processes to tangible neural correlates. While we offer a high-level definition of what, for instance, a newly abstracted representation might look like (e.g., containing fewer constituents than related representations), it remains unclear how exactly this manifests in network activations or connectivity patterns. Future research should formalize and explore the precise signatures of abstraction, differentiation, and other processes in the neural activities, ultimately grounding these conceptual descriptions in measurable evidence.

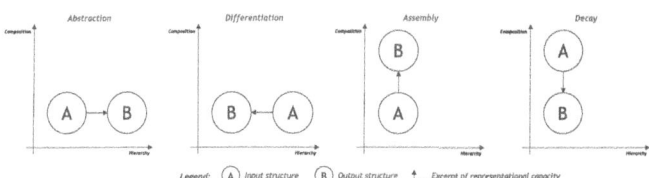

Fig. 5. Minimal set of processes describing representational development "completely"

Disclosure of Interests. The author has no competing interests to declare that are relevant to the content of this article.

References

1. Murphy, G.L.: The big book of concepts (The big book of concepts.). Cambridge, MA, US: Boston Review, p. 555 (2002)
2. Hubbard, T.L.: What is mental representation? And how does it relate to consciousness? J. Conscious. Stud. **14**(1), 37–61 (2007)
3. Bengio, Y., Kaelbling, L., Kawaguchi, K.: Generalization in deep learning. In: Grohs, P., Kutyniok, G. (eds.) Mathematical Aspects of Deep Learning, pp. 112–148. Cambridge University Press, Cambridge (2022)

4. Zhang, C., Bengio, S., Hardt, M., Recht, B., Vinyals, O.: Understanding deep learning (still) requires rethinking generalization. Commun. ACM **64**(3), 107–115 (2021). https://doi.org/10.1145/3446776
5. Shanahan, M., Mitchell, M.: Abstraction for deep reinforcement learning. In: Presented at the Proceedings of the Thirty-First International Joint Conference on Artificial Intelligence, Vienna, Austria (2022)
6. Mitchell, M.: Abstraction and analogy-making in artificial intelligence. Ann. N. Y. Acad. Sci. **1505**(1), 79–101 (2021). https://doi.org/10.1111/nyas.14619
7. Saxe, A.M., McClelland, J.L., Ganguli, S.: A mathematical theory of semantic development in deep neural networks. Proc. Natl. Acad. Sci. **116**(23), 11537–11546 (2019). https://doi.org/10.1073/pnas.1820226116
8. Meng, K., Bau, D., Andonian, A., Belinkov, Y.: Locating and editing factual associations in GPT. In: Presented at the Advances in Neural Information Processing Systems, New Orleans, USA (2022)
9. Guo, W., Wang, J., Wang, S.: Deep multimodal representation learning: a survey. IEEE Access **7**, 63373–63394 (2019). https://doi.org/10.1109/access.2019.2916887
10. Nimtz, C., Langkau, J.: Concepts in philosophy - a rough geography. Grazer Philosophische Studien **81**, 1–11 (2010)
11. Wang, H., Raj, B.: On the Origin of Deep Learning (2017). http://arxiv.org/pdf/1702.07800v4
12. Margolis, E., Laurence, S.: Concepts. The Stanford Encyclopedia of Philosophy. https://plato.stanford.edu/archives/fall2023/entries/concepts/. accessed
13. Mandler, J.M.: Perceptual and conceptual processes in infancy. J. Cogn. Dev. **1**(1), 3–36 (2000). https://doi.org/10.1207/s15327647jcd0101n_2
14. Carey, S.: Precis of 'The Origin of Concepts'. Behav. Brain Sci. **34**(3), 113–24 (2011). https://doi.org/10.1017/S0140525X10000919
15. Sloutsky, V.M., Sophia Deng, W.: Categories, concepts, and conceptual development. Lang. Cogn. Neurosci. **34**(10), 1284–1297 (2019). https://doi.org/10.1080/23273798.2017.1391398
16. Versace, E., Martinho-Truswell, A., Kacelnik, A., Vallortigara, G.: Priors in animal and artificial intelligence: where does learning begin? Trends Cogn. Sci. **22**(11), 963–965 (2018). https://doi.org/10.1016/j.tics.2018.07.005
17. Liu, S., Brooks, N.B., Spelke, E.S.: Origins of the concepts cause, cost, and goal in prereaching infants. Proc Natl Acad Sci U S A **116**(36), 17747–17752 (2019). https://doi.org/10.1073/pnas.1904410116
18. Spelke, E.S., Kinzler, K.D.: Core knowledge. Dev. Sci. **10**(1), 89–96 (2007). https://doi.org/10.1111/j.1467-7687.2007.00569.x
19. Martin, A.: The representation of object concepts in the brain. Annu. Rev. Psychol. **58**, 25–45 (2007). https://doi.org/10.1146/annurev.psych.57.102904.190143
20. Ebitz, R.B., Hayden, B.Y.: The population doctrine in cognitive neuroscience. Neuron **109**(19), 3055–3068 (2021). https://doi.org/10.1016/j.neuron.2021.07.011
21. Chung, S., Abbott, L.F.: Neural population geometry: an approach for understanding biological and artificial neural networks. Curr. Opin. Neurobiol. **70**, 137–144 (2021). https://doi.org/10.1016/j.conb.2021.10.010
22. Zucker, L., Mudrik, L.: Understanding associative vs. abstract pictorial relations: an ERP study. Neuropsychologia **133**, 107127 (2019). https://doi.org/10.1016/j.neuropsychologia.2019.107127
23. Kiefer, M., Pulvermüller, F.: Conceptual representations in mind and brain: theoretical developments, current evidence and future directions. Cortex **48**(7), 805–825 (2012). https://doi.org/10.1016/j.cortex.2011.04.006
24. Pulvermüller, F.: How neurons make meaning: brain mechanisms for embodied and abstract-symbolic semantics. Trends Cogn. Sci. **17**(9), 458–470 (2013). https://doi.org/10.1016/j.tics.2013.06.004

25. Parthemore, J.: The unified conceptual space theory: an enactive theory of concepts. Adapt. Behav. **21**(3), 168–177 (2013). https://doi.org/10.1177/1059712313482803
26. Gärdenfors, P.: Conceptual spaces: The geometry of thought (Conceptual spaces: The geometry of thought), pp. x, 307-x, 307. The MIT Press, Cambridge (2000)
27. Beckmann, P., Köstner, G., Hipólito, I.: An alternative to cognitivism: computational phenomenology for deep learning. Mind. Mach. **33**(3), 397–427 (2023). https://doi.org/10.1007/s11023-023-09638-w
28. Poldrack, R.A.: The physics of representation. Synthese **199**(1–2), 1307–1325 (2020). https://doi.org/10.1007/s11229-020-02793-y
29. Anderson, M.L., Champion, H.: Some dilemmas for an account of neural representation: a reply to Poldrack. Synthese, **200**(2) (2022). https://doi.org/10.1007/s11229-022-03505-4
30. Thomson, E., Piccinini, G.: Neural representations observed. Mind. Mach. **28**(1), 191–235 (2018). https://doi.org/10.1007/s11023-018-9459-4
31. Morris, M.: Why there are no mental representations. Mind. Mach. **1**, 1–30 (1991)
32. Thagard, P.: Cognitive science. The Stanford Encyclopedia of Philosophy. https://plato.stanford.edu/archives/win2023/entries/cognitive-science/ (accessed
33. Barsalou, L.W., Dutriaux, L., Scheepers, C.: Moving beyond the distinction between concrete and abstract concepts. Philos. Trans. R. Soc. Lond. B Biol. Sci. **373**(1752) (2018). https://doi.org/10.1098/rstb.2017.0144
34. Bengio, Y., Courville, A., Vincent, P.: Representation learning: a review and new perspectives. IEEE Trans. Pattern Anal. Mach. Intell. **35**(8), 1798–1828 (2013). https://doi.org/10.1109/TPAMI.2013.50
35. LeCun, Y., Bengio, Y., Hinton, G.: Deep learning. Nature **521**(7553), 436–444 (2015). https://doi.org/10.1038/nature14539
36. Bengio, Y., Delalleau, O.:On the expressive power of deep architectures. In: Algorithmic Learning Theory, (Lecture Notes in Computer Science, 2011, ch. Chapter 3, pp. 18–36
37. Fodor, J.A., Pylyshyn, Z.W.: Connectionism and cognitive architecture: a critical analysis. Cognition, **28**(1), 3–71 (1988). https://doi.org/10.1016/0010-0277(88)90031-5
38. Rumelhart, D.E., Hinton, G.E., Williams, R.J.: Learning representations by back-propagation errors. Nature **323**, 533–536 (1986)
39. Olah, C., Mordvintsev, A., Schubert, L.: Feature Visualization. Distill, **2**(11) (2017). https://doi.org/10.23915/distill.00007
40. Bau, D., Zhou, B., Khosla, A., Oliva, A., Torralba, A.: Network dissection: quantifying interpretability of deep visual representations (2017). https://doi.org/10.48550/arXiv.1704.05796
41. Kästner, L., Crook, B.: Explaining AI through mechanistic interpretability (2023)
42. Nanda, N., Chan, L., Lieberum, T., Smith, J., Steinhardt, J.: Progress measures for grokking via mechanistic interpretability (2023)
43. Olah, C.: Mechanistic interpretability, variables, and the importance of interpretable bases. vol. 2022, ed. Transformer Circuits Thread (2022)
44. Matsuo, Y., et al.: Deep learning, reinforcement learning, and world models. Neural Netw. **152**, 267–275 (2022). https://doi.org/10.1016/j.neunet.2022.03.037
45. Petkov, G., Petrova, Y.: Relation-based categorization and category learning as a result from structural alignment. the rolemap model. Front. Psychol. **10**, 563 (2019). https://doi.org/10.3389/fpsyg.2019.00563
46. Marcus, G.: Innateness, AlphaZero, and Artificial Intelligence (2018). https://arxiv.org/ftp/arxiv/papers/1801/1801.05667.pdf. Accessed 27 Dec 2023
47. Locke, J.: An Essay Concerning Human Understanding, pp. 601–605. (no. 5). Oxford University Press (1689)
48. Silver, D., et al.: Mastering the game of Go without human knowledge. Nature **550**(7676), 354–359 (2017). https://doi.org/10.1038/nature24270

49. Barabasi, D.L., Beynon, T., Katona, A., Perez-Nieves, N.: Complex computation from developmental priors. Nat. Commun. **14**(1), 2226 (2023). https://doi.org/10.1038/s41467-023-379 80-1

50. Mandler, J.M.: On the birth and growth of concepts. Philos. Psychol. **21**(2), 207–230 (2008). https://doi.org/10.1080/09515080801980179

51. Mandler, J.M.: The spatial foundations of the conceptual system. Lang. Cogn. **2**(1), 21–44 (2014). https://doi.org/10.1515/langcog.2010.002

52. Carey, S.: The origin of concepts. J. Cogn. Dev. **1**(1), 37–41 (2000). https://doi.org/10.1207/s15327647jcd0101n_3

53. Chalmers, D.J., French, R.M., Hofstadter, D.R.: High-level perception, representation, and analogy: a critique of artificial intelligence methodology. J. Exp. Theor. Artif. Intell. **4**(3), 185–211 (1992). https://doi.org/10.1080/09528139208953747

54. Scholkopf, B., et al.: Toward causal representation learning. Proc. IEEE **109**(5), 612–634 (2021). https://doi.org/10.1109/jproc.2021.3058954

55. Aslin, R.N., Smith, L.B.: Perceptual development, (in Eng). Annu. Rev. Psychol. **39**, 435–473 (1988). https://doi.org/10.1146/annurev.ps.39.020188.002251

56. Martin, K.A.: A brief history of the "feature detector". Cereb Cortex, **4**(1), 1–7 (1994). https://doi.org/10.1093/cercor/4.1.1

57. Eimas, P.D., Corbit, J.D.: Selective adaptation of linguistic feature detectors. Cogn. Psychol. **4**, 99–109 (1973)

58. Pelli, D.G., Burns, C.W., Farell, B., Moore-Page, D.C.: Feature detection and letter identification. Vis. Res. **46**(28), 4646–4674 (2006). https://doi.org/10.1016/j.visres.2006.04.023

59. Ronacher, B.: Innate releasing mechanisms and fixed action patterns: basic ethological concepts as drivers for neuroethological studies on acoustic communication in Orthoptera. J. Comp. Physiol. A Neuroethol. Sens. Neural Behav. Physiol. **205**(1), 33–50 (2019). https://doi.org/10.1007/s00359-018-01311-3

60. Li, Y., Wang, S., Tian, Q., Ding, X.: A survey of recent advances in visual feature detection. Neurocomputing **149**, 736–751 (2015). https://doi.org/10.1016/j.neucom.2014.08.003

61. Yu, L., Liu, H.: Efficient feature selection via analysis of relevance and redundancy. J. Mach. Learn. Res. **5**, 1205–1224 (2004)

62. Higgins, I., et al.: SCAN: learning hierachical compositional visual concepts. In: Presented at the International Conference on Learning Representations, Vancouver, Canada (2018)

63. Wasserman, E.A., Miller, R.R.: What's elementary about associative learning? Annu. Rev. Psychol. **48**, 573–607 (1997)

64. Solomon, K., Medin, D., Lynch, E.: Concepts do more than categorize. Trends Cogn. Sci. **3**(3), 99–105 (1999)

65. Welling, H.: Four mental operations in creative cognition: the importance of abstraction. Creativity Res. J. **19** (2007). https://doi.org/10.1080/10400410701397214

66. Gibson, J., Gibson, E.: Perceptual learning: differentiation or enrichment? Psychol. Rev. **62**(1), 32–41 (1955)

67. Caviezel, M.P., et al.: The neural mechanisms of associative memory revisited: fMRI evidence from implicit contingency learning. Front Psychiatry **10**, 1002 (2019). https://doi.org/10.3389/fpsyt.2019.01002

68. Kiefer, M., Barsalou, L.W.: Grounding the human conceptual system in perception, action, and internal states. Action Sci. 381–407 (2013)

69. Barsalou, L.W.: Grounded cognition. Annu. Rev. Psychol. **59**, 617–645 (2008). https://doi.org/10.1146/annurev.psych.59.103006.093639

70. Mitchell, C.J., De Houwer, J., Lovibond, P.F.: The propositional nature of human associative learning. Behav. Brain Sci. **32**(2), 183–98 (2009). https://doi.org/10.1017/S0140525X09000855

71. Asmuth, J., Gentner, D.: Relational categories are more mutable than entity categories. Q J Exp Psychol (Hove) **70**(10), 2007–2025 (2017). https://doi.org/10.1080/17470218.2016.121 9752

72. Ullman, S., Assif, L., Fetaya, E., Harari, D.: Atoms of recognition in human and computer vision. Proc. Natl. Acad. Sci. U S A **113**(10), 2744–2749 (2016). https://doi.org/10.1073/pnas.1513198113

73. Voulodimos, A., Doulamis, N., Doulamis, A., Protopapadakis, E.: Deep learning for computer vision: a brief review. Comput. Intell. Neurosci. **2018**, 7068349 (2018). https://doi.org/10.1155/2018/7068349

74. Li, D., Wang, R., Chen, P., Xie, C., Zhou, Q., Jia, X.: Visual feature learning on video object and human action detection: a systematic review. Micromachines (Basel), **13**(1) (2021). https://doi.org/10.3390/mi13010072

75. Gentner, D., Hoyos, C.: Analogy and abstraction. Top. Cogn. Sci. **9**(3), 672–693 (2017). https://doi.org/10.1111/tops.12278

76. Frankland, S.M., Greene, J.D.: Concepts and compositionality. in search of the brain's language of thought. Annu. Rev. Psychol. **71**, 273–303 (2020). https://doi.org/10.1146/annurev-psych-122216-011829

77. Burgoon, E.M., Henderson, M.D., Markman, A.B.: There are many ways to see the forest for the trees: a tour guide for abstraction. Perspect. Psychol. Sci. **8**(5), 501–520 (2013). https://doi.org/10.1177/1745691613497964

78. Borghi, A.M., Binkofski, F., Castelfranchi, C., Cimatti, F., Scorolli, C., Tummolini, L.: The challenge of abstract concepts. Psychol. Bull. **143**(3), 263–292 (2017). https://doi.org/10.1037/bul0000089

79. Buckner, C.: Deep learning: a philosophical introduction. Philos. Compass, **14**(10) (2019). https://doi.org/10.1111/phc3.12625

80. Voudouris, K., et al.: Direct human-AI comparison in the animal-AI environment. Front. Psychol. **13**, 711821 (2022). https://doi.org/10.3389/fpsyg.2022.711821

81. Smith, C., Carey, S., Wiser, M.: On differentiation: a case study of the development of the concepts of size, weight and density. Cognition **21**, 177–237 (1985)

82. Goldstone, R.L.: Perceptual learning. Annu. Rev. Psychol. **49**, 585–612 (1998)

83. Bjotk, E., Bjork, R.A., Anderson, M.: Varieties of goal directed forgetting. In: Golding, J.M., MacLeod, C.M., (eds.) Intentional forgetting: Interdisciplinary approaches, pp. 103–137. Lawrence Erlbaum Associates Publishers (1998)

84. Williams, M., Hong, S.W., Kang, M.S., Carlisle, N.B., Woodman, G.F.: The benefit of forgetting. Psychon. Bull. Rev. **20**(2), 348–355 (2013). https://doi.org/10.3758/s13423-012-0354-3

85. Timm, I.J., et al.: Intentional forgetting in artificial intelligence systems: perspectives and challenges. In: KI 2018: Advances in Artificial Intelligence, (Lecture Notes in Computer Science, Chapter 30, pp. 357–365 (2018)

86. Ellwart, T., Kluge, A.: Psychological perspectives on intentional forgetting: an overview of concepts and literature. KI - Künstliche Intelligenz **33**(1), 79–84 (2018). https://doi.org/10.1007/s13218-018-00571-0

87. Markovitch, S., Scott, P.D.: The role of forgetting in learning. In: Presented at the Proceedings of the Fifth International Conference on Machine Learning, Ann Arbor, Michigan (1998)

88. Jung, H., Ju, H., Jung, M., Kim, J.: Less-forgetful learning for domain expansion in deep neural networks. In: Presented at the Thirty-Second AAAI Conference on Artificial Intelligence (2018). https://doi.org/10.1609/aaai.v32i1.11769

89. Kirkpatrick, J., et al.: Overcoming catastrophic forgetting in neural networks. Proc. Nat. Acad. Sci. USA **114**(13), 3521–3526 (2017). https://doi.org/10.1073/pnas.1611835114

90. Ebrahimi, S., et al.: Remembering for the right reasons: explanations reduce catastrophic forgetting. Appl. AI Lett. **2**(4) (2021). https://doi.org/10.1002/ail2.44

Author Index

J. Proença et al. (Eds.): SEFM 2024, LNCS 15551, p. 291, 2026.
https://doi.org/10.1007/978-3-031-94748-3

The manufacturer's authorised representative in the EU is Springer
Nature Customer Service Centre GmbH, Europaplatz 3, 69115 Heidelberg,
Germany. If you have any concerns regarding our products, please
contact ProductSafety@springernature.com

Printed and bound by CPI Group (UK) Ltd, Croydon, CR0 4YY

28/04/2026

02098527-0002